Sons of Cambria

The Who's Who of Welsh International Football Players

Volume I – 1876-1946

Wales v Ireland, at Solitude in Belfast, on 23 March 1901. Ephraim Williams (208), wearing the halved shirt, is challenging the Ireland goalkeeper. Wales won 1-0.

Sons of Cambria

The Who's Who of Welsh International Football Players

Volume I – 1876-1946

Ian Garland and Gareth M Davies

St David's Press
Cardiff

Published in Wales by St. David's Press, an imprint of

Ashley Drake Publishing Ltd
PO Box 733
Cardiff
CF14 7ZY

www.st-davids-press.wales

First Impression – 2021

ISBN
Paperback: 978-1-902719-795
eBook: 978-1-902719-887

© Ashley Drake Publishing Ltd 2021
Text © Ian Garland & Gareth M Davies 2021

The right of Ian Garland & Gareth M Davies to be identified as the authors of this work has been asserted in accordance with the Copyright Design and Patents Act of 1988.

All rights reserved. No part of this publication may be reproduced, stored in a retrieval system, or transmitted, in any form or by any means without the prior permission of the publishers.

Every effort has been made to contact copyright holders. However, the publishers will be glad to rectify in future editions any inadvertent omissions brought to their attention.

Ashley Drake Publishing Ltd hereby exclude all liability to the extent permitted by law for any errors or omissions in this book and for any loss, damage or expense (whether direct or indirect) suffered by a third party relying on any information contained in this book.

British Library Cataloguing-in-Publication Data.
A CIP catalogue for this book is available from the British Library.

Typeset by Prepress Plus, India (www.prepressplus.in)

CONTENTS

Introduction xi
Acknowledgements xiii
Map of Wales xv
Abbreviations xvi

1 Edwin Alfred Cross	1	**34** John Roberts	17
2 Alfred Davies	1	**35** John Vaughan	18
3 William Henry Davies	1	**36** George Woosnam	18
4 John Hawley Edwards	2	**37** Thomas Henry Boden	19
5. William Addams Williams Evans	2	**38** Harry Hibbott	19
6 Daniel Grey	3	**39** William Pierce Owen	20
7 John Jones	3	**40** Edward Bowen	21
8 Samuel Llewellyn Kenrick	4	**41** William Strafford Bell	21
9 David Thomson	5	**42** Uriah Goodwin	22
10 George Frederick Thomson	6	**43** Thomas Lewis	22
11 William Wiliams	6	**44** Robert John McMillan	22
12 Thomas Blundell Burnett	7	**45** John Roberts	23
13 John Hughes	7	**46** Harry Adams	23
14 Alexander Fletcher Jones	7	**47** Frederick William Hughes	24
15 John Richard Morgan	8	**48** Charles Frederick Ketley	24
16 John Price	8	**49** Edward Gough Shaw	25
17 Thomas Johnson Britten	9	**50** Walter Hugh Roberts	25
18 James Davies	10	**51** Henry Phoenix	26
19 Charles Edwards	10	**52** Thomas Burke	26
20 Henry Valentine Edwards	11	**53** John Phillip Davies	26
21 George Garnet Higham	11	**54** William Roberts	27
22 Edward Phennah	11	**55** Richard Thomas Gough	27
23 John Powell	12	**56** John Jones	28
24 George Foulkes Savin	13	**57** Robert Davies	28
25 George William Glascodine	13	**58** John Arthur Eyton-Jones	29
26 Dennis Heywood	14	**59** Charles Conde	29
27 Thomas Owen	14	**60** Walter Thomas Davies	30
28 William Digby Owen	14	**61** William Tanat Foulkes	30
29 William Roberts	15	**62** Peter Griffiths	31
30 Watkin William Shone	15	**63** Robert Albert Jones	31
31 Knyvett Crosse	16	**64** Elias Owen	31
32 John Davies	16	**65** Morris/Maurice Jones Evans	32
33 James William Lloyd	17	**66** William Owen	32

67 Joseph Harry Williams	33	115 Allen Pugh	57
68 Robert Roberts	33	116 Samuel Gladstone Gillam	57
69 John Edward Davies	34	117 Richard Herbert Jarrett	58
70 Robert Davies	34	118 Patrick Leary	58
71 George Farmer	35	119 Thomas Patrick McCarthy	59
72 Frederick Robert Jones	35	120 John Charles Henry Bowdler	59
73 Humphrey Jones	36	121 Abel Hayes	60
74 William Lewis	37	122 David Morral Lewis	60
75 Robert Herbert Mills Roberts	37	123 Robert Humphrey Lee Roberts	61
76 George Thomas	39	124 Albert Richard Wilcock	61
77 Thomas Vaughan	39	125 Walter Gwynne Evans	62
78 Job Wilding	39	126 David Oswald Davies	62
79 Seth Powell	40	127 Albert Thomas Davies	63
80 Alfred Owen Davies	40	128 Benjamin Lewis	63
81 John Roach	41	129 Robert Arthur Lloyd	64
82 Herbert Sisson	41	130 John Mates	64
83 John Owen Vaughan	41	131 Robert Roberts	64
84 Thomas Bryan	42	132 Richard Edward Turner	65
85 Albert Malcolm Hersee	42	133 William Hughes	65
86 Richard Hersee	43	134 Charles Frederick Parry	66
87 Robert Roberts	43	135 Smart Arridge	67
88 William Roberts	43	136 Archie Middleship Bastock	68
89 Thomas Davies	44	137 Robert Davies	68
90 John Doughty	44	138 Caesar Augustus Llewellyn Jenkyns	69
91 Richard Parry Williams	45	139 John Owen	70
92 John Bonamy Challen	45	140 Joseph Hudson Turner	71
93 Edward Clement Evelyn	46	141 Tom William Egan	71
94 William Haighton Turner	46	142 John Evans Butler	71
95 George Griffiths	47	143 Edwin James	72
96 Edward Percival Whitley Hughes	47	144 Edward Morris	72
97 Alexander Hunter	47	145 James Vaughan	73
98 Samuel Jones	48	146 Edwin Houghland Wiliams	73
99 Henry Wilmshurst Sabine	48	147 Harry Ernest Bowdler	73
100 Alfred William Townsend	49	148 Frederick William Jones	74
101 Richard Jones	49	149 Samuel Jones	74
102 William Ernest Pryce Jones	50	150 Oliver David Shepston Taylor	75
103 James Morris	50	151 George Williams	75
104 James Trainer	51	152 John Evans	75
105 Joseph Davies	52	153 Thomas Chapman	76
106 Roger Doughty	53	154 Robert Samuel Jones	76
107 Edmund Gwynne Howell	53	155 John Charles Rea	77
108 Reuben Humphreys	54	156 Abel Hughes	77
109 David Jones	54	157 Hugh Morris	77
110 George Alfred Owen	54	158 Thomas Worthington	78
111 John Hallam	55	159 James Alfred Edwards	78
112 William Parry Jones	55	160 John Leonard Jones	78
113 Arthur Lea	56	161 William Henry Meredith	79
114 Joseph Davies	56	162 William Parry	81

163 Harry Trainer	82	211 Roger Evans	108
164 Albert Westhead Pryce Jones	82	212 Thomas Jenkins	109
165 John Samuel Matthias	83	213 Hugh Jones	110
166 Arthur Grenville Morris	84	214 Richard Morris	110
167 David Henry Pugh	85	215 Walter Martin Watkins	111
168 Joseph Rogers	85	216 Llewellyn Griffiths	111
169 Price Ffoulkes White	85	217 Joseph Owens	112
170 John Garner	86	218 Thomas Davies	112
171 Sydney Darvell	86	219 William Davies	113
172 Morgan Maddox Morgan-Owen	87	220 William Wynn	113
173 William Nock	88	221 Lloyd Davies	114
174 William Roberts Jones	88	222 Arthur Davies	114
175 John Henry Edwards	88	223 David Davies	115
176 Albert Lockley	89	224 John Hughes	116
177 John Morris	89	225 George Latham	116
178 Thomas John Thomas	89	226 Alfred Oliver	117
179 Richard Samuel Jones	90	227 Albert Thomas Jones	118
180 Alfred Ernest Watkins	90	228 William `Lot' Jones	118
181 Thomas Bartley	91	229 William Mathews	119
182 John Taylor	91	230 John Tracey Morgan	120
183 Robert Atherton	92	231 Robert Ernest Evans	120
184 Horace Elford Blew	93	232 Edwin Hughes	121
185 David Charles Davies	94	233 John Love Jones	122
186 Edward Hughes	94	234 Richard Jones	122
187 William James Jackson	95	235 John Lewis	123
188 Fredrick Charles Kelly	95	236 James Roberts	124
189 George Richards	96	237 Llewellyn Davies	124
190 Charles Edwin Thomas	96	238 Arthur Howell Hughes	124
191 Ralph Stanley Jones	96	239 Gordon Peace Jones	125
192 Trevor Owen	97	240 George Owen Williams	125
193 Thomas James Buckland	97	241 Ioan Hayden Price	126
194 William Clare Harrison	98	242 William Charles Davies	127
195 William Thomas Butler	98	243 Albert Victor Hodgkinson	127
196 Frederick John Griffiths	98	244 Jeffrey Woodward Jones	128
197 Richard Jones	99	245 Thomas Daniel Jones	129
198 Samuel Meredith	100	246 Ernest Peake	129
199 Charles Richard Morris	100	247 George Arthur Wynn	130
200 Thomas David Parry	101	248 Evan Jones	130
201 Samuel James Brookes	101	249 Thomas John Hewitt	132
202 Robert Morris	102	250 Edward Thomas Vizard	132
203 Leigh Richmond Roose	102	251 Joseph Thomas Jones	133
204 Hugh Morgan-Owen	104	252 Moses Richard Russell	134
205 John Owen Jones	105	253 John William Williams	135
206 William James Jones	105	254 David Walter Davies	136
207 Maurice Pryce Parry	106	255 John Evans	136
208 Ephraim Williams	106	256 Leonard Frank Newton	137
209 Arthur William Green	107	257 William Ellis Bailiff	138
210 Robert Owen Evans	107	258 Walter Otto Davies	138

#	Name	Page
259	Edward James Roberts	139
260	Edward John Peers	139
261	William Jennings	140
262	Thomas James Matthias	141
263	Alfred Stanley Rowlands	142
264	Stanley Davies	142
265	Ivor Jones	143
266	Frederick Charles Keenor	144
267	Harry Millership	145
268	Richard William Richards	146
269	David John Collier	146
270	Francis Hoddinott*	147
271	David Rees Williams	148
272	William James Hole	148
273	Robert William Matthews	149
274	Leonard Stephen Davies	150
275	Herbert Price Evans	151
276	James Henry Evans	152
277	Edward Parry	152
278	Robert Idwal Davies	153
279	George Alfred Godding	153
280	Robert Frederick John	154
281	David Sidney Nicholas	154
282	Albert Gray	155
283	William Davies	156
284	John Jenkins	156
285	John Barry Lewis Nicholls	157
286	George Harold Beadles	157
287	Frederick Cook	158
288	William Williams	159
289	Jack Fowler	160
290	Edwin Samuel Jenkins	160
291	Ernest James Morley	161
292	Daniel Edgar Thomas	161
293	James Jones	162
294	John Reginald Blackwall Moulsdale	162
295	Jesse Thomas Williams	163
296	Samuel Raymond Bennion	164
297	James John Lewis	164
298	Arthur Ivor Brown	165
299	David Evans	165
300	Thomas Jones	166
301	John Newnes	166
302	Charles Jones	167
303	William John Pullen	168
304	Thomas John Evans	168
305	Tom Percival Griffiths	169
306	Daniel Lewis	170
307	Wilfred Leslie Lewis	170
308	Harry Thomas	171
309	Sidney John Vivian Leonard Evans	171
310	Ernest Robert Curtis	172
311	Benjamin David Williams	173
312	Hywel Davies	173
313	Stanley James Bowsher	174
314	Arthur Albert Lumberg	175
315	Albert William Mays	175
316	Eugene O'Callaghan	176
317	Frederick Windsor Warren	176
318	Richard Prytherch Finnegan	177
319	Arthur Ronald Hugh	177
320	Edward Lawrence	178
321	Tudor James Martin	178
322	John Pugsley	179
323	Bertie Williams	180
324	Thomas Bamford	180
325	William Elvet Collins	181
326	Wynne Crompton	182
327	Frederick Thomas Dewey	182
328	Emrys Ellis	183
329	John Edward Neal	183
330	Walter William Robbins	184
331	William Rogers	185
332	William Rees Thomas	185
333	Leslie Williams	186
334	David John Astley	187
335	Wilfred Bernard James	187
336	William Ronald John	188
337	Cuthbert Phillips	188
338	David Thomas Richards	189
339	Thomas Edwards	190
340	Ernest Matthew Glover	190
341	Philip Henry Griffiths	191
342	Aneurin Glyndr Richards	191
343	Benjamin Ellis	192
344	Hugh Edward Foulkes	193
345	Sidney Wilfred Lawrence	193
346	Thomas John Jones	194
347	John Edward Parris	194
348	David Jenkin Lewis	195
349	James Patrick Murphy	195
350	William Evans	196
351	William Edward Richards	197
352	Leslie Jenkin Jones	197
353	Alfred Day	198
354	Harry Hanford	199

355 David Owen Jones	199	**365** William Marshall Hughes	206
356 Thomas James Edward Mills	200	**366** Edwin Perry	207
357 Ronald Williams	200	**367** George Henry Green	207
358 Idris Morgan Hopkins	201	**368** Thomas George Ronald Jones	208
359 John Iorwerth Hughes	202	**369** Reginald Horace Cumner	210
360 Brynmor Jones	203	**370** William John Whatley	210
361 Charles Wilson Jones	204	**371** Donald John Dearson	211
362 Seymour Morris	204	**372** Leslie Mervyn Boulter	211
363 Herbert Gwyn Turner	205	**373** George Poland	212
364 John Warner	205	**374** John James Williams	213

Appendix 1: Official International Matches 1876-1939   215
Appendix 2: Unofficial International Matches 1876-1946   233
    A - Canada 1891   233
    B - Victory Internationals 1919   234
    C - FAW Tour of Canada 1929   235
    D - War-time Internationals 1939-1946   237
    E - War-time Wales XI Matches 1941-44   243
Appendix 3: Edward Robbins   249
Appendix 4: Caps Awarded 1876-1939   250
Appendix 5: Goal Scorers 1876-1939   252
Appendix 6: Captains 1876-1939   254
Appendix 7: Clubs Represented 1876-1939   255
Appendix 8: Birthplaces of Welsh Internationals 1876-1939   259

Player Index   262

*To all the pioneers of the game in Wales who contributed so much
and enabled the game to develop into what it is today.*

*On a personal note I'd like to dedicate this book to the players and supporters of Wrexham,
Holyhead Town ('The Harbourmen'), Holyhead Hotspur and of course Wales who have made
this book a labour of love. I'm also very proud that my paternal grandfather's second cousin,
Llew Griffiths, is featured in the book having won his single cap in 1902.*

Gareth M Davies

INTRODUCTION

The Who's Who of Welsh International Soccer Players was first published in 1991 as one volume covering all the players who had appeared for Wales at full international level between 1876 and 1991. At that time the number of books on Welsh soccer was fairly modest but in the intervening year we have been pleased to witness an upsurge in titles, not least prior to and after Euro 2016. It was always our intention to publish a second edition and any correlation between the recent success of the national side and the timing of this book is entirely coincidental.

We have been able to benefit from the many more sources that have become available since 1991, as well as those previously available becoming much more accessible. The sheer amount of information available, and the number of players capped over more than 140 years, means that it is no longer feasible to accommodate it all in one book. Consequently, it was decided to split the work into three volumes and close the first book at the end of the Second World War. We have been able to revise and update many of the entries and correct the few errors that crept into the earlier volume. Needless to say, the authors are solely responsible for any errors in the present volume.

We have decided, in contrast to the earlier book, to list the players in the chronological order in which they appeared for Wales. Where there was more than one debutant in a match, we have numbered those players alphabetically by surname. So, for the first international match against Scotland in 1876, in which all the players were making their debut for Wales, we begin with Edwin Cross as number 1 and have William Williams at 11. The final player to make his debut before war intervened in 1939 was John James Williams and he was the 374th Wales player since that first match at the West of Scotland Cricket Ground in 1876. A player index is provided to help the reader locate a particular individual. In the second volume we will pick up the story in the 1946-47 season with player number 375. For the sake of completeness, for the period covered by this first volume, we have included in the appendices details of those players whose only recognition by the FA of Wales (FAW) was in unofficial international matches. They fall into four groups – the matches against the Canadian touring team in 1891, the Victory internationals of 1919, the FAW's first overseas tour in 1929 and the war-time internationals played by Wales XIs between 1939 and 1946. Players whose only appearance was in an unofficial match are not included in the chronological numbering.

All players were amateurs prior to the legalization of professionalism in England in 1885. The FAW followed suit in 1892 but the South Wales and Monmouthshire FA did not allow professionals until 1900. As an amateur, a player could appear for a different team every week. We believe that we have captured the players' extended club associations but it is entirely possible that for some early amateurs there are a few one-off matches that may have escaped our radar.

As we mentioned in 1991, it would not have been possible for us to have completed a book of this nature without the help of many individuals and organizations. Firstly, we would like to thank the staff of the British Newspaper Library at Colindale, in particular those who never made it to St Pancras where the British Library now has its Newsroom. We are grateful to the FA of Wales, in particular the late Alun Evans, the National Library of Wales, David Barber, late librarian at the English FA, Denbighshire Archives, Gwynedd Archives at Caernarfon, University College Bangor Archives, Ynys Mon Archives and the Wrexham Archives. Mike Davage was an enormous help with the original publication and the indefatigable Jim Creasy built on his valuable previous input by continuing to furnish us with information on Welsh players active during the inter-war years. Our gratitude is also extended to the assiduous Cris Freddi for his very helpful contributions and enthusiasm for the project. We hope he's not disappointed with the result.

ACKNOWLEDGEMENTS

The help we have received from Dave Sullivan, Barry Riley, Dr Michael Leman Trip, Bruce Steele-Gray, Craig Jones, Roger Titford, Bob McPherson and Phil Stead is greatly appreciated. Ken Davies (Newtown) and Trevor Beal produced snippets of information which enabled us to fill in gaps in the later careers of a couple of players, Danny Richards (Cardiff) who helpfully provided us with some photographs from the 1920s, and Pat who runs the excellent website www.doingthe92.com generously allowed us to use some of the images in his card museum for which we are most grateful.

We remain indebted to those soccer historians who supplied information and photographs for the original book. They include Michael Braham, Gary Chalk, Dennis Clareborough, D Downs, Garth Dykes, John Eastwood, D Farmer, Terry Frost, A Futter, Ray Goble, Frank Grande, John Harding, G Haynes, J Helliar, R Hockings, Bryan Horsnell, M Jay, A Jenkins, D Jenkins, Paul Joannou, C Jones, Trefor Jones, Doug Lamming, S Marland, W Martin, J Matthews, Tony Matthews, Brian Mellowship, R Middleton, A Mitchell, D Orme, G Parry, A Porter, G Porter, F H C Robertson, Rev Nigel Sands, Ray Spiller, D Smith, P Taylor, L Triggs, D Turner, Gil Upton, M Whelan, A Wilson and S Woodhead. Sheila Murphy at the Football League helped to clarify details of several players. We also received a significant amount of help from Malcolm Brodie (Belfast Telegraph), Karl Woodward (Western Mail), John Burgum (South Wales Evening Post), Mrs Gwawr Pugh (Denbigh Free Press), Mike Neasom (Portsmouth Mail), Robin C B Stirling (former editor of the Motherwell Times) and Bob Turner (Nottingham Evening Post), all of whom generously provided invaluable assistance regarding specific players. John Jenkins aided the project substantially in the early 1990s by helping with the research at the National Library of Wales and suggesting new avenues for exploration. Our appreciation is also extended to Ceri Stennett of Cardiff for his assistance with the original book.

Thanks must also go to the following people who were happy to share their knowledge of particular players when we first embarked on this endeavour: the Rev L O Arridge, Janice Balmain, C Barrett, C Bayliss, S Beckett, Simon Bird, Mrs C Bingham, G Bodgers, Mrs V M Bond, Mrs A Brown, Mrs E Byrne, B Carter, M L Charlesworth (Old Salopians), G H Chesterton (Old Malvernians), R Collier, S Crompton, J Daniels, Mrs M E Davies, C Davies, Mr and Mrs D Davies, Miss F Davies, Mrs G Davies, Mrs. R L Davies, J Doherty, Mrs D Edwards, Mrs E Edwards, V Emmanuel, C Evans, D Evans, G Evans, W Evans, R Ewing, Mrs D French, R Gate, Mrs M Gentle, H Gillbanks, Reverend D Griffiths, Mrs R Goodwin, Mrs B Harrison, F Hewitt, Mrs E Hibbott, P H Hinks, C Holmes, Mrs R Hugh, D R Hughes, DE S Ingram, Mrs Jackson, G James, Mrs S Johnson, Mrs C Jones, R Jones, E Jones, P Jones, Mrs E Jones-Griffiths and family, Mrs A Leach, D Leahy, Mrs E Lloyd, J G Lloyd, P McGrath, M McKeown, R Mansell, R Matthews, Mr E F Mills (Jesus College, Cambridge), John Maddox Morgan-

Owen, Alan Morris, Arthur Morris, J Moulsdale, R Neal, H Owen, Mrs J Parry, M A Pengelly, Mr and Mrs Powe, Mrs M Powles, Mrs E Preston, Mr and Mrs Price, Mr D A Price-White, Mr D Roberts, Mrs N Roberts, H Roy, Mr and Mrs Russell, C Sargeant, the Sabine family, Mrs J Scudder, Mr D Slattery, Richard Shepherd, D Smith, Mrs B Squires, A Sutton, J A Thomas, J Thomas, Mrs Y Thomas, P Wain, M Gwen Walch, K Wallace, B Wardell, B Wareing, J Watmough, Mrs A Williams, Gerald Williams, Gerry Williams, H Williams, Mrs P Williams, T Ceiriog Williams and N Wynne. We apologise if we have inadvertently omitted anyone.

We must also thank Brian Lile, Peter Parry and Donald Griffiths for permission to quote from *The Old Black and Green - Aberystwyth Town FC 1884-1994*, the late Dr Percy Young for allowing us to quote from his book *Bolton Wanderers*, and the University of Wales Press for granting permission for us to use the map of Wales that was originally published in the *Encyclopaedia of Wales* (2008). We are also grateful to Dr Philip Goodwin, who would probably be surprised to see himself mentioned in a book on the round ball game, Rob Sawyer, and also the Scottish Football Museum, Hampden Park, Glasgow.

Finally, but no less importantly, we'd like to thank Ashley Drake at St David's Press for readily agreeing to take on the publication of this work and for his guidance, enthusiasm, encouragement and good humour along the way.

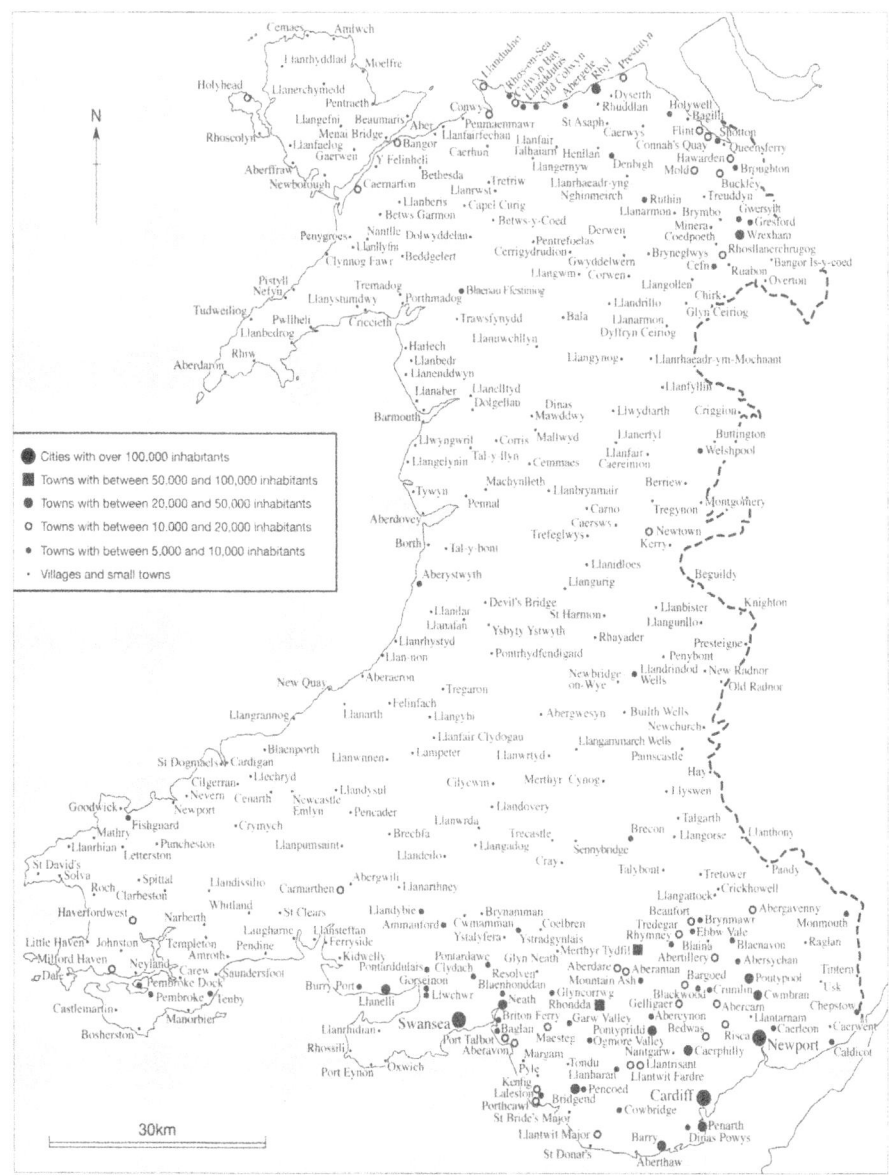

[Map originally published in *The Welsh Academy Encyclopaedia of Wales* (University of Wales Press, 2008). Reproduced with permission of the University of Wales Press.]

ABBREVIATIONS

apps	appearances	G Sch	Grammar School
Alb	Albion		
Alex	Alexandra	H	Hotspur
Ath	Athletic		
		Ire	Ireland
bapt	baptised	lge	league
B C	British Championship		
		N E	North End
C	City		
Can	Canada	Rgrs	Rangers
Co	County	Rov	Rovers
Comb	Combination	RWF	Royal Welsh Fusiliers
c/season	close season		
coll	college	S E	South End
		Sch	School
Dist	District	Sco	Scotland
Div	Division	SL	Southern League (Eng)
Eng	England	T	Town
Gl / gls	goal / goals	Utd	United
		Univ	University
F	Forest		
FA	Football Association (Eng)	Vic	Victoria
F Alliance	Football Alliance (Eng)		
F Comb	Football Comb (Eng)	Wdrs	Wanderers
FL	Football League (Eng)	Wed	Wednesday
Fra	France		

1 Edwin Alfred Cross
B: Wrexham; 1848
D: Old Colwyn; 19 Jan 1924
Half back
2 caps: (Wrexham) v Sco 1876; v Sco 1877

Career: Wrexham, 1872-79; Wrexham Hare & Hounds. Also, **N Wales** v Birmingham (1877), v Sheffield (1876 & 1878), v Lancashire (1879).

Although primarily a cricketer, Cross played a pivotal role in early Welsh football as a pioneer with Wrexham and helped to form the FAW in 1876. Cross had been a member of Wrexham Football Club as early as 1869 and in 1873 was playing in 15-a side matches against a Provincial Insurance XI. He was an energetic wing half who had the distinction of appearing in the first Wales international and the first Welsh Cup final. Some reports credit him with being the first footballer to play in the position of centre half. After concluding his time at Wrexham he played the occasional match for local junior clubs and, for several years, Cross continued to be a leading batsman for Wrexham CC. A clerk with the Alliance Insurance Company at the time of his appearances for Wales, Cross later worked at the Shrewsbury office before becoming an accountant in around 1889. He retired in 1902 and resided with his nephew in Liverpool. His nephew, also E A Cross, was later a director of Wrexham FC and a Wrexham alderman.

Honours:
Wrexham - Welsh Cup 1878; finalists 1879

2 Alfred Davies
B: Wrexham; 1850
D: Wrexham; 6 Apr 1891
Forward
2 caps: (Wrexham) v Sco 1877

Career: Wrexham, 1872-81. Also, **N Wales** v Sheffield, v Birmingham, v Staffordshire (all 1877); **Denbighshire**.

Davies, along with his brother James, was one of the members of the Wrexham Cricket Club who gravitated to the local football club to keep themselves occupied on Saturday afternoons during the winter months. He began in 16-aside matches in the days when the goal posts were connected by a tape. Alf Davies was one of a six-man attack in both his international matches, but the 'Sons of Cambria', as the team were dubbed by one newspaper, went down to defeat in both games without managing a goal. A Sunday school teacher and a lieutenant in the Wrexham volunteer fire brigade, he became an umpire for Wrexham on retiring from playing. Davies was a stonemason by trade and died at the early age of 40 from a chest complaint.

Honours:
Wrexham - Welsh Cup 1878

3 William Henry Davies
B: Oswestry (Eng); 1855
D: Oswestry (Eng); 14 Nov 1916
Halfback/forward
4 caps (1 gl): (Oswestry T) v Sco 1876; v Sco 1877; v Eng 1879; v Eng 1880

Career: St Oswalds (Oswestry), 1874-77; Oswestry White Stars, 1880; Oswestry T, 1880-84. Also, **N Wales**; v Sheffield (1876).

Davies was a pioneer of soccer in Oswestry and was present at the meeting of Oswestry Cricket Club on 4 September 1875 to form an association club. He had earlier captained St Oswalds, the first football club in the town. Davies was equally at home as a forward or half back, could pass the ball accurately and possessed good dribbling skills. Although sometimes criticized for selfishness, his presence as a forward always meant danger for opposing defences. Davies had the distinction of scoring the first international goal for Wales (v England), latching on to a clever centre from William Roberts and kicking the ball under the tape.

Davies began his working life in the office of the County Court Registrar and subsequently became an accountant to a firm of solicitors in Oswestry. He also held the part-time post of Registrar of Births for Oswestry. A strong churchman, Davies was active in the temperance movement for many years.

Honours:
Oswestry T - Welsh Cup finalists 1884

4 John Hawley Edwards
B: Shrewsbury (Eng); 1850
 (bapt. 8 May)
D: Old Colwyn; 13 Jan 1893
Forward
1 cap: (Wanderers) v Sco 1876

Career: Shropshire Wdrs, 1873-80; Shrewsbury, 1876-80; Wanderers, 1873-74, 1875-76 (3 apps).

Hawley Edwards was one of the foremost pioneers of soccer in the border counties in the 1870s. He served on the Birmingham Association and founded and captained the Shropshire Wanderers. The team of gentleman amateurs, which reached the semi-final of the FA Cup in 1875, did much to foster the game in Shropshire and eastern Denbighshire. Edwards was an industrious, unselfish forward who could dribble strongly but was apt to overrun the ball. A team mate of Edwards, who played with him in the 1870s, described him as 'one of the most determined players I ever met and although he was never safe, one or both of his knees being liable to give way at any time, he would always be to the fore.' In 1874, Edwards appeared for England against Scotland. The Shropshire man was well known on the soccer field and an attempt by Druids to bolster their ranks by playing Edwards under the name of `Jones' caused much ill-feeling among their opponents Wrexham.

Edwards, who represented Shropshire at cricket in the early 1870s, became treasurer on the formation of the FAW and was invited by Llewellyn Kenrick, himself a former Shropshire Wanderers player, to take part in the first ever Welsh international. 'There are few better dribblers in this part of the country, his only fault being that he prefers a crooked course to a straight one' was how the Shrewsbury Chronicle described Edwards. His playing days were ended around 1880 by knee injuries and he switched to the more sedate pursuit of angling. From 1871 Edwards worked as a solicitor and was later clerk to the Shrewsbury Magistrates. He died at a young age from a throat infection while convalescing at Old Colwyn.

Honours:
The Wanderers - FA Cup 1876

5. William Addams Williams Evans
B: Usk; 1853 (bapt. 17 Oct)
D: Llanddewi Rhydderch;
 23 Apr 1919
Full back
2 caps: (Oxford Univ) v Sco 1876; v Sco 1877

Career: Shrewsbury Sch, 1870-72; St John's Coll (Oxford), 1872-77 (no soccer blue).

Evans was the son of the vicar of Usk and holds a special place in Welsh soccer as the first man from South Wales to play for the Principality. No doubt he had been immersed in the game during his time at Shrewsbury School, a soccer stronghold. Previews of the 1876 match in the Welsh newspapers made great play of the recruitment of the university men, including Evans. Despite a 4-0 reverse, a match report commented 'Evans and Kenrick, the backs, played splendidly for Wales. Indeed better men never toed a ball'. After taking a BA degree in 1877, Evans was ordained and served as Curate of Barwell (Leicestershire) for six years, then at All Saints, Northampton and Harrowden (Bedfordshire) before returning to Monmouthshire in 1885. He was subsequently rector of Llanthewy and Llandegfeth, near to his birth place, until his death in 1919. Evans, who was a brother in law to G F Thomson, was named after his grandfather William Addams Williams of Llangibby Castle, County Magistrate for Monmouthshire.

6 Daniel Grey

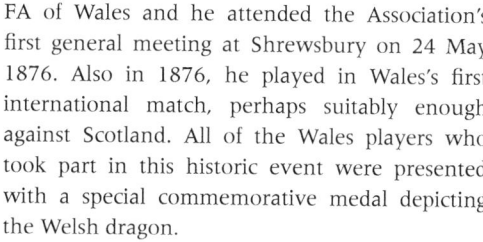

B: New Mills (Sco); 1848
D: Ruabon; 26 Feb 1900
Half back/forward
2 caps: (Druids) v Sco 1876; v Sco 1878

Career: Ruabon Rov, 1873; Plasmadoc; Druids, Jan 1876-80. Also, **N Wales** v Birmingham (1876, 1877 & 1878), v Sheffield (1876, 1877 & 1878), v Staffordshire (1878).

In the early 1870s Daniel Grey worked as an assistant surgeon in Calderbrook, Rochdale and joined the medical register in 1875 after obtaining his medical degree at Glasgow University. He moved to Ruabon around 1872 to start a medical practice and as a keen sportsman soon joined Ruabon Rovers. He then captained Plasmadoc, alongside the Thomson brothers and later Llewellyn Kenrick. Gray's interest in soccer led to him becoming a founder member of the FA of Wales and he attended the Association's first general meeting at Shrewsbury on 24 May 1876. Also in 1876, he played in Wales's first international match, perhaps suitably enough against Scotland. All of the Wales players who took part in this historic event were presented with a special commemorative medal depicting the Welsh dragon.

Grey, a busy player and a tremendous worker, took part in the very first Welsh Cup tie when Druids played Newtown in October 1877. Appropriately, he had contributed £15 to the Association's fund to purchase a trophy. He retired from active participation in the game in the late 1870s but retained his interest as a spectator. He was often called onto the field in his medical capacity to attend to injured players. When, in 1889, Wrexham and Westminster Rovers figured in a particularly violent Welsh Cup tie, Dr Grey was called upon to lecture the players about their behaviour before the replay got underway. His strictures were effective and the match passed off peacefully.

According to one newspaper article it was Dr Grey and the Thomson brothers that came up with the idea of the Druids club, with Llewellyn Kenrick and Bobby Lythgoe joining a little later. The Druids name first appears in football reports in January 1876 and the club may well have been a restructuring of Plasmadoc FC which was set up as early as 1869 and also played at Plasmadoc Park.

Honour:
Druids - Welsh Cup finalists 1878

7 John Jones

B: Ruabon; c. 1856
D: unknown
Forward/wing half
1 cap: (Druids) v Sco 1876

Career: Ruabon Rov; Plasmadoc; Druids, 1876-78; Oswestry T, 1879-80; Druids,

1879-82; Small Heath All, 1882-83; Druids, 1883-86. Also, **N Wales** v Sheffield (1876), v Staffordshire (1878).

John Jones worked as a coal miner and was known in North Wales soccer circles as 'Dirty Jack', a nickname that had nothing to do with the state of his kit. A tough and vigorous opponent who gave no quarter, he was a player perfectly in tune with the style of football which predominated in the early 1880s. Jones, who appeared for Druids against Blackburn Olympic in the 1881 FA Cup, began as a forward and played for Ruabon alongside T B Burnett and James Lloyd. He later played at half back and ended his career as a goalkeeper. Jones was a faithful servant to the Druids but broke his allegiance when the club were without a ground and also turned out for Small Heath Alliance. He also made what might be termed a 'guest appearance' for Oswestry in 1882 when he helped them win the Shropshire Cup. A John Jones (Ruabon) was elected to the FAW in 1891, serving until 1893, and may have been the former Druids player.

Honours:
Druids - Welsh Cup 1880, 1881, 1882; finalists 1878, 1883

8 Samuel Llewellyn Kenrick

B: Ruabon; 9 Jun 1847
D: Ruabon; 29 May 1933
Full back
5 caps: (Druids) v Sco 1876; v Sco 1877; (Oswestry T) v Eng, Sco 1879; (Druids) v Eng 1881

Career: Priorslee (Shifnal); Ruabon Rov; Plasmadoc, 1874-76; (also Shropshire Wdrs 1874-75); Druids, 1876-78; Oswestry T, 1878-79; Druids, 1879-80.

Llewellyn Kenrick was the son of a Ruabon ironmaster and came from a family long established in the area. He was an early soccer enthusiast, playing in matches against Oswestry School as early as 1866 and appeared for the Shropshire Wanderers in the 1874-75 FA Cup semi-final. He also had a hand in the transformation of the Plasmadoc club into Druids. On leaving Ruabon Grammar School Kenrick trained as a solicitor (admitted 1871) and opened a practice in Ruabon. Undoubtedly his greatest contribution to Welsh soccer came in January 1876 when he founded the Football Association of Wales. A London Welshman, G Clay-Thomas, had suggested in The Field newspaper that a Welsh team be formed to play Scotland or Ireland at rugby. Kenrick's enthusiasm was fired by the idea and he inserted notices in the sporting newspapers seeking players born in Wales or with sufficient residence in the Principality. He corresponded with several Welsh clubs and the universities in order to raise a team but ran into criticism for allegedly overlooking players from the south. In fact, one South Walian appeared in Wales' first international and Kenrick was anxious to spread the game throughout Wales.

Kenrick was a tall, muscular player and a full back with a reputation as a fearsome shoulder charger. He made his last appearance for Wales at Blackburn in 1881 when Jack Powell missed his train connection at Chester and Kenrick turned out in his everyday clothes to give a splendid performance despite carrying a knee injury. In 1884, he left the FAW, probably because of the trend towards professionalism but couldn't divorce himself from the game entirely. When Chirk won the Welsh Cup in 1890, Kenrick was one of the honoured guests at the celebration dinner. After commenting how encouraged he was to see the game in a much more healthy state than 15 years previously, he remarked, in typical Victorian sentiments, on the character-building of the game: 'Football was the means of employment and enjoyment for the youth of the neighbourhood and it makes them better citizens and better men'. Kenrick made an unexpected return to football administration in Wales in February 1897, when the FAW Secretary was charged with fraud, and he guided the Association through its most testing crisis. He made the final break a few months later over the minor issue of the allocation of gate money to Welsh Cup semi-finalists and finalists. But he clearly retained a fondness for the game and it was reported in 1914 that he was present at the Racecourse when Wales played Ireland. Wrexham journalist George Lerry, a perceptive commentator and one-time FAW councillor paid this tribute to Kenrick in 1909: 'The Welsh Association have a great deal to thank the gentleman for. Probably but for him there would not have been a Welsh Association. He was undoubtedly the finest organiser, the best captain and one of the best backs that ever went on the field. No man has done more for football in Wales than Mr Kenrick'.

Kenrick was Clerk to the Ruabon Magistrates from 1896 and was appointed Coroner for East Denbighshire in 1906, a post he held until his death. Shortly after his appointment, he presided over an inquest into the death of a footballer at Chirk and, after amusing himself with a remark that the jury probably knew more about the game than he did, made the following comment on the game: 'Football was one of the best English pastimes which young men could engage in and within reasonable limits and provided that it was indulged in simply as a pastime only. It was far better for a young man to take part in football, cricket or any other healthful experience in the fresh air than to be hanging around billiard tables and public houses in an atmosphere meeting with tobacco smoke and the smell of intoxicating liquor'. When, in September 1922, eight schoolboys appeared before him at Ruabon Petty Sessions for playing football on open spaces at Cefn, Kenrick ordered them to pay a fine of one shilling each. He then paid the fines himself but at the same time warned them that footballers had to obey the law.

One writer who knew Kenrick well described him as 'thoroughly straightforward and conscientious. He has never been the man to court favour and popularity. His somewhat brusque manner perhaps offended many, but no one ever doubted his sincerity'. Kenrick married the daughter of the headmaster of Ruabon Grammar School; his brother-in-law Charles Taylor played nine matches for the Wales rugby XV and was Welsh pole vault champion. Taylor was killed on board HMS Tiger at the Battle of the Dogger Bank in the North Sea in 1915.

Honours:
Druids - Welsh Cup 1880; finalists 1878

9 David Thomson
B: Halesowen (Eng);
5 Nov 1847
D: Ruabon; 14 Sep 1876
Goalkeeper
1 cap: (Druids) v Sco 1876

Career: Ruabon Rov; Plasmadoc/Druids, 1869-76.

David Thomson, a brother to George, was the first ever Wales goalkeeper and had a tough international baptism. At least one of Scotland's four goals was scored by Ferguson charging Thomson and ball over the line. His club was given as Shropshire Wanderers, although he was regularly turning out for Druids. A captain in the Royal Denbighshire Militia, he was one of the originators of the Plasmadoc club and was later Druids president. He was present at the first FAW meeting in June 1876 at which the Association decided to adopt English Football Association rules. Thomson, who was also an excellent cricketer with Wynnstay CC, died suddenly in September 1876 and as a mark of respect the Druids players wore black armbands throughout the '76-77 season. Thomson played cricket for the Gentlemen of Staffordshire (1868-74) and the Gentlemen of Shropshire (1871-73)

10 George Frederick Thomson
B: Halesowen (Eng);
    28 Sep 1853
D: Cheltenham (Eng);
    15 May 1937
Forward
2 caps: (Druids) v Sco 1876;
v Sco 1877

Career: Plasmadoc/Druids, 1869-80; (also Ruabon Rov, and Shropshire Wdrs, 1874-75). Also, **N Wales** v Birmingham (1876), v Sheffield (1876 & 1878); **Denbighshire** v Birmingham (1877).

Younger brother of David Thomson, Fred was a hard working forward whose forte was running with the ball but was none too accurate in his shooting.

Together with his brother and Dr Gray, all three individuals played a prominent role in the foundation of the FAW and G F Thomson was a member of the original committee of the Association.

Thomson worked as a timber merchant but later assisted his father who was manager of the New British Iron Works in Ruabon. He was also a shareholder in the Llangollen Iron Ore Company Ltd. Thomson retired from soccer in 1880 but remained active in the Wynnstay Cricket Club. When the iron company went into liquidation over Christmas 1887, he left Ruabon and eventually moved to Quendon in Essex. There, in a radical change of career, he became an artist. Thomson later lived in Bedford and settled in Cheltenham before the First World War. His two sons, Aubrey and George, were both killed in the conflict. Thomson was a brother-in-law to William Addams Williams Evans, a teammate in the first international match in 1876.

Honours:
Druids - Welsh Cup finalists 1878

11 William Wiliams
B: Ruabon; 1856:
D: Acrefair; 21 Jan 1921
Halfback
11 caps: (Druids) v Sco 1876;
v Sco 1878; (Oswestry T)
v Eng, Sco 1879; (Druids)
v Eng 1880; v Eng, Sco 1881;
v Ire, Eng, Sco 1882; v Ire 1883

Career: Ruabon; Plasmadoc/Druids, 1874-78; Oswestry T, 1878-79; Druids, 1879-90. Also, **N Wales** v Sheffield (1877 & 1878).

'Little Billy', as he was known, was a phenomenon of early Welsh soccer and, by the standards of the times, enjoyed a remarkably long career. Of the first 15 international matches, Billy failed to gain a place in the team on just four occasions. He invariably reserved his best performances for the national team for the meetings with the Scots and this earned him the nicknames of 'Scotty' and 'Bill Williams Scot'. While never a subtle player, Billy could run all day and had endless reserves of stamina. His strong points were his 'perfect tackling' and vigorous support to the forwards. One reporter commented: "he puts a stop to many a dangerous run, he is a most effective player though not one of the fastest".

A chimney top maker by trade, Billy kept going until 1890 and outlasted all his contemporaries. He also made occasional appearances for Bootle where Bobby Lythgoe, the former Druids official, was club secretary. In later life he lived in Acrefair and worked as a brick presser at a local brickworks.

Honours:
Druids - Welsh Cup 1880, 1881, 1882, 1885, 1886;
    finalists 1878, 1883, 1884

12 Thomas Blundell Burnett

B: Southport (Eng); 1852
D: Buxton (Eng); 22 Oct 1918
Goalkeeper
1 cap: (Ruabon) v Sco 1877

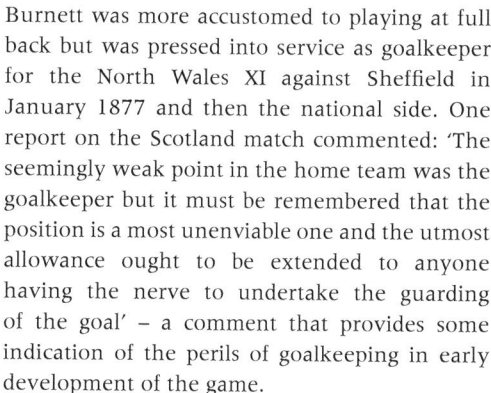

Career: Ruabon, 1876-80; Southport, 1881-86.

Burnett was more accustomed to playing at full back but was pressed into service as goalkeeper for the North Wales XI against Sheffield in January 1877 and then the national side. One report on the Scotland match commented: 'The seemingly weak point in the home team was the goalkeeper but it must be remembered that the position is a most unenviable one and the utmost allowance ought to be extended to anyone having the nerve to undertake the guarding of the goal' – a comment that provides some indication of the perils of goalkeeping in early development of the game.

Burnett was also a keen cricketer and chairman and opening bat of Wynnstay CC in Ruabon. In the winter of 1880, he moved to Southport where he played rugby for the local club and took part in its first association match in November 1881 (v Bootle Second). A burly full back and a vigorous player, Burnett was Southport secretary in October 1882 when the team faced Liverpool Ramblers in their first-ever FA Cup tie. The Southport club folded in 1886 and he transferred to the local lacrosse club rather than join Southport Wanderers. Burnett was an apprentice corn merchant as a youngster and then variously an accountant, coal merchant and insurance agent. His mother owned a number of houses and by his early forties he was able to live in retirement in Formby on private means. In the 1870s Burnett played cricket for Denbighshire alongside E A Cross and Charles Edwards. His best performance as a bowler was the nine wickets in an innings he took for Wynnstay against Wrexham in June 1876.

13 John Hughes

B: Llanbadarn Fawr; 1855
D: Bloomsbury (Eng); 2 Oct 1914
Forward
2 caps: (Cambridge Univ) v Sco 1877; v Sco 1879

Career: Shrewsbury Sch; Jesus Coll (Cambridge), 1874-78.

Jack Hughes, the son of an Aberystwyth solicitor, was introduced to soccer at Shrewsbury School where he played in the first eleven in 1872-73. At Cambridge University he was awarded soccer blues in 1875, 1876 and in 1877, when he appeared in the same team as his Jesus College contemporary J R Morgan, the Wales full back. Hughes was Aberystwyth's 'first great exponent of the association game' and the driving force behind the formation of the Aberystwyth club. One commentator observed many years later: 'The pre-eminence of Jack Hughes cannot be over-emphasized, recalling that he was one of the best forwards in the United Kingdom. At that period combination was unknown and a single good player in a team counted a lot, so that Aberystwyth in virtue alone of their possession of a footballer of so much renown held a high place in the football world'. Hughes gave up the Aberystwyth captaincy in 1879 when he left the town to become a solicitor in London.

14 Alexander Fletcher Jones

B: Dumfries (Sco); 1854
D: Bristol (Eng); 16 Feb 1878
Forward
1 cap: (Oxford Univ) v Sco 1877

Career: Oswestry Sch; Brasenose Coll (Oxford); (also Shrewsbury, Jan 1878).

Jones was educated at Oswestry School and was the first pupil to win a school scholarship before going up to Brasenose College, Oxford. At Oxford, he was a brilliant scholar and took first class degrees in both mathematics and natural sciences. Jones earned his selection on the basis of his performance for North Wales against Sheffield in January 1877 and his varsity background was no drawback. In those days, Llewellyn Kenrick and his fellow selectors had a healthy regard for university soccer. One report described him as 'an admirable centre player'.

Jones became a master at Clifton College, Bristol in May 1877 but lost his life the following year in a bizarre accident. The boys had been to Sea Mills for shooting practice and on the return journey by train a loaded gun was accidentally discharged and killed Jones in the next compartment. Apparently, a boy had been demonstrating the fault of a competitor when the gun went off. Jones is commemorated with memorial windows at both Oswestry School and Clifton College.

15 John Richard Morgan

B: Llangyfelach; 1 Oct 1854
D: Bath (Eng); 11 Apr 1937
Full back
10 caps (2 gls): (Cambridge Univ) v Sco 1877; (unattached) v Sco 1879; (Derby Sch) v Eng, Sco 1880; v Eng, Sco 1881; v Ire, Eng, Sco 1882; (Derby Midland) v Eng 1883

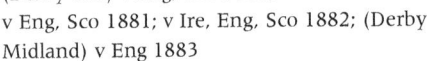

Career: Oundle Sch; St John's (Leatherhead); Jesus Coll (Cambridge), 1874-77; Reading, Oct 1878-Mar 1879; Derby Sch, Aug, 1879; Notts Co, 1879; Derby Midland, 1883.

The son of the curate of Llansamlet, Morgan was born in Wales but educated in England, – at Oundle School and St John's, Leatherhead. He was a student at Cambridge between 1874 and 1877, gaining his soccer blue in 1877 and an athletics blue for the shot putt. He was prominent in the University's progress to the 1876-77 FA Cup semi-final in which they lost to eventual winners, Wanderers. Morgan was a strong, athletic back who was an automatic choice for his country and captained Wales during their first faltering steps in international football. In the 1881 match against England he was said to have 'captained his team in first-rate style'.

After university, Morgan was appointed assistant master at Park House School, Reading and joined the local amateur club Reading FC, again appearing in the FA Cup. While with the Berkshire club he appeared in two England trial matches held at the Kennington Oval in February 1879 to select a team to face Scotland, but whether he was a realistic candidate for selection is not clear. Although 'Swansea' was appended to his name in the Wales team, there was no soccer club in Swansea at that time of his appearances for the national side. After Reading he was an assistant master at Derby School from August 1879. He left Derby in 1883 and taught briefly at Somersetshire College in Bath before, in 1885, becoming the founder and headmaster of Connaught House prep school in Weymouth. Morgan was the author of the text book 'A Preparatory English Grammar'.

16 John Price

B: Wrexham; 1854
D: Wrexham; 30 Nov 1907
Centre forward
12 caps (4 gls): (Wrexham) v Sco 1877; v Sco 1878; v Eng 1879; v Eng, Sco 1880; v Eng, Sco 1881; v Ire, Eng, Sco 1882; v Sco, Ire 1883

Career: Wrexham Grosvenor; Civil Service, Wrexham; Wrexham, 1877-83. Also, **N Wales** v Birmingham (1877), v Staffordshire (1878 & 1880), v Lancashire (1879, 1880 & 1881).

For five seasons Johnny Price was an automatic choice for Wales and, remarkably, missed only three of the first fifteen internationals. In 1882 at Wrexham, he created a goal-scoring record by notching four goals against Ireland (see also R Doughty). Equally good with his head and feet, Price was said never to have played a 'foul game'. Although he played the occasional match for Bolton he remained faithful to the Wrexham club, declining all offers.

Price had first appeared as full back for the Civil Service but Charles Murless, the Wrexham captain, persuaded him that he stood a better chance of Welsh Cup success if he changed allegiance. Murless decided to move Price to centre forward where his remarkable speed made him 'a difficult opponent to stop in front of goal'. The strength of the Wrexham forward line allowed Murless to pull one of his front men to the half back line to field a 2:3:5 formation – a pattern not adopted by other clubs until around 1880. Price's play in an age of individualism was modern in style, skilfully involving his fellow forwards, particularly the wingmen. By 1883, he had practically given up football and it was something of a surprise when the out-of-practice Price was chosen to play against Ireland. Away from football, Price, who worked as a leather dresser in a Wrexham leather works, was noted as a good wicketkeeper, angler, sprinter and rifle shot. The bearers at his funeral were four Welsh internationals players: John Davies, Harry Edwards, Sam Jones and Bob Roberts.

Honours:
Wrexham - Welsh Cup 1878; finalists 1879

17 Thomas Johnson Britten

B: Byton (Eng); 6 Mar 1858
D: Johannesburg (SA); 24 Oct 1910
Forward (5ft 8ins)
2 caps: (Parkgrove) v Sco 1878;
v Sco 1880

Career: Doncaster G Sch; Parkgrove; Grantham 1878; Nottingham F, 1879; Brentwood, 1883-86 (also guested for Bootle); Crusaders (Leyton), 1886-87. Also, Glasgow v Sheffield (1878); **London FA XI**.

As a youngster Thomas Britten was sent to board at Doncaster Grammar School where he was once upbraided for playing with a ball during school hours. While he was apprenticed as an engineer to Messrs. John Elder & Co in Glasgow he began playing for Parkgrove. Britten was subsequently employed by Messrs. R Hornsby and Sons, of Grantham and later in the London area. A player of great speed, energy and determination, Britten was the only Welsh forward to trouble the Scots in the 1878 match. By 1879 the Football Association had clearly realized that, despite some suggestions that Britten hailed from Carmarthen, he was English and he was called for a trial match for England v The Rest at Stoke. When he was subsequently chosen by Wales to play against England, Britten's qualification was objected to and he stood down.

A qualified mining engineer, Britten went out to South Africa in June 1887 as the representative of Messrs Hornsby and played a major role in the development of mining in the Transvaal. He opened up many of the most profitable mines and in 1893 turned to mine management and practised in Johannesburg on his own account. Britten was subsequently general manager of the Wolhuter Gold Mines to 1905, and consulting engineer to Messrs Abe Bailey and Company. He was elected an associate member of the Institution of Civil Engineers in December 1896. In 1904, he was awarded a £500 prize by the Transvaal Chamber of Mines and a gold medal for devising a spray atomiser which minimized dust in mines and prevented phthisis, a tubercular disease of the lungs. The 1903 patent described the gadget for 'Improvements in Apparatus for Laying or Settling the Dust or Pulverised Rock Created in the Boring and Blasting of Holes in Mining'.

Britten, who married Cecilia Johanna Botha, a cousin of General Louis Botha, first Prime

Minister of the Union of South Africa, was a great polo player and a member of the Hand and Johannesburg Turfs Clubs.

18 James Davies
B: Wrexham; 1844 (bapt. 16 Jun)
D: Wrexham; 1 Oct 1924
Centre forward
1 cap: (Wrexham) v Sco 1878

Career: Wrexham, 1872-80. Also, **N Wales** v Birmingham (1877).

James Davies was at the heart of Welsh football in the 1870s and was a key member of the Wrexham Football Club as player and instigator. He served on the committee from 1873 and did much to nurture the game in the town. Davies was 'a fearless player' and 'a deadly shot at goal'. Athletic News described him as 'an excellent centre forward, very fast and thoroughly unselfish'. On his retirement in 1880, as a result of a knee injury, he was said to have scored more goals for Wrexham than any other player, with the exception of Johnny Price. Most important of all his goals was the one he scored in the dying moments of the first Welsh Cup final to give Wrexham the trophy. The ball was rushed through the posts with Davies getting the crucial touch; the effort lacked finesse but was typical of soccer at that time.

In 1876, Davies helped Llewellyn Kenrick establish the Football Association of Wales and he served as the body's president in 1891. He was also chairman of the Welsh League – the first soccer league in North Wales – during its initial seasons. Davies, who was in business in Wrexham as a master mason, employing several men, inscribed the slab on the tomb of Elihu Yale that was given to Yale University.

Honours:
Wrexham - Welsh Cup 1878

19 Charles Edwards
B: Aberdovey; 27 Jul 1855
D: Llanymynech; 25 Dec 1943
Half back
1 cap: (Wrexham) v Sco 1878

Career: Llangollen, 1877; Wrexham, 1877-81. Also, **N Wales** v Birmingham (1876), v Sheffield (1878).

The son of Edward Edwards of the Hand Hotel, Llangollen, Charles Edwards had a brief dalliance with soccer. A bank clerk by profession, he featured in the Wrexham side which won the first ever Welsh Cup competition. Edwards gained international honours in somewhat unusual circumstances. The FAW had notified the Scottish FA that they were unable to raise a side for the international match but the indefatigable SFA secretary Mr Dick was determined that the match should be played. At his prompting, FAW officials toured the Wrexham area and rounded up a team to represent the Principality.

Edwards, who later took the name Gore-Edwards, wound down his soccer activity after 1881 and a few years later moved to London where he worked as a commercial clerk for a telephone company. He was a brother to Sir Francis Edwards, one time Liberal MP for Radnorshire, and brother-in-law to Alfred George Edwards, Archbishop of Wales from 1920 to 1934. His son Sylvanus Rupert Gore-Edwards claimed to be the true Prince of Wales, as a direct descendant of Prince Llewellyn, the last native-born ruler of Wales.

Honours:
Wrexham - Welsh Cup 1878; finalists 1879

20 Henry Valentine Edwards

B: Wrexham; 1856
D: Wrexham; 16 Aug 1913
Half back
8 caps: (Civil Service, Wrexham) v Sco 1878; (Wrexham) v Eng 1880, Sco 1880; v Eng, Sco 1882; v Sco 1883; v Ire 1884; (Wrexham Olympic) v Ire 1887

Career: Civil Service, Wrexham, 1876-79; Wrexham, 1879-84; Wrexham Olympic, 1884-88. Also, **N Wales** v Lancashire (1879 & 1880), Staffordshire (1880 & 1881), v Liverpool & Dist (1883).

Described as 'a splendid athlete', Harry Edwards was a solid half back, much admired for his capacity for hard work and his ability to 'back up his forwards'. His enthusiasm sometimes got the better of him and an element of roughness could creep into his play. Captain of the Civil Service team, he moved to the senior Wrexham club in 1879 and four years later led Wrexham to their second Welsh Cup win. For most of the 1880s, his name invariably found his way onto the selectors' short list for the international matches.

Edwards retired in 1888, playing his final match for Wrexham at Anfield in the Argus Silver medal tournament. He worked as a cabinet maker for many years but later kept dining rooms in Wrexham.

Honours:
Wrexham – Welsh Cup 1883

21 George Garnet Higham

B: Oswestry (Eng); 1855
D: Drwysynant; 20 Oct 1925
Full back
2 caps: (Oswestry T) v Sco 1878; v Eng 1879

Career: Oswestry T, 1875-81. Also, **N Wales** v Sheffield (1876).

Higham was one of the founders of the Oswestry Football Club in September 1875 and retained a lifelong interest in soccer. Oswestry captain in 1878-79, he was described as 'a formidable full back, clean with his kicks and charges well and with judgement'. In those early days Higham was usually the Wales reserve to Llewellyn Kenrick and J R Morgan and on occasions assumed the captaincy.

He gave up playing in the early 1880s but remained an Oswestry committee member for over 40 years. Higham was a gunsmith by profession and kept a sports outfitters shop in Oswestry with a branch in Welshpool. A keen motorist, he had been out for a drive with his wife in his Austin Seven when the car was found overturned in a river at Drwysynant. The couple had died by drowning but their small terrier was found alive. The police investigations failed to establish how the tragic accident had occurred.

22 Edward Phennah

B: Birkenhead (Eng); 1859
D: Ruabon; 18 May 1923
Goalkeeper
1 cap: (Civil Service, Wrexham) v Sco 1878

Career: Civil Service, Wrexham, 1876-77; Wrexham, 1877-78; Civil Service, Wrexham, 1878-80. Also, **N Wales** v Sheffield (1878).

Ted Phennah's soccer career was short and he subsequently channelled his enthusiasm for the game into the administration side. He was a leading member of the Civil Service club, a junior soccer and cricket club which played its matches at the Rhosddu Recreation ground. Ted was asked by Edward Evans of the Wrexham club to throw in his lot with them for the 1877-

78 season. Wrexham reached the first ever final of the Welsh Cup and won 1-0, thanks in part to Phennah's brave stop from Fred Thomson of Druids, close to goal. He always believed that his performance in the final, and in particular that save, impressed the Welsh selectors.

Later that year, he returned to the Civil Service but dislocated his arm in a practice match. The injury was a bad one and he retired from soccer to become an umpire and then a referee. Phennah was treasurer of Wrexham FC and a member of the FAW for several years. On 15 March 1890, he chaired the meeting at the Lion House Wrexham to launch the first association football league in North Wales. Many years after giving up the game Phennah made the following observation on goalkeeping in the early days of Welsh soccer: 'modern goalkeepers would be surprised if they were suddenly called upon to play under the conditions that obtained when I played. It was the practice for one forward to charge the goalkeeper and another to deliver the shot'. Ted was steward of the Wrexham Conservative Club and subsequently kept the Masons Arms in Cefn Bychan until his death. He also served on the committee that administered the Denbighshire & Flintshire Charity Cup Association competition – the Soames Cup.

Honours:
Wrexham - Welsh Cup 1878

23 John Powell

B: Ffrwd, Wrexham;
25 Mar 1859
D: Wrexham; 16 Mar 1947
Right back (6ft 2ins, 14st)
15 caps: (Druids) v Sco 1878; v Eng, Sco 1880; v Ire, Eng, Sco 1882; v Eng, Sco, Ire 1883; (Bolton Wdrs) v Eng 1884; (Newton Heath) v Eng, Sco 1887; v Eng, Ire, Sco 1888

Career: Druids, 1878-83; Bolton Wdrs, Oct 1883-86; Newton Heath, Mar 1886-91. Also, **N Wales** v Sheffield (1878), v Lancashire (1879 & 1880), v Staffordshire (1880 & 1881).

Jack Powell always maintained that he had never played soccer competitively before joining Druids and yet after just three games for the Ruabon club he was selected in 1878 to play for Wales. A week after his international debut, he lined up for Druids in the first ever Welsh Cup final. At that time, Jack, who was employed at the Newbridge Iron Works, was considered a colossus and his massive build earned him the nicknames 'The Welsh Giant' and 'The Lion of Wales'. He captained Druids for several seasons and was usually partnered at full back by his brother Albert. In the 1882-83 season Druids, under Jack's leadership, reached the quarter-final of the FA Cup, losing 4-1 to eventual winners Blackburn Olympic.

Bolton Wanderers, beaten by Druids, were so impressed with their opponents that Jack was persuaded to join the Lancashire club – making him, in effect, the first professional footballer produced by Wales. His career at Bolton ended in unusual circumstances. Professionalism in England was legalized in July 1885 and the FA Cup rules allowed pros to compete, provided they were qualified by birth or residence for two years within six miles of the ground or headquarters of the club for which they played. After losing to Preston in December 1885, Bolton entered a protest claiming that their opponents had violated this rule as two of their players had been working in Scotland during the compulsory qualifying period. Preston conducted their own investigations which showed that Powell had broken the rules by taking a temporary job in Ruabon. He had kept quiet and subsequently denied that he had been paid for the work. The Bolton officials had been put in an impossible position and Jack had to leave the club. The FA ruled that both clubs be disqualified from the competition.

In 1886, he joined Newton Heath and moved to Manchester to become a fitter with the

Lancashire and Yorkshire Railway Company. Powell proved to be a highly influential signing for the club formed in 1878; he was appointed captain and in September 1889 guided the club into the Alliance League. In the 1890 Manchester Cup final against Royton, Powell, who was returning from injury was given a less active role and was fielded in goal! Jack was regarded as a tough but generous adversary and one opponent was quoted by Percy Young in Bolton Wanderers (1960) as saying 'I don't believe Jack would wilfully hurt an opponent. He is very good humoured and generously maintains his equanimity. But when he goes into a scrimmage it's a case of ware hawk, nothing seems to bar his progress'.

After retiring from football, he continued to work for the railway company for a while, but then became a publican in Manchester and subsequently at the Cross Keys Inn, Wrexham. He made his last appearance on a football field in 1908 but remained a fervent follower of the game until his death and invariably attended league matches and internationals at the Racecourse. For many years Jack was caretaker of the livery stables owned by FAW secretary Ted Robbins.

Honours:
Druids - Welsh Cup 1880, 1881, 1882; finalists 1878, 1883
Newton Heath - Manchester Cup 1888, 1889

24 George Foulkes Savin

B: Oswestry (Eng);
    27 Jan 1860
D: Oswestry (Eng);
    29 Nov 1901
Wing half/Inside forward
1 cap: (Oswestry T) v Sco 1878

Career: Oswestry T, 1877-80. Also, **N Wales** v Lancashire (1879).

After completing his education at Oswestry Grammar School, Savin trained as an engineer at Brown Brothers of Edinburgh. His availability for the Oswestry club was limited by the demands of his apprenticeship. Savin's one appearance for Wales was an unhappy experience as the side were crushed 9-0 by the Scots. He was a member of the Welsh side recruited largely at the instigation of Mr Dick, the SFA secretary, and found himself playing international football at the age of barely 18.

Savin later took work in London but subsequently became works manager of the Western Railway Company in Argentina. His father Thomas Savin, who was mayor of Oswestry in 1863, had been a great promoter of railway construction in Wales in the mid nineteenth century, in particular the Vale of Clwyd line and the Cambrian Railway. George's health broke down in 1900 and he was invalided home to Oswestry where he died a few months after his former footballing colleague Digby Owen.

25 George William Glascodine

B: Isle of Wight (Eng);
    7 Aug 1856
D: Oswestry (Eng);
    15 Dec 1943
Goalkeeper
1 cap: (Oswestry T) v Eng 1879

Career: St Oswalds (Oswestry), 1875-77 and Oswestry T, 1876-1880; (also Wrexham and Chester Coll). Also, **N Wales** v Lancashire (1879).

George Glascodine moved to Wales at a young age when his father became village schoolmaster at Llanyblodwel. He began playing football as a centre forward for St Oswalds – a church team – in 16-a-side matches. Glascodine was one of nine Oswestry players who faced England at the Kennington Oval in a match played in a snowstorm before some 150 spectators. His defence of the Wales goal wasn't helped by the mixture of snow and sleet that fell during most of the game. Glascodine's selection and that of eight other Oswestry men owed a lot to the refusal of most of the Wrexham players to be considered and to the selection committee being chaired by the Oswestry club chairman in an Oswestry hotel! Glascodine trained as a teacher at Chester College, Ellesmere and held posts in Willoughton and Corringham, Lincolnshire for 43 years before returning to Oswestry in the 1920s.

26 Dennis Heywood
B: Prestwich (Eng); 1854
D: Middleton (Eng); 7 Oct 1919.
Forward
1 cap: (Wrexham) v Eng 1879

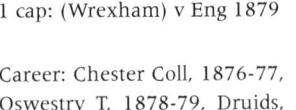

Career: Chester Coll, 1876-77, Oswestry T, 1878-79, Druids, 1879-82. Also, **N Wales** v Staffordshire (1878 & 1880), v Lancashire (1879).

'A fast runner but erratic shooter', Dennis Heywood preferred to play as what would now be known as a right winger. While capable of 'brilliant runs' and outpacing defenders, he was sometimes criticized as being slow to cross the ball. Heywood was another of the Oswestry players chosen to face England at Kennington Oval, although newspaper reports gave his club as Wrexham. He had an unhappy game eventually having to leave the field of play because of injury. Heywood, who worked as a teacher at Trevor, near Llangollen, severed his connection with the Druids when he returned to Lancashire in 1882. He was later a schoolmaster in Ebberstone, Yorkshire then South Stoneham and concluded his career in Stepney in London.

Honours:
Druids - Welsh Cup 1880, 1881, 1882

27 Thomas Owen
B: Unknown
D: Unknown
Half back
1 cap: (Oswestry T) v Eng 1879

Career: St Oswalds (Oswestry), 1876-77; Oswestry T, Oct 1878-79. Also, **N Wales** v Lancashire (1879).

Owen was a member of the Oswestry contingent who was drafted into the Wales team side to play in the very first international meeting with England. The Wrexham players refused to be considered, Druids were inactive having lost their ground and this left way open for the Oswestry players. Owen's strengths lay at half back and he was said to be excellent at 'backing up'. Although he occasionally played full back, he was 'more at home at half back'. It was thought that Owen was the father of Wilfred Owen, the war poet, and brother-in-law of E G Shaw who played for Wales in 1882 and 1884. However, an article in a 1909 Oswestry newspaper indicated that Owen had a connection with the town of Pwllheli and was a member of the Castle Blues team that won the Shropshire Cup in 1882. This would rule out Wilfred's father from being the international player. Additionally the family of Wilfred Owen have confirmed that Wilfred's father never mentioned playing soccer for Wales. The international player moved to Shrewsbury in 1880 and played for Shrewsbury Engineers then Shrewsbury Castle Blues. It is now believed that Owen worked as a tax official and died in 1932 aged 82.

28 William Digby Owen
B: Oswestry (Eng); 1857
D: Oswestry (Eng); 2 Jun 1901
Forward
1 cap: (Oswestry T) v Eng 1879

Career: Oswestry G Sch; Oswestry T, 1876-80 (intermittently); Trinity Coll

(Oxford Univ), 1876-80. Also, **N Wales** v Sheffield (1877), v Lancashire (1879); **Shropshire** v Staffordshire (1879).

Digby Owen was a fine athlete and a noted exponent of the dribbling game so popular in the 1870s. He joined the Oswestry club in its second year of existence but his appearances were limited by academic studies and other commitments. An Oxford graduate (BA Trinity College 1878), Owen missed his soccer blue through illness. He got the call-up for Wales as part of the large Oswestry contingent selected to face England. After 1880, he reverted to his first love and played cricket for the Oswestry club for many years and also represented Shropshire. A private tutor by profession, Owen died of pneumonia while in his early forties.

29 William Roberts

B: Prestatyn; 1859
D: Birkenhead (Eng);
   9 Aug 1910
Forward
7 caps (2 gls): (Llangollen) v Eng, Scot 1879; v Eng, Sco 1880; (Berwyn Rgrs) v Eng, Sco 1881; v Sco 1883

Career: Llangollen, 1878-80; Crewe Alex; Northwich Vic, Oct 1880; Berwyn Rgrs (Llangollen), 1881-82; Aston Villa, 1882-84; Berwyn Rgrs (Llangollen); also Small Heath Alliance. Also **N Wales** v Staffordshire (1878 & 1800), v Lancashire (1880).

Roberts gained his first cap as replacement for his Llangollen colleague and namesake Jack Roberts as one of only two non-Oswestry players in the Principality's team for the first international match against England. With Wales trailing 1-2, he managed to put the ball between the English posts to secure what his colleagues believed was an equaliser but a foul on Davies had been allowed and the ball was brought back. In the words of one newspaper: 'The Welshmen, who thought matters were now brought level, were rather surprised that their efforts had been thrown away, and the goal could not be reckoned'. In 1881 he had the distinction of scoring Wales' first ever goal against Scotland.

Roberts was unusual, and something of a pioneer, in that he appeared for top English clubs several years before professionalism, even of an unofficial nature, became common. At Villa, he made five FA Cup appearances and played alongside such greats as Howard Vaughton and Archie Hunter. One report commented: 'He can scamper down the wing with his mates to the right of him and curl the leather plum in front of goal, neatly and deftly'. Villa's 6-1 defeat at the hands of Queens Park, in January 1884, signalled the end of his career at the midlands club. Roberts 'seemed unable to make any headway at all' and in the close season returned to Llangollen. He worked as stone mason and in the 1890s moved to the Merseyside area. His obituary described him as 'having been the father of Association Football in the Llangollen district' and commented that with Jack Roberts 'they were terrors for their size and made their mark in the very front rank as exponents of the winter game'.

30 Watkin William Shone

B: Birmingham (Eng);
   10 Mar 1858
D: Oswestry (Eng);
   20 Sep 1930
Outside right
1 cap: (Oswestry T) v Eng 1879

Career: St Oswalds (Oswestry), 1875-77; Oswestry T, 1876-80 (and Oswestry White Stars, 1880 and 1882); Stafford Road (Wolverhampton), 1880-82.

Shone was a very popular player with the spectators, who admired his head-down, high speed dashes for goal. He had joined the Oswestry club early in its existence but subsequently left to join the midlands club Stafford Road in 1880. Shone partnered Charles Crump, later senior vice president of the FA, in the team that competed against the likes of Aston Villa and Wolverhampton Wanderers.

In a 1909 interview Shone recalled his playing career, which had begun with a club 'promoted by the Church of England Young Mens' Society', and involved matches against teams such as Ruabon, All Saints (Shrewsbury), The Ramblers (Shrewsbury), Gwersyllt, Whittington and Wrexham. Oswestry cricketers formed a club and subsequently amalgamated with St Oswalds to form Oswestry Town which Shone also represented against the likes of Wrexham, the Druids, Stafford Road (Wolverhampton) and Chester College. He retired from playing in the 1880s and confessed in 1909 that the game had greatly improved: 'In my days it was all individual play and there was very little passing. It was all dribbling, now combination has taken its place, and the game has undoubtedly advanced'.

Shone had left school to work for the Oswestry Cooperative Society but then got an apprenticeship in the mechanical engineering department of the Cambrian Railway. He was employed as an engine fitter and remained with the company until it was taken over by the Great Western in 1924. Shone's one appearance for Wales was as part of the large Oswestry contingent drafted into play England at the Kennington Oval.

31 Knyvett Crosse
B: Pontesbury (Eng); 1855
D: Liverpool (Eng);
   19 Nov 1916
Half back/Forward
3 caps (1 gl): (Druids) v Sco 1879; v Eng, Sco 1881

Career: Druids, 1877-78; Ruabon, 1878-79; Druids, 1879-83, also Oswestry T, 1880. Also, **N Wales** v Lancashire (1879, 3 matches), v Staffordshire (1878).

On leaving school Crosse was employed as a parcels clerk at Ludlow station and then as a bookstall manager for W H Smith at Ruabon station. He frequently played under the pseudonym 'C K Smith' as he was anxious that his employers should remain unaware of his footballing activities and took the company's name to conceal his identity. Crosse was a well-built player, ideally suited to the robust style of play adopted by Druids. Although a hard working player, his lack of consistency limited his appearances for Wales.

Crosse was the licensee of the Cross Foxes, Ruabon for several years until the public house was closed by Sir Watkin Williams Wynn, patron of the Druids club. In December 1889 Crosse moved to the Star Hotel in the Bangor High Street (opposite the Cathedral) and it was here that the Wales and Ireland teams were entertained after the international match in Penrhyn Park in March 1892. Crosse was active in the sporting life of the town, playing cricket for the Bangor club from 1890 to 1895 and serving as captain of the club, and he took a leading role in the football club. A sporting activity of a different kind saw Crosse prosecuted in 1894 for trespassing in pursuit of game on Lord Penrhyn's land at Siliwen Woods. He was fined 5s (25p). The following year a gas explosion damaged the Star Hotel and he received £12 compensation from Bangor Council. Crosse moved to the Horns Inn, Wrexham in 1899 and remained the licensee until he retired to live in Marchwiel.

Honours:
Druids - Welsh Cup 1880, 1881, 1882

32 John Davies
B: Bersham; 1856
D: Glyn Ceiriog; 22 Jun 1929
Goalkeeper
1 cap: (Wrexham) v Sco 1879

Career: Wrexham, 1878-83.

John Davies had only a brief career as a goalkeeper and

played his most important role as FAW secretary from 1897 to 1903. He took over the reins of the FAW in the wake of the imprisonment of John Taylor, the previous incumbent. A senior official at the Wrexham County Court, Davies brought much needed integrity to the position of FAW secretary and put the Association back on an even keel. In 1905, he became president of the FAW and held the post for six years. In August 1911 he declined to be re-elected and was succeeded by R T Gough. The imposing figure of the bearded Davies can be seen in many of the team photographs taken during his time with the FAW. In his one appearance for Wales, Davies had a hard time – the Scots 'charged the goal five times consecutively but Davies frustrated all their efforts by thrusting the ball back or throwing it over the posts, some of the challenges being very heavy.' A keen cricketer, Davies worked as a County Court official for 54 years.

33 James William Lloyd
B: Ruabon; 10 Mar 1861
D: Wallasey (Eng); 8 Jan 1944
Wing half/Centre forward
2 caps: (Wrexham) v Sco 1879; (Newtown) v Sco 1885

Career: Ruabon, 1877-78; Wrexham, 1878-80; Druids, 1880-82; Oswestry T, Oct-Dec 1882; Druids, 1883; Newtown, 1884-87. Also, **N Wales** v Staffordshire (1880).

Jimmy Lloyd was an early starter in soccer and played for Ruabon at the age of 16 against Newtown White Star in the inaugural Welsh Cup competition. During 1877, he joined the North and South Wales Bank at Wrexham and he subsequently changed clubs as he moved from branch to branch. A splendid dribbler, Lloyd was said to have improved his game by 'a systematic course of training and running' – no doubt invaluable preparation for his part in Druids' quarter-final FA Cup run of 1883.

When Lloyd was transferred to Newtown, he found football interest to be at a low ebb. He called a meeting in August 1884 but only five people turned up. Lloyd decided to call on the various woollen mills and factories in the area and 150 turned up to a second meeting to successfully re-launch senior soccer in the town. In 1887, he retired from playing but served as FAW treasurer from 1889 to 1891 when he moved to the Wirral.

Honours:
Druids - Welsh Cup 1881; finalists 1883
Wrexham - Welsh Cup finalists 1879, 1886

34 John Roberts
B: Cerrigydrudion; 1857
D: Llangollen; 4 Jan 1921
Forward
6 caps (1 gl): (Corwen) v Sco 1879; v Eng, Sco 1880; v Ire, Sco 1882; (Berwyn Rgrs) v Eng 1883

Career: Llangollen, 1878; Corwen, 1879-81; Berwyn Rgrs (Llangollen), 1882-83; Corwen, 1883-1889. Also, **N Wales** v Cheshire (1879, 1881, 1882), v Lancashire (1879, 1880), v Staffordshire (1880, 1881, 1882).

Jack Roberts excelled at the skill of dribbling and he was capable of 'dodging all opponents with his swift runs and was said to be one of the pioneers of soccer in the Corwen area. A popular player, he was secretary and organizer of the Corwen club until the early 1890s, and secretary of Corwen Cricket Club. Roberts worked as a barman in his father's hotel but was subsequently in business on his own account, owning two public houses and a guest house. He was also for some years a member of the local District Council. Roberts refereed the Wales v England match in March 1882, a match in which he was selected to play. The FAW had arranged for 'one of the members of the Scotch Football Association to act as referee in the match' and Roberts stepped into the breach and his place in the team was taken by William Roberts (Llangollen). Wales won the match 5-3 and there was some muttering among the English contingent that at least one of the home side's goals was offside.

Roberts was the subject in October 1881 of what the local newspapers headlined as a 'serious charge under the licensing act'. The landlord of the Woolpack Inn, Llangollen, was charged with illegal opening of his premises, while three other men including Roberts and fellow Wales international William Roberts were charged with being on licensed premises during prohibited hours. They had travelled from Corwen to attend a football committee meeting at Llangollen, which did not end until eleven o'clock and as their usual lodgings were full they were invited to be guests of the landlord of the Woolpack. When the police entered the premises, they found John Roberts with a glass on a table before him partly filled with ale, and bread and butter and cheese. The magistrates, after a lengthy discussion in their private room, returned into court, and Lord Trevor said that after duly considering the case they thought the police quite right in bringing the case forward, but as the evidence for the prosecution was weak they dismissed it

35 John Vaughan
B: Ruabon; 1858
D: Acrefair; 1 Nov 1935
Outside left
11 caps (2 gls): (Oswestry T) v Sco 1879; (Druids) v Sco 1880; v Eng, Sco 1881; v Ire, Eng, Sco 1882; v Eng, Sco, Ire 1883; (Bolton Wdrs) v Eng 1884

Career: Druids, 1876-78; Oswestry T, 1878-79; Druids, 1879-83; Bolton Wdrs, Oct 1883-85; Druids, Oct 1885-90. Also, **N Wales** v Lancashire (1879, 1889 & 1881), v Staffordshire (1882).

Jackie Vaughan was a durable and hard working player who had the distinction of scoring the only goal of the match when Wales beat England for the first time, at Blackburn in 1881. After taking part in the first ever Welsh Cup final in 1878, he left Druids when the club were temporarily without a playing field and joined Oswestry. This was a deeply unpopular move within the footballing fraternity as previously players had been expected to show loyalty to their villages or town. Vaughan, Bill Williams and Llewellyn Kenrick considerably strengthened the Oswestry side but took their share of criticism.

Vaughan, who was employed at a terracotta works, was one of the Druids contingent which joined Bolton in 1883 and must have made an impression. Fifty years later, when the Bolton directors heard of Vaughan's death they sent a letter of condolence to his son 'in memory of an old and respected player of the Bolton club from its Pike Lane days'. In 1885, Vaughan returned to Druids and finally retired five years later.

Honours:
Druids - Welsh Cup 1880, 1881, 1882, 1886; finalists 1878, 1883

36 George Woosnam
B: Newtown; 1860
D: Newtown; 21 Oct 1935
Outside right
1 cap: (Newtown Excelsior) v Sco 1879

Career: Newtown Excelsior, 1878-80; Newtown White Stars, 1880-83.

Woosnam was reputedly one of the first men to play association football in Newtown and helped to form the local club in the mid 1870s. When the club was wound up around 1880, Woosnam joined the White Stars, a rival organization in the town. Although lightly built, he was an immensely tricky player who relied on skill and speed. In the 1878 Welsh Cup semi-final against Druids,

Woosnam dribbled the whole length of the field to score. The White Stars team were notorious for roughness and fighting amongst themselves, but Woosnam had a reputation as a clean player. From 1883 onwards he concentrated on cricket and played for Newtown CC for many years. He worked for the Royal Welsh Warehouse woollen manufacturing company of Sir Pryce Pryce Jones for over fifty years.

Honours:
Newtown White Stars - Welsh Cup 1879; finalists 1881

37 Thomas Henry Boden
B: Wrexham; 7 Jul 1860
Died: South Africa; 1918
Forward
1 cap: (Wrexham) v Eng 1880

Career: Penybryn Wdrs (Wrexham), 1874-77; (also Grosvenor Boys); Wrexham Hare & Hounds, 1877-78; Wrexham, 1878-80.

Tom Boden was a brewery worker in Wrexham and appeared in the Penybryn team alongside Jim Trainer. A very promising player, he developed a good understanding in the Wrexham team with John Price, first choice centre forward for Wales. The FAW selectors fielded the partnership against England but Boden was badly kicked on the instep close to half time and thereafter was a virtual passenger. He was not selected again and in late 1880 he emigrated to South Africa and joined the Cape Mounted Rifles. Boden later served as a constable in the Cape Town Police Force until his retirement in 1907.

Boden appeared for North Wales v Staffordshire, Lancashire (captain) and Cheshire in 1880. He also played cricket for Penybryn Wanderers.

Honours:
Newtown White Stars - Welsh Cup 1879; finalists 1881

38 Harry Hibbott
B: Newtown; Jul 1859
D: Newtown; 4 Mar 1933
Goalkeeper/Centre forward
3 caps: (Newtown Excelsior) v Eng, Sco 1880; (Newtown) v Sco 1885

Career: Newtown Amateurs; Newtown Excelsior, 1878-80; Newtown White Stars, 1880-83; Newtown, 1884-89. Also, **N Wales** v Lancashire (1879 & 1880), v Staffordshire (1880).

As a goalkeeper, Harry Hibbott was said to be 'quick, adroit, difficult to pass' and possess 'cat-like agility'. The Excelsior club was short lived and when Jimmy Lloyd rekindled soccer interest in the town Hibbott took up the centre forward position for the new club. An excellent dribbler, Harry showed good positional play and had a turn of speed, but struggled at international level. He was called up to face the Scots when Topham of Oswestry cried off but was 'decidedly a failure' – probably because he was better equipped to play as a winger. Nevertheless, he remains the only man to have been selected by Wales as a goalkeeper and an outfield player.

A good athlete, Hibbott had to give up soccer in 1889 when he suffered a badly broken leg which left him with a limp for the rest of his life. He turned to refereeing but continued to play cricket for Newtown for many seasons. A versatile individual, he excelled at snooker and billiards, played in the local brass band and sang in the church choir. In 1903, the people of Newtown marked his emigration to South Africa with the presentation of an illuminated address and a 'purse of gold'. Hibbott remained there for three years until his wife's illness prompted him to return to Wales. A keen territorial and rifleman, he was called up when war broke out and served as a sergeant in the 2/7th Royal Welsh Fusiliers but was invalided out of the Army in 1917. He worked for many years as a carpenter and undertaker and from 1917 was steward at the Newtown Comrades club. His second wife later kept the Market Vaults in Newtown and it was there that George Latham and the victorious Cardiff team displayed the FA Cup in 1927 on their visit to the town. Harry's grandson Bobby Hibbott was capped by Wales as an amateur in 1949-50.

Honours:
Newtown White Stars - Welsh Cup finalists 1881
Newtown - Welsh Cup finalists 1886, 1888

39 William Pierce Owen

B: Llanllechid; 20 Nov 1860
D: Llanbadarn Fawr;
   13 Dec 1937
Winger/Wing half
12 caps (7 gls): (Ruthin) v Eng, Sco 1880; v Eng, Sco 1881; v Ire, Eng, Sco 1882; v Eng, Sco 1883; v Ire, Eng, Sco 1884

Career: Friars Sch (Bangor), 1877; Christ College (Brecon); Ruthin, 1879-84.

W P Owen was a brother to goalkeeper Elias Owen and a cousin to Hugh and Morgan Morgan-Owen. He was one of several international players produced by Friars School, Bangor, where he studied before attending Christ College in Brecon. Owen was an excellent winger who was equally proficient at wing half. He was a member of the victorious Wales side which defeated England for the first time and many years later recalled the occasion: 'We travelled to Manchester by the 8 o'clock train from Ruthin, and on the way to the station I asked Uriah Goodwin where were his football clothes. Oh! he replied, "I've got them on". They were underneath his ordinary clothes! At Manchester we met the rest of the team, mostly Druids, except Bell and McMillan of Shrewsbury. We arrived at Blackburn a man short and took the field with only ten men. To the best of my recollection the ground was nearly 200 yards long and 100 yards wide. The spectators stood on foot planks along the touch lines. It was snowing and hailing and we had been playing for some time, when I saw what I thought was a spectator breaking into the field and making a violent attack upon Marshall and Rostrom, the English right wing. Upon closer inspection I found it was Llewellyn Kenrick of Ruabon. He was dressed in long tweed trousers, wore ordinary boots and sported a smart Oxford shirt. He played with the utmost vigour until unfortunately his knee gave way and once more Wales had only ten men on the field. The only goal of the match was scored by Jack Vaughan from a pass I gave him; he was materially aided by Uriah Goodwin, who impeded the goalkeeper, as he was quite entitled to do in those days. We had to leave Blackburn immediately after the match; so we commandeered from the dining room some fowls and ham to eat on the homeward journey. We stopped at Chester for the night and then travelled on to Mold by train. In addition to our train fare we were given 10s (50p) to pay for a trap from Mold to Ruthin. Goodwin and I made arrangements whereby I was to stand him a pint at the Loggerheads, a far-famed hostelry between Mold and Ruthin, if he carried my bag, and we agreed to divide the 10s and to walk the ten miles across the moor. We reached Ruthin just as the people were coming out of church. We thought ourselves the greatest heroes, having vanquished the English XI'.

Owen gave up soccer to train for the legal profession with Lewis & Edwards of Ruthin. With his great friend and fellow solicitor Llewellyn Kenrick, he represented the FAW at the international association board meetings. On his marriage in 1892, Owen spent the first night of his honeymoon at Kenrick's home at Wynn Hall. He had been admitted as a solicitor in 1886 and practised for a short time in Bala before settling in Aberystwyth. He became patron of the FAW in 1896 and was a committee member of Aberystwyth Town FC. Owen was

Clerk to the Talybont Justices from 1897, the Llandbadarn Justices from 1920 and Registrar of the Aberystwyth County Court. Away from sport, W P, as he was known in north and mid Wales, was a keen antiquarian. Owen played for Wales before caps were awarded but was honoured later and his cap was on display at the Ceredigion Museum in Aberystwyth in the 1980s. W P's eldest son Billy was given the middle name Kenrick and as Lt William Henry Kenrick Owen served in the Great War with the 9th Battalion Royal Welsh Fusiliers. He was wounded at Festubert and died in October 1915 aged just 21.

Honours:
Ruthin - Welsh Cup finalists 1880

40 Edward Bowen
B: Rhosymedre; 1861
D: Llangollen; 9 Oct 1921
Full/Half back/Forward
2 caps: (Druids) v Sco 1880; v Sco 1883

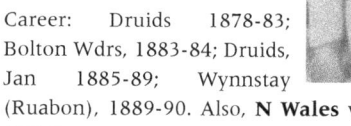

Career: Druids 1878-83; Bolton Wdrs, 1883-84; Druids, Jan 1885-89; Wynnstay (Ruabon), 1889-90. Also, **N Wales** v Staffordshire (1889).

Always known as Ned, Bowen 'had a capacity for playing in all positions and was regarded as a speed merchant of the first water'. He once played in goal at Sunderland in a friendly match and gave a thrilling exhibition. Although very much a 'play anywhere' man and something of a goal scorer, Bowen was undoubtedly strongest at full back. In 1878 he appeared with Druids in the first Welsh Cup final and went on to feature in a further seven finals. This record of eight appearances in the final was shared with Billy Williams and stood for some time.

Bowen, who worked as a colliery labourer, was a robust player who could give a good account of himself, no matter how rough the game. In 1883, he was one of several Druids players to join Bolton, but he was not as successful as Jack Powell, Jack Vaughan and Bob Roberts and he eventually returned to Ruabon. After he ceased playing he lodged with fellow Wales international 'Bob Bolton' in Cefn, Ruabon but later moved to Llangollen and worked as a bricklayer's labourer.

Honours:
Druids - Welsh Cup 1880, 1881, 1882, 1885, 1886; finalists 1878, 1883, 1884

41 William Strafford Bell
B: Newtown; 22 Aug 1860
D: Small Heath (Eng); 1930
Centre half
5 caps: (Shrewsbury Engineers) v Eng, Sco 1881; (Crewe Alex) v Ire, Eng, Sco 1886

Career: Shrewsbury Engineers, 1878; Swifts, 1883-84; Crewe Alex, 1884-90.

Bell's father was a stone mason from Yorkshire who settled in Newtown but when he died his mother remarried and the family, including the young Bell, moved to Shrewsbury. His unusual second name was his mother's maiden name. A strapping pivot with a powerful tackle and a great capacity for hard work, Bell was described in the mid 1880s as: 'one of the finest half backs in the country' – an assessment that was probably not far off the mark. Another report had him as: 'a brilliant defender who plays a hard game'. As was the custom in those days, his name was submitted by Shrewsbury Engineers for consideration by the FAW and he made his debut against England at Blackburn. The match took place on a ground covered with snow and slush and he helped Wales to an unexpected victory.

While playing for Shrewsbury, Bell worked as an iron turner and later kept the Neptune Inn at Coppenhall, later still the Albion Inn and the Lord Nelson in Crewe. In early 1885 Bell was involved in what one newspaper described as a 'most unpleasant incident'. During the interval of a Welsh Cup tie between Oswestry and Crewe, the crowd became ugly and officials had some difficulty holding them back. C J Hughes, secretary of the Cheshire FA, got within the ropes to speak to the players but Bell, as the Crewe captain, ordered him out. When Hughes persistently refused to leave, he was ejected 'with violence'. The Cheshire FA decided to suspend Bell from all cup matches but the FAW took the view that they had overstepped the mark as the match was played under Welsh rules and Bell was 'only engaged in keeping order'.

The defender was one of the Crewe stars in their progress to the semi-final of the FA Cup in 1887-88. He was awarded a benefit match against Port Vale in 1890, which attracted over 4,000 spectators, and after retirement he refereed in the Football Alliance and served on the Crewe committee for a number of years.

Honours:
Shrewsbury Engineers - Shropshire Cup winners 1880

42 Uriah Goodwin

B: Llanfwrog; 1859
D: Ruthin; 13 Dec 1924
Inside forward
1 cap: (Ruthin) v Eng 1881

Career: Ruthin, 1879-89. Also, **N Wales** v Lancashire (1880 & 1881).

'Little Uriah', as he was known, was called up by Wales as a replacement for William Roberts of Berwyn Rangers and according to some reports provided the cross for Jackie Vaughan to score the only goal of the 1881 match against England. W P Owen, his Ruthin colleague, later claimed to have made the goal, with Goodwin 'providing material support by impeding the goalkeeper'. Goodwin had a long connection with football at Ruthin, first as a player and then as a committee member for over forty years. According to one report he was employed at the Ruthin Soda Water works (later the Cambrian Mineral Water Works) for many years but in fact spent time as a bricklayer's labourer. After retiring from playing he seldom missed a Ruthin match.

Honours:
Ruthin - Welsh Cup finalists 1880

43 Thomas Lewis

B: Wrexham
D: unknown
Outside right
2 caps: (Wrexham) v Eng, Sco 1881

Career: Wrexham, 1880-81.
Also, **N Wales** (1880) v Lancashire (1880).

Something of a mystery man, Lewis's career at Wrexham was short-lived but spectacular. A fast and skilful player, he was a hard worker who supplied a stream of accurate crosses for the inside men. Lewis participated in Wales's first-ever victory over England, at Blackburn, but he was lost to the Wrexham club at the end of just one season, possibly to pursue employment outside Wales. Efforts to establish his birthplace have been unsuccessful; one possibility is that he hailed from Oswestry but confirmation has proved elusive.

44 Robert John McMillan

B: Lima (Peru); 16 Nov 1856
D: Gorseinon; Nov 1928
Goalkeeper
2 caps: (Shrewsbury Engineers) v Eng, Sco 1881

Career: Stoke, 1877-79; Thursday Wdrs (Stoke), 1879; Stoke; Shrewsbury Engineers, 1880-84; Shrewsbury Castle Blues. Also, **Staffordshire** v N Wales (date), v Lancashire (1880).

Peruvian-born McMillan was a member of the Welsh team who achieved the first-ever victory over England, at Blackburn in 1881. He was said to have kept goal 'in the very best style', while another report commented 'McMillan and Morgan played so well that each attempt (at goal) was futile'. For three quarters of the match Wales were under pressure but 'McMillan was impassable'.

The goalkeeper had made the Wales team on the basis of Shrewsbury Engineers's participation in the Welsh Cup and implied FAW membership. Earlier, he had acted as secretary of Stoke Thursdays. McMillan had been born in South America, where his father was working as a gas engineer. He later followed that profession, becoming manager of a gas works in Hull, but some time between 1905 and 1911 moved to Swansea where he worked as a waterman for the local council. In E D H Sewell's 'Rugby International Roll of Honour' it was suggested that Richard Garnons-Williams, a Wales rugby international player, may have kept goal in the 1881 England match. The authors have found no evidence to support the suggestion.

Honours:
Stoke - Staffordshire Cup 1879

45 John Roberts
B: Ruthin; 1858
D: Ruthin; 23 Dec 1918
Full back
2 caps: (Ruthin) v Sco 1881; v Sco 1882

Career: Ruthin, 1878-86. Also, **N Wales** v Lancashire (1880-81), v Staffordshire (1881-82).

Much admired as a 'fine and brilliant full back', Johnny Roberts greatly impressed the Ruthinians with his ability to kick the ball from goal to goal. Probably of greater value to the Ruthin team were the other dimensions to his play – safe defence, fine tackling and spirited encouragement to his team mates. In the early years of the Welsh League, which had been formed in 1890, he acted as a referee. Roberts became chief clerk to a solicitor and was later deputy clerk to Denbighshire County Council. He served on the Denbigh Borough Council for many years, was made an alderman but declined the mayoralty.

Honours:
Ruthin - Welsh Cup finalists 1880

46 Harry Adams
B: Crick (Eng); 1855
D: Ellesmere (Eng);
    13 Jul 1910
Goalkeeper
4 caps: (Berwyn Rgrs) v Ire, Eng 1882; (Druids) v Eng, Ire 1883

Career: Berwyn Rgrs (Llangollen), 1879-82; Druids, 1882-83; Ellesmere, 1883-95; also Ellesmere Volunteers; Ellesmere Rgrs, 1900. Also **N Wales** v Cheshire (1881 & 1882), v Staffordshire (1881).

Harry Adams was born in England of Welsh parents and was first capped while playing for the local club at Llangollen, where he worked as a plumber. He was praised in his first international match for his 'judicious kicking', an important skill in the days when a goalkeeper needed to clear the ball quickly to protect his person. Adams was retained for England match at the Racecourse, which saw Wales gain their first home win over a strong English eleven. But, despite this success, he lost his place to Harry Phoenix for the Scotland game, the final international match of the 1881-82 season. Druids recognized his ability and he kept goal in their remarkable progress to the quarter-final of the 1882-83 FA Cup. After a 5-0 defeat by England in February 1883, Adams lost his place in the Welsh side to R T Gough. Although he was not originally selected for the match against Ireland, he was called up for the trip to Belfast but for the final 30 minutes of the match had to leave the field through injury. When Adams returned to Ellesmere, where his parents lived, he moved out of the FAW's orbit and was not selected again. He continued to turn out for Ellesmere teams until his forties and was a keen cricketer for the local club. Outside soccer, Adams had his own plumbing business in Ellesmere and was a keen bandsman and rifleman. In 1899 Adams stood for election to the FAW but was unsuccessful.

Honours:
Druids - Welsh Cup finalists 1883

47 Frederick William Hughes

B: Witton (Eng); 1860
D: Northwich (Eng); Nov 1923
Full/Half back
6 caps: (Northwich Vic) v Eng, Ire 1882; v Eng, Sco, Ire, 1883; v Sco 1884

Career: Northwich Vic, 1876-85. Also: **Cheshire** v N Wales (1882), v Lancashire (1879 x 2), Staffordshire (1884).

Fred Hughes, the son of a Northwich tile manufacturer, was the most accomplished player in the local side – two footed and very quick. A good all round athlete, he was described as 'the ideal of what a sportsman should be – he never did a shady trick on or off the field'.

His selection by Wales is explained by the fact that Northwich played in the Welsh Cup and the club were looked upon as a member club of the FAW. It was while playing in the competition that he came to the selectors' attention. When Wales played England at the Kennington Oval in February 1883, the English FA opposed Hughes' appearance but they had left it so late – 30 minutes before kick off – that Wales were not prepared or able to field a replacement and the matter was dropped. The following year English FA secretary Charles Alcock again objected to Fred Hughes, and to any member of the Wrexham club playing for Wales, the latter no doubt because the Wrexham club had been banned by the FA for crowd trouble in a match against Oswestry. But Hughes' international career was not quite at an end – he made his last such appearance in March 1884 against the Scots when the FAW must have been aware that he was ineligible. After six appearances for the Principality, his birth qualification was objected to, found to be 'inaccurate on investigation' and he stood down.

Hughes was a builders' merchant in Northwich for many years and went missing on a foggy night on 10 November 1923. His body was found in the river Dane six weeks later and it was likely that he had lost his footing and fallen into the swollen river.

Honours:
Northwich Vic - Welsh Cup finalists 1882

48 Charles Frederick Ketley

B: Ruabon; 1856
D: Syracuse (NY, USA); 23 Sep 1934
Inside forward
1 cap: (Druids) v Ire 1882

Career: Druids, 1876-83; Liverpool Cambrians, 1884; Bootle Wdrs, 1888. Also, **N Wales** v Sheffield (1878).

A neighbour of the Doughtys and the Davies brothers of Cefn, Ketley was a powerful forward and a prolific goalscorer for Druids, but inclined to selfishness. He was described as being 'as strong as a horse' and his methods were not noted for their subtlety. Ketley was a master painter by profession and had lost an arm in an accident (see also Arthur Lea) but his game was completely unaffected by this loss. Ketley later worked in Liverpool and played for the Liverpool Cambrians, a club set up in 1884 and playing at Stanley Park. In a match against Everton in January 1885 Ketley was criticized for rough play and the game was halted 'because of Kettley's (sic) violent conduct'. He had a brief spell at Bootle Wanderers in 1888 before emigrating to New York in March of that year. He worked in the United States as a painter and decorator, mostly in Syracuse but with a spell in New Jersey.

Honours:
Druids - Welsh Cup 1880, 1881, 1882; finalists 1878, 1883

49 Edward Gough Shaw
B: Llanforda (Eng); 1863 (bapt 31 Dec)
D: unknown
Centre forward/Wing
3 caps (2 gls): (Oswestry T) v Ire 1882; v Ire, Sco 1884

Career: Oswestry White Stars, 1880; Oswestry T, 1880-87.

Something of a precocious talent, Shaw took an active part in FAW affairs both on and off the field. He was adept at running with the ball, an excellent dribbler and not loath to provide scoring chances for his colleagues. In his second match for Wales he hit two goals against Ireland in a 6-0 win at Wrexham in February 1884.

His international career came to a temporary halt in March 1884 when his qualification for Wales was successfully objected to by England. Despite this difficulty the FAW selectors recalled him for the team to face Scotland later that month.

Shaw, who worked in his father's hardware and ironmongery shop in Oswestry, served on the local club's committee from 1882. He also represented the club at FAW meetings and frequently took the chair. Shaw's drinking and general lifestyle brought him into conflict with his family and in the late 1880s he disappeared from the family home. In 1893 he was thought to be in Denver, Colorado, which is believed to be the last that was heard of him. The authors have failed to pick up any later trace of him in their research and it is entirely possible that he changed his name. Shaw, whose father was at one time mayor of Oswestry, was an uncle to Wilfred Owen, the famed First World War poet.

Honours:
Oswestry T - Welsh Cup 1884

50 Walter Hugh Roberts
B: Ruthin; 1858
D: Rhyl; 23 Jun 1886
Forward/Half back
6 caps (1 gl): (Ruthin) v Eng, Sco 1882; v Eng, Sco, Ire 1883; (Rhyl) v Sco 1884

Career: Ruthin, 1878-82; Rhyl, 1880-85. Also, **N Wales** v Staffordshire (1881), v Cheshire (1882); **Flintshire** v Carnarvonshire (1882)

Almost forty years after his death some Ruthinians still spoke admiringly of the footballing skill of Walter Roberts. He was reputed to be 'one of the best players Ruthin ever possessed'. A dashing centre forward, Roberts was described as 'a splendid captain with a good command of players'. He divided his playing time between Ruthin, for whom he was qualified for cup ties by domicile, and Rhyl where he worked. He was employed by the London and North Western Railway at Rhyl as head of the parcels department and was secretary to the Rhyl club in 1884. He fell ill towards the end of 1885 and died at the young age of 28.

51 Henry Phoenix

B: Bersham; 1856
D: Bersham; 23 Apr 1937
Goalkeeper
1 cap: (Wrexham) v Sco 1882

Career: Wrexham Alb; Wrexham, 1880-83; Wrexham Alb. Also, **N Wales** v Staffordshire (1881).

Harry Phoenix took the place of Adams, the first choice goalkeeper who was unavailable for the 1882 Scotland match. He had joined Wrexham as a full back but quickly found himself playing in goal. Phoenix, who worked as a general labourer, was said to show 'skill and coolness' between the posts. When Jim Trainer took up goalkeeping with Wrexham, Phoenix lost his place and returned to the Albion, a junior club in the town. He was later a collier/stoker.

52 Thomas Burke

B: Wrexham; 1863
D: Moston (Eng); 9 Feb 1914
Half back
8 caps (1 gl): (Wrexham) v Eng 1883; (Wrexham Olympic) v Sco 1884; v Eng, Sco, Ire 1885; (Newton Heath) v Eng, Sco 1887; v Sco 1888

Career: Wrexham Grosvenor, 1880-82 (also Wrexham Ath); Wrexham, Feb 1882-84; Wrexham Olympic, 1884-86; Liverpool Cambrians; Newton Heath, 1886-89; Wrexham Vic, 1890-91. Also, **Denbighshire** v Staffordshire (1883, 1884), v Liverpool & Dist (1883), v Staffordshire (1884).

Tom Burke was the son of an Irish painter and began his footballing career at Wrexham Grosvenor alongside James Trainer. Burke was a capable half back with a sure kick who made intelligent use of the ball. When Wrexham were banned from the FA Cup in March 1884 following disturbances at a cup-tie, Burke was recruited by Olympic, their successor club. He made his international debut at the Kennington Oval as a late replacement for Ned Bowen of Druids and came in for some harsh criticism from 'Taffy', who seemed to have plenty to say in a letter to the *Wrexham Advertiser*. Nevertheless, the selectors persisted with Burke and he was given the captaincy against England in 1885, a match in which the 'Welsh half backs formed a strong line of defence'.

Burke was a painter by trade and one of several footballers from north Wales in the 1880s to join Newton Heath, predecessors of Manchester United, and take work with the Lancashire and Yorkshire Railway Company. He remained with the club until 1889, but when they moved to the Football Alliance, and a higher standard of football, he lost his first team place. Faced with playing for Newton Heath reserves, Burke returned to Wrexham and took up playing for Victoria, alongside Job Wilding, Billy Harrison and Harry Trainer. By 1911 he was living and working in Trafford, Manchester but three years later died from lead poisoning, almost certainly caused by his work as a painter.

Honours:
Wrexham - Welsh Cup 1883
Newton Heath - Manchester Cup 1888

53 John Phillip Davies

B: Gwyddelwern; 1853
D: Johannesburg (SA); 1929
Forward/Half back
2 caps: (Corwen) v Eng, (Druids) v Ire 1883

Career: Corwen, 1877-79; Berwyn Rgrs (Llangollen), 1879-81; Druids, 1881-83; Berwyn Rgrs (Llangollen), 1883-88. Also, **N Wales** v Lancashire (1880), v Staffordshire (1880).

J P Davies was one of the early enthusiasts of soccer in Llangollen, helping to form a club in October 1877 and serving as its secretary.

Davies, who had his own drapery shop in Castle Street, Llangollen, was a member of the Druids side that defeated Bolton in the FA Cup. One description of his play was 'useful but not very ornamental', while a more generous assessment praised his 'able and dashy play'. He was said to have 'played splendidly' against England at the Oval on a difficult pitch. Although some reports named him as a 'Corwen' player, he was in fact playing for Druids at the time. He wound down his soccer activities in 1888 but continued to turn out for Llangollen Cricket Club during the summer months.

Davies was active in municipal life and was a member of Llangollen Local Board and served on the sub-committee that in 1893 proposed bringing electric light to Llangollen. Around 1899 Davies, his wife and four children emigrated to South Africa, settling in Queenstown in the Cape Colony.

Honours:
Druids - Welsh Cup 1882

54 William Roberts
B: Rhyl; 15 Feb 1863
D: unknown
Forward
1 cap: (Rhyl) v Eng 1883

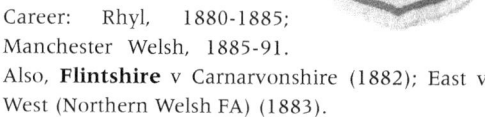

Career: Rhyl, 1880-1885; Manchester Welsh, 1885-91.
Also, **Flintshire** v Carnarvonshire (1882); East v West (Northern Welsh FA) (1883).

Roberts was something of a controversial choice by Wales to replace the unavailable Britten, and was subsequently much criticised for his display in his only international. One correspondent said of the young and inexperienced Roberts: 'He may play fairly well for his own club but cannot be said to have been a success against England'. Captain of the Rhyl club and the first international player produced by the town, he was a good opportunist and excelled at 'individual runs'. Nevertheless, his form was variable and he could be brilliant or hopeless. A good dribbler and very tricky, he was not a selfish player and combined well with his colleagues. Roberts found local matches more congenial and his goal scoring took Rhyl to the Northern Welsh FA Cup final in 1883. A butcher by trade, he moved to Manchester but in the 1890s, having married in London, gravitated to the English capital where he became a greengrocer.

Note: In some reference books, Roberts' appearance was recorded against the name of William Roberts (Llangollen).

55 Richard Thomas Gough
B: Worthen (Eng); 1860
D: Oswestry (Eng);
   2 Feb 1934
Goalkeeper
1 cap: (Oswestry T) v Sco 1883

Career: Oswestry T, 1877-88.

Tom Gough was the son of the Deputy Chief Constable of Shropshire and, uniquely, was a member of the English FA Council at the same as he was president of the FAW. His playing career had been fairly modest and was very much overshadowed by his contribution in later years, first as a referee and then as an administrator. After leaving school, Gough joined Oswestry as a half back with the reserve side but took up goalkeeping in 1880, and began appearing for the first team that same season. In 1883 he was selected to play for Wales in all three internationals despite not being one of the three goalkeepers used in the trial match. Some newspaper reports indicated he was attached to the Oswestry White Stars club but he appears to have been a player with the town club throughout his playing career. Because of his work commitments as a teacher he could only take part in one international – at Wrexham.

In 1903 he was described as 'an excellent goalkeeper in the days when a goalkeeper required iron nerves if he wished to come off the field in any way but on a stretcher'. One of his strong points was the distance he was able to achieve when punching the ball. In an interview in 1928 he reflected on his one appearance for Wales; "I well remember the game, for Dr Smith, the centre forward for Scotland, took the skin off my jaw. I used to keep goal in knee breeches and stockings. The breeches were buttoned at the knees and were lined with lamb's wool because the goalkeeper sometimes had a cold job". He went on: "I have lived to see many changes in legislation by which goalkeepers have benefited. In my time the 'keeper was not given much protection. One forward made for the goalkeeper and the other looked after the ball. Today the goalkeeper cannot be touched unless in possession of the ball". Appropriately for a former goalkeeper, Gough chaired the International Board in June 1912 at which Law 8 was altered so that a goalkeeper was allowed to handle the ball only within his own penalty area.

Gough gave up the game in 1888 and became a referee, officiating at several Welsh Cup finals and a number of international matches. He also became a member of the Shropshire FA and held the posts of secretary, treasurer and, later, president. A school board attendance officer, he served as President of the FAW from August 1911 until his death and was awarded a national testimonial in 1928, subscribed to by all four home associations. Gough was also an accomplished cricketer and demon fast bowler, playing for Shropshire against the MCC and a number of the first-class counties. His best bowling analysis of 16 wickets for seven runs was achieved in a match against Welshpool.

Honours:
Oswestry T - Welsh Cup 1884; finalists 1885
 - Shropshire Cup 1883, 1885

56 John Jones

B: Llangollen; c.1858
D: Llangollen; 25 Mar 1902
Half back
3 caps: (Berwyn Rgrs) v Sco, Ire 1883; v Sco 1884

Career: Berwyn Rgrs (Llangollen), 1878-86; also Small Heath Alliance, 1882-83 (11 FL apps); Denbigh, 1886-87; Vale of Llangollen, 1887-88; Ruthin, 1888-89.

A gritty and tireless worker, John Jones was complimented in 1886 by one reporter for his 'truly magnificent half play'. He was much admired for his skill at backing up. Mostly a Llangollen player, he had spells with Denbigh and Ruthin, but after 1888 his appearances became occasional. Jones was found shot dead in a field on his farm in the early hours of 25 March 1902. One explanation was that his gun could have discharged as he was climbing over a gate, and the inquest found that 'there is nothing to indicate whether he had taken his own life or an accident had taken place'.

57 Robert Davies

B: Wrexham; c.1861
D: Wrexham; 16 Aug 1911
Forward
3 caps: (Wrexham) v Ire 1883; v Ire 1884; (Wrexham Olympic) v Ire 1885

Career: Civil Service (Wrexham), 1879; Wrexham, 1881-84; Wrexham Olympic, 1884-88: Wrexham, 1888-92. Also, **Denbighshire** v Staffordshire (1883, 1884), v Liverpool & Dist (1883).

Robert Davies was a player who excelled at ball control and dribbling. A slightly-built individual with much natural ability, he was full of attacking instinct and was reckoned to be 'a very accurate shot'. He also put his footballing talents to good use by winning a number of football dribbling contests - popular competitions in the early 1880s. 'Bob Pugh', as he was known in Wrexham, was 'a capable forward, described by old footballers as one who saw the change from the individualism of the 1880s to the combination so generally adopted'. Davies was widely regarded in the town as 'one of the players who helped to introduce the new idea'. He gained the last of his three caps when Richard Parry Williams of Carnarvon Town was ruled out by injury. A one-time FAW referee, he worked as a stationery engine driver and later kept the Albion Hotel in Wrexham.

Honours:
Wrexham - Welsh Cup 1883; finalists 1890

58 John Arthur Eyton-Jones
B: Wrexham; 1860
D: Birkenhead (Eng); 3 Mar 1940
Wing half/Forward
4 caps (1 gl): (Wrexham Hare & Hounds) v Ire 1883; (Wrexham) v Ire, Eng, Sco 1884

Career: Wrexham, 1882-84, also Wrexham Hare & Hounds; Wrexham Olympic, 1884-85; Bootle, 1885-87. Also **Denbighshire** v Staffordshire (1883 & 1884), v Shropshire (1885); **Lancashire** v Ulster (1886).

Eyton-Jones first began playing soccer with Wrexham Hare and Hounds - a local sports club. His father was a doctor in Wrexham and at one time mayor of the town. An athletic player, Eyton-Jones was full of dash and enthusiasm; his strongest suit was constructive play but he was an erratic shot. As one report put it 'he passed well but was less impressive in front of goal'. Against Ireland, in his first international, he was described thus: 'he has speed, is smart on the ball, passes with judgement and appears to be able to stay - an essential quality'.

When Jones moved to Liverpool to study medicine, he joined the Bootle club but was also on Everton's books as an amateur. After qualifying in 1889, he practised medicine in Wrexham until shortly before the First World War, later practised at Oldham and later still was house surgeon at Liverpool Royal Infirmary. During the war, he served as a captain in the RAMC and was also with the 1st Welsh Border Mounted Brigade. For some years before his death in 1940 a GP in Birkenhead. His brother, also a doctor, was a medical missionary to China.

Honours:
Wrexham - Welsh Cup 1883

59 Charles Conde
B: Chirk; 1 Mar 1859
D: Chirk; 25 Mar 1936
Full back
3 caps: (Chirk) v Ire, Eng, Sco 1884

Career: Chirk, 1877-84; Crewe Alex, 1884-89.

Conde was a powerfully-built full back who was valued for his leadership qualities as well as defensive skills. He began his working life in the coal mines at the age of 10 and became a founder member of both the Chirk football and cricket clubs. Conde also had a liking for goalkeeping and twice appeared in that position for the Denbighshire County XI.

He was the first of many Welsh international players to leave the village to join a leading English club but reputedly remained an amateur throughout his career. The consistent Conde captained Chirk, and more notably Crewe in the Staffordshire side's progress to the FA Cup semi-final in 1887-88 (lost 0-4 to Preston). In his early career he also turned out for Oswestry and represented North Wales on three occasions (v Cheshire in 1880 & 1882, and v Staffordshire in 1881). Conde, who was awarded a benefit match against Chester in 1889, lived in Crewe for many years before returning to Chirk shortly before his death. He was employed in Crewe as a steel caster for the LNWR railway company. A distant relative of Jimmy Conde, the former Scunthorpe United and Bangor City striker who was a prolific goalscorer in the 1960s.

60 Walter Thomas Davies
B: Wrexham; 1864
D: Wrexham; 1931
Full back
1 cap: (Wrexham) v Ire 1884

Career: Wrexham Vic; Wrexham, Dec 1882-84; Wrexham Olympic, 1884; Derby Co, 1884; Wrexham Gymnasium.

A well-built full back, Walter Davies captained Wrexham Victoria before being persuaded to join the premier club in the town. His excellent defensive performances, including his part in Wrexham's surprise victory in the 1883 Welsh Cup final, led to interest from clubs further afield and in November 1884 he appeared for Derby County. Davies returned to Wrexham in 1886 and was 'rumoured to be about to don the Wrexham jersey again'. Competition for places was strong and he instead linked up with a junior club in the town, living in Bersham where he worked as a tailor.

Honours:
Wrexham - Welsh Cup 1883

61 William Tanat Foulkes
B: Llanrhaiadr; 1863
D: Oswestry (Eng);
   8 Feb 1937
Half back
2 caps: (Oswestry T) v Ire 1884; v Sco 1885

Career: Oswestry Sch; Oswestry T, 1882-86; Oswestry Harriers, 1893; Oswestry Utd, Jan 1895.

The son of a farmer, Bill Foulkes captained Oswestry Town to their first Welsh Cup success in 1884 - the first occasion for the trophy to leave Wales. The defensive qualities he displayed against Queens Park in a third round FA Cup tie in December 1883 impressed the FAW selectors. In spite of his side's 7-1 defeat, Foulkes had done well against top calibre forwards of the likes of the fearsome Scottish international player Dr John Smith. According to one reporter, Foulkes was 'a sturdy half who could give and take knocks'. Foulkes, who also appeared at full back for his club, made his second appearance for Wales alongside Humphrey Jones at the Racecourse. The Scots ran up an 8-1 victory and the name of Foulkes was quietly erased from the selectors' future plans.

Foulkes was a steam engine maker/fitter and later a marine engineer. He holds what is probably a unique place among Wales international players in that, in July 1895, he was sued for breach of promise. The lady in question was named Letitia Allmand, who was described in press reports as being of 'prepossessing appearance'. It appears that Foulkes first became engaged to Miss Allmand in 1886 when she was 18. Subsequently, Foulkes decided to go to Australia to improve his prospects; he returned in 1894 for 12 months, then again left in May 1895. At the time of the legal action he was in Freemantle, Western Australia and reputed to be earning £6 a week, in addition to which he had an annuity and two properties in Llansantffraid. The jury found for Miss Allmand and assessed the damages at the then huge sum of £250. The couple did eventually marry, but not to each other. Foulkes died in 1937 in a barber's chair in Oswestry.

Honours:
Oswestry T - Welsh Cup 1884; finalists 1885

62 Peter Griffiths

B: Chirk; 17 Sep 1861
D: Chirk; 29 Mar 1952
Half back
6 caps: (Chirk) v Ire, Eng 1884; v Eng 1888; v Ire, Sco 1890; v Ire 1891 (also **Wales XI** v Can 1891)

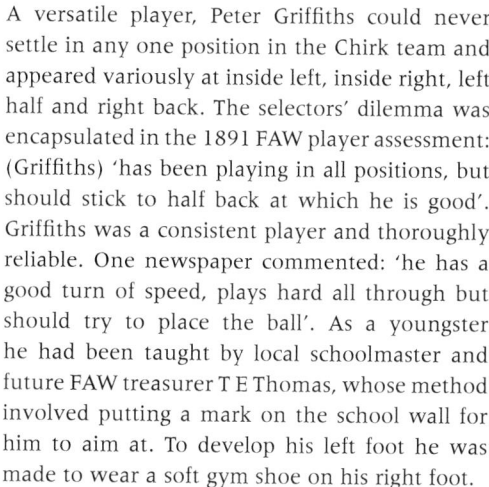

Career: Chirk, 1879-91. Also, **Denbighshire** v Staffordshire (1883), v Liverpool & Dist (1883).

A versatile player, Peter Griffiths could never settle in any one position in the Chirk team and appeared variously at inside left, inside right, left half and right back. The selectors' dilemma was encapsulated in the 1891 FAW player assessment: (Griffiths) 'has been playing in all positions, but should stick to half back at which he is good'. Griffiths was a consistent player and thoroughly reliable. One newspaper commented: 'he has a good turn of speed, plays hard all through but should try to place the ball'. As a youngster he had been taught by local schoolmaster and future FAW treasurer T E Thomas, whose method involved putting a mark on the school wall for him to aim at. To develop his left foot he was made to wear a soft gym shoe on his right foot.

Griffiths had been born next door to Billy Meredith in Long Row, Chirk, and remained a coal miner throughout his working life. He was forced to retire from football in October 1891 after sustaining a bad injury in a friendly against Accrington. A benefit match for Peter Griffiths and his brother George, between Oswestry and Chirk, was played in May 1894. He remained fascinated by soccer, was Chirk trainer and groundsman in the 1890s and in later years liked nothing better than to yarn about football in the old days.

Honours:
Chirk - Welsh Cup 1887, 1888, 1890

63 Robert Albert Jones

B: Ruabon; 1864
D: Ruabon; 22 Sep 1925
Outside left
4 caps (2 gls): (Druids) v Eng, Ire, Sco 1884; v Sco 1885

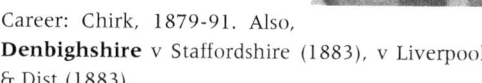

Career: Ruabon G Sch; Druids, 1882-85; Ruabon; Wynnstay, 1889-90.

Albert Jones was a good all-round athlete and began playing for the Druids after leaving Ruabon Grammar School. He got into the first team in 1882 and his 'complete ball control' and 'fine dribbling qualities' made him the ideal left wing partner for Jack Vaughan. In 1886, he was promoted from Ruabon goods station to booking clerk at Market Drayton, after which his football appearances became rarer. Work commitments forced him to turn down an invitation to face Ireland in 1886. By 1890, he had his own grocery and provisions business in Ruabon and had virtually retired from soccer. Jones became a councillor in Ruabon, was later made an alderman of Denbighshire County Council and served on the Druids FC committee. He must have been well respected in the business community as he was one of the judges at the International Grocers' Exhibition held at the Agricultural Hall in London. Jones, who played cricket for Ruabon, was a keen supporter of the national side and regularly accompanied the Wales team.

Honours:
Druids - Welsh Cup 1885; finalists 1884

64 Elias Owen

B: Llanllechid; 1863
D: Ruthin; 20 Sep 1888
Goalkeeper
3 caps: (Ruthin G Sch) v Ire, Eng, Sco 1884

Career: Ruthin G Sch, 1880-85; St David's Coll (Lampeter), 1888.

Elias Owen was the son of the Reverend Elias Owen, a diocesan inspector of schools who published *Welsh Folk-Lore*, a collection of tales based on a prize-winning essay at the National Eisteddfod of 1887, and also authored *Old Stone Crosses of the Vale of Clwyd*. A brother to W P Owen and cousin to the Morgan-Owen brothers, Elias was a half back who took up goalkeeping in 1882. Jim Trainer's non-availability for the Denbighshire match against Liverpool Association gave Owen the opportunity to impress the FAW selectors and gain international recognition. He performed well against Ireland and England drawing the comment, 'acquitted himself admirably and in important contests it will be a difficult matter to entrust the important task of defending goal to a more competent player'. In the Scotland match, Wales conceded four goals and the selectors dropped Owen from their plans.

In 1885, Owen went to St David's College to study theology where he played for the college team at half back, the position he had originally favoured before taking up goalkeeping. Tragically, Owen, who had been studying for the ministry, took his own life in September 1888. There was a suggestion that he was depressed over the outcome of his final examinations but the story within the family was that he returned from college to find that his wife Zillah was having an affair. In a depressed state he went into the churchyard with some leather reins with which he hanged himself.

65 Morris/Maurice Jones Evans
B: Llanfyllin; 1859
D: Droylsden (Eng);
   18 Oct 1910
Half back
1 cap: (Oswestry T) v Eng 1884

Career: Oswestry White Stars, 1880-82; Oswestry T, 1882-87.

Morris (Maurice in some records) Jones Evans came into the Welsh team as a replacement for Fred Hughes, the Northwich defender, whose qualification had been objected to by England. The Oswestry wing half played alongside his club colleague Joe Williams and 'didn't disgrace himself'. An excellent tackler, Evans was a tenacious defender and 'a thorn in the side of forwards'. A blacksmith by profession, he left the Oswestry district in 1887 to move to Manchester but by the early 1890s was living in Llanfyllin. Evans later returned to the Manchester area, where he continued to work as a blacksmith but suffered from heart problems and died at a young age.

Honours:
Oswestry T - Welsh Cup 1884

66 William Owen
B: Chirk; 10 Aug 1861
D: Chirk; 2 Mar 1946
Forward
16 caps (4 gls): (Chirk) v Eng 1884; v Ire 1885; v Eng 1887; v Eng 1888; v Eng, Sco, Ire 1889; v Ire, Sco 1890; v Ire, Eng, Sco 1891; v Eng, Sco 1892; v Sco, Ire 1893

Career: Chirk, 1876-99 (also Bolton Wdrs, Newton Heath 1887, and Sep-Oct1888, Port Vale, Chester, Crewe Alex, and Oswestry T).

Billy Owen was described in the FAW 1891 player assessment as 'a hard-working player, can play in any position, very tricky but rather selfish'. Billy Meredith, his right wing partner in the Chirk team of 1893, later maintained that Owen was 'the sort of player who displayed that unselfishness that makes a player shine'. Nevertheless, Owen loved to show off his footballing skills and in 1886 one writer described him as: 'a very clever dribbler but he plays to the gallery and loses too much time crossing the ground going backwards and forwards instead of going for goal'.

Owen was nicknamed 'the John L Sullivan of inside forwards', after the last bare-knuckled world heavyweight boxing champion. He was a stalwart of the Chirk team for many seasons but, surprisingly, never sought to join a senior club on a permanent basis. He had a period on Bolton's books as an amateur and a few brief flirtations with Newton Heath. Owen 'retired' in 1895 to become a referee in the Welsh League but was still turning out for Chirk Reserves in 1899. He was awarded a benefit match against the full Manchester City Football League team in March 1901, a suitable recognition for a player described in one newspaper as 'a more genuine sportsman never toed a football'. The former coal miner's later years were far from secure financially and several benefit matches were arranged for him, some of which featured his old pal and former Chirk colleague Billy Meredith. Owen, a brother to Jack Owen who played for Wales in 1892, had to wait until the age of 72 to receive a Welsh cap. The omission was rectified at the Racecourse in January 1934 when Horace Blew made the presentation.

Honours:
Chirk - Welsh Cup 1887, 1888, 1890, 1892, 1894; finalists 1893

67 Joseph Harry Williams
B: Oswestry (Eng); 13 Sep 1857
D: Oswestry (Eng); 26 Sep 1941
Full back/Centre half
1 cap: (Oswestry T) v Eng 1884

Career: St Oswalds (Oswestry), 1870-76; Oswestry T, 1880-86.

Joe Williams began playing soccer as early as 1870, with St Oswald - a church club in Oswestry. His own description was: 'Initially we played in our trousers but after we had played one season we obtained striped jerseys and stockings. It was at the start almost a game from hedge to hedge in the field where we played. We had goalposts but no touchlines. We had no crossbar; the goals were spanned by a piece of string only. Then in those good old days we had no offside rule to trouble us. It was all individual; a player used to get the ball and go as far as he could by himself. There were six forwards, two halves, two backs and a goalkeeper'.

Joe was a strong tackler but also a good athlete - 20ft 6ins in the long jump and 5ft 8ins in the high jump. He was one of the Oswestry players who took part in a floodlit match against Wrexham in 1883, 'rare fun' according to Joe. For his appearance against England, he was given a white shirt and a badge which depicted the Welsh dragon with the words 'Cymru am byth' and 'The Football Association of Wales' worked around the figure of the dragon. International caps only being introduced some time later.

A cabinet maker by profession, he later ran his own business and was well known throughout Shropshire as an expert in antique furniture and pictures, and assisted at many country house sales in Shropshire and the border counties. Joe was also an FAW referee and his favourite relaxation outside soccer was playing the clarinet.

Honours:
Oswestry T - Welsh Cup 1884; finalists 1885
 - Shropshire Cup 1882

68 Robert Roberts
B: Ruabon; Jul 1864
D: Wrexham; 15 Mar 1932
Wing half/Full back
 (5ft 11ins, 14st)
8 caps (1 gl): (Druids) v Sco 1884; (Bolton Wdrs) v Sco

1887; v Eng, Sco 1888; v Eng 1889; v Sco 1890; v Ire, (Preston N E) v Sco 1892 (also **Wales XI** v Can 1891)

Career: Druids, 1882-84; Bolton Wdrs, Apr 1884-92 (1889-92, 71 FL apps, 3 gls); Preston N E, Mar 1892 (5 FL apps). Also, **Denbighshire** v Liverpool (1883).

A good athlete and a useful boxer, Bob Roberts had a 'burly frame' and was one of the stars of Druids' 1882-83 FA Cup run. He had replaced the injured Albert Powell for the replay against Bolton and retained his full back place for the quarter-final against eventual winners Blackburn Olympic. Roberts made his Wales debut when he again deputised for the luckless Powell.

The former terracotta works employee was probably the most successful of the Druids players who joined Bolton. In his first match for his new club he helped them defeat a Preston side unbeaten in many months. Roberts was converted to wing half and in 1889 was described as 'a very fast man (120 yards in 13 seconds), a splendid dribbler and difficult to overcome in possession of the ball'. One newspaper dubbed him 'the best half back in England' and he would have featured more often for Wales if his club had been prepared to release him. Although he was selected to play against Scotland in April 1889, and his name appears in some match reports, his place was in fact taken by Percy Hughes of Bangor. Once, he missed his train connection at Chester and the railway company laid on a special train to take him to the Racecourse for an international match. He arrived in time for the start of the game and on taking the field was given a rousing reception by the crowd.

On completing his soccer career he was briefly the trainer for Leicester Fosse before returning to the Wrexham area where he worked as a coal miner. Towards the end of his life he lived in the alms houses at Ruabon. He was known, inevitably, as `Bob Bolton' and the walls of his room were said to be covered with photographs of Bolton, Preston and Wales, with little space for anything else.

Honours:
Druids - Welsh Cup finalists 1883, 1884

69 John Edward Davies

B: Oswestry (Eng); 1862
D: Ellesmere (Eng);
  19 Jun 1913
Forward
1 cap: (Oswestry T) v Eng 1885

Career: Oswestry White Stars, 1880-82; Oswestry T, 1883-87. Also, **Shropshire** v Denbighshire (1885)

John Davies was originally an inside forward but later moved out to the wing to accommodate Johnny Roach in the Oswestry team. He was a careful player with a reputation for accurate kicking, particularly from corner kicks. Davies caught the selectors' eye on just one occasion and participated in Wales' 1-1 draw against England at Blackburn. By 1887, he was one of the older members of the Oswestry team and he gave way to younger talent. Davies served on the Oswestry committee for several years and ran a restaurant in the town. He also acted as an agent for the Prudential Assurance Company. He was out for a Saturday afternoon cycle ride when he collapsed and died at Ellesmere.

Honours:
Oswestry T - Welsh Cup finalists 1885

70 Robert Davies

B: Cefn; Ruabon, 1863
D: Manchester (Eng);
  9 Oct 1922
Wing half
1 cap: (Druids) v Eng 1885

Career: Druids, 1883-86; (also Ardwick).

Second eldest of the Davies brothers of Cefn, Bob was a splendid utility player but seen to best advantage at wing half. When Denbighshire played Shropshire in January 1885, Davies had an outstanding game, no doubt persuading the selectors that he was worthy of place against England. Although 'the Welsh half backs formed a strong line of defence' in the 1-1 draw against England, Davies gave way to Humphrey Jones for matches v Scotland and Ireland. A keen competitor and a tough tackler, after leaving Druids Davies played much of his soccer in the Manchester area and at one time assisted Ardwick (later Manchester City).

Davies, who at one time worked as a general labourer in Manchester, was something of a rolling stone. His employment included coalmining in Barnsley and as an erector of iron works in Upton-on-Severn before returning to Manchester.

Honours:
Druids - Welsh Cup 1885; finalists 1884

71 George Farmer

B: Oswestry (Eng); 1863
D: West Derby (Eng);
    4 May 1905
Inside forward (5ft 6ins, 11st)
2 caps: (Oswestry T) v Eng,
v Sco 1885

Career: Oswestry White Stars, 1880-83; Oswestry T, 1883-85; Everton, 1885-90 (31 FL apps, 1 gl); Liverpool Caledonians; Liverpool South End; Rock Ferry.

George Farmer joined Everton in 1885 along with George Dobson of Bolton Wanderers and the pair were reportedly the first professionals ever signed by the club. He was paid 30 shillings (£1.50) a week which compared favourably with a working man's wage at the time. Farmer had worked in Oswestry as a skinner and leather dresser and helped the local club take the Welsh Cup over the border for the first time in 1884. A clever and constructive player, he was noted as 'a fine passer' who was capable of 'beautiful work'. Farmer scored Everton's first goal in the FA Cup in October 1887 against Bolton Wanderers, but their opponents lodged an appeal that seven Everton players were amateurs who had been offered money to play and were therefore ineligible. The outcome was that the club was suspended for a month. More of a provider than a goalscorer, Farmer set up both goals for George Fleming in the Merseyside club's first Football League fixture in September 1888 against Accrington. Tom Gough, FAW President, who had played with Farmer, described him as 'the finest corner kicker I ever saw'. Farmer missed only one match during Everton's debut season in the Football League and his neat displays earned him the description – 'one of the most skilful forwards in the league'. He later settled into the left half position where his defensive tackling found 'full scope'. Farmer, who was employed as a glass cutter and later a tinsmith, wound down his career with Liverpool South End in the Liverpool and District League. In October 1905 the receipts of the Combination match between Everton and Stockport County went to the benefit of his widow and children.

Honours:
Oswestry T - Welsh Cup 1884; finalists 1885

72 Frederick Robert Jones

B: Bangor; 1863
D: Liverpool (Eng);
    3 Jan 1905
Full back
3 caps (1 gl): (Bangor) v Eng,
Ire 1885; v Sco 1886

Career: Friars Sch (Bangor), 1877; Bangor, 1882-86; (also Liverpool Cambrians 1884-85). Also, **Caernarvonshire** v Flintshire (1882); **Denbighshire** v Lancashire 1885.

The son of John Jones, a Bangor Police Superintendent, Fred Jones made his debut for Wales in the same team as his Bangor colleague Humphrey Jones. Curiously, Fred was one of the original team, chosen by the FAW selectors, but his more illustrious team mate only made the side when Bob Roberts dropped out. A precocious full back, Fred was participating in local representative matches at the age of 17 while still a Friars schoolboy. An exceedingly quick defender, his weakness was his inclination to 'wander a bit and get caught out of position'. Jones was also an excellent sprinter, an accomplished cricketer and front-line bowler for Bangor Cricket Club. After leaving Bangor, he was employed by the Post Office in Liverpool and played for Liverpool Cambrians, frequently alongside Charles Ketley.

73 Humphrey Jones

B: Bangor; 7 Dec 1862
D: Gateshead (Eng);
   10 Jun 1946
Half back (5ft 8ins, 11st 9lbs)
14 caps: (Bangor) v Eng, Sco, Ire 1885; v Ire, Eng, Sco 1886; (Queens Park) v Eng 1887; (East Stirlingshire) v Eng, Sco 1889; v Ire, Eng, Sco 1890; (Queens Park) v Eng, Sco 1891

Career: Friars Sch (Bangor); Christ's Coll (Brecon), 1879-82; (also Bangor, 1879-86); Peterhouse Coll (Cambridge), 1882-85; London Swifts, 1885-86; Queen's Park, 1886-87; London Swifts, 1887-88; East Stirlingshire, 1888-89; Queens Park, 1889-92; also Corinthians, 1888-90 (3 apps). Also, **N Wales** v Liverpool & Dist (1884); London v Birmingham (1884); **Denbighshire** v Staffordshire (1884).

Humphrey Jones and his brother Richard, a Bangor doctor, were important soccer influences in the fledging local club. The brothers, sons of a Bangor builder, were the outstanding performers in the local team. Humphrey had learnt his soccer at the local Friars School but later at Christ College, Brecon, he captained the school rugby XV. While at Peterhouse College, Cambridge he played for the Bangor team when available, and under his leadership they won the Northern Welsh FA Cup on four occasions between 1882 and 1885. Humphrey, though captain of Wales, was denied a place in the Cambridge University side because he would not adapt to their method of playing the ball along the ground to the point where the man would be in a position to collect the ball.

In April 1886, he became classics master at Blair Lodge School, Polmount, Stirlingshire and joined the famous Queens Park club. A club handbook later commented – 'There is no one who is more widely respected or held in higher esteem than our evergreen half back Humphrey Jones'. The Welshman was apparently involved in a bizarre incident in November 1886 in a match between Queens Park and Clyde. An accidental clash of heads between the defender and Clyde's 20-year old Claude Lambie put Lambie on the ground. According to reports 'He lay there for a short time, but it was thought he was only winded, and the usual remedies applied. He was soon apparently alright again and refused to leave the field, playing on to the end. On reaching home he complained of feeling ill and a doctor was called'. Lambie was said to have died of brain fever a few days later but was then miraculously resurrected as newspapers corrected earlier accounts and reported that the player was hale and hearty.

What little football Jones played during the '87-88 season was with the Swifts. The 1891 FAW assessment of him was – 'the best centre half for years, uses judgement and tackles fearlessly'. Jones was a frequent visitor to Wales in later years and retained his connection with the FAW. He once turned down a trial for the Wales rugby union team, refereed England's matches against Ireland and Scotland in 1896 and the following year was called on to take charge of the Welsh Cup final when Wrexham objected to Tom Gough's Oswestry background. From 1892,

Jones concentrated on his employment at Blair Lodge School but later gave up teaching and in a radical change of direction moved to London to work in the wine and spirits trade. Jones is one of a handful of individuals who have played in the Welsh Cup, Scottish Cup and English FA Cup.

74 William Lewis
B: Bangor; 1864
D: Manchester (Eng); 1935
Centre forward/Winger
26 caps (7 gls): (Bangor) v Eng 1885; v Eng, 1886; v Eng, Sco 1887; v Eng 1888; v Eng, Sco, Ire 1889; (Crewe Alex) v Eng 1890; v Eng, Sco 1891; (Chester) v Ire, Eng, Sco 1892; v Ire, Eng, Sco 1894; v Ire, Eng, Sco 1895; v Ire, Eng, Sco 1896; (Manchester C) v Sco, Eng 1897; (Chester) v Ire 1898 (also **Wales XI** v Can 1891)

Career: Bangor Rov; Bangor, 1882-88; Everton, Sep 1888 (3 FL apps, 1 gl); Bangor, Jan-Oct 1889; Crewe Alex, Oct 1889-91; Chester, Nov 1891-96; Manchester C, Sep 1896-97 (12 FL apps, 4 gls); Chester, Sep 1897. Also: **Northern Welsh FA**; v Liverpool (1884)

Billy Lewis was a Bangor stonemason who became the local club's star player and eventually the first professional footballer produced by Bangor. He was known in the town as 'Billy Cae Top' ('Billy Top Field') and invariably took the honours at the town's athletics competitions. In 1888 Lewis joined Everton as an amateur and played in their first ever Football League match, but his connection with the club was short lived and he was soon back in the Bangor side. During the 1880s Bangor were one of the best sides in north Wales and in 1889 they became the first north west Wales club to win the Welsh Cup. Billy Lewis, who had been on a football tour with Crewe, joined up with the Bangor team at Chester to travel to Wrexham for the final, against Northwich, where two defenders marked Lewis and 'debarred his usual playing'.

Lewis became a permanent fixture in the Welsh team, usually appearing as a winger or in his best position of centre forward. The FAW assessment of 1891 commented: 'a speedy forward and very clever - does not use sufficient judgement'. In 1896, he joined Manchester City and made twelve first-team appearances, playing alongside Billy Meredith. Years later, Meredith gave his verdict on Lewis: 'speedy, clever in combination and a deadly shot in his day'. For several years Lewis held the record for appearances for Wales until he was finally overhauled by Meredith in 1913. Outside soccer, he was a publican and kept the Duke of York in Chester for a time. In April 1907 he was granted a benefit match between Chester and Wrexham.

Honours:
Bangor - Welsh Cup 1889

75 Robert Herbert Mills Roberts
B: Penmachno; 5 Aug 1862
D: Bournemouth (Eng); 27 Nov 1935
Goalkeeper (5ft 8ins, 11st)
8 caps: (St Thomas' Hospital) v Eng, Sco, Ire 1885; v Eng 1886; v Eng 1887; (Preston N E) v Eng, Ire 1888; (Llanberis) v Eng 1892

Career: Friars Sch (Bangor); Univ Coll Wales (Aberystwyth); Aberystwyth T, 1879-82 (4 apps); St Thomas' Hosp (London); United Hospitals; Crusaders (Brentwood); Barnes, 1884-85; Casuals, 1886-87; Preston N E, 1887-89; Warwick Co; Mitchell St George; Corinthians, 1884-88 (7 apps).

Although born in Penmachno, Mills Roberts moved to Ffestiniog at the age of three months when his father, who had been a village schoolmaster, became accountant for Oakeley Quarries and later general manager. Mills Roberts played both soccer and rugby at Friars School, Bangor where he was a contemporary of

W P Owen, A O Davies, and Humphrey Jones. Following his studies at Aberystwyth University he entered the teaching hospital at St Thomas' in 1882 to complete his medical degree. In London, he gave up ideas of playing rugby, took up goalkeeping for the hospital team and appeared for several amateur clubs including the Casuals, the Corinthians, the Crusaders and Barnes. The slightly-built goalkeeper was brave, agile and not afraid to take risks. Medical duties curtailed his sporting activities in the '86-87 season and he decided, reluctantly, to give up soccer after the England game at the Kennington Oval in February 1887. The week before the match he sprained both wrists playing for London against Staffordshire and, unable to bend or move either wrist despite attending hospital for daily treatment, he was pronounced unfit to play. On the Friday, Mills Roberts persuaded his medical colleagues to put both wrists in plaster and he was fixed up with splints to his elbows which left his fingers and thumbs free to punch the ball. England won 4-0 but Mills Roberts thought his performance, for which he was given a great reception, to be one of the best he had given and he went back on his decision to quit.

An appearance for the Corinthians against Preston at the Jubilee football festival of 1887 at the Oval before the Prince of Wales led to an invitation to join the Lancashire club. Regular keeper Jim Trainer, as a pro', had to serve a two-year qualification period to be eligible for FA Cup matches, whereas an amateur only had to register for a month. In 1888, Preston lost 2-1 to West Brom in the final and Mills Roberts described their performance as: 'stale - they had played 44 matches in succession without defeat and were playing under tremendous pressure. Every club was endeavouring to beat them. We met our Waterloo in the final but wiped out the disappointment in the following year'. Remarkably, Preston's success in the 1888-89 FA Cup was achieved without conceding a goal. Mills Roberts qualified as a surgeon in 1887 and very often had to travel from his Stroud home by horse and carriage to catch a train from Gloucester to wherever Preston were playing. He became house surgeon at Birmingham General Hospital in February 1888 and, when not playing for Preston, appeared in the occasional game for Warwick County, Mitchell St George and Birmingham. An athletic journal of March 1888 offered the following verdict: 'As a goalkeeper he is cool and quick, always on the alert, gets rid of the ball quickly, rarely makes a mistake. The best goalkeeper of the day'.

Mills Roberts was successively resident surgeon at Leicester Infirmary, Royal United Hospital, Bath, and South Devon and East Cornwall Hospital in Plymouth. In November 1890, he was appointed quarry surgeon at the Dinorwic Hospital in his native north Wales and moved to live in Llanberis where he established the local football club, playing occasionally until 1909. Strangely, although he hadn't played for a couple of years, he was selected again by Wales in 1892. Mills Roberts served in the Boer War with the team that established the Welsh Hospital at Springfontein in Transvaal, and moved to Pretoria in July 1900, where he was awarded the CMG in recognition of his war service. The former goalkeeper remained a keen military man and was an officer with the 6th Btn Royal Welsh Fusiliers from 1906 to 1915. Mills Roberts also served as a Lieutenant Colonel with the RAMC during the First World War, in particular at the 41st Stationary Hospital, and was mentioned in despatches. After the war, he became Deputy Commissioner of Medical Services for north Wales and Shropshire, living in Chester and based at Wrexham, until he retired in 1927. He returned to live in Ffestiniog and died in a Bournemouth nursing home in 1935. Although newspaper reports invariably referred to him as 'Mills-Roberts', his birth was registered as Roberts; Mills was his mother's maiden name and he did not adopt the hyphen.

Honours:
Preston N E - FA Cup 1889; finalists 1888

76 George Thomas

B: Wrexham; 1857
D: Wrexham; 16 Dec 1929
Full back
2 caps: (Wrexham Olympic) v Eng, Sco 1885

Career: Civil Service (Wrexham), 1878-81; Wrexham, 1881-84; Wrexham Olympic, 1884-87.

George Thomas was a tall, well-built full back: strong in the air and an awkward opponent. When Jack Powell was detained on club duty in March 1885, Thomas deputised for him against England. The Wrexham-born defender had 'a fine game' and kept his place for the Scottish match. At club level, he formed a solid full back partnership with Harry Edwards and captained Wrexham Olympic in '84-85. In his early years he was employed in a mineral water factory at Pentrefelin but then branched out on his own. From 1886, he began to concentrate on his mineral water business and his Wrexham appearances became intermittent until he retired in 1887.

Honours:
Wrexham - Welsh Cup 1883

77 Thomas Vaughan

B: Rhyl; 1864
D: St. Asaph; 26 Aug 1908
Outside right
1 cap: (Rhyl) v Eng 1885

Career: Rhyl, 1882-86; Rhyl Colts, 1886-88; Rhyl, 1888-90. Also, **Flintshire** v Carnarvonshire (1888).

Tom Vaughan was a cousin to J O Vaughan and the pair frequently appeared together in the Rhyl team. A light and nippy winger, Vaughan made his one appearance for Wales when C A Lloyd Jones of Shrewsbury Castle Blues was unable to play because of injury. He had recently recovered from illness and didn't do himself full justice. His health later broke down and Vaughan, a joiner by trade, died in his early forties at St Asaph Infirmary after a long illness.

78 Job Wilding

B: Wrexham; 12 Oct 1865
D: Chester (Eng); 15 Mar 1947
Outside left/Centre forward
9 caps (4 gls): (Wrexham Olympic) v Eng, Sco, Ire 1885; v Ire, Eng 1886; (Bootle) v Eng 1887; v Ire, Sco 1888; (Wrexham) v Sco 1892

Career: Wrexham Crown, 1881-84; Wrexham Olympic, 1884-85; Everton, Oct 1885; Bootle, Nov 1886-88; Wrexham, Nov 1888-90; Westminster Rov, 1890-91; Wrexham, 1891-92; Westminster Rov, 1892-96. Also, **Denbighshire** v Cheshire, v Shropshire (1885); **Liverpool & Dist** (2 apps).

'Joby' Wilding played his first match for Wrexham aged 17, against Birmingham Excelsior, but it wasn't until 1884 that he became a regular member of the town's senior club. Olympic were formed in the aftermath of the banning of Wrexham FC by the English FA, and Wilding was recruited for the new outfit. His performances for his new club earned him the description 'never flurried, invariably acts with discretion and plays an admirable game'.

Wilding spent three years in Liverpool during which time he worked for the Municipal Corporation and played for Everton and then Bootle. A reporter at the Everton v Wrexham match at Anfield Road in January 1886 (six years before the formation of Liverpool FC) commented: 'Of the Everton players, none performed as well as Wilding'. He returned to Wrexham in 1888 but eventually threw in his lot with Westminster Rovers - a colliery team. Wilding captained the Rovers from the centre half position and although a hard working defender was 'inclined to ramble too much'. Wilding was a moulder by trade, having served an apprenticeship with an agricultural implement maker, but later worked as an iron founder at Chester. A Welsh League referee and one-time assistant trainer to Wrexham FC, 'Joby' was also a fine wicket keeper for Wrexham CC. He was a brother-in-law to Ben Lewis.

Honours:
Wrexham - Welsh Cup finalists 1890
Westminster Rov - Welsh Cup finalists 1892, 1894

79 Seth Powell
B: Cerney (Wrexham); 1862
D: Oswestry; 3 Feb 1945
Full back
7 caps: (Oswestry T) v Sco 1885; v Ire, Eng 1886; (West Bromwich Alb) v Eng, Sco 1891; v Eng, Sco 1892

Career: Summerhill (Wrexham); Oswestry T, 1884-89; West Bromwich Alb, 1890-Jul 1892 (29 FL apps); Burton Swifts; Chester, Oct 1892; Oswestry Utd, Sep 1893.

Seth Powell was a strongly-built defender who tackled crisply and distributed the ball quickly and accurately. In the FAW 1891 player assessment, Powell was described in the following terms: 'plays a cool game and tackles well, justified his selection. Also played a good game v England'. Powell moved to Oswestry in 1883 to become an assistant schoolmaster at the Oswestry Board School, and he played for the local club for five years until he was signed by WBA as a professional on £2-a-game plus expenses. Powell moved to Burton Swifts in 1892, then to Chester in the Combination before returning to Oswestry and the newly formed United club. After giving up the playing side of the game he became a referee and, from 1900 until his retirement in September 1930, Powell was district relieving officer for the Oswestry Board of Guardians. He was secretary of Oswestry Football Club for some time and spent twenty years as a member of the 2nd Volunteer Battalion of the King's Shropshire Light Infantry.

Honours:
Oswestry T - Welsh Cup 1884; finalists 1885

80 Alfred Owen Davies
B: Barmouth; 1863
D: Machynlleth; 8 Sep 1932
Full back
9 caps: (Barmouth) v Ire 1885; v Eng, Sco 1886; (Swifts) v Eng, Sco 1887; v Eng, Ire 1888; (Wrexham) v Sco 1889; (Overton) v Eng 1890

Career: Friars Sch (Bangor); Ardwyn House Sch (Aberystwyth), 1878-81; Aberystwyth Mechanics; Aberystwyth T, 1881 (2 apps); Edinburgh Univ; Swifts, 1886-88; Casuals, 1886-87, also Corinthians, 1886-88 (15 apps); Wrexham, 1888-89; Overton, Oct-Dec 1889; Crewe Alex, 1889.

In *Association Football*, published in 1900, 'Pa' Jackson offered the following description of A O Davies: 'a terrible fellow he was to opposing forwards, dashing, almost to recklessness, a very strong and heavy charger, a splendid header and a clever kick. His weak points were an inability to combine with the rest of the defence'. Davies had begun playing football seriously while studying medicine at Edinburgh and helped the university to victory over Hearts in the Edinburgh Cup final of 1883. He qualified in 1886 and for a time assisted the London Swifts, scoring seven of Swifts's nine goals v Forest School in November 1886, before moving to the Wrexham area. He also guested for Preston North End and Bolton Wanderers and, being an amateur, played for both Wrexham and Druids. He also found time to start a soccer club at Overton in October 1889 and to instigate the founding of the Welsh League in March 1890.

Davies had a spell with Crewe in the Football Alliance, but in 1890 he returned to Wales to become a medical practitioner in Machynlleth. He later became medical officer and finally coroner for the town until his death in 1932. Davies, who was said to be largely responsible for starting soccer in Machynlleth, remained deeply interested in the game and was chairman of the local club. He stood for election to the FAW unsuccessfully in 1925, losing by a narrow margin.

Davies was one of four brothers, three of whom became doctors – Thomas in Kensington, London and Edward in Croydon, with the fourth brother unfortunately dying at a young age. A O died while out fishing at a spot known as Fir Tree Pool, not far from Dovey Bridge. He collapsed on the river bank and fellow fisherman George Roberts sought help from the Dovey river bailiff. A O's brother, Dr Thomas Davies, who had been fishing lower down the river, arrived too late to help. Davies, who was an uncle by marriage to the England full backs A M and P M Walters, was the first Welshman to appear in the Welsh, Scottish and English FA Cup competitions.

81 John Roach

B: Oswestry (Eng); 1862
D: Oswestry (Eng);
   18 Feb 1929
Outside /Inside left
1 cap (2 gls): (Oswestry T) v Ire 1885

Career: St Oswalds (Oswestry), 1880; Oswestry T, 1880-93; Oswestry Utd, 1893.

Johnny Roach was an Oswestry stalwart throughout the 1880s and one of their principal goal scorers, particularly with his head. He had a memorable introduction to international football in Belfast, playing alongside his club colleague George Farmer, scoring a brace of goals in an 8-2 victory. Strangely, not only was he subsequently overlooked by the FAW selectors but he never even made the international trial matches. Roach, who worked as a labourer in a manure works at the time of his selection, was on Everton's books in 1886 but made few first team appearances. After retiring from playing he became a referee.

Honours:
Oswestry T - Welsh Cup 1884; finalists 1885

82 Herbert Sisson

B: Wrexham; 7 Aug 1862
D: Hackney (Eng);
   3 May 1891
Centre forward
3 caps (4 gls): (Wrexham Olympic) v Ire 1885; v Ire, Sco 1886

Career: Grove Park Sch (Wrexham); Wrexham, 1882-84; Wrexham Olympic, 1884-86. Also, **N Wales** v Lancashire (1885); **Denbighshire** (3 apps)

Sisson learnt his football at the Grove Park School in Wrexham, and later played for the works team at his father's Cambrian Brewery where he was employed. He was valued by Wrexham, and its successor club Wrexham Olympic, for his ability to score goals regularly. On his debut for Wales, although not a particular fast player, he notched a hat-trick at Belfast. Sisson was treasurer of the FAW for twelve months until he left Wrexham in 1886 to study medicine. It was while pursuing his studies in London that Sisson contracted diphtheria and died.

83 John Owen Vaughan

B: Rhyl; 17 May 1863
D: Holywell; 5 Oct 1952
Half back
4 caps (1 gl): (Rhyl) v Ire 1885; v Ire, Eng, Sco 1886

Career: St Thomas' Coll (Rhyl), 1876-81; Rhyl, 1881-86; Rhyl Colts, 1886-88; Rhyl, 1888.

Vaughan first took up soccer at school, as centre forward for St Thomas'. During his five years in the team they were reputedly unbeaten in all matches. He joined Rhyl as a centre forward but when Walter Roberts arrived in 1883 Vaughan switched to left back. After being selected as reserve half back for two international matches, Vaughan made his debut against Ireland in Belfast. He remained first choice half back for Wales but towards the end of 1886 began to suffer problems with eyesight. Several operations interrupted his career and he gave up the game finally around 1888.

Vaughan recovered his fitness to become a trooper in the Denbighshire Hussars Yeomanry and served in the Boer War. He was also quite a swimmer and was said to have saved about a dozen people from the sea at Rhyl. Certainly, in August 1886, he rescued a young woman from the sea at his fourth attempt, and the following year saved a man and two young children. For each of the rescues he was awarded a bronze medal from the Royal Humane Society. In early life, Vaughan had worked for a time in his father's baths, then as a draper's assistant before returning to take over the baths. He was an authority on coastal erosion and an accomplished trumpet player.

84 Thomas Bryan
B: Banbury (Eng); 1866
D: Shrewsbury (Eng);
  8 Oct 1934
Forward
3 caps (1 gl): (Oswestry T)
v Ire, Eng, Sco 1886

Career: Oswestry Academy; Oswestry Colts; Oswestry T, 1883-88.

Tom Bryan was an energetic forward who, in the words of a contemporary report, 'plays a pretty game but should pass more'. Perhaps because of this selfishness he was quite a goalscorer, knocking in four against Bollington in an 1886 FA Cup tie and found the net in his second match for Wales. Bryan was lightly built, fleet of foot and carried a fair shot; he was said to have formed 'a very good left wing' against Ireland. He set up Hersee for the third goal but for the match against Scotland, Bangor's Willie Lewis got the selectors' nod. Although some match reports had Lewis in the team, he was unable to play and Bryan took his place. Bryan was a former pupil at the Oswestry Academy in Willow Street, run by Oxford-educated Owen Owen, later the first chief inspector for the Central Welsh Board for Intermediate Education. His brother Benjamin was also a pupil there and also played for the school team. Bryan's father was an itinerant dealer and hawker who eventually settled in Llanfyllin and, on his death in 1916, left the then staggering sum of over £19,000. Tom Bryan became a farmer and dealer in Llanymynech and, in September 1934, he was knocked off the pillion of his son's motor bike. Although his injuries were limited to a badly broken elbow, he tragically died under anaesthetic during an operation to re-set the bone.

Honours:
Oswestry T - Welsh Cup 1884; finalists 1885

85 Albert Malcolm Hersee
B: Llandudno; 1864
D: Deganwy; 8 Jan 1922
Goalkeeper
2 caps: (Bangor) v Ire, Sco 1886

Career: Llandudno Swifts, 1882-85; Bangor, 1885-86; Llandudno Swifts, 1886-88; Rhyl, Sep- Dec 1888; Chester, Dec 1888-89; Port Vale, 1889; Rhyl, Jan 1890; Llanrwst, Mar 1890; Blackburn Rov, 1890; Rhyl, Nov 1891; Llandudno Swifts, 1892-94. Also, **N Wales** v Liverpool & Dist (1884), v Lancashire (1885, 1886); **Denbighshire** v Lancashire (1885).

The much-travelled Malcolm Hersee was a familiar figure on the north Wales soccer scene but he failed in his two attempts to establish himself at a senior level. With Mills Roberts unavailable for the 1886 Scotland match, the FAW selectors were faced with the choice of Hersee or R Evans of Welshpool for the goalkeeper's position. Hersee did well in the trial and got the selectors' nod. He was retained for the second match but the more experienced Mills Roberts was preferred against England. At club level Hersee also had several outings as a forward and he was said to 'play a very unselfish game but with not quite enough dash'. He later worked as a house painter in Wallasey before returning to the Llandudno area.

86 Richard Hersee
B: Llandudno; 25 Nov 1867
D: Llandudno; 5 May 1922
Outside left/Centre forward
  (5ft 10ins, 9st 10lbs)
1 cap (1 gl): (Bangor) v Ire 1886

Career: Gloddaeth Rov (Llandudno), 1882-86; Bangor, 1886-1889; Rhyl, 1889-92; Llandudno Swifts, 1892-94; (also appeared for Bootle and Liverpool Cambrians).

Although Dick Hersee played his one international match at outside left, he was a versatile individual at club level, appearing at centre forward, full back and finally in goal. He was reputed to be one of the founders of football in Llandudno and an originator of Gloddaeth Rovers, where he captained the club for five seasons until moving to Bangor. As a forward, he was reckoned to be 'a good dribbler and very tricky'.

His three-year spell as captain and full back of Rhyl was brought to a close in 1891 by a serious illness. On recovery, he resumed playing with Llandudno Swifts as a goalkeeper. Hersee, a brother to Malcolm, with whom he appeared in his one international match, was subsequently a well-known referee in the North Wales Coast League. A part-time superintendent with the Llandudno Fire Brigade, he was a painter and decorator but later kept the Pier Hotel in the town. He died within months of his elder brother

87 Robert Roberts
B: Wrexham; 1863
D: Wrexham; 24 Mar 1950
Full back
3 caps: (Wrexham Olympic) v Ire 1886; v Ire 1887

Career: Rhostyllen; Wrexham Olympic, 1884-88; Wrexham, 1888-92.

A hard-working player and a sound defender, Bob Roberts was one of the first signings made by the Wrexham Olympic club after its formation. His performance in the 1886 North v South trial led to his selection against Ireland, but A O Davies was preferred for the matches against England and Scotland. Roberts was said to 'kick and head the ball well' but the following year had to demonstrate talents of a slightly different type when he was emergency goalkeeper in Belfast in 1887.

Captain of the Wrexham club, he retired in 1892 and subsequently served as trainer for several years. Roberts worked at Bersham Colliery in his early life and was a keen Territorial. He was a brother to William Roberts, who also played for Wrexham Olympic and Wales.

Honours:
Wrexham - Welsh Cup finalists 1891

88 William Roberts
B: Wrexham; 18 Mar 1859
D: Wrexham; 12 Jun 1945
Forward
4 caps (1 gl): (Wrexham Olympic) v Eng, Ire, Sco 1886; v Ire 1887

Career: Wrexham, 1879-83; Wrexham Olympic, 1883-88; Rhostyllen, 1888.

Bill Roberts was the type of player who was 'always in the thickest of the fight'. One scribe said that he was 'tricky and comical, occasionally brilliant'. He gained all of his caps during a lengthy spell with Wrexham clubs. After leaving Wrexham, he joined his brother Robert Roberts, the Wrexham and Wales full back, at Rhostyllen. Bill worked as a collier, then as a brickmaker and was later employed at a leather works.

Honours:
Wrexham - Welsh Cup 1883

89 Thomas Davies
B: Oswestry (Eng); 1865
D: Flint; 17 Dec 1902
Centre forward
1 cap: (Oswestry T) v Eng 1886

Career: Oswestry T, 1882-87; (also Oswestry White Stars 1882); Chester, 1891; Chester Police Athletic Club. Also, **Denbighshire** v Lancashire (1886).

'Darky' Davies emerged from the Oswestry reserve team in 1884 as a potential successor to E G Shaw. A tricky dribbler, he was at first thought to be too light but soon filled out. Although he was not selected for the 1886 Welsh trial match, withdrawals from the side brought Davies an unexpected call to fill the problem position of centre forward. He later adopted a half back role with Oswestry but eventually moved to Chester where he found work as a painter and played for the local club. Subsequently, he was manager of the Cestrian Hotel, then the Salmon's Vaults before becoming landlord of the Royal Oak Hotel in Flint. His brother George was a footballer with Kettering.

90 John Doughty
B: Bilston (Eng); 1864
D: Manchester (Eng); Apr 1937
Centre forward
8 caps (6 gls): (Druids) v Sco 1886; (Newton Heath) v Ire, Sco, 1887; v Eng, Ire, Sco 1888; v Sco 1889; v Eng 1890

Career: Druids, 1882-86; Newton Heath, 1886-91 (F Comb 1888-89, F Alliance 1889-91 - 26 apps, 12 gls).

Jack Doughty shot to prominence in his first season with Druids when he scored the only goal of the match against Bolton to give the Ruabon team a sensational FA Cup victory. Doughty, surprisingly, was not among the players lured from Ruabon to Lancashire but remained with the Druids to enjoy considerable Welsh Cup success. In 1886, Doughty, possibly persuaded by Jack Powell, joined Newton Heath for a fee of 10s a week to cover a meal and his train fare to north Wales. Previously a coal miner, he was found employment with the Lancashire and Yorkshire Railway, in the carriage works, and turned professional with the associated Newton Heath club for 30s a week. At one time the club had several players from the Wrexham area in the team including Tom Burke, Joe Davies and Jack Owen. Doughty was admired for his unselfish play, and the sturdy forward, who was extremely fast with the ball at his toes, seldom failed to get him name on the score sheet. He became the first Newton Heath player to hit 100 goals and managed 42 in his best season. Percy Young, in his 1960 book, *Manchester United*, described Doughty as 'a crasher of the first order' and 'a terror to opposing defences'. He was charged with rough play by the English FA in March 1889 but the Council decided to take no action.

Jack scored four goals in Wales' 11-0 win over Ireland in 1888, and hit three later that season in Newton Heath's 7-1 Manchester Cup win over Denton. One report commented that the brothers 'played a rattling good game'. In April 1892, Newton Heath faced a team of Welsh international players for Jack's benefit game, which included Trainer, Jack Powell, Dai Jones, Joe and Bob Davies, Joe Davies (Millwall), Morris and Egan. A total of 4,000 spectators attended and 'it was a mark of the respect in which he was held that all of the selected players turned up'. Doughty's robustly physical approach to the game had taken its toll; an injury at Stoke in January 1891 meant the end of his playing career. Long after retiring from football, Doughty remained in employment with the railway company, as a steam pipe fitter and lived within sight of the old Newton Heath ground. `The Warrior', as he was known, was reputedly the first Wales international player to be awarded a cap; previously, players were presented with a jersey and badge. The evidence suggests that the Doughty brothers were born in England of an Irish father and Welsh mother and moved to Ruabon as youngsters.

Honours:
Druids - Welsh Cup 1885, 1886; finalists 1883, 1884
Newton Heath - Manchester Cup 1888

91 Richard Parry Williams

B: Caernarfon; 1863
D: Bulawayo (Zim);
    27 Jul 1934
Wing half
1 cap: (Carnarvon Ath) v Sco 1886

Career; Friars Sch (Bangor); Carnarvon Ath, 1883-86.

Dick Parry Williams was the son of Robert and Ellen Williams of the Ship and Castle Hotel, Caernarfon, and after early education at the local national school he became a pupil at Friars School in Bangor - a soccer stronghold. In January 1885, he took part and scored in the Welsh trial match and, on the strength of his performance, was subsequently selected to face Ireland. An injury ruled him out and he had to wait until the following year for his one and only Wales appearance. His *forte* was said to be 'speed and skill'.

Williams trained as a chemist but was, for a while, manager of the Ship and Castle with his brother Tom. When the local Athletic football club was turned into a limited company in 1888, Williams became a shareholder. He went out to South Africa in January 1902 to work as an assayer for a mining company in Johannesburg, and at one time was said to be 'prospecting in Swaziland'. Williams retained his connection with his home town and was a frequent visitor when on holiday.

92 John Bonamy Challen

B: Ruthin; 26 Mar 1863
D: Eastbourne (Eng);
    5 Jun 1937
Forward
4 caps: (Corinthians) v Eng, Sco 1887; v Eng 1888, (Ruthin & Corinthians) v Eng 1890

Career: Marlborough Coll, Sep 1878-Dec 1879; Trinity Coll (Dublin), 1885-88; Wellingborough G Sch; Corinthians, Dec 1887-91 (35 apps, 20 goals); (also Swifts 1886-90).

John Challen was the son of the Reverend J L Challen and studied at Trinity College, Dublin, after attending Marlborough College. An exceptionally fast and troublesome winger, he was a member of both the Swifts and the Corinthians. In the latter's match against Preston North End in December 1887 Challen, despite the array of talent on the field, was described as 'the pick of the teams', and scored his side's goal in a 1-1 draw. He was also Wales' finest forward in the Scotland match of 1887. As an amateur, Challen featured in a number of teams including the Wellingborough Grammar School XI, which was made up of masters and boys at the school.

He was successively a master at Ruthin Grammar School and Wellingborough Grammar School before getting the headmastership of Queen Elizabeth School, Crediton. A fine cricketer, Challen played for Somerset for many years; his best seasons were in the early 1890s when he scored 1,317 runs in the 1890 and 1891 seasons and knocked 109 in two hours in 1893. Described as a 'hard hitting middle order bat and altogether excellent cover point', his first-class career lasted from 1884 to 1899, and in 52 matches he accumulated 1,656 runs. Challen left Crediton to become headmaster at Devon County School in West Buckland, then at the North Devon School, in Barnstaple. His final teaching appointment was as an assistant schoolmaster at a private school in Eastbourne. In retirement he lived in Eastbourne and was an enthusiastic member of the local opera and dramatic society.

93 Edward Clement Evelyn
B: Presteigne; 18 Nov 1862
D: Scotts Bluff (NE, USA);
   6 May 1936
Inside forward
1 cap: (Crusaders) v Eng 1887

Career: Malvern Coll, 1877-81; Crusaders; Brentwood, 1882-86; Crusaders; Corinthians, 1882 (5 apps, 1 goal).

E C Evelyn captained both the cricket and football elevens at Malvern College and went into the legal profession after leaving school, practising as a solicitor in Westminster between 1887 and 1892. 'A dashing forward with a sure kick', he spent several seasons with the amateurs of Brentwood, usually appearing alongside fellow Welsh international player T J Britten. Unfortunately for Evelyn, the Welsh selectors decided to play him at wing half and he was not a conspicuous success. Wales lost 4-0 and only the efforts of Jack Powell and A O Davies kept the score down.

Evelyn was also a splendid cricketer and the Malvern College summary of the 1881 season commented: 'Malvern has had, and will doubtless again have, better XIs than the present, but it never had, and, we venture to prophecy it never will have, a better captain than Evelyn'. He emigrated to the United States of America in 1908 and began farming at Scotts Bluff in Nebraska. Evelyn became a naturalized US citizen in March 1918 and remained in Nebraska until his death in 1936.

94 William Haighton Turner
B: Wrexham; 1867
D: South Africa; 9 May 1955
Forward
5 caps: (Wrexham) v Eng, Ire 1887; v Sco 1890; v Eng, Sco 1891

Career: Wrexham Vic, 1882-84; Wrexham Lever, 1884-86; Wrexham, 1886-92.

A utility forward who preferred the centre forward berth, Bill Turner was capped on five occasions by Wales, and on each occasion the team went down to defeat. In 1887, in Belfast, he took the place of Lewis who was unable to make the trip. One writer described him as 'a dashing centre forward who passes well to his wings', while another had him as 'a fair shot but rather rash'. The luckless Turner also appeared in two Welsh Cup finals but fared no better than in his international games, ending up on the losing side on both occasions. He made a guest appearance for Everton in March 1891, against Notts County, but didn't impress sufficiently.

Turner and his brother Dick emigrated to South Africa in the early 1890s and were later partners in a business in Cape Town. By 1919 he was employed as a municipal superintendent of works.

Honours:
Wrexham - Welsh Cup finalists 1890, 1891

95 George Griffiths
B: Chirk; 11 Apr 1864
D: Leigh (Eng); 7 Jul 1918
Outside left (5ft 3ins, 8st 3lbs)
1 cap: (Chirk) v Ire 1887

Career: Chirk,1881-92.

George Griffiths followed his brother Peter into the Chirk team and developed a reputation as a goalscoring winger. The two often played together on the left wing and made a fine combination. George was a neat player, with a deft touch and always eager to shoot for goal, but made only rare appearances in the first team after 1892, giving way to Albert Lockley. A coal miner in Chirk, he later moved to Leigh in search of work and at one time was employed in an iron works and later as a collier. He was a member of the Leigh Volunteers and joined the Army Service Corps in June 1915, giving his age as 48 when he was actually 51 years old. Griffiths served in France from August 1915 until November 1916 but suffered an accident at Merecourt when a heavy bale of hay fell off a lorry and struck his left knee. This left him lame, unable to fully extend his leg, and requiring the aid of a stick to walk. He had also been gassed in France and was medically discharged from the Army in March 1917 on account of this knee injury. Sadly, just 15 months later he succumbed to cancer.

Honours:
Chirk - Welsh Cup 1887, 1888, 1890

96 Edward Percival Whitley Hughes
B: Dwygyfylchi; 9 Mar 1868
D: East Grinstead (Eng);
   3 Sep 1941
Half back
4 caps: (Bangor) v Ire 1887; v Eng, Sco, Ire 1889

Career: Friars Sch (Bangor); Bangor, 1886-Dec 1890; London Welsh, 1891-92; East Grinstead.

In the late 1880s, Bangor were fortunate to find in Percy Hughes a worthy successor to the great half back Humphrey Jones. Hughes, the son of a farmer, had received his early schooling at Friars, Bangor, and later became captain of the fine Bangor side which won the Welsh Cup in 1889. One report commented on Hughes – 'besides being a fine judge of the game he has great pace combined with accurate place kicking'.

He left Bangor in December 1890 to train as a solicitor in London. When available, he turned out for the enthusiastic London Welsh XI and one judge thought so highly of him as to describe him as 'the best centre half in London'. Hughes moved to East Grinstead in 1892 and was appointed Clerk to the Local Justices in 1896 and subsequently County Court Registrar. He was active in the life of the town for many years, a freemason, and held several public appointments.

Honours:
Bangor - Welsh Cup 1889

97 Alexander Hunter
B: Tiverton (Eng); 1862
D: Shrewsbury (Eng);
   16 Dec 1899
Centre half
1 cap: v Ire 1887

Alex Hunter holds a unique place in Welsh soccer history as the FAW secretary who was called on in an emergency to play in the national team. In those early days the Irish trips always presented a problem to the FAW Committee; several players were unwilling to undertake the journey while others travelled but didn't play because of the after effects of the crossing. Hunter, who was expected to act as an umpire, was a late substitute for Humphrey Jones (Percy Hughes in some reports) and one newspaper commented: 'Mr Hunter the secretary of the Welsh Association filled up the gap in the Welsh team by playing half back, but it is needless to say it was neither strengthened nor stabilised by his presence. He must have thought it a good joke to get playing or he would never have donned the jersey, for whatever his knowledge may be of the theory, he was glaringly deficient in practice'. He was not a total novice at the game, having played for junior club Wrexham Hare and Hands in the early 1880s.

Hunter, the son of a clergyman, was at one time based in Llangollen and had trained as an architect and surveyor, becoming a partner in 1886 in the firm of Richardson & Hunter. He was FAW secretary from September 1883 to 1887 and, although a capable administrator, his period in office was marked by an unfortunate incident when in July 1885 a fire at his office in Temple Row, Wrexham caused considerable damage and destroyed the FAW's papers: Preston NE later played Wrexham and District to raise money to cover part of the loss. On one occasion, he submitted his resignation after complaining about his work load and malicious allegations that he was feathering his nest. The FAW committee increased his honorarium and he remained in post.

Hunter, who refereed the Scotland v Wales match in 1886 relinquished his post as secretary the following year, but in 1889 took on the position of treasurer. Along with FAW secretary John Taylor he represented the association at the International Board meeting at Glasgow in May 1891 which changed the laws to introduce penalty kicks and replace umpires with linesmen. He severed his connection with the FAW around 1892 but became a referee in the Football Alliance and served on the committee of the Shropshire Charity FA. Hunter moved to Shrewsbury in the early 1890s to become the town's sanitary inspector and died at the young age of 37.

98 Samuel Jones
B: Mold; 1867
D: Caergwrle; 13 Nov 1932
Full back
2 caps: (Wrexham Olympic) v Ire 1887; (Chester) v Sco 1890

Career: Caergwrle, 1883-84; Wrexham Olympic, 1884-87; Chester, Dec 1887-91; Wrexham, 1891-92; Caergwrle Wdrs, 1892-95.

A tall, rangy full back, Sam Jones was a tireless worker with a powerful kick and was an early recruit to Wrexham Olympic, following Wrexham's ban by the English FA. Although very much a reserve man for Wales, Jones remained on the fringes of selection for several seasons, even after returning to junior football with Caergwrle. He spent a lengthy period with Chester and was with the club when they became founder members of the Combination League in 1890. In September 1894 he was reinstated as an amateur. Jones began work as a coal miner in his early teens and continued to work in the pits until his retirement. Outside soccer, he was a member of the Territorial Army and a keen bandsman.

99 Henry Wilmshurst Sabine
B: Oswestry (Eng); 9 Jan 1865
D: Harrogate (Eng); 13 Aug 1955
Outside right
1 cap (1 gl): (Oswestry T) v Ire 1887

Career; Oswestry T, 1882-89; Oswestry Old Boys (also secretary); Oswestry Utd, 1893.

At various times, Henry Sabine captained the cricket, hockey and soccer clubs in Oswestry. He was also awarded the Royal Humane Society medal in 1892 for rescuing a person from the river Severn. Sabine, the son of a solicitor, also participated in local amateur dramatic presentations and had a gift for song writing. Although there was some doubt about him being eligible to play for Wales, he was able to qualify on 'grounds of partial ancestry'. He was said to be good passer of the ball but needed to feed his partners more often. Sabine joined the North & South Wales Bank in Oswestry at the age of 16, and his transfer to Wrexham in December 1897 drew the following tribute: 'Oswestry football and cricket have lost a rare good man in Mr H. W. Sabine. He was one of those good all round men whom it was a pleasure to meet, as he was a thorough sportsman and gentleman to boot. He could fight desperately hard to win a game for his side, but he could take a licking with a smiling face'. Two years later he moved to Liverpool, and was then manager for the successor company, the London, City & Midland Bank at Harrogate from 1910 until 1930. An avid cricket follower, Sabine was on his way to the county ground in Harrogate when he was tragically knocked down by a bus. He died in hospital a week later, from shock.

An excellent all-rounder, who often bowled in tandem with R T Gough for Oswestry, he represented Shropshire at cricket and faced the MCC in July 1895. His son Charles Shirley Wilmshurst Sabine was a dental surgeon in Harrogate and served in France in the Second World War with the British Expeditionary Force.

100 Alfred William Townsend
B: Birmingham; 1864
D: Newtown; 15 May 1936
Full back (5ft 10ins, 11st 9lbs)
2 caps: (Newtown) v Ire 1887; v Ire 1893

Career: Newtown, 1884-96.

The athletically-built Townsend started at half back but spent most of his career at full back or as a goalkeeper. He made his first appearance for Wales in Belfast when Jack Powell, along with several other players were unable to appear. When he was called up to replace Smart Arridge in 1893 against Ireland, he partnered Oliver Taylor: the first time Wales had fielded a pair of full backs from the same club. This 'model defender' had to don the goalkeeper's jersey in the 1895 Welsh Cup final when Goodwin was sent off.

Alf Townsend turned to refereeing after his playing days were over and was prominent in Newtown cricketing circles. His father had been a brewer in Newtown and Townsend, a painter in early life, subsequently went into the licensed trade and kept the New Inn at Newtown for many years until his death.

Honours:
Newtown - Welsh Cup 1895, finalists 1886

101 Richard Jones
B: Bangor; 1864
D: Crewe (Eng); 24 Mar 1936
Forward
3 caps: (Bangor) v Sco 1887; v Eng 1889; (Crewe Alex) v Eng 1890

Career: Bangor, 1882-89; Crewe Alex, 1889-92 (46 FL apps).

Dick Jones was one of the stars of Bangor's 1889 Welsh Cup success, a victory which broke the north east Wales and border clubs' monopoly on the trophy. 'A brilliant winger', he had 'good dribbling qualities' and was in particularly fine form against Northwich Victoria. Jones and his colleague Billy Lewis had been lined up by Crewe and signed for the Cheshire club after the final. As an inducement, Jones was fixed up with a clerical job in the railway accountant's office, a common practice for the Crewe club. He partnered Jackie Pearson, 'popular marksman and idol of the Crewe crowd', in the Second Division side but his career was brought to an end in 1892 by an accident. In 1890, he was described in the following terms: 'gives valuable service up front but shows some inclination to be selfish allowing himself to be robbed'. He continued to work in the accountant's office of the LNWR until his retirement in 1927. A brother to John Owen Jones (#205).

Honours:
Bangor - Welsh Cup 1889

102 William Ernest Pryce Jones

B: Newtown; 29 Dec 1867
D: Tywyn; 14 Mar 1949
Forward (5ft 8ins, 10st 4lbs)
5 caps (3 gls): (Cambridge Univ) v Sco 1887; v Eng, Ire, Sco 1888; v Ire 1890

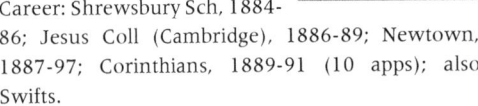

Career: Shrewsbury Sch, 1884-86; Jesus Coll (Cambridge), 1886-89; Newtown, 1887-97; Corinthians, 1889-91 (10 apps); also Swifts.

While not so much of an all-rounder as his brother, 'Mr Ernest' was a more accomplished footballer. Pryce Jones gained a soccer blue in 1889 and was, for a period, a member of the Corinthians XI. He returned to Newtown from college, became chairman of the local club and began placing it on a firm footing. In later years the club was known as Newtown RWW, after the family business. When the team reached the Welsh Cup final, Pryce Jones arranged, at his own expense, for the entire team to prepare for the match at Borth on the west Wales coast.

'Mr Ernest', like 'Mr Bertie' was a captain in the 5th volunteer battalion South Wales Borderers, known as The Dandy Fifth. For many years, after giving up soccer around 1910, Pryce Jones was a permanent feature of the Newtown cricket team, as a batsman and leg break bowler, and also represented Shropshire and Montgomeryshire. He continued to work for the family firm as a director until it was taken over in 1937 by Messrs Lewis. It was while spending the winter at a private hotel in Aberdovey that Pryce Jones was taken ill and died.

Honours:
Newtown - Welsh Cup 1895; finalists 1897
 - Shropshire & Dist Lge champions 1893

103 James Morris

B: Trefonen (Eng); 1864
D: Oswestry (Eng); 16 Jul 1915
Half back
1 cap: (Oswestry T) v Sco 1887

Career: Trefonen, 1881-84; Oswestry T, 1884-91.

Jim Morris made his only Welsh appearance against the Scots in 1887 when he stood in for the indisposed Humphrey Jones. The previous year he had featured in the FAW's North v South trial match at Wrexham but didn't get the nod. At one time, Morris was the defensive strong man and captain of the village side Trefonen, but his association with Oswestry lasted over 30 years as he was a long-time committee member after giving up the game. Morris was a bricklayer but relinquished building to become landlord of the Five Bells Inn in Oswestry.

104 James Trainer

B: Wrexham; 7 Jan 1863
D: London (Eng); 5 Aug 1915
Goalkeeper (5ft 11ins, 12st)
20 caps: (Bolton Wdrs) v Sco 1887; (Preston N E) v Sco 1888; v Eng 1889; v Sco 1890; v Sco 1891; v Ire, Sco 1892; v Eng 1893; v Ire, Eng 1894; v Ire, Eng 1895; v Sco 1896; v Ire, Sco, Eng 1897; v Sco, Eng 1898; v Ire, Sco 1899

Career: Penybryn Wdrs, 1876; Challenger B C; Wrexham Vic, 1876-78; Wrexham Grosvenor, 1878-81; Wrexham, 1881-83; Great Lever (Bolton), Dec 1883-85; Bolton Wdrs, 1885-87; Preston N E, Aug 1887-1900 (253 FL apps).

Jim Trainer played junior football as a centre half and centre forward and was a reluctant convert to goalkeeping. He played his first senior match for Wrexham in November 1882 and before long had established a reputation as an excellent goalkeeper. In November 1883, he was elected a member of the Everton club but was not prepared to accept reserve team football and left, or so it was said. Whatever the truth, the following week he was back in the Wrexham team.

Trainer, a time-served coach builder, left Wrexham under a cloud, following a particularly rough FA Cup tie between Wrexham and Oswestry in December 1883. He was alleged to have 'insulted the referee' and the English FA banned Wrexham from the competition and reported Trainer's offence to the FAW. By the time the FAW met, in February 1884, to formulate a rule to expel players from the Association for misconduct, Trainer was well out of their jurisdiction. In an earlier match for Wrexham, Trainer had played against Great Lever and when the Lancashire club's goalkeeper got injured, they remembered 'the yon' man fra' Wrexham' and sent for him - an approach he must have welcomed. He was given 30s a week and the promise of work, but no job materialised, so to retain his services in the close season the club made the novel decision to pay him 13s a week summer wages.

Bolton were soon aware of the talented Trainer and, after offer and counteroffer from Lever, got their man for 50s a week. The club, to forestall any attempt at further bidding, gave Trainer £5 and packed him and his girlfriend off to the Isle of Man for a fortnight until the '85-86 season started. The Great Lever chairman commented: 'I hope when he's coming home his boat will go down, and everybody will be saved excepting him'.

Trainer enjoyed his greatest success at Preston as a member of the `Invincibles'. Curiously, he'd impressed Preston while playing for Bolton at Deepdale in a match in which he let in 12 goals. It was said that but for Trainer's efforts the score would have reached 40! He was reckoned to be 'as safe as a sandbag'. The removal of J J Bentley from the Bolton secretaryship was an influential factor in Trainer leaving the club for Preston. For several years, Trainer was a publican in Preston, running the Royal Consort, and a director of North End, but his domestic life was far from harmonious; in 1898 Trainer's petition for divorce on the grounds of his wife's adultery was rejected.

At the time of Trainer's separation from his wife and six children, in 1904, it was reckoned that the couple had once been worth £2,000. He resigned his Preston directorship the following year to become involved with an indoor exhibition soccer scheme at London Olympia. The venture failed, the participants were banned by the FA and the one-time 'Prince of Goalkeepers' was out of work. Trainer died in poverty in 1915 of 'consumption of the throat', having received some financial help in his later years from Leigh Roose. He had worked in London as a boot finisher but ended his days in Paddington Infirmary, adjacent to

Paddington Workhouse. It was only as a result of an appeal for information by journalist and FAW councillor George Lerry through the coluimns of the Wrexham Leader in the 1930s that it was discovered that the 'Prince of Goalkeepers' had died in poverty and obscurity.

It was probably during Trainer's time at Preston that he had a remarkable confrontation with a footballing elephant. Sanger's Circus, owners of this unusual beast, arranged for Trainer to take three penalty kicks against the elephant and then for him to go in goal and face the animal. 'When Trainer was shooting, he was placed about 12 yards distance and the ball was 2ft 6ins in diameter. It was practically impossible to get this through the goal for the elephant when turned end on filled the area. When the animal's turn came, it was brought to within six or seven yards. Trainer stopped the first shot though the force was nearly enough to break his arm. He also kept out the second but the elephant proved not only a deadly shot but a trickster. For his third effort it walked up to the ball as before and raised its foot to kick, then it put its foot down again as if intending to go back and walk up again. Trainer, therefore, who had not expected to find the real cunning of a footballer in an elephant, relaxed his vigilance, but quick as lightning the animal took the kick unexpectedly and the goal was scored. However, Trainer was adjudged to have performed so well that he was given the prize.'

Honours:
Preston N E - FL 1st Div champions 1889, 1890
            - FL 1st Div runners-up 1891, 1892, 1893
Wrexham - Welsh Cup 1883

105 Joseph Davies
B: Cefn Mawr; 3 Feb 1865
D: Cefn Mawr; 7 Oct 1943
Half back
7 caps: (Newton Heath) v Eng, Ire, Sco 1888; v Sco 1889; v Eng 1890; (Wolverhampton Wdrs) v Eng 1892; v Eng 1893

Career: Druids,1882-86; Newton Heath, 1886-90 (21 F Alliance apps in 1889-90); Wolverhampton Wdrs, Aug 1890-93 (34 FL apps); Druids, 1894-95.

Joe Davies was one of five brothers who played for Druids, four of whom were capped by Wales (see also Lloyd, Robert and Thomas). While uncapped Walter played for Druids, there's no indication that a sixth brother – Edward, the eldest – played the game. Joe, whose first employment was as a horse driver in a coal mine, gained an early taste of top class soccer as a 17-year-old when he was a member of the Druids team which faced Blackburn Olympic in the quarter-final of the FA Cup. Joe was a solidly built, totally reliable player whose enthusiasm drew the best out of his colleagues. He enjoyed a reputation as a very keen, aggressive player who was strong in the tackle.

Joe was the first of the Welsh contingent to leave Newton Heath; after some 160 appearances and Manchester Cup success in 1888, he signed for Wolves and it was at the midlands club that he was said to have suffered his greatest footballing disappointment. Wolves met Everton in the 1893 FA Cup final, but there was no place for Joe even though he had played in 18 league matches that season. Wolves were supposedly intent on fielding an all-English team, as West Brom had done previously, and Joe was so disappointed that he never again kicked a ball for the club, or so the story goes. In fact, Joe had not appeared in any of the cup games but made a subsequent league appearance for Wolves and later resumed playing for Druids, albeit very briefly. On retiring from soccer he became a successful farmer and kept a butcher's shop in Cefn until his death. Joe married Jane, sister of the distinguished professor of veterinary science Professor J Share-Jones, and was at one time a member of the Wrexham and District Master Butchers Association.

106 Roger Doughty

B: Cannock Chase (Eng); c.1870
D: Prestwich (Eng); 18 Dec 1914
Forward/Wing half
(5ft 8ins,12st)
2 caps (2 gls): (Newton Heath)
v Ire, Sco 1888

Career: Druids, 1884-86; Newton Heath, 1886-93 (F Comb 1888-89, F Alliance 1889-92, 54 apps, 2 gls); Fairfield, 1893-94; West Manchester, 1894-96)

Roger Doughty worked as a horse driver in a local colliery and followed his brother Jack into the Druids team. The two brothers lived in Crane Street, Ruabon, home of the Davies brothers and several other Druids notables. They had a fine understanding and usually played alongside each other. Their loyalty to their teammates was said to be legendary. Roger moved to Newton Heath in 1886 but wasn't considered to be as classy as Jack and only received £1 a week. He was also given work with the Lancashire and Yorkshire Railway Company and stayed with the company for a time after retiring from the game. By 1894, Roger had joined West Manchester as a full back, having started his career as a forward. Following his playing career, Doughty became a publican at the Museum Inn in Failsworth, Manchester. His only son, Tom, served with the Royal Marine Light Infantry in the Dardenelles and was killed in action in northern France in February 1917 aged 20.

Honours:
Druids - Welsh Cup 1885, 1886

107 Edmund Gwynne Howell

B: Builth; 1867
D: Transvaal (SA); 1943
Forward
3 caps (3 gls): (Builth T) v Ire 1888; v Eng 1890; v Eng 1891

Career: Builth T, 1886-99.

The son of Marmaduke Howell, a Builth solicitor, Ned Howell was very much a gentleman amateur, one of the early mainstays of the club and was the first Builth player to be selected for Wales, an occasion which gave rise to much celebration. On his return from Wrexham, 'a crowd of well wishers greeted him at the station, a horse-drawn omnibus which was well laden inside and out took him to the club headquarters at the Lion Hotel where he was lustily cheered'.

Ned was again the Builth hero when he scored in the club's victory over Cardiff in the South Wales and Monmouthshire Senior Cup final of 1894 but, in 1897, he gave up the club captaincy as 'he could no longer expend the time and trouble'. The local paper described him as 'one of the finest forwards in the district and possibly at one time one of the best inside forwards in Wales. He has an extraordinary command over the ball; he gets away with such ease and grace and is positively the trickiest shot I have seen. Ned is a grand coach, a masterly tactician and a gentlemanly player'; he was also known for his 'delightful dribbling and swift shooting'. A keen and skilled cricketer, he was also a stalwart of the Builth Cricket Club alongside his brother. Howell was a captain in the South Wales Borderers and took part in the Boer War of 1900-02, a conflict in which his brother Herbert also served. By 1911 he was living in Oswestry with his young wife and daughter and working as a law clerk. He resigned his commission in January 1914 and the following year was the subject of an arrest warrant for failing to maintain his daughter, but the police were unable to establish his whereabouts. There is some mystery about his subsequent life. It appears that he returned to South Africa in the early 1920s and later remarried after the death of his wife in 1940. By the early 1940s he was also using the name Edmund Gwynne White and was diamond prospecting in the Transvaal, but he was not successful and never struck it rich - the solicitors dealing with his estate after his death found that he'd left just a few personal effects.

108 Reuben Humphreys

B: Cefn Mawr; 13 Sep 1865
D: Oswestry (Eng); 23 Apr 1944
Half back
1 cap: (Druids) v Ire 1888

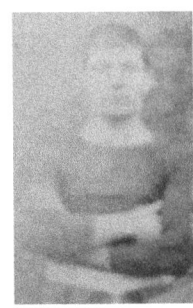

Career: Druids, 1886-94.

A versatile Druids player, Humphreys had spells at wing half, full back and inside right before settling into the centre half position towards the end of his career. Said to 'kick well' and 'use judgement', he had an easy time in his one international against Ireland as the side ran up a record 11-0 victory. It was such a comfortable win that A O Davies, W Pryce-Jones and Ned Howell left after the tenth goal to catch their trains!

Humphreys was a coal miner at the Wynnstay colliery in Ruabon but sustained a serious injury in 1907 that left him disabled and forced him to give up work.

109 David Jones

B: Trefonen (Eng); 1867
D: Bolton (Eng); 27 Aug 1902
Left back
   (5ft 10½ins, 13st 12lbs)
14 caps: (Chirk) v Ire, Sco 1888; (Bolton Wdrs) v Eng, Sco, Ire 1889; v Eng 1890; v Sco 1891;

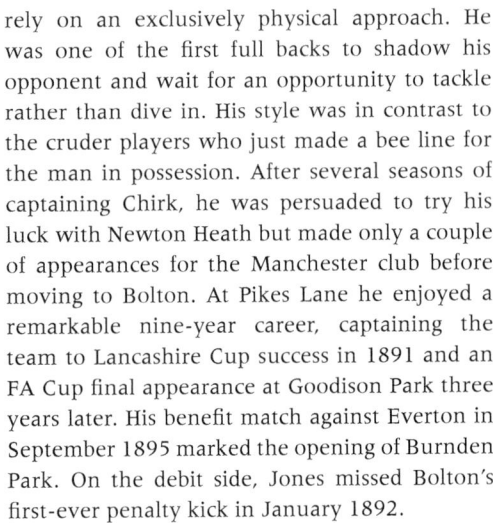

v Ire 1892; v Eng 1893; v Eng 1894; v Eng 1895; v Sco 1898; (Manchester C) v Eng, Ire 1900

Career: Chirk, 1883-88; Newton Heath; Bolton Wdrs, Mar 1888-1898 (228 FL apps, 4 gls); Manchester C (£50), Sep 1898-Aug 1902 (114 FL apps, 1 gl).

Di Jones was a typical product of Chirk football, preferring to use skill and guile rather than rely on an exclusively physical approach. He was one of the first full backs to shadow his opponent and wait for an opportunity to tackle rather than dive in. His style was in contrast to the cruder players who just made a bee line for the man in possession. After several seasons of captaining Chirk, he was persuaded to try his luck with Newton Heath but made only a couple of appearances for the Manchester club before moving to Bolton. At Pikes Lane he enjoyed a remarkable nine-year career, captaining the team to Lancashire Cup success in 1891 and an FA Cup final appearance at Goodison Park three years later. His benefit match against Everton in September 1895 marked the opening of Burnden Park. On the debit side, Jones missed Bolton's first-ever penalty kick in January 1892.

Billy Meredith played an important part in persuading his old friend to move to Manchester City in 1898 and, although 31 years of age - a veteran by early football standards - Jones showed no diminution in his footballing powers. In August 1902, while taking part in a pre-season practice match, he sustained a cut knee which at first sight seemed to be nothing more than a straightforward injury. However, treatment at the local hospital was limited to the stitching of the wound, tetanus set in and Jones was dead within ten days. Thousands lined the streets of Bolton as the coffin made its way to the station for burial at Froncysyllte.

Honours:
Bolton Wdrs - FA Cup finalists 1894
Manchester C - FL 2nd Div champions 1899
Chirk - Welsh Cup 1887, 1888

110 George Alfred Owen

B: Chirk; 10 Apr 1865
D: Chirk; 29 Jan 1922
Inside forward
4 caps (2 gls): (Chirk) v Sco 1888; (Newton Heath) v Sco, Ire 1889; (Chirk) v Ire 1893

Career: Chirk, 1880-89; Newton Heath, 1889-90 (12 F Alliance apps, 2 gls); West Manchester; Chirk, 1891-93; Druids, 1893-95; Chirk, 1895-96.

George Owen, a pupil teacher in his youth, was involved in Chirk football from the early days and played alongside T E Thomas, the future mentor of so many international players for Wales. A constructive player with an excellent shot, he was regularly on target for his hometown team. Owen had a spell at Newton Heath with the large north Walian contingent and appeared for them in a Manchester Cup final which featured no fewer than six Welsh caps. He made his debut for Wales in 1888, standing in for his Chirk colleague Billy Owen, after being chosen as a reserve. An ever reliable performer, Owen retired in 1896 to become a referee in local league football. A half brother to Tom Egan.

Honours:
Chirk - Welsh Cup 1887, 1888, 1892; finalists 1893
Newton Heath - Manchester Cup 1889

111 John Hallam
B: Oswestry (Eng);
   26 Jun 1869
D: Swindon (Eng);
   7 Mar 1949
Outside right
1 cap: (Oswestry T) v Eng 1889

Career: Oswestry Cambrian, 1885-87; Oswestry Crescent, 1887-88; Oswestry T, 1888-90; Small Heath, Jan 1890-96 (1890-92, 51 F Alliance apps, 21 gls), 1892-96 (82 FL apps, 33 gls); Swindon T, Aug 1896-97 (14 SL apps, 4 gls); Trowbridge, 1897-98; Swindon T, 1898-99 (2 SL apps).

A winger in the traditional mould, Jack Hallam was a lively player said to display 'clever tactics with the ball'. He served a lengthy apprenticeship with Oswestry clubs before breaking into senior soccer with Small Heath. When, in February 1889, Billy Owen was unavailable to play against England, Hallam took his place, but he was overlooked for further honours. One report described his performance thus: 'he showed great speed but was evidently nervous and hesitated too much'. He made his last league appearance for Small Heath at Christmas 1895 but took part in the end of season test matches against Liverpool and Manchester City.

Hallam later moved south to Swindon to join the Southern League outfit and to take work at the Great Western Railway works. He made first-team appearances in the 1896-97 and 1898-99 seasons, either side of a single campaign with Trowbridge. Hallam, who was said to have retired from playing in 1901, continued to work as a foreman for GWR until his retirement.

Honours:
Small Heath - FL 2nd Div champions 1893
             - FL 2nd Div runners-up 1894

112 William Parry Jones
B: Corwen; 23 Mar 1870
D: Ruabon; 17 Apr 1953
Full back
4 caps: (Druids) v Eng, Ire 1889; (Wynnstay) v Ire, Sco 1890

Career: Druids, 1887-90; Wynnstay (Ruabon), 1890-92; Druids, 1896-97.

A native of Corwen, W P Jones lived in Ruabon for the greater part of his life and was employed as a clerk in the office of the Wynnstay estate for 50 years. He was called up for his first international in place of the unavailable A O Davies, and he partnered Di Jones of Bolton in his first two internationals, displaying fine defensive qualities and 'good judgement and playing of the ball'. Jones had succeeded Albert Powell in the Druids team, but in 1890 left the club to help form Wynnstay - a team of employees of the landowner Sir Watkin Williams-Wynn, bolstered by some veteran ex-Druids. The club was short-lived and after a four year break from soccer, Jones made a brief comeback with Druids before playing a few games for Chirk and representing Denbighshire at cricket.

113 Arthur Lea

B: Wrexham; 23 Nov 1866
D: Marchwiel; 23 Mar 1945
Half back/Inside forward
4 caps: (Wrexham) v Eng 1889; v Ire, Sco 1891; v Ire 1893

Career: Wrexham Grosvenor, 1881-83; Wrexham, 1883-94.

Arthur Lea had only one arm but even with this disadvantage he was an accomplished footballer. 'Arthur became famous in football circles not only because of his handicap but because of his all-round skill on the field. He possessed a natural flair with the ball, made his debut at the age of 15 when he helped to launch the Wrexham Grosvenor and took up his position at full back and on the left wing when called upon. He was also noted for his tremendous and powerful kick'. A few years after the Grosvenor team was formed, he was picked up by Wrexham as a second team player and was quickly promoted to the first XI. As a professional he was paid 5s a week but when he made guest appearances the figure was increased to 10s. He was then reputedly the highest paid player in Wales. Lea, who first played for Wales in place of original selection George Owen, fulfilled his greatest ambition in 1893 when he captained Wrexham to victory over Chirk in the Welsh Cup final. In the same year, he captained Wales against Ireland at Belfast.

Shortly afterwards, Lea fell seriously ill and at one point was threatened with the loss of a leg. He was awarded a benefit match, then began playing again in the 1894-95 season but the comeback was short lived and ended in unfortunate circumstances. In a Soames Charity Cup final, Wrexham played Druids in an ill-tempered match. Wrexham won by a single goal but at the end of the match they were so roughly handled by some of the spectators they had to hurriedly leave the field and make their way back to Wrexham as best they could. Lea was said to have expressed the opinion that 'if that was what football was all about, it was the end for him'. The game marked his last pro' appearance but on a few occasions he played for Wrexham's second team.

The FAW 1892 player assessment described Lea as, 'a good hard working player - called upon at the last moment and had to play in the wrong position, appeared nervous. Played a good game against Ireland at left half'. Lea combined playing with his daytime job as a postman. He sometimes reported for work at 5.30am, did an 18-mile round and then caught the 9.20am train to an away match. In the evening, he would return to Chester after the last train to Wrexham, walk home and be back on duty at 5am! By 1900, he was reckoned to have travelled over 80,000 miles on foot in the service of the Post Office. After retiring in May 1927, he became landlord of the Wrest Hotel, Marchwiel. Lea also played for Wrexham Cricket Club, where at one time he was a pro', principally as a bowler but he was also a useful bat and made a number of half centuries.

Honours:
Wrexham - Welsh Cup 1893; finalists 1890, 1891, 1895

114 Joseph Davies

B: Pant, Rhosllanerchrugog; 27 Aug 1871
D: Featherstone (Eng); 1957
Outside right (5ft 7ins, 11st)
11 caps: (Everton) v Sco, Ire 1889; (Chirk) v Ire 1891, (Ardwick) Eng, Sco 1891; (Sheffield Utd) v Ire, Eng, Sco 1895; (Manchester C) v Eng 1896; (Millwall Ath) v Eng 1897; (Reading) v Eng 1900

Career: Chirk, 1887-88; Everton, Oct 1888-89 (8 FL apps, 2 goals); Gloddaeth Rov (Llandudno), Oct 1889; Chester, 1889; Chirk; Ardwick, Feb 1891-94 (16 FL apps, 8 gls); Sheffield Utd, Jan 1894-95 (12 FL apps, 3 gls); Manchester C, Nov 1895-96 (11 FL apps, 4 gls); Millwall Ath, May 1896-98 (29 SL apps, 16 gls); Reading, Mar 1898-1900 (42 SL apps, 5 gls); Manchester C, 1900-01 (8 FL apps); Stockport Co, Aug 1901-02 (29 FL apps, 5 gls).

The 1891 FAW player assessment of Millwall's first international player described Davies as 'a good outside right with a splendid shot and plays well with William Owen (Chirk) his partner. The only drawback is that he is rather selfish'. Davies had excellent ball control and a fierce drive. He featured in the Everton squad for their first Football League season but was not retained and gravitated back to north Wales. In February 1891, Ardwick officials were sufficiently impressed with Davies to offer him a three year contract - the first of three spells at the club which was later re-named Manchester City.

At Sheffield United, Davies found himself in trouble with the directors for taking lodgings in a public house and he was suspended for two weeks. It wasn't the first time he'd lodged in a pub – during his first spell at Ardwick (later renamed Manchester City) he stayed at the Hyde Road Hotel, adjacent to the ground. When City were keen to sign two of United's players in 1895, the Sheffield club insisted that Davies form part of the deal. He later gravitated to the Southern League and was described at Reading as an energetic and clever winger. His dribbling was a conspicuous part of his game and he could be a nightmare opponent for any full back. Davies was called up for his first international match at the tender age of 17 years and seven months, making him Wales' youngest international player. Joe's record stood until 1998 when it was ceded to Ryan Green.

In later life Joe Davies is believed to have worked as a coal miner in the Wakefield area, and died in 1957.

115 Allen Pugh
B: Esclusham; 27 Oct 1869
D: Rhostyllen; 7 Feb 1942
Goalkeeper (5ft 5ins, 13st 9lbs)
1 cap: (Rhostyllen) v Sco 1889 (sub)

Career: Rhostyllen, 1884-85; Wrexham Olympic, 1885-86; Rhostyllen, 1886-96.

Alf Pugh's fleeting appearance on the international stage came on Monday, 15 April 1889 when he unexpectedly found himself in the Wales goal facing the Scots. Jim Trainer, the selected goalkeeper, failed to appear despite the kick-off being delayed until 4.20pm and Pugh was asked to deputise. Meanwhile, the Welsh FA also hurriedly sent for Sam Gillam who seems to have been regarded as Trainer's deputy. Pugh's international career lasted all of 30 minutes, during which he kept a clean sheet, before being substituted - possibly the first such instance in competitive football. While never a serious contender for international honours, Alf Pugh was a competent goalkeeper who had begun playing for Rhostyllen at the age of 14. He appeared for Denbighshire on two occasions - against Shropshire in January 1885 at the age of 15 and Lancashire the following November. Pugh was at one time secretary of a junior soccer club and kept the Union Vaults public house in Wrexham. Subsequently he was employed as a clerk of works for an engineering company.

116 Samuel Gladstone Gillam
B: Swindon (Eng); 1868
D: Chard (Eng); 13 Oct 1938
Goalkeeper (6ft 1in)
5 caps: (Wrexham) v Sco, Ire 1889; (Shrewsbury) v Ire, Eng 1890; (Clapton) v Sco 1894

Career: Wrexham Lever, 1884-86; Wrexham Olympic, 1886-88; Everton, Jul

1888; Bolton Wdrs, Nov 1888; Wrexham, 1888-89; Shrewsbury T, Oct 1889-90; Chirk, Sep-Oct 1890; London Welsh, 1890-93; Clapton, 1893; Brighton Ath; West Hampstead, 1898.

Gillam succeeded Alf Pugh as Wrexham Olympic goalkeeper and in 1889 the two men figured in a notable substitution incident. Selected goalkeeper Jim Trainer was unable to secure his release from Preston to face the Scots but the selectors were not informed until shortly before kick-off. Pugh stood in for the first thirty minutes of the match, giving way to substitute Gillam, who had been summoned urgently. Gillam was the son of a Wrexham coal merchant and had first caught the selectors' eye when representing Denbighshire against Walsall in 1887. The following year he played for Bolton Wanderers against Everton, and Preston. In the Everton match, Gillam 'defended his charge in marvellous fashion, accounting for shot after shot in a style that brought forth hearty cheers'.

In October 1890, Gillam moved to London and captained London Welsh for a time. His last international appearance, like his first, was as a replacement for Jim Trainer. Once described by a newspaper as 'the man of many clubs', from 1900 business commitments put his footballing career into semi-retirement but four years later he was still on West Hampstead's books. In the 1920s, Gillam was vice president of London Welsh AFC and made the following comment on his first international: 'my first experience of international football was naturally to me, then 21 years of age, a wonderful event. We drew without any goals being scored and when we assembled at the Wynnstay Arms (Wrexham) in the evening to dine together there was a heated argument as to whether Scotland had not actually scored a goal with a shot which I tipped over the bar, there were no nets in those days. Anyway the Scotch players took it rather badly and swore that I had swindled them out of a win'. Gillam was later an hotelier in Cullompton before taking charge of the Crown Hotel in Chard.

117 Richard Herbert Jarrett

B: Corwen; 9 Oct 1870
D: St Louis (MO, USA); 29 Jan 1935
Forward
2 caps (3 gls): (Ruthin) v Ire 1889; v Sco 1890

Career: Ruthin, 1887-90; Chester; Bolton Wdrs, 1890-91.

The son of a Corwen farmer, Richard Jarrett moved to Ruthin to become a solicitor's clerk. On his international debut he bagged a hat-trick but, despite earning the tag 'the best goal-getter we have', was selected for only one further match. Jarrett played for several clubs but never stayed anywhere for long and always returned to Ruthin. He had spells with Rhyl and Ardwick, and played five league games for Bolton during the 1890-91 season. In a selection system heavily based on nomination by clubs, Jarrett's wanderings worked against him. In February 1891, he emigrated to Canada before heading south to Chicago where he became a naturalised US citizen in 1893. By 1910 Jarrett was working as a clerk in a tobacco factory in St Louis, Missouri and he was subsequently employed by the local authority for several years before his death in 1935.

118 Patrick Leary

B: Bethesda; 4 May 1864
D: Cuckfield (Eng); 1944
Half back (5ft 6ins, 10st 2lbs)
1 cap: (Bangor) v Ire 1889

Career: Bangor, 1883-1889; Gainsborough Trinity, 1889-90; Preston (Sussex), 1894.

The son of an Irish fishmonger, Patsy Leary was a member of the Bangor side which won the Welsh Cup for the first time in April 1889. Five days after that victory, he gained his only

Wales cap at Belfast. During the 1889 close season, he moved to Midlands League club Gainsborough Trinity but had great difficulty in breaking into the first team. Leary was said to play 'a remarkably grand game' and was adept at providing a service for the front man with short or long passes. An extremely accurate kicker, he had several run outs in the senior side, getting excellent press notices but failing to convince the club's officials. In the early 1890s Leary moved to the Brighton area where he worked as a coach painter for a railway company. He renewed acquaintance with his former Bangor colleague Percy Hughes in November 1894 as a full back for East Grinstead against Preston.

Honours:
Bangor - Welsh Cup 1889

119 Thomas Patrick McCarthy
B: Wrexham; 1868
D: Chester (Eng); 14 Feb 1945
Centre half
1 cap: (Wrexham) v Ire 1889

Career: Wrexham Excelsior, 1885-88; Wrexham, 1888-Sep 1889; Chester, Sep 1889-90.

One of two brothers who both played for Wrexham and Chester, but with very different styles, Tom McCarthy was a cool and stylish defender whereas brother Ted had an unenviable reputation as a rough and often violent player. Tom had learned the game at the junior club Wrexham Excelsior, but first came to notice in the Wrexham side that lost 1-3 to the London Swifts in the 1888-89 FA Cup. When he took work in Chester he joined the local club, but the association was brought to a premature end when he sustained a broken leg in an FA Cup tie at Lincoln in January 1890.

McCarthy made his only appearance for Wales in Belfast in a match described in one report thus:

'Everything considered, it cannot be said that at any point the play was of such a character to be worthy of an international character'. He made an abortive come back at the start of the 1890-91 season but was soon forced to quit. The injury ended the career of a promising defender who might well have found his way into the Football League. A printer by trade, Tom McCarthy worked for several years at the office of the *Chester Chronicle*.

Note: Appeared in many match reports and some reference books under the surname 'Carty'.

120 John Charles Henry Bowdler
B: Shrewsbury (Eng);
   8 Sep 1868
D: Shrewsbury (Eng);
   18 Jul 1927
Winger/Inside left
4 caps (4 gls): (Shrewsbury T)
v Ire 1890; (Wolverhampton
Wdrs) v Sco 1891, Ire 1892; (Shrewsbury) v Eng 1894

Career: Shrewsbury Sch; Shrewsbury T, 1885-90; Wolverhampton Wdrs, 1890-Apr 1892 (23 FL apps, 3 gls); Blackburn Rov, 1892-Apr 1893 (24 FL apps, 5 gls); Shrewsbury T, 1893-99.

Bowdler attended Shrewsbury School, a soccer stronghold, and in 1886 helped found the town club. He was undoubtedly the club's best player and in 1890 became the first Shrewsbury man to join a league club. Charlie Bowdler could perform equally well on either wing or at inside forward, had speed, good ball control and packed a strong shot. Shrewsbury won their first ever FA Cup tie in 1887, against Macclesfield, mainly due to the skill of Bowdler, for whom arriving late after missing his train was not a problem: 'The moment he stepped onto the field he seized the ball and, making straight for goal, scored'. He appeared in two FA Cup semi-finals - for Wolves when Blackburn won the trophy, and vice versa. In January 1892 Blackburn had been fined £25 by the Football League for approaching Bowdler at Wolves before the required 14 days had expired. Bowdler was articled to Hawley Edwards and from 1895, when he qualified as a solicitor, his appearances on the football field became rarer but usually at wing half. Blackburn made a fruitless attempt to re-sign him in October 1895.

Bowdler retained his footballing connection for many years, serving as Shrewsbury secretary and then chairman. In 1901, he came to the club's financial rescue and used his own resources to keep the club afloat for a whole month. He was also a member of the Shropshire FA, served on Shrewsbury Town Council from 1901, and for some years he acted as agent to the local MP. The firm of solicitors he established – J C H Bowdler & Sons of Shrewsbury – continues to this day. Bowdler would have had made more appearances for Wales but an injured ankle put him out of the Ireland match in 1891 and, two years later, illness caused him to miss the England match at Stoke. Intriguingly, in 1894 a newspaper reported that, although Bowdler hailed from Shrewsbury, he was born in Rhayader, which was probably a ruse by the FAW to justify his selection.

Honours:
Shrewsbury T - Shropshire Cup 1887, 1888, 1889

121 Abel Hayes
B: Wrexham; 21 Dec 1865
D: Wrexham; 20 Jul 1941
Half back
2 caps: (Wrexham) v Ire 1890; v Ire 1894

Career: Wrexham Crown, 1883-84; Wrexham Olympic, 1884-85; Everton, Oct 1885-86; Bootle, 1886-88; Wrexham, Nov 1888-90; Wrexham Hibernian, Sep-Oct 1890; Wrexham, 1890-95; Rhostyllen, Dec 1895-97; Rhos Eagle Wdrs, Jan 1897-98.

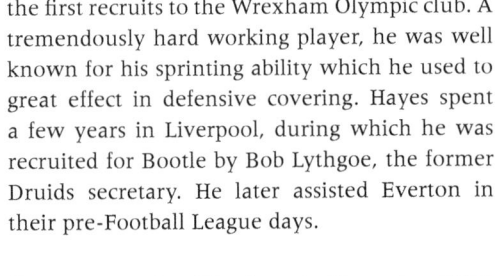

Along with Job Wilding, Abel Hayes was one of the first recruits to the Wrexham Olympic club. A tremendously hard working player, he was well known for his sprinting ability which he used to great effect in defensive covering. Hayes spent a few years in Liverpool, during which he was recruited for Bootle by Bob Lythgoe, the former Druids secretary. He later assisted Everton in their pre-Football League days.

Hayes returned to Wrexham in November 1888, as a reinstated amateur, and his experienced defensive play greatly benefited the club in their first few seasons in organised league competition. He later worked as a bricklayer's labourer. In the 1920s and '30s, he could usually be found at the Racecourse on Saturday afternoons, alongside his pal and fellow Welsh international player, Jack Powell.

Honours:
Wrexham - Welsh Cup winners 1893; finalists 1890, 1891, 1895

122 David Morral Lewis
B: Dolgellau; 1 Feb 1871
D: Durban (SA); 16 Nov 1925
Forward
2 caps (2 gls): (Bangor) v Ire, Sco 1890

Career: Friars Sch (Bangor); Bangor, 1887-90.

The son of the Rev. Evan Lewis, Dean of Bangor, David Lewis was another international player produced by the soccer stronghold of Friars School, Bangor. The well-built Lewis was a 'smart' forward, a fast dribbler and a useful goalscorer. He was called up as stand-in against Ireland for the injured P R Farrant of Corinthians, the original selection. Lewis did little in the first half but improved considerably after the interval and played a part in one of the Welsh goals. He retained his place for the Scotland match after his namesake and former Bangor colleague Billy withdrew from the team.

In October 1890, he left Bangor for London apparently giving up soccer. He later emigrated to Southern Africa and was eventually head of the Rhodesian police force in Bulawayo. Lewis took part in the suppression of the Matabele uprising in 1896 and served as a captain in the South African Defence Force during WW1. He later lived in British East Africa and was on his way to England in 1925 when he was taken ill and put ashore at Durban, where he died.

Honours:
Bangor - Welsh Cup 1889

Note: In some reference books, Lewis' appearances were mistakenly added to those of William 'Billy' Lewis (#74).

123 Robert Humphrey Lee Roberts

B: Walthamstow (Eng); 21 Dec 1866
D: Milford Haven; 2 Mar 1943
Full back (5ft 11ins, 10st)
1 cap: (Chester) v Ire 1890

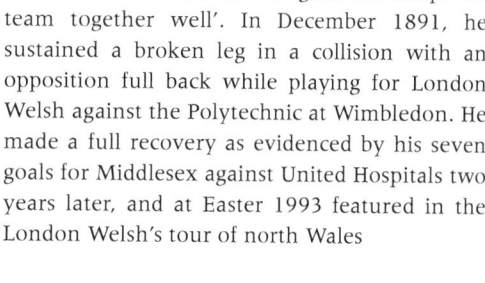

Career: Chester, 1888 - Dec 1890; London Welsh, 1891-1902; Brentwood.

It had been thought that Roberts hailed from Ynys Môn, his mother's county, but he was actually born in Walthamstow. At one time the family lived at Red Hill in Beaumaris and Roberts was a fluent Welsh speaker. 'Bob Lee', as he was known, captained Chester before moving back to London in 1891 and joining the recently formed London Welsh club. Capped as a full back, Roberts was converted to a free-scoring centre forward with London Welsh and represented Essex and Middlesex. One report commented: 'his play is remarkable for unnerving judgement, together with great speed...besides being a good dribbler he is a fine shot at goal and keeps his team together well'. In December 1891, he sustained a broken leg in a collision with an opposition full back while playing for London Welsh against the Polytechnic at Wimbledon. He made a full recovery as evidenced by his seven goals for Middlesex against United Hospitals two years later, and at Easter 1993 featured in the London Welsh's tour of north Wales

Roberts, who was on Everton's books at one time, was employed in early life by Shoolbreds of Gower Street – a large departmental store in the capital – but later lived on private means. In 1928, Roberts married the granddaughter of the founder of the Bland Shipping Line and settled at Dale Fort in Pembrokeshire. According to one report, 'His knowledge of Wales and Welsh matters was considerable and he was very proud of his fluency in his native language'. His brother, Will, who became an underwriting member of Lloyds, was also a prominent footballer with London Welsh at both rugby and association.

124 Albert Richard Wilcock

B: Newtown; 31 Oct 1867
D: Manchester; 1 Jul 1932
Inside forward
1 cap: (Oswestry T) v Ire 1890

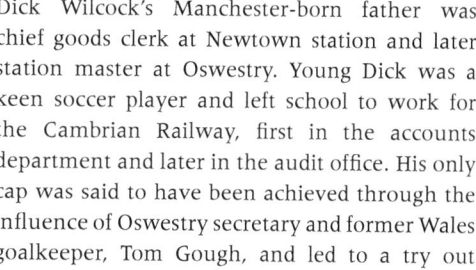

Career: Oswestry Orleton; Oswestry T, 1887-90; Small Heath, Feb 1890, (4 FL apps, 2 gls); Oswestry T, 1890-91; Oswestry Utd, Sep 1893; Oswestry Old Boys.

Dick Wilcock's Manchester-born father was chief goods clerk at Newtown station and later station master at Oswestry. Young Dick was a keen soccer player and left school to work for the Cambrian Railway, first in the accounts department and later in the audit office. His only cap was said to have been achieved through the influence of Oswestry secretary and former Wales goalkeeper, Tom Gough, and led to a try out with Small Heath. He made his debut alongside Caesar Jenkyns and John Hallam and showed neat close-passing skills. Although he scored on his international debut with an excellent goal, it was clearly not enough and did not convince the selectors that he had justified his retention. With the demise of the town club in November 1891, Wilcock became less active on the soccer front but when the new Oswestry United club was formed in 1893, he was soon among the line up. Wilcock emigrated to Canada in 1906 to take a job with the Canadian Pacific Railway. In June 1915 he joined the 61st Winnipeg Battalion, knocking ten years off his real age on his attestation papers, to become a member of one of the first Canadian contingents to arrive in Europe. Wilcock fought at Ypres, where he was severely wounded. He returned to Canada after the war but eventually settled in Manchester, Lancashire where he worked as a storekeeper at an engineering works.

125 Walter Gwynne Evans

B: Builth; 1867
D: Builth; 10 May 1897
Full back (5ft 8ins, 13st 10lbs)
3 caps: (Builth T) v Eng 1890, (Aston Villa) Eng 1891; v Eng 1892

Career: Builth T; Bootle, 1889-90 (4 FL apps); Aston Villa, Jul 1890-93 (40 FL apps); Builth T, 1893-97.

The son of a Builth butcher, Evans excelled at rugby, cricket and soccer and made his first appearance for the national side when Bolton Wanderers refused to release Bob Roberts. Newspaper reports at the time mistakenly listed his birthplace rather than his current club. The FAW player assessment of 1891 described Evans as 'a very good back, tackles unflinchingly and a safe kick – done himself credit'. After spells with Bootle and Villa, during which time he appeared in the 1892 FA Cup final, Evans returned to Builth to become landlord of the Lamb Inn, and the public house became headquarters and changing rooms for Builth FC. Evans went on the become the club's secretary in 1894. His brothers George and Fred also played for Builth. In May 1897 Evans reputedly caught a chill while attending a funeral and died within days, although some reports gave the cause of death as blood poisoning. His loss was described as 'a calamity for the Builth club'

Honours:
Aston Villa - FA Cup finalists 1892

126 David Oswald Davies

B: Llanfyllin; 10 Aug 1865
D: Barmouth; 22 May 1917
Outside right
1 cap: (Wrexham) v Sco 1890

Career: Llangollen, 1887-88; Grove Park Sch, 1888-89; Wrexham, 1889-92; Barmouth, 1897.

Oswald Davies was educated at the Congregational School in Lewisham and became a classics master at Grove Park School in Wrexham. He had played rugby for Stroud and Gloucester in 1885 before turning to soccer, and was said to have 'a good command of the ball, a strong shot and any amount of pluck and will tackle the biggest back or half back'. Described as 'a brilliant footballer but needs a little weight', Davies 'played hard from start to finish'. His employers objected to him playing for the town club and for the first few weeks of the '89-90 season his Wrexham appearances were spasmodic. This may well have been because Davies was also studying at UCW Aberystwyth where he gained a BA degree in 1892. In a change of career, he became articled to Messrs Minshall & Co, Llangollen, and was admitted as a solicitor in April 1896. Davies moved to Barmouth and entered into a partnership with W R Davies' practice in Dolgellau, before succeeding to run the legal firm on the death of his partner. From 1901 he also had an office in the Old Shire Hall at Barmouth. Davies, who was clerk to Tywyn

Petty Sessions from August 1914 and clerk to the governors of Dr Williams School, Dolgellau, was a friend of William George, brother of David Lloyd George. In August 1914, Davies, a member of the Territorial Army, was mobilised as a lieutenant in the 7th Battalion Royal Welsh Fusiliers. He was forced to later relinquish his commission because of ill health and died in May 1917 as a result of illness contracted while serving with the Army.

Honours:
Wrexham - Welsh Cup finalists 1890, 1891

127 Albert Thomas Davies

B: Shrewsbury (Eng); 9 Nov 1869
D: Shrewsbury (Eng); 11 Sep 1940
Centre forward
1 cap (1 gl): (Shrewsbury T) v Ire 1891

Career: Shrewsbury Castle Blues; Shrewsbury T, 1886-91

Alty Davies was described in the 1891 FAW player assessment as 'a centre with a good reputation', while another verdict was 'a good dribbler, he would run opponents off their legs and plague the life out of them.' He gained his only cap on the strength of Shrewsbury's successful Welsh Cup run which culminated in their thrashing of Wrexham. Davies however failed to reproduce his club form and his reputation counted little with the selectors. Earlier, Davies had played for Shrewsbury Castle Blues and helped form the Shrewsbury Town club in 1886. He played in the club's initial match and scored Shrewsbury's first ever goal in a 1-1 draw against Wellington Town. Davies, who worked in the printing trade as a compositor for many years, sadly ended his days in Shrewsbury Asylum.

Honours;
Shrewsbury T - Welsh Cup 1891

128 Benjamin Lewis

B: Leeswood; 1 Mar 1864
D: Wrexham; Apr 1944
Centre forward/Winger
10 caps (1 gl): (Chester) v Ire 1891; (Wrexham) v Ire, Eng, Sco, 1892; (Middlesbrough) v Eng, Sco 1893; (Wrexham) v Ire, Eng, Sco 1894; v Sco 1895

Career: Wrexham, 1883; Chester; Bootle, 1887-88; Chester, 1888-91; Wrexham, 1891-92; Middlesbrough, 1892-93; Wrexham, 1893-95; Chester, Sep 1895-96; Wrexham, Sep 1896-99; Buckley Vic, Aug 1900-01.

A regular goalscorer and 'effective passer', Ben Lewis was said to possess 'admirable judgement and a well directed shot'. The FAW player assessment of 1891 described the young Lewis as 'a very good forward, works hard but did not combine well with Robert Roberts (Rhosllanerchrugog)'. He played the majority of his soccer in the Combination League with Chester and Wrexham but spent one season in the Northern League with Middlesbrough. Controversially, Lewis was dropped by Wrexham on the eve of their 1899 Welsh Cup final replay against Druids. This was described in the press as 'a great mistake by the Committee' and Lewis understandably severed his connection with the club.

In January 1890, 'Cestrian' was sufficiently impressed by Lewis, and his wing colleague Bob Davies, also a Wales international, to devise a new version of *Hearts of Oak* which included the following verse:

Ben Lewis's play has become quite a treat

He dribbles and dodges and passes so neat

While his partner, the clever and quick little Bob

At centring and shooting is well on the job

Lewis was a brother-in-law to his former Bootle and Wrexham wing partner, Job Wilding.

Honours:
Wrexham - Welsh Cup 1897; finalists 1895, 1898

129 Robert Arthur Lloyd
B: Ystalyfera; 12 Mar 1868
D: Clevedon (Eng); 10 Jan 1942
Full back
2 caps: (Ruthin) v Ire 1891; v Sco 1895

Career: Ruthin, 1883-91; Rhyl, 1891-92; Denbigh, 1892-93; Ruthin, 1894; Rhyl, 1898; Trinity College (Dublin), 1899-1902.

As a schoolboy in Ruthin, Arthur Lloyd played at centre forward and was said to possess 'well-measured dribbling, great strength and speed'. He was described in 1891 as 'a cool defender, fast on the ball with a large kick and never loses confidence'. However, a more caustic description was: 'he has no idea of tackling but kicks well'. Lloyd was an assistant master at Ruthin Grammar School and turned out at full back for the local XI. He stood in for original selection Seth Powell against Ireland in 1891 and for Jim Edwards four years later. When his selection for Wales was announced, the school gave the pupils a half-day holiday. An amateur, he also appeared for Blackburn Rovers, Nottingham Rangers, Lincoln, Sheffield Wednesday and Grimsby but 'resisted overtures from leading clubs'. After several years as a schoolmaster, Lloyd took a degree at Trinity College Dublin and went into the church. He was ordained in 1902 and became a deacon in Liverpool before being appointed as curate at Bootle. In 1914, he moved to Newton le Willows and subsequently served at Aughton. From 1929 until shortly before his death, he was rector at Much Wenlock in Shropshire.

130 John Mates
B: Chirk; 28 Feb 1870
D: Chirk; 25 Nov 1938
Centre half
3 caps: (Chirk) v Ire 1891; v Sco, Eng 1897

Career: Chirk, 1889-1901; (also Oswestry).

Jack Mates was described in the FAW player assessment of 1892 as: 'a very good centre half - tackles well and kicks with judgement; played far below form against Ireland'. He spent almost his entire footballing career with Chirk, shunning all offers to try his luck with front rank clubs. Mates was a pillar of the Chirk sides of the 1890s and was rated by Charlie Parry as the best centre half in Wales. He was 'always on the ball, here, there and everywhere'. Fellow Welsh international Maurice Parry described Mates in the following terms: 'He is one of the finest centre halves playing football – a wonderful player, especially clever with his head and seemed to me to be more than a match for two opponents at any time'. The FAW selectors didn't share these opinions and his disappointing performance against the Irish kept him out of the reckoning until 1897, when he deputised for Caesar Jenkyns. Mates, a coal miner throughout his working life, also played the occasional game for Crewe, Chester, Northwich and Gainsborough and was a member of the Chirk FC committee in the 1920s.

Honours:
Chirk - Welsh Cup 1890, 1892, 1894; finalists 1893

131 Robert Roberts
B: Johnstown, Wrexham; 6 Aug 1866
D: Crewe (Eng); 1 Oct 1945
Outside left
2 caps (1 gl): (Rhosllanerchrugog) v Ire 1891; (Crewe Alex) v Eng 1893

Career: Rhosllanerchrugog, Oct 1891-92; Crewe Alex, 1892-94 (38 FL apps, 17 gls).

As a youngster Bob Roberts was captain of a joint Rhos and Johnstown team, and then became a prime mover in the Rhos team. He was described in the 1892 FAW player assessment as 'a good outside left, passes well, requires the same partner regularly'. In both of his Wales appearances he replaced the injured Charlie Bowdler, the original selection. Roberts was noted for 'his dashes down the left wing and his good centres', while one writer commented approvingly on 'his continual raids into the visitors' territory'.

He joined Crewe shortly after becoming Wrexham captain and, for a time, travelled 104 miles each week to play for the Cheshire club. Roberts retired in 1894 and became a committee member of the Crewe club, later serving as a director. During the early part of twentieth-century he was a well-known Football League referee and handled several important matches including Welsh Cup finals. He worked as a clerk for the LNWR company in Crewe.

132 Richard Edward Turner
B: Wrexham; 1866
D: South Africa; 29 Sep 1926
Goalkeeper
2 caps: (Wrexham) v Ire, Eng 1891

Career: Wrexham Vic, 1881-83; Wrexham Lever, 1883-85; Wrexham, 1885-92.

Dick Turner was described in the FAW 1892 player assessment as: 'a good goalkeeper – nervous – played much below his form, played a good game against Ireland'. Typically, he had begun playing soccer as an outfielder and 'undoubtedly would have been capped at half back but for a premature smash to an ankle'. This severe dislocation of the ankle, in the late 1880s, virtually ended his outfield career and he took up goalkeeping. Sam Gillam's departure from Wrexham conveniently created a vacancy for Turner. He was rated a 'very cool' custodian who showed 'wonderful form and did his work in an easy manner'. In his first international match, Turner captained Wales and despite his hesitant start he was retained to face the English.

His association with the Wrexham club had begun in 1885 when he was invited to play for them against Bootle and did so well that a permanent transfer followed. Turner and his brother William subsequently emigrated to South Africa.

Honours:
Wrexham - Welsh Cup finalists 1890, 1891

133 William Hughes
B: Liverpool (Eng); 1865
D: Birkenhead (Eng); 14 Nov 1919
Wing half
3 caps: (Bootle) v Eng 1891; v Ire, Sco 1892

Career: Anfield Rd Sunday Sch (Liverpool); Oakfield Rov, 1885-86; Bootle, 1887-93 (1889-92, 56 F Alliance apps), (1892-93, 22 FL apps, 1 gl); Liverpool, 1893.

Billy Hughes was a product of Sunday school football and part of a nucleus of players from the Anfield Road club who got together to form Oakfield Rovers. He captained the side for two years before being invited to join Bootle, the leading club in the area, where he spent some time in the reserves as understudy to Johnny Holt. When Holt moved to Everton, he took his opportunity.

The FAW assessment of 1892 described Hughes as 'a very pretty half back, rather light but never tires, plays with judgement'; while another write-up commented: 'never flags from start to finish, feeds his forwards with skill and dexterity, has great command of the ball and a good shot'. Hughes was called up by Wales in March 1891 as a reserve against England and came into the team when Joe Davies (Wolves) couldn't play. He retained his place in the team for the Scotland game but did not play. Hughes was at the ground but at the last minute found himself unable to play and was replaced by Arthur Lea. The reason was not apparent but he could have been objected to on grounds of qualification. Although he was described in reports as 'Bootle and Carnarvon' he was in fact born in Liverpool and, despite his mother hailing from Beaumaris, was not qualified to play for Wales under the rules that pertained at the time.

Hughes featured in the same Bootle team as Smart Arridge and was an ever present during the club's one and only season in the Football League. In August 1893 the club resigned from the Lancashire Senior Cup. This withdrawal was followed by a meeting at the club's Hawthorne Road ground at which a resolution was passed to voluntarily wind up the club and appoint a liquidator. The directors were told that the club had been badly affected by the rise of Everton. While Arridge signed for Everton, Hughes joined Liverpool but made only one first-team appearance – against Northwich Victoria in February 1894 – and became a stalwart of the reserve team in the Lancashire League. When Liverpool Reserves played Newton Heath in March the following year, Hughes drew the following comment: 'The surprise of the half back line was the old Bootle captain W Hughes. Nothing but praise could be meted to him for his defensive work'.

A later report said that 'Heading was his great forte and one could hardly 'tell him' when he had finished a match because he was mud-bespattered from top to toe. Jumping like a deer, he was always in the thick of the game and enjoyed his sport as much as those who watched him play'. Hughes worked as an ironer but in later life joined the White Star Line and served as a chief steward on ships such as the SS Lapland. Hughes was riding his motor cycle and side car in Birkenhead in 1919 when he fell from his machine and died from heart failure. According to a press report of the incident 'the last act he performed was to shut off the engine of his machine and save his friend, who accompanied him, from accident'.

134 Charles Frederick Parry

B: Llansilin; 1870
D: Oswestry (Eng); 4 Feb 1922
Half/Full back
 (5ft 8ins, 12st 2lbs)
13 caps: (Everton) v Eng, Sco 1891; v Eng 1893; v Eng 1894; v Eng, Sco 1895; (Newtown) v Ire, Eng, Sco, 1896; v Ire 1897; v Ire, Sco, Eng 1898

Career: St Oswalds (Chester), 1889; Everton, 1889-1895 (86 FL apps, 5 gls); Newtown, Dec 1895-99; Aberystwyth T, 1899-1900 (31 apps, 4 gls); Oswestry Utd, 1900-06.

Charlie Parry was discovered in junior football by Will Nunnerley (later FAW secretary) and signed by the St Oswalds club. Everton were very keen to sign the youngster but Charlie was reluctant because he thought he was not 'class enough'. The league club convinced him and Parry became a valuable asset to the club and an 'exceedingly popular player'. He made his Everton debut on the opening day of the Football League's second season, grabbing one of his side's goals in a 3-2 win over Blackburn. Very much the versatile player, he was equally comfortable at full back or wing half, possessing good positional sense, a strong tackle and good speed. An extremely accurate kicker, Parry was able to place a free kick over 60-70 yards 'on the required spot', but had an 'unenviable name for bashing goalkeepers'.

In the FAW player assessment of 1891, Parry was described as 'a good half back but out of condition and got injured, played a splendid game v England'. Remarkably, in 13 appearances for his country he featured in six different positions. One of his finest displays for Wales was in the 1895 1-1 draw against England at Queens Club. Parry's opinion of the Welsh team of the 1890s survives: 'Wales had a magnificent defence but no forwards'.

After leaving Everton, he became at the Oak Arms public house in Newtown and joined the local club. Parry then moved to Aberystwyth in 1899 before returning closer to his birthplace and settling in Oswestry. When the local club were unable to find a goalkeeper, Charlie became their regular custodian and performed creditably. In a newspaper interview given in 1906, Parry suggested that 'the first class players are overworked and the number of matches in which they have to take part is too great'. He also deplored the abolition of bonuses to players. Charlie retired as a player in 1906 and became a referee in the Birmingham and District League. When ill health forced him to retire from officiating, the Oswestry club provided him with work as a groundsman/caretaker. By 1921 he had fallen on 'evil days' and Everton generously played a friendly at Oswestry to raise funds for their former player. Sadly, he died in February of the following year, aged only 51, leaving a widow and six children.

Honours:
Everton - FL 1st Div champions 1891
Aberystwyth T - Welsh Cup 1900
Newtown - Welsh Cup finalists 1897

135 Smart Arridge

B: Sunderland (Eng); 21 Jun 1872
D: Bangor; 20 Oct 1947
Full back
(5ft 10ins, 11st 10lbs)
8 caps: (Bootle) v Ire, Sco 1892; (Everton) v Ire 1894; v Ire 1895; v Eng 1896; (New Brighton Tower) v Ire, Eng 1898; v Eng 1899

Career: Friars Sch (Bangor); Bangor, 1888-92; Bootle, 1892-93 (21 FL apps); Everton, Aug 1893-97 (51 FL apps); New Brighton Tower, Aug 1897-01 (22 FL apps); Stockport Co, Jul 1901-03 (64 FL apps); Bangor, 1903-06.

Although born in the north east of England, Smart Arridge, the son of a boot and shoe dealer, moved to Bangor with his family at an early age. A chorister at Bangor Cathedral, he left Friars School to go on a voyage round the world which, in the words of one scribe, 'divorced him from his favourite pastime'. On his return he joined the Bangor club and played his first match at Holyhead in March 1888, as a left winger. He displayed such form and stamina in this and subsequent matches that he was quickly drafted into the first team and became a favourite of the club and its followers. His first name, which was not a nickname as some thought, was a gift for the press and inevitably match reports referred to him as 'the smartest on the field'. In March 1890, he was switched to defence by Percy Hughes, the Bangor captain, and was an immediate success. Two years later, as Bangor captain, Arridge was seen playing for Bangor against Everton and invited to Bootle for a successful trial.

Arridge was not a typical full back for his era – he was very speedy and keen to move forward with the attack. When the Bootle club collapsed in 1893, he moved to Everton, on £3 a week, where he played in all the early rounds of the

1896-97 FA Cup, but was not selected for the semi-final or the final (v Aston Villa). He relied, unsurprisingly, on his speed, kicked well with either foot, and as a former left winger loved to move up in support of the attack. He was described in some reports as the 'gentleman footballer', while the *Athletic News* commented on his international debut in 1892: 'Smart Arridge, one of the full backs assisting Wales against Ireland on Saturday, was perhaps the youngest that ever played in that position. He is a splendid kicker, smart and fearless tackler and likely to make a great name for himself'. Despite a reputation as a fair player, his trademark was the shoulder charge, which were 'events to be thought over long after the person had been the recipients of such a favour'. His brother Will kept goal for Bangor while another brother Jack was a half back with the local team.

In later years, Arridge was a part-time trainer with Bangor City and had a second-hand furniture business. Subsequently, he worked on the *Clio*, an industrial training ship, then for the local council on Bangor pier and finally as a stevedore in Port Penrhyn.

136 Archie Middleship Bastock

B: Hereford (Eng); 19 Mar 1869
D: Eastleigh (Eng); 13 Oct 1954
Centre forward
1 cap: (Shrewsbury T) v Ire 1892

Career: Singers (Coventry); Smethwick Carriage Works, 1890-91; St George (Birmingham), 1891-92; Shrewsbury T, 1892; West Bromwich Alb, Jul 1892-May 1894 (24 FL apps, 11 gls); Burton Swifts, May 1894; Eastleigh Ath, Nov 1894-1906.

Bastock, who moved to Smethwick as a young boy, first tasted serious soccer with a Sunday school team and gained a reputation with the local club as a goalscorer. He turned professional with Birmingham St George, and despite being a neat player he was a little on the slow side. Bastock spent a short time with Shrewsbury before being enticed to join Albion for a weekly wage of £2 5s. He made his last appearance for the club in the team that shared the Birmingham Senior Cup with Wolves, scoring two goals. Later that year he moved south to Eastleigh in Hampshire to take work with a railway company as a coach builder. Bastock remained with the local club until 1906, captaining them from half back, and helped them to a league and cup double. In March 1895, Bastock was alleged, during a match at Christchurch, to have deliberately jumped on the opposition goalkeeper, a melee ensued and a spectator tried to strike Bastock. Not cautioned by the referee, it was at Bastock's instigation that the game was stopped, yet a subsequent charge of rough play against the veteran was not proved. Bastock, who also represented Eastleigh at meetings of the Hampshire FA, made his final appearance on a football field at the age of 52. Although he made only one appearance for Wales, he was also selected against England in 1892 but did not play. Earlier, as an amateur, he had played for a Birmingham FA XI against Leicestershire in April 1890

Honours:
West Bromwich Alb - Birmingham Senior Cup joint-winners 1894
(The game against Wolverhampton Wdrs ended 3-3. The clubs had been told there would be extra time but Birmingham FA neglected to inform the referee so the result stood.)

137 Robert Davies

B: Caergwrle; 3 Jan 1868
D: Caergwrle; 1940s
Forward
2 caps: (Wrexham) v Ire, Eng 1892

Career: Wrexham; Chester, Dec 1888-91; Wrexham, 1891; Caergwrle Wdrs, 1891-92; Wrexham, 1893-95; Caergwrle.

Slight of build, Bobby Davies was a capable enough winger in domestic competition but was described as 'weak' on his couple of forays into the international scene. In both his matches for Wales he stood in for original selection Joe Davies (Ardwick), and missed some good scoring chances but was not helped by an ankle injury.

An orthodox wingman, he had pace and showed neat skills during his two seasons with Wrexham. The 1895 Welsh Cup final marked the end of his senior career and he resumed playing for his village club. Davies worked as a coal miner and during the cricket season was a notable bowler for Caergwrle Cricket Club. Davies was later re-instated as an amateur and was still playing in 1913.

Honours:
Wrexham - Welsh Cup 1893; finalists 1895

138 Caesar Augustus Llewellyn Jenkyns

B: Boughrood; 24 Aug 1866
D: Birmingham (Eng);
   23 Jul 1941
Centre half (6ft 3ins, 14st)
8 caps (1 gl): (Small Heath) v Ire, Eng, Sco, 1892; v Eng 1895; (Woolwich Arsenal) v Sco 1896; (Newton Heath) v Ire 1897; (Walsall) v Sco, Eng 1898

Career: Southfield; St Andrews (Small Heath); Walsall Swifts; Small Heath Alliance, Apr 1884; Unity Gas (Birmingham Lge), 1886-88; Small Heath, 1888-95 (75 FL apps, 11 gls); Woolwich Arsenal, May 1895-96 (27 FL apps, 6 gls); Newton Heath, May 1896-97 (35 FL apps, 5 gls); Walsall (£45), Nov 1897-1901 (63 FL apps); Coventry C (coach), Nov 1902-03; Unity Gas; Saltley Wed, 1904; Walsall, 1905.

Jenkyns joined Small Heath (Birmingham) from Unity Gas in 1889 and was in the side when the club joined the Football League three years later. A big, burly fellow, who at one time was known as 'The Mighty Caesar', or 'Jumbo', to opponents, Jenkyns was a player of no little skill and a master of the shoulder charge. He was reputed to have a fearsome but fair charge and woe betide any opponent who thought they could get the better of him in this respect – one reporter described him as having 'an atomic shoulder charge'. Jenkyns was said to have charged one opponent from the centre of the field to the wire ropes surrounding the playing field!

The powerful Jenkyns had a heart as big as his huge frame and was a source of great inspiration to his teammates, and leading, inevitably, to him captaining each of his clubs. His strong physique enabled him to get tremendous distance with his heading and kicking; he once won a long distance kicking competition by sending a 'dead' ball from one end of the field to the other. The physicality of his game got him into trouble with referees on a number of occasions, being sent off three times in his career, and he became a player opposition supporters loved to hate. On occasions, matters boiled over and in March 1895 Small Heath decided to dispense with his services and suspend him for the remainder of the season for attempting to assault two spectators at Derby. A few months later, Jenkyns, by then a Woolwich Arsenal player, refused to leave the field when ordered off by the referee, drawing the comment, 'Jenkyns is a heavyweight and it is possible that gives him a character as a foul player he does not deserve'. William McGregor, 'Father of the League', speaking in 1895 gave his view: 'I dare say that most footballers have seen or heard of the redoubtable ex-policeman, Caesar Jenkyns, of Builth, Small Heath, Royal Arsenal, Newton Heath, Walsall, and Welsh international fame. There never was a man more sinned against than Jenkyns. He earned a bad reputation, I admit, and no man gets such a reputation undeservedly but, having acquired that reputation, spectators, players, and referees were apparently united in their determination that he should never lose it. I have seen men deliberately rush at him in a most unfair way; they have rolled off his burly frame and gone to the earth, and the referee has penalised Jenkyns. The Welshman's great and unforgivable fault is that he is big, strong, clumsy, and awkward. Such a man could do nothing right'.

While playing for Walsall at Luton, prior to the match he visited a hairdresser for a shave. During the process the barber and another customer discussed the prospects for the match. The barber observed, 'I hope they have not brought that big blighter of theirs, Caesar Jenkyns. I should like to see him 'done in'; Caesar did not open his mouth until the shaving operation was finished and then, rubbing his face, observed to the barber: 'Thanks very much, old chap, you never had a better chance of doing the blighter in than you have just had' and thereupon revealed his identity.

Jenkyns was again in hot water with the football authorities towards the end of his career. He was banned for taking part in an amateur match while still officially registered as a professional with Coventry. By 1905 the ban had been lifted and he was registered at the FA as a professional with Walsall but his career was all but over. For much of the later part of his playing career Jenkyns kept a series of pubs, including The George in Moxley, near Wednesbury. During the First World War he also worked at BSA. In the 1880s, Jenkyns was an apprentice printer but reputedly followed in the footsteps of his father and his brother Plato, who were both police officers, and the press often referred to him as 'the former policeman'. In later life he may well have returned to the printing industry as a compositor.

Jenkyns, who was Arsenal's first international player, finally received his cap in November 1933. It was pointed out to FAW secretary Ted Robbins that Jenkyns had nothing to show for his services and the association decided to honour him by giving him a belated cap. 'The presentation was made by Mr William Bassett, chairman of West Bromwich Albion, who was England's outside right in Jenkyns' time'.

Honours:
Small Heath - FL 2nd Div champions 1893

139 John Owen
B: Chirk; 4 Apr 1865
D: Manchester (Eng); Oct 1915
Half back
  (5ft 6½ins, 11st 10lbs)
1 cap: (Newton Heath) v Eng 1892

Career: Chirk, 1883-87; Newton Heath, Oct 1887-93 (52 F Alliance apps, 2 gls).

Jack Owen was a very effective player and 'equally good in attack and defence'. A centre half with Chirk, his greatest asset was his consistency but he was famed for the remarkable distances he could achieve from throw-ins. Owen had joined Newton Heath with his brother Billy, and remained after Billy had returned to Chirk. The brothers' departure for Manchester in 1887 was described thus: 'The Chirk club has sustained a great loss with the secession from their ranks of J and W Owens [sic] who are playing with Powell's Newton Heath team'. Jack gave good service to Newton Heath for several seasons, making over 200 appearances for the Heathens. When, eventually, the club decided to look to Scotland for players, he lost his first team place to one of the new imports. He remained in Manchester, however, and worked as a railway labourer, lodging for many years at a public house run by a Mr and Mrs Hole. Owen became a brewer's drayman and married the widowed Mrs Hole in 1907, taking over the running of the pub in Newton until his early death.

In some reference books Owen's one appearance for Wales was incorrectly credited to George Owen.

Honours:
Chirk - Welsh Cup 1887
Newton Heath - Manchester Cup 1889

140 Joseph Hudson Turner
B: Wrexham; 1872
D: Caergwrle; 8 Mar 1937
Forward
1 cap: (Wrexham) v Eng 1892

Career: Wrexham, 1890-93; Wrexham Gymnasium.

Joe Turner was one of five brothers, two of whom – Richard and William – were also capped by Wales. Their father was borough surveyor of Wrexham for some 50 years and owned a considerable amount of property in the town. When Joe was called upon to stand in for Joe Davies (Ardwick) against England in 1892, he was described in match reports as 'a novice on the left wing'. There was also a surprising suggestion that he was unfit to play.

Turner, who was a brother in law to Horace Blew, long retained his sporting interests and was later instructor at the Wrexham Gymnasium for a lengthy period. He was in business in Wrexham for many years, as a master plumber, but towards the end of his life became the licensee of the Crown Inn, Caergwrle.

Honours:
Wrexham - Welsh Cup 1893; finalists 1891

141 Tom William Egan
B: Chirk; 29 Apr 1872
D: Tibshelf (Eng); 1946
Inside left
1 cap: (Chirk) v Sco 1892

Career: Chirk, 1889-92; Fairfield, 1892-93; Ardwick, 1893-94 (7 FL apps); Burnley, 1894-95 (10 FL apps, 3 gls); Ashton N E, May 1895; Sheffield Utd, Nov 1895-96 (16 FL apps, 4 gls); Lincoln C, Oct 1896-97 (16 FL apps); Birdwell, Nov 1897-98; Altofts, Oct 1898-99; Darwen (Lancs Lge), Jun 1899-00; Royston Utd, Aug 1901; Stockport Co, Sep-Oct 1901.

Egan graduated from Chirk Reserves to the first team in 1891 and was soon taken up by the Manchester club Fairfield. A diligent forward with a good turn of speed, he was described as a 'tricky player' with 'a fine shot at goal'. A broken leg, while playing for Burnley at Blackburn in the East Lancashire Charity Cup in September 1894, proved a temporary setback. Nevertheless, Egan was thought by Sheffield United, in 1895, to be the answer to their attacking problems and he, was signed to replace another Chirk man – Jos Davies. After one season he moved on to Lincoln, and had several other non-league clubs before returning to Chirk around 1903. Egan subsequently moved to Derbyshire where he worked as a miner. A half brother to George Owens, Egan's sons Harry and Douglas also became professional footballers.

Honours:
Chirk - Welsh Cup 1892

142 John Evans Butler
B: Pontrobert; 27 Mar 1868
D: Chirk; Oct 1956
Centre forward/Centre half
3 caps: (Chirk) v Eng, Sco, Ire 1893

Career: Chirk, 1887-93; Wrexham, 1893-94; Chirk, 1894-98.

Selected at centre forward for Wales, Jack Butler had a reputation as 'an erratic shot' but was inclined to overdo things. He was far more effective as a defender – a position he occasionally occupied for Chirk. He was said to be 'a formidable centre half', determined and vigorous to the point of roughness. Butler had trials with Bolton in September 1890 and the following month played a couple of games at centre forward for West Bromwich Albion Reserves, but neither led to a permanent engagement. A coal miner by employment, later a colliery overman underground, he was also a leading light in the Chirk Cricket Club.

Honours:
Chirk - Welsh Cup 1890, 1892; finalists 1893

143 Edwin James
B: Chirk; 1869
D: Chirk; 25 Mar 1958
Outside left/Centre forward
8 caps (2 gls): (Chirk) v Eng, Ire 1893; v Ire, Eng, Sco 1894; v Sco, Eng 1898; v Ire 1899

Career: Chirk, 1890-1908 (also apps for Fairfield and Burnley).

A long time Chirk stalwart, James gave almost 20 years service to the club. He was already an established member of the village side by the time Billy Meredith emerged and was one of several mentors to the young winger. James, who worked as a coal miner, was an integral part of Chirk's rise to premier club status in Wales in the 1890s and was still turning out for the club years after the glory had faded.

One assessment of 1899 described him in the following terms: 'A very good centre indeed, he is speedy, combines splendidly and keeps his wings well in hand and is generally about the goal when scoring is to be done'. However, his shooting could be erratic on occasions and he missed several chances against Ireland in 1899, a match that turned out to be his final international. James continued to play for Chirk until 1908, and was awarded two benefit matches, against Druids in 1900 and a further benefit against Crewe Alex in Feb 1908, after a remarkable 18 seasons with Chirk.

Honours:
Chirk - Welsh Cup 1892, 1894; finalists 1893

144 Edward Morris
B: Trefonen (Eng); 1872
D: Chirk; 4 Dec 1957
3 caps: (Chirk) v Eng, Sco, Ire 1893

Career: Black Park, 1889-90; Chirk, 1890-93; Accrington, Mar 1893; Whitchurch, 1893-95; Knighton.

The son of a Chirk miner, Edward Morris graduated to the local side via school football and Black Park – a colliery team. He left school at the age of 11 to work in a local colliery, leading pit ponies for 1s a day. In 1891 his football ability, pace and power gained him a place in Chirk's first team. Morris' selection for all three international matches in 1893 was the pinnacle of his footballing career. When Accrington were relegated in April 1893, and decided not to compete in the Second Division because of substantial debts, he abandoned his plans for a career in soccer and joined the Shropshire police force.

While stationed at Whitchurch and Wem, Morris, who was an extremely fast half back, played in the Shropshire and District League. He made full use of his sprinting ability in the police sports, winning the 100 yards dash six years in succession, and took many athletics trophies in competitions in the region. Morris also served in Market Drayton, Ludlow, Oakengates and spent 14 years at Pontesbury. He was promoted to superintendent in 1920 and became Deputy Chief Constable of Shropshire in January 1934. In all, he spent over 40 years in the force until his retirement in 1935. Years later he recounted one of the more fraught incidents of his police career when he was searching outbuildings in Market Drayton for vagrants. Morris disturbed the black bear of a travelling Russian dancing master and leapt over a nearby wall in shock.

Honours:
Chirk - Welsh Cup 1892

145 James Vaughan

B: Ruabon; 1868
D: Australia; Apr 1926
Outside right
4 caps: (Druids) v Eng, Sco, Ire 1893; v Eng 1899

Career: Druids, 1888-1900; Chirk; Ashton N E.

Younger brother of Jackie Vaughan, Jim was a player in the same mould – 'a very clever dribbler' and 'a brilliant forward'. His one fault was an inclination to overdo his fancy footwork and 'exhibit his tricks'. The two brothers generally formed a right wing partnership for Druids until Jackie retired in 1890. Vaughan, who worked as a coal miner, remained a loyal servant to Druids until 1900 and was rewarded in March 1899 with a benefit match against Manchester City, then Second Division champions. That same month, he returned to the Wales team after a six year break to replace Kelly and play alongside Billy Meredith. Vaughan emigrated to Australia in 1925 but sadly died not long afterwards.

Honours:
Druids - Welsh Cup 1898, 1899

146 Edwin Houghland Wiliams

B: Saltney; 5 Nov 1868
D: Nantwich (Eng); 14 May 1950
Half back
2 caps: (Crewe Alex) v Eng, Sco 1893

Career: Saltney; Over Wdrs; Crewe Alex, Oct 1890-94.

A strong and agile player, Williams allied speed to his undoubted skill and was an accomplished sprinter, once defeating the England amateur 100 yards champion. One report described him as 'a thoroughly reliable player and a resolute tackler with excellent judgement'. Williams, who succeeded William Bell as Crewe centre half, revelled in muddy conditions and was said to 'upset the combination of opposing forwards'. He had to wait for international recognition and the opinion in Crewe was that 'he had not received justice at the hands of the Welsh Association'.

Williams, who retired in December 1894 because of ligament trouble, was a prominent Cheshire journalist and worked for the *Crewe Chronicle* for 65 years, 57 of which were spent as the paper's Nantwich correspondent. He took a keen interest in agricultural matters and was at one time the hunting correspondent for the *Chronicle*.

147 Harry Ernest Bowdler

B: Shrewsbury (Eng); 1872
D: Shrewsbury (Eng); 24 May 1921
Outside left
1 cap: (Shrewsbury T) v Sco 1893

Career: Shrewsbury Sch; Shrewsbury Wdrs, 1891; Shrewsbury T, 1893-1901.

The Bowdler brothers (see also J C H Bowdler) were reputedly responsible for setting up, in 1886, the club that became known as Shrewsbury Town. Ernie was a clever winger but had little chance to shine on his one international appearance as Wales went down 8-0 to Scotland. Nevertheless, match reports described him as the fastest of the Welsh forwards and 'best in front of goal'. Bowdler had been called up as one of five replacements for a Wales side that had to be completely remodelled because of absentees. Like his father before him, Bowdler was a rate collector and assistant overseer of the poor in Shrewsbury. He died at the early age of 47 following an operation for appendicitis.

148 Frederick William Jones
B: Llandudno; 1869
D: Llandudno; 27 Dec 1910
Full back (6ft 1in)
1 cap: (Small Heath) v Sco 1893

Career: Gloddaeth Rov, 1885-90; Llandudno Swifts, 1890-92; West Manchester, 1892; Port Vale; Newton Heath; Small Heath, Dec 1892-93 (8 FL apps); Lincoln C, Aug 1893-94 (7 FL apps); Reading, Aug 1895-96 (1 SL app); Llandudno Swifts, 1896-1900; Carnarvon Ironopolis, Nov 1901-02; Llanrwst, Mar 1903.

'Fred Fawr' (Big Fred) played football seriously from the age of 16 and had a varied career, travelled far, but always returned to Llandudno. A solidly built full back with a powerful physique, Fred cleared the ball well and was not afraid of hard work. Despite several attempts, he never entirely established himself with a senior club, but in 1892 was a member of the first Small Heath side to play in the Second Division of the Football League. Aston Villa took an interest in him in 1893 but no offer materialised.

Fred's only cap was against Scotland in 1893, as replacement for Di Jones, but the Welsh side lost 8-0 and his performance was described as 'weak' and 'a complete failure'. In his 30s, he formed the Llandudno Corinthian club and became secretary of a Wednesday League in the town for shop assistants. Fred 'trained unsuccessfully for the law' and became a bookkeeper for a large store in Llandudno. He retired from soccer at the end of the 1909-10 season and plans to mark his 25 years in the game with a presentation were abandoned at his untimely death. Fred was found dead in a Llandudno street in 1910 by a milkman in the early hours of a December morning; the subsequent inquest returned a verdict of death by apoplectic seizure.

149 Samuel Jones
B: Wrexham; 1870
D: Wrexham; 12 Nov 1931
Goalkeeper (5ft 8ins, 13st)
6 caps: (Wrexham) v Sco, Ire 1893; (Burton Swifts) v Sco 1895; v Ire, Eng 1896; (Druids) v Eng 1899

Career: Wrexham, 1889-93; Burton Swifts, Aug 1893-96 (85 FL apps); Shrewsbury T, 1896-97; New Brompton, May 1897-98 (10 SL apps); Druids, 1898-1901.

A product of the Wrexham reserve team, Sam Jones was a stocky but agile goalkeeper who understudied regular Welsh custodian, Jim Trainer, in the 1890s. He had trials with Accrington in January 1892 and, although nothing came of the approach, 18 months later he joined Burton Swifts, remaining with the Second Division club for three seasons. A beacon of reliability in a poor side, Jones was thought by some judges to be wasting his talents at Burton. The move to a better club did not materialise and Jones eventually settled for Combination League football with Druids. A member of the Denbighshire Militia, he interrupted his footballing activities with Druids to fight in the Boer War. Jones, who worked as a collier, was also attached to the Royal Welsh Fusiliers as a volunteer for over 20 years. He continued to play football well into his thirties and in 1905 was reinstated as an amateur.

Honours:
Wrexham - Welsh Cup 1893
Druids - Welsh Cup 1899

150 Oliver David Shepston Taylor

B: Newtown; 25 February 1869
D: Newtown; 29 Apr 1945
Full back
4 caps: (Newtown) v Sco, Ire 1893; v Ire, Sco 1894

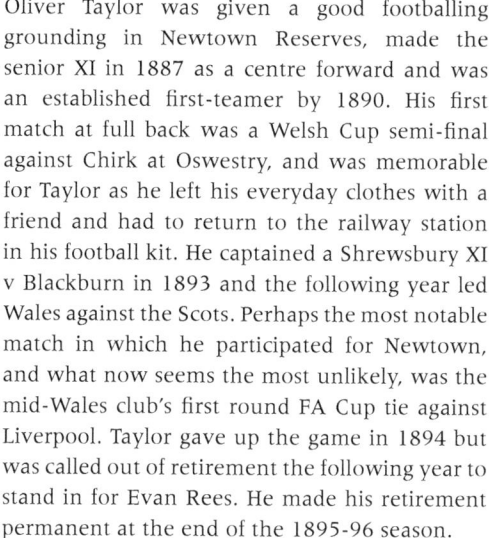

Career: Newtown, 1884-94, 1895-96.

Oliver Taylor was given a good footballing grounding in Newtown Reserves, made the senior XI in 1887 as a centre forward and was an established first-teamer by 1890. His first match at full back was a Welsh Cup semi-final against Chirk at Oswestry, and was memorable for Taylor as he left his everyday clothes with a friend and had to return to the railway station in his football kit. He captained a Shrewsbury XI v Blackburn in 1893 and the following year led Wales against the Scots. Perhaps the most notable match in which he participated for Newtown, and what now seems the most unlikely, was the mid-Wales club's first round FA Cup tie against Liverpool. Taylor gave up the game in 1894 but was called out of retirement the following year to stand in for Evan Rees. He made his retirement permanent at the end of the 1895-96 season.

As a young man, Taylor was employed by the Newtown gas works, becoming manager in 1894. He subsequently went into business as a retail and wholesale tobacconist and confectioner. A cricketer and keen golfer, with a single figure handicap, he was at one time chairman of the North Wales Hockey Association.

151 George Williams

B: Chirk; 1862
D: Blackpool (Eng); 1944
Wing half
6 caps: (Chirk) v Sco 1893; v Sco 1894; v Sco, Ire, Eng 1895; v Ire 1898

Career: Black Park; Chirk, 1891-1902.

George Williams worked as a coal miner at Black Park colliery and played alongside Edward Morris and Billy Meredith in the pit team. When he first joined Chirk, Williams was primarily a reserve, but by 1893 was firmly established in the right half position. A durable, hard-working player, he was skilful, persistent and packed a good long-range shot. Against the Scots in 1894, he was described as 'the pick of the half backs'. Williams was granted a benefit match by Chirk in May 1900, and enjoyed his last full season with the club in 1901-02, but he continued to turn out occasionally until 1904. A brother-in law to Ephraim Williams.

Honours:
Chirk - Welsh Cup 1894; finalists 1893

152 John Evans

B: Oswestry (Eng); 1859
D: Oswestry (Eng);
 14 Sep 1939
Half back/Inside forward
3 caps: (Oswestry T) v Ire 1893; (Oswestry Utd) Ire, Eng 1894

Career: Oswestry Sch; St Oswalds (Oswestry); Oswestry T; Oswestry White Stars, 1880-82; Oswestry T, 1882-91; Oswestry Old Boys; Oswestry Utd, 1893-94.

Jack Evans was a versatile player who, because Oswestry Town were inactive at the time, won his first cap while playing for Oswestry Old Boys. A tough individual with plenty of stamina, his methods could at times be none too subtle. He was once suspended for two months for injuring the Ludlow goalkeeper in an over exuberant challenge! Nonetheless, his industry and application led to approaches from several professional clubs but he would not be tempted.

Evans gave years of service to football in Oswestry, firstly as a player, then captain of

Oswestry United and finally as a committee member. He was also a FAW referee in the late 1890s and early 1900s. Evans was employed for over 50 years at Parry and Jones, the tannery company run by the father of Maurice and Tom Parry.

Honours:
Oswestry T - Welsh Cup 1884; finalists 1885

153 Thomas Chapman

B: Newtown; 1871
D: Hull (Eng); 25 Dec 1918
Half back (5ft 10ins, 12st 4lbs)
7 caps (2 gls): (Newtown) v Ire, Eng, Sco 1894; v Ire, Sco 1895; (Manchester C) v Eng 1896; v Eng 1897

Career: Newtown, 1886-95; Manchester C, Jun 1895-96 (26 FL apps, 3 gls); Grimsby T, May 1896-98 (51 FL apps); Chatham, Sep 1898-1901; Maidstone, 1901-7.

One of Newtown's most accomplished players, Tom Chapman, who was known as 'War Horse' and had a major role in their Welsh Cup success of 1895. When he moved to Man City, he became the first Newtown man to play for a league club. A newspaper of 1894 offered the following description of him: 'plays a resolute game and is never beaten, not tall but well built and is a hard nut to crack', while a pen picture said '[he] plays a cool and judicious game, feeds his forwards admirably'.

Chapman was also attack minded and loved to move forward and shoot at goal at every opportunity. Billy Meredith called him: 'a capital centre half who never knew when he was beaten, and game as a pebble'. In 1898, he settled in Kent but his association with Chatham came to an abrupt end in 1901 when the club went into liquidation. Chapman signed for Maidstone, then playing in the South Eastern League and the Thames and Medway League, and settled into the left half slot where he was described as 'great at making openings for the front men' and 'extremely good in his attacking work'. By the time his association with Maidstone ended in March 1907, he had chalked up a very substantial number of appearances for the club.

Chapman worked as a carpenter's labourer but, following the death of his first wife, moved to Hull where he was employed as a general labourer. While playing for Newtown against Stafford Rangers in 1894, Chapman appeared fatigued towards the end of the game and had to be helped off the field. Remarkably, he was found to be suffering from sunstroke – in March!

Honours:
Newtown - Welsh Cup 1895

154 Robert Samuel Jones

B: Wrexham; 1868
D: Salford (Eng); 25 May 1939
Defender (5ft 7ins)
1 cap: (Everton) v Ire 1894

Career: Challenger Boys' Club (Wrexham); Wrexham Grosvenor; Everton, Jun 1888-94 (7 FL apps, 1 gl); Manchester C, Jun 1894-95 (18 FL apps).

A product of Wrexham junior soccer, Bob Jones featured in the same side as Arthur Lea. He played in Everton's very first Football League match in September 1888, but was mostly a reserve at the club, playing in the Combination team.

Jones was a versatile defender who put in his best performances at full back. In spite of this he played at right half in the Welsh trial of 1894 and was selected for that position. After a long spell with Everton, he moved to Man City and ran up a string of appearances at centre half. A burly half back, Jones was 'an invaluable defender' and 'a most unassuming player'. In March 1895, he broke his ankle in a Manchester Senior Cup tie against Bolton and retired from the game. Jones later worked as a dock labourer.

155 John Charles Rea
B: Aberystwyth; 21 Dec 1868
D: Aberystwyth; 6 Feb 1944
Inside left/Outside left
9 caps: (Aberystwyth T) v Ire, Eng, Sco 1894; v Sco 1895; v Ire, Sco 1896; v Ire, Sco 1897; v Ire 1898

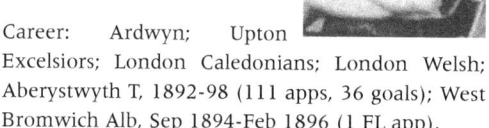

Career: Ardwyn; Upton Excelsiors; London Caledonians; London Welsh; Aberystwyth T, 1892-98 (111 apps, 36 goals); West Bromwich Alb, Sep 1894-Feb 1896 (1 FL app).

One of the founder members of London Welsh in 1890, Jack Rea served as club secretary for a while and did much to foster soccer among the expatriates in London. Rea was also a leading light on the field of play, being 'very fast with a good command over the ball and a good shot', and was selected at county level by the London FA. Reae returned to Aberystwyth in 1892 and while indelibly connected with the town club, was also on WBA's books as an amateur.

Rea retired in 1898 to devote his time to the family's hotel and grocery business. A major in the Cardiganshire Battery of the Field Artillery during WW1, he eventually reached the rank of colonel. Rea's hotel in Aberystwyth, the White Horse, preserved the family name in decorative stained glass and coloured tiles.

156 Abel Hughes
B: Rhosllanerchrugog; 1869
D: Cheadle Hume (Eng); 12 Aug 1946
Full back/Half back
2 caps: (Rhosllanerchrugog) v Eng, Sco 1894

Career: Rhosllanerchrugog, 1892-94; Liverpool, 1894-95; Rhosllanerchrugog, Sep 1895-97; Rhos Rgrs, 1907.

Abe Hughes was reputedly one of the founders of Rhosllanerchrugog FC, rivals to Wrexham in the 1890s. He made his debut for Wales at half back, alongside Tom Chapman, and was retained for the Scottish match at full back. A Wrexham newspaper commented on his performance: 'he kicks and tackles well but his roughness is against him'. Hughes was signed by Liverpool, newly promoted to the First Division, as cover but he never got a first team call: his one credited appearance was in fact made by fellow Wales international player William Hughes.

Abel Hughes working career was varied: he worked for some years for the Johnstown Gas Company in Wrexham, then as a tobacconist, and served on the local council as a ratepayer representative. He later became successively landlord of the Grapes Inn in Johnstown, the Moreton Inn, also Johnstown, and finally the Nags Head in Rhosllanerchrugog. At the Grapes Inn, Hughes was said to have 'raised the house from a not very respectable one to one of the most respectable houses in the district', but his application for an unlikely wine licence was turned down.

157 Hugh Morris
B: Chirk; 3 Jan 1872
D: Chirk; 20 Sep 1897
Inside forward/Winger
  (5ft 4ins)
3 caps (2 gls): (Sheffield Utd) v Sco 1894; (Manchester C) v Eng 1896; (Grimsby T) v Eng 1897

Career: Chirk, 1889-91; Ardwick, May 1891-93; Sheffield Utd, Dec 1893-95 (32 FL apps, 11 gls); Manchester C, Nov 1895-96 (16 FL apps); Grimsby T, May 1896-97 (21 FL apps, 1 gl); Millwall Ath, May 1897.

An industrious little forward, Hugh Morris first made his mark with Chirk in Welsh Cup matches. He was taken up by Ardwick, then in the Football Alliance, and later returned to the club for a second spell after it had been renamed Manchester City. One writer dubbed Morris 'an exceedingly clever player' but his play was not always productive and another reporter criticised him for being 'inclined to pass to and fro when a well aimed shot was needed'. Morris died in September 1897, from tuberculosis at aged just 25, without having made any appearances for his new club, Southern League Millwall.

Honours:
Chirk - Welsh Cup 1890

158 Thomas Worthington
B: Newtown; 11 Jul 1864
D: Massachusetts (USA); 1920s
Wing half/Inside forward
  (5ft 9ins, 10st 13lbs)
1 cap: (Newtown) v Sco 1894

Career: Newtown, 1884-96.

A sturdy player of all-round abilities, Tom Worthington began playing soccer as a left winger and appeared in virtually every position for Newtown before settling on half back. Full of stamina, he was a formidable opponent who packed a strong shot. When the future of football in Newtown looked in doubt in 1888, Worthington was one of the individuals who rallied to Captain E Pryce-Jones' call to ensure the continuation of a senior club in the town. He is believed to have later worked as a collier in south Wales at one time and then as a ganger at a water works.

Worthington emigrated to the United States in July 1903, his wife and family following in December that year. They settled in Methuen, Massachusetts where Worthington worked as a night watchman in a bed factory.

Honours:
Newtown - Welsh Cup 1895; finalists 1888

159 James Alfred Edwards
B: Dudleston (Eng); 1874
D: Oswestry (Eng); 5 May 1939
Full back
3 caps: (Oswestry Utd) v Ire 1895; v Ire, Eng 1897

Career: Oswestry Harriers; Oswestry Utd, 1893-1901.

'A very good back, safe and reliable' was an 1895 description of Edwards, while against England in 1897 he was described as 'wonderfully quick to get in his kick, and rarely out of his place, he is very safe as a rule and tackles nicely'. Jim Edwards, a thoughtful player who cleared the ball neatly and constructively, remained a stalwart of the Oswestry team until his retirement in 1901, and served the club in an administrative capacity until the First World War. Maurice Parry, the Wales and Liverpool wing half, had a high opinion of the footballing talents of Edwards, describing him as 'the best full back Oswestry had for years'. Edwards was also selected for the Scotland match in 1897 but couldn't play and his place was taken by Matthias. Like his father before him, Edwards was a master tailor by profession.

Honours:
Oswestry Utd - Welsh Cup 1901

160 John Leonard Jones
B: Rhuddlan; 1866
D: Sunderland (Eng);
  24 Nov 1931
Forward/Half back
  (5ft 10ins, 12st 8lbs)
21 caps: (Sheffield Utd) v Ire, Eng, Sco 1895; v Ire, Eng, Sco 1896; v Ire, Sco, Eng 1897; (Tottenham H) v Ire, Sco, Eng

1898; v Ire, Sco 1899; v Sco 1900; v Ire, Eng, Sco 1902; v Eng, Sco, Ire 1904

Career: Rhuddlan, 1882; Bootle, 1886-90; Stockton, 1890-93; Grimsby T, May 1893-94 (28 FL apps, 7 gls); Sheffield Utd, Sep 1894-97 (30 FL apps, 3 gls); Tottenham H, May 1897-1904 (132 SL apps, 6 gls); Watford, May 1904; Worcester C, Jun 1905; Stoke, Nov 1905; Crewe Alex, Nov 1907; Middlesbrough, Jun 1908.

According to a 1902 report, J L Jones had to travel from Rhuddlan to Liverpool to play football as there was no team in his home town. He had, in fact, played for a Rhuddlan team in the early 1880s, but learned 'the technicalities of the game' with a Bootle Reserve team who went through the season undefeated. Jack scored on his debut for Sheffield United in their 2-1 win against West Brom in September 1894, the second goal coming from Hugh Morris. The pair repeated the feat in the next match at Wolves. Jones was described as 'a most capable half, very speedy on the ball, supports the front rank well and generally plays a judicious game', while another report had him as 'a clever utility player, not showy but passes nicely at every opportunity and places well to his forwards'.

A useful cricketer, Jones was found employment as a coach at Rugby School by J Westinholm, secretary of Yorkshire County Cricket Club, and his Sheffield connection ended in 1897 when he joined Southern League Tottenham Hotspur. Two United players – McKay and Cain – followed Jones to Spurs, causing some bitterness in the Yorkshire club because Spurs, who were not a member of the Football League, were not obliged to pay transfer fees. In 1901, Jack captained the London side to victory in the FA Cup - the last occasion on which a team outside the Football League has won the trophy. In October 1904, Jones produced 'a treatise on the popular game', said to include: 'the qualification necessary for players in various positions and hints on training'.

Jones was part of a group of players putting on exhibition matches at Olympia on an 'imitation turf carpet', but this early venture into indoor football didn't catch on. In March 1906, the company failed so Jones returned to work that summer as a cricket coach, at one time at Rugby School. By 1907, however, he had turned professional, playing cricket for Leinster, later travelling to South Africa to play for a club in Durban before returning to Britain in the early 1920s to take up the post of coach/groundsman at Whitburn Cricket Club in Sunderland.

In later life he was employed as a pattern maker at Messrs Jennings Winch and Foundry Ltd, where he fell down a 12-foot stairway, sustaining head injuries which proved fatal: there were suggestions of a faulty handrail or that he could have been taken ill.

Honours:
Tottenham H - FA Cup 1901
          - SL champions 1900

161 William Henry Meredith

B: Chirk; 30 Jul 1874
D: Manchester (Eng); 19 Apr 1958
Outside right
(5ft 8ins, 11st 8lbs)
48 caps (11 gls): (Manchester C) v Ire, Eng 1895; v Ire, Eng 1896; v Ire, Sco, Eng 1897; v Ire, Eng 1898; v Eng 1899; v Ire, Eng 1900; v Eng, Ire 1901; v Eng, Sco 1902; v Eng, Sco, Ire 1903; v Eng 1904; v Sco, Eng 1905; (Manchester Utd) v Ire, Sco, Eng 1907; v Eng, Ire 1908; v Sco, Eng, Ire 1909; v Sco, Eng, Ire 1910; v Ire, Sco, Eng 1911; v Sco, Eng, Ire 1912; v Ire, Sco, Eng 1913; v Ire, Sco, Eng 1914; v Ire, Sco, Eng 1920

Career: Black Park; Chirk (also Wrexham), 1890-94; Northwich Vic, 1893-94 (FL 5 apps, 5 gls); Manchester C, Oct 1894-1905 (339 FL apps, 146 gls); Manchester Utd, Dec 1906-21 (303 FL apps, 35 gls); Manchester C, Jul 1921-24 (28 FL apps).

Once described as 'the football wonder of all time', Billy Meredith was the outstanding soccer personality of his age and one of the most famous of all Welsh footballers. His total of 48 caps (the FAW inaccurately had a figure of 51), at a time when the national side played only three international matches each season, was thought in the 1920s to be unsurpassable. He was in fact selected on 60 occasions.

The youngest of ten children, he won his first soccer medal in a dribbling competition aged ten. Meredith, like so many early international players from Chirk, was coached at the local school by T E Thomas, an FAW member who was a firm believer in keeping the ball on the ground. Billy left school at the age of 12 and took work in the pits as a pony driver, 'unhooking the tubs' and later 'hutching' – pushing the tubs along the line. His ambition at that time was to go in for engineering like his father and engine driver brother Elias, yet he spent ten years in the mines and continued to work there for some time after joining Manchester City.

Originally a centre forward, Meredith was a prolific scorer for the local team and it wasn't long before senior clubs were taking notice of the Chirk youngster. He appeared for Wrexham in the Combination before joining the struggling Northwich Victoria during their final season in the Football League. Looking for a new club, Billy was reluctant to agree terms with Manchester City and reputedly engaged their officials in a two day battle of wits before he was signed by Josh Parlby, their secretary. His reluctance was borne out of his mother's disapproval of soccer, and four days after signing for City, 'Di' Jones tried to persuade her son to join Bolton whose secretary-manager J J Bentley, in her opinion, had 'shilly-shallied' over the move. Meredith was not for turning, however, and was convinced that Bentley believed he was 'too young' and 'too light'

Initially, Billy remained at Chirk so he could continue to work at Black Park colliery. In 1919 he wrote 'I do remember one of my earliest games for the Manchester XI. On the Friday I went to work in the pit at Chirk early in the evening and stayed on, working hard until past six the next morning. Then home for a wash and I caught the nine o'clock train for Manchester. Arriving there I played in a match against the far-famed Preston North End team, and after the game returned to Chirk and put in another whole night's work before having any sleep on the Sunday'. He gained the first of his many caps in March 1895, commenting: 'When I got my invitation to play against Ireland and my club gave consent I felt as if I was walking on air'. On the crossing to Ireland, he got seasick and crawled down a ladder into the engine room where the warmth sent him to sleep. Before finding him, the rest of team had hunted high and low for the missing youngster and Jim Trainer said: 'I hope the bounder hasn't done as he threatened to do and thrown himself overboard'. Later that year 'Free Critic' rhapsodised: 'I don't suppose there is a man playing better football in the three kingdoms than Meredith. Nature has certainly endowed him with advantages above the common, and, lithe of foot, an awkward customer to tackle, slippery as an eel, and a rare 'buttocker' as they say in Cumberland, with shooting powers extraordinary, he is a real gem'.

Man City were promoted to the First Division in 1899 and Meredith finally got to perform in the top flight, scoring the club's first goal at the highest domestic level – against Newcastle. The team made a bad start to the 1901-02 season and, despite some new signings, City failed to retrieve the situation and were relegated. Under new manager, Tom Maley, the Welshman found the ideal inside partner in Jimmy Bannister and flourished, captaining City to the Second Division title in 1903. The following year he scored the only goal in the FA Cup final against Bolton at Crystal Palace. In April 1905 City, who were now chasing the First Division title, were involved in a fractious match at Aston Villa which saw some ugly confrontations and crowd trouble which required police reinforcements to deal with the situation. The inevitable FA inquiry followed but its findings, when announced in August 1905 contained a veritable bombshell. The commission found that Meredith had offered a sum of money to a Villa player to throw the match, a finding he vehemently denied, and he was banned until April 1906. His persistent efforts to obtain wages from City during his inactivity led to the discovery that players had been receiving more than the maximum wage and Meredith was transferred at the end of his suspension to Manchester United. He was very aware of his value to his club and once commented: 'In 18 seasons I don't think I was ever badly hurt or had a real illness. I don't think I have cost £3 in doctors' fees'. Meredith deplored the fact that bonus payments by clubs were illegal yet players could be bought in by transfer fees. A natural rebel, he was also a prominent member of the Players' Union and a leading light in the organisation's struggle with the FA in 1909.

For some time Meredith was a partner in the sports outfitters Pilling & Briggs, but he was not a successful businessman and, following a fire at the shop, was declared bankrupt in 1909. In fact, that same year he re-signed for United in Manchester County Court! In 1915, despite taking ownership of the Church Hotel in Manchester, he still had plenty of matches to play. One scribe wrote: 'Like the brook, he dribbles on forever'. It was not until 1924 that he played his last major match, for City – losing to Newcastle in an FA Cup semi-final.

Meredith was presented with a gold medal in August 1920 to mark what the FAW believed was his 50th cap and he enjoyed a number of testimonial matches over the years. After retiring from playing he continued to run the Church Hotel and, in 1930, moved to the Stretford Road hotel. His *Sunday Dispatch* column provided him with an opportunity to give his views on the game. In 1929 he commented 'Personally, I think one of the things that is wrong with the game today is that we have too many players, trainers, managers and officials who worship at the shrine of 'kick and run'. When the ball is kicked a long way ahead of them, they go after it like greyhounds. As I see it, a player ought to be valued, not at the pace he can go on the running track, but at the pace at which he can travel while keeping the ball under control'.

Commenting in 1937, when reminiscing about his long career, he said: 'I was always learning up until the time I retired. I made mistakes of course but every time I made a mistake I took a ball out the next week and practised until I felt sure I could do what I wanted to do'. Meredith was the first man to win winner's medals in both the Welsh and FA cups and, until the 1990s, held the record as the oldest player to appear in an international match. 'Old Skinny', as he was sometimes known, was said never to play without a toothpick in his mouth, and usually prepared before a match with a crust of toast. In his career which spanned 34 years, he played in almost 700 league games, and innumerable other matches – possibly as many as 1,600 in total – and enjoyed the international stage for 25 years. Meredith was quite simply a footballing phenomenon.

Honours:
Chirk - Welsh Cup 1894; finalists 1893
Manchester C - FA Cup 1904
                - FL 2nd Div champions 1899, 1903
Manchester Utd - FL 1st Div champions 1908, 1911
                - FA Cup 1909

162 William Parry

B: Newtown; 1873
D: Newtown; 7 June 1923
Outside right
  (5ft 6ins, 12st 8lbs)
1 cap: (Newtown) v Ire 1895

Career: Newtown, 1891-1904; Newtown RWF; Newtown N

E, 1904-06; Newtown Royal Welsh Warehouse, 1907-08.

Newtown's successful Welsh Cup run of 1894-95 – and a particularly fine game in Newtown's 1895 Boxing Day encounter with Manchester City – prompted the FAW selectors to recognize Bill Parry at international level. Unusually for a winger, Parry had occasional games at centre forward but he was never comfortable in that position. As with many of the Newtown players, Parry was a member of the Dandy Fifth - a South Wales Borderers volunteer unit founded by the Pryce Jones brothers. He joined the Royal Welsh Fusiliers at the outbreak of the First World War but was declared unfit for service. Parry worked as a Post Office clerk for 37 years until his early death.

Honours:
Newtown - Welsh Cup 1895; finalists 1897

163 Harry Trainer

B: Wrexham; 1872
D: Wrexham; 15 May 1924
Centre forward
3 caps (2 gls): (Wrexham) v Ire, Eng, Sco 1895

Career: Wrexham Vic, 1890-91; Wrexham Grosvenor, 1891-93; Westminster Rov, 1893-94; Wrexham, 1894-Jan 1895; West Bromwich Alb (£20), Feb 1895; Wrexham, Mar-Sep 1895; Leicester Fosse, May 1895-97 (32 FL apps, 13 gls); Sheppey Utd, Jun 1897-99 (43 SL apps, 17 gls); Wrexham, 1899-1900; Oxcroft Colliery; Poolsbrook Utd.

Harry Trainer, the son of an Irish-born bricklayer, was signed by Wrexham from Westminster Rovers, a colliery team with an aggressive approach to the game. A cousin to Jim Trainer, he was a forceful centre forward but his form could be erratic, and his scoring sporadic. He did well in the 1895 Welsh trial and was selected for all three international matches. Trainer combined well with Billy Meredith and Joe Davies (Chirk), and hit two goals in the Irish match. Meredith later said: 'Trainer led the line with skill and courage'. By contrast, he had a poor game in the 1895 Welsh Cup final.

After a reported move to West Bromwich Albion for a fee and an exhibition match, it transpired that Trainer was 'never properly transferred' and he reverted to Wrexham. His transfer to Second Division Leicester was free of such hitches and he remained with the club for two seasons. Trainer returned to Wrexham from Sheppey in 1899 but a serious knee injury sidelined him for a long period. He was also no stranger to the local police – in March 1894 he was arrested by a constable at Wrexham railway station as he was waiting for the train to take him to Ruabon, where the Druids v Westminster Rovers tie was to be played. He was taken to the police-station but was bailed by a magistrate and conveyed by cab to the station, where he was just in time to catch the excursion train to Ruabon.

Trainer, a coal miner, is believed to have taken employment in the Derbyshire coalfields in 1902 and played for Oxcroft Colliery and Poolsbrook Utd. He was fined for using indecent language in December 1902 and the following year penalised for being drunk & disorderly at Poolsbrook.

Honours:
Westminster Rov - Welsh Cup finalists 1894, 1895

164 Albert Westhead Pryce Jones

D: Newtown; 7 Jun 1923
D: Buenos Aires (Arg); 17 Aug 1946
Winger (5ft 10ins, 10st)
1 cap: (Newtown) v Eng 1895

Career: Shrewsbury Sch, 1884-89; Clare Coll (Cambridge), 1889-93; Newtown, 1888-97 (intermittently); Corinthians, 1893 (1 app v Derby Co).

A W Pryce Jones was the son of Sir Pryce Victor Pryce Jones, owner of the Royal Welsh Warehouse (RWW) woollen manufacturing business and one time MP. He was one of four brothers – as well as fellow Wales international Ernest Pryce Jones, there was also Edward Pryce Jones and Henry Pryce Jones. 'Mr Bertie', as he was known, was a man of many sports. He headed the bowling and batting averages at Shrewsbury School, Clare College, Cambridge and for Montgomeryshire CC. He also gained two soccer blues (1891 and 1893), a tennis blue and captained his college at cricket and soccer. In addition, he was an expert billiards player, a crack rifle shot and once sank a hole in one at golf! He was called to the Bar and admitted to the Inner Temple.

On leaving Cambridge, Pryce Jones became a director of the RWW, firstly in Wales and then with the Canadian subsidiary firm. In 1911, the firm of which the Pryce Jones brothers were directors – Pryce Jones (Canada) Ltd – had, among its trustees Alfred Lyttelton, the former England footballer and cricketer. The Calgary-based business was, however, a not a conspicuous success and was wound up in 1915, eventually being sold for a break-even price.

During the First World War, Pryce Jones served as a major with the Royal Welsh Fusiliers and then, as a lieutenant-colonel, with the Canadian Saskatchewan Regiment in France. He saw service on the Western Front before being assigned to the occupation force staff, and was awarded the OBE at the end of the war. After living in London for much of the inter-war years, he joined his son in Argentina in 1938 and died in South America eight years later.

Honours:
Newtown - Welsh Cup 1895
             - Shropshire & Dist Lge 1893

165 John Samuel Matthias

B: Broughton; Wrexham 1872
D: Moss, Wrexham; 16 Nov 1938
Full back
5 caps: (Brymbo Institute) v Ire, Sco 1896; (Shrewsbury T) v Sco, Eng 1897; (Wolverhampton Wdrs) v Sco 1899

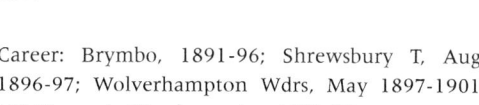

Career: Brymbo, 1891-96; Shrewsbury T, Aug 1896-97; Wolverhampton Wdrs, May 1897-1901 (43 FL apps); Wrexham, Aug 1901-02.

According to one report, John Matthias began playing for Brymbo as a 13-year-old but he was certainly with the club in the early to mid-1890s and won his first cap, as a precocious full back, when he was preferred to Smart Arridge. In August 1896 he turned professional with Shrewsbury, making him one of the club's first paid players and one of five internationals on their books. His reputation as a clever defender became firmly established in the Birmingham and District League and First Division Wolves soon stepped in to take him to Molineux.

In his final international match Matthias collided heavily with a Scottish opponent and sustained a severe knee injury which meant that Blew was called up for the England match. It was another injury – a broken leg while with Wolves – that reportedly ended his Football League career. Wrexham took him on at the start of the 1901-02 season but he made few appearances and eventually turned to refereeing in the North Wales League and the Birmingham and District League. Matthias worked at the Brymbo Steel Works for many years and was a leading light in the works band, and the nearby Broughton Cricket Club. At the time of his death he was caretaker of the local church where he was also a Sunday School teacher.

166 Arthur Grenville Morris

B: Builth; 13 Apr 1877
D: Nottingham (Eng); 27 Nov 1959
Inside left
(5ft 10ins, 11st 10lbs)

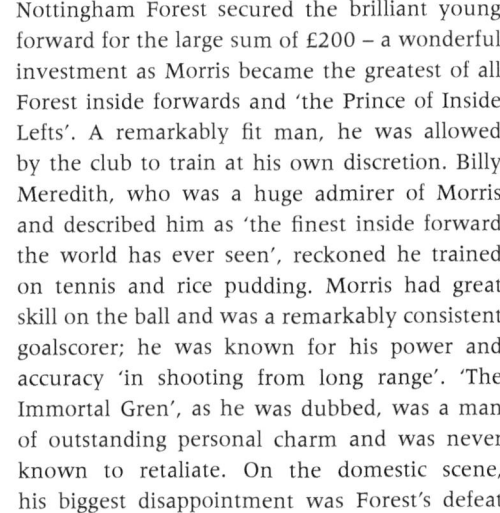

21 caps (9 gls): (Aberystwyth T) v Ire, Eng, Sco 1896; (Swindon T) v Eng 1897; v Sco 1898 (Nottingham F) v Sco, Eng 1899; v Eng, Sco 1903; v Sco, Eng 1905; v Sco, Eng 1907; v Eng 1908; v Sco, Eng, Ire 1910; v Ire, Sco, Eng 1911; v Eng 1912

Career: Builth T, 1892; Aberystwyth T, 1893-97 (75 apps, 111 gls); Swindon, Oct 1897-98 (29 SL apps, 21 gls); Nottingham F, Nov 1898-1913 (420 FL apps, 199 gls).

Gren Morris took up soccer at St Oswald College, Ellesmere, where he was a pupil, and also appeared for Builth as a 15-year-old. It is reported that when he played for Builth against South Wales Borderers he was so skilful he was marked by seven men. When Morris became an apprentice engineer at Green's foundry in Aberystwyth, he turned out for the local team, scoring over 100 goals in 75 games. Morris also represented Mid Wales at the age of 17. In 1896 – as an inducement to sign for Southern League club – he was offered a job in the drawing office of the GWR works at Swindon, and was switched from his customary position of centre forward to inside left to protect him from rough treatment! He settled quickly into his new role and, in a match against New Brompton on a heavy pitch, scored a remarkable goal. Morris tricked his way past all of the opposition and collapsed unconscious into the net, on top of the ball, after scoring. It was reputedly fully half an hour before he knew he had won the match for Swindon!

Nottingham Forest secured the brilliant young forward for the large sum of £200 – a wonderful investment as Morris became the greatest of all Forest inside forwards and 'the Prince of Inside Lefts'. A remarkably fit man, he was allowed by the club to train at his own discretion. Billy Meredith, who was a huge admirer of Morris and described him as 'the finest inside forward the world has ever seen', reckoned he trained on tennis and rice pudding. Morris had great skill on the ball and was a remarkably consistent goalscorer; he was known for his power and accuracy 'in shooting from long range'. 'The Immortal Gren', as he was dubbed, was a man of outstanding personal charm and was never known to retaliate. On the domestic scene, his biggest disappointment was Forest's defeat against Bury in the 1900 FA Cup semi-final. Curiously, he had been on Bury's books while at Aberystwyth and played his first and last matches for Forest against the Lancashire club.

Morris won his first cap at the age of 18, scoring on his debut against Ireland, and alongside Billy Meredith ranks as the greatest forward of the first 50 years of Welsh international soccer. Indeed, for years after his retirement the FAW selectors bemoaned the loss of 'The Immortal Gren'. Morris, who played his final match for Forest against Fulham at the City Ground in April 1913, was also a fine lawn tennis player and, on his retirement from football as a professional, sought reinstatement as an amateur so he could participate in tennis tournaments. He had won one tennis championship in 1911 but had then been promptly banned due to his professional status. Morris' application was unsuccessful – the FA refused to even consider it – so he turned to coaching instead, becoming coach to the Nottinghamshire LTA in 1926 in addition to maintaining his business as a coal merchant. His brother, John Morris, played for Bradford City reserves and for Bargoed, at left back.

167 David Henry Pugh
B: Wrexham; 4 Mar 1875
D: Waddington (Eng);
  26 May 1945
Outside right
7 caps (2 gls): (Wrexham) v Ire, Sco 1896; v Ire, Sco 1897; (Lincoln C) v Sco 1900; v Sco, Eng 1901

Career: Wrexham Grosvenor; Wrexham, 1895-97; Stoke, May 1897-98 (18 FL apps, 1 gl); Lincoln C, Mar 1898-1902 (91 FL apps, 10 gls).

An orthodox winger with good dribbling qualities and excellent centring ability, Harry Pugh was one of the Wrexham stars during the 1896-97 Welsh Cup competition before signing for First Division Stoke where he started off well. Brilliant on his day, Pugh was said to 'display plenty of pluck even if roughly handled' but needed 'to be supported and well supplied with the ball'. Despite his pluck, he was generally unhappy playing against big, muscular defenders and was tried at inside right in a struggling Stoke side, but was released in March 1898. Pugh joined Second Division Lincoln where he found life more congenial, with one newspaper describing him as 'the best forward in Lincolnshire'.

He made his final two appearances for Wales in 1901, as replacement for Billy Meredith against Scotland and for Gren Morris against England. A keen cricketer, Pugh worked as a joiner and, appropriately, lived at Sincil Bank.

Honours:
Wrexham - Welsh Cup 1897; finalists 1896

168 Joseph Rogers
B: Brymbo; 12 Sep 1869
D: Wrexham; 26 Nov 1943
Wing half
3 caps: (Wrexham) v Ire, Sco, Eng 1896

Career: Brymbo Inst, 1891-95; Wrexham, 1895-1901; Coedpoeth, Jul 1908.

Rogers was a very strong, aggressive player and reputedly 'one of the fastest defenders Wrexham ever possessed'. He was a sharp tackler, cool under pressure and his great speed brought him local fame as an athlete and many sprint trophies.

He was one of those players whose love of the game was so strong that he was still turning out for junior clubs in his 40s and, after retirement, he retained a close connection with Wrexham, working at the Racecourse turnstiles for over 30 years. Rogers spent all his working life as a coalminer, firstly at Gatewen Colliery, Brymbo for 35 years and later Plas Power colliery. Outside soccer, Rogers was a talented musician and successful choir conductor.

Honours:
Wrexham - Welsh Cup finalists 1896, 1898, 1899

169 Price Ffoulkes White
B: Bangor; 25 Apr 1873
D: Bangor; 10 Jan 1952
Centre half
1 cap: (London Welsh) v Ire 1896

Career: Bangor, Nov 1890-1892; London Welsh, Mar 1892; Aberystwyth T, 1896 (4 apps); Clapton, 1898.

Price White was another of the Friars schoolboys who graduated to the ranks of the local team. He captained Bangor in 1891-92 but moved to London at the end of the season to become an apprentice in the electrical section of the Post Office Telegraph Department, where he shared a bench with a young Guglielmo Marconi but could not be persuaded by his colleague to leave the Post Office and strike out with the young inventor into radio development.

He gained his single Welsh cap when first choice Jack Mates withdrew. White, an amateur throughout his career, also had games for Spurs, Sheffield United and Leicester Fosse and was described as a 'grand tackler and stubborn defender'. In an era when most footballers sported moustaches, White's was a fine example and something of a trademark for him. He returned to Bangor in 1900 to become manager of the corporation's electricity plant, taking an additional responsibility for the gas department in 1906. 'His wife Charlotte was the driving force in the Bangor branch of the National Union of Women's Suffrage Societies, and one of the first members of the Women's Institute at Llanfairpwll in 1915'. White became secretary of London Welsh in 1896 and a vice president of the club in the 1920s. His son, David Price White, was briefly MP for Caernarvon Boroughs after the Second World War.

170 John Garner
B: Aberystwyth;
 11 Jan 1871
D: Ludlow (Eng);
 23 Sep 1948
Forward
1 cap: (Aberystwyth T) v Sco 1896

Career: Ystwyth Rov; Aberystwyth G Sch; Aberystwyth T, 1888-96 (100 apps, 86 gls)

Aberystwyth's premier marksman, Jack Garner, 'rendered invaluable service to the club during the halcyon days of the 1890s'. He made his single Welsh appearance when the FAW selectors opted for an all-Aberystwyth inside forward trio of Garner, Gren Morris and Jack Rea. Unlike his two colleagues, Garner never gained the international recognition he perhaps deserved and he retired a few months after being capped. 'A genial and popular captain', Garner gave up the game for what were described as business reasons: he worked in the family bakery and eventually found that working during Friday nights and playing football on Saturdays affected his health.

A grateful club presented him, in 1897, with a gold watch in recognition of his services, summing up his qualities thus: 'though he had said little on the field he had been a unique influence and a good leader'. Another report described him in the following terms: 'the unostentatious but very excellent captain. He plays with skill and care, and is altogether unselfish, and he captains the team without their knowing it, which is a great merit in a commander'. Garner was an Aberystwyth club official for several years, an FAW referee and served as a magistrate in the town. He retired from the bakery in 1920 to become the Cardiganshire representative of a firm of Swansea millers. Garner was later captain of Aberystwyth Golf Club and president of the local bowling club

171 Sydney Darvell
B: Rossett, Wrexham;
 17 May 1874
D: Kencot (Eng);
 22 Jun 1944
Wing half
2 caps: (Oxford Univ) v Ire, Sco 1897

Career: Charterhouse Sch, Oxford Univ, 1893-97; Old Carthusians; Gresford; Corinthians, 1897-1900 (20 apps).

Rossett-born Darvell was the son of a wealthy clergyman and the family lived in some style with servants, a coachman, a butler, and young Sydney had a governess. He attended Charterhouse School before going up to Keeble College, Oxford. Darvell was not included in the 1897 Wales trial match but came to the selectors' attention through Old Carthusians' FA Amateur Cup exploits. After leaving university, Darvell was employed for a short time as a master at Tonbridge School but after two years at Holdersham House School, Broadstairs, he became a private tutor in 1900. He was first selected for Wales, against Scotland in February 1900, but he was unable to appear and Harrison stepped in.

In the First World War Darvell served as a captain in the Denbighshire Hussars, attached to the Royal Welsh Fusiliers, and was reported missing in May 1918. Two months later news was received that he had been captured by the Germans and he spent several months in a prisoner of war camp, only being repatriated in December 1918. Darvell moved to Kencot Manor in 1923 and was secretary of the Oxfordshire Agricultural Wages Committee in the 1920s. His only son, Lieutenant Richard W Darvell of the Royal Welch Fusiliers, died in May 1944 of wounds received in action the previous month.

Honours:
Old Carthusians - FA Amateur Cup 1897

172 Morgan Maddox Morgan-Owen

B: Cardiff; 20 Feb 1877
D: Willington (Eng); 14 Aug 1950.
Centre forward/Half back

12 caps (2 gls): (Oxford Univ) v Ire, Sco 1897; v Sco, Eng 1898; v Sco 1899; (Corinthians) v Sco, Eng 1901; v Sco 1903; v Sco, Eng, Ire 1906; v Eng 1907

Career: Colet Sch (Rhyl); Shrewsbury Sch; Rhyl; Oriel Coll (Oxford), 1896-1900 (soccer blues in 1897, 1898 & 1900); Corinthians, 1897-13 (170 apps, 24 gls); also Casuals, 1903-13; Nottingham F, 1901.

Morgan-Owen was aptly described by Norman Creek, the Corinthians' historian, as 'the greatest Corinthian of the Edwardian period'. He was a leading supporter of the amateur game and, during the split with the professionals in 1906, was instrumental in the formation of the Amateur Football Association. Morgan-Owen's attachment to the public school/amateur ethos was so strong that on one occasion, with his brother 'H', he withdrew from a Welsh international team chosen to face England in order to play for the Old Salopians in the final of the Arthur Dunn Cup.

Morgan-Owen wrote in Annals of Corinthians (1906): 'to be successful, a half back must always be cool and collected and the possessor of great patience and endurance', but it was his leadership and organisational skills that Wales most valued. As captain of the Corinthians, he led the team on tour to the Netherlands, Germany, Austria, Canada and Brazil. Morgan-Owen also played many times for Rhyl and Welshpool, where he had family connections, and in April 1901 made a solitary league appearance for Nottingham Forest.

From 1905 he served, as a territorial, with the Essex Regiment, becoming a captain in the regular army at the outbreak of war. Morgan-Owen saw action at Gallipoli, was gassed in France and was severely wounded at the Second Battle of Cambrai on Good Friday 1918. He was twice mentioned in despatches and demobbed as a lieutenant-colonel, being awarded the DSO. 'MM' was a schoolmaster at Forest School, Walthamstow, until 1909 and then Repton School, Derby, until his retirement in 1937. Oddly enough, he had played in Shrewsbury School's first public school match, against Repton, in 1894. A cousin to William Pierce Owen (Player 39), he remained active in public life as a magistrate and councillor, and enjoyed shooting, riding, fishing and philately. His son John, who was born when MM was in his late fifties, became High Sheriff of Derbyshire. The family retained a great attachment to Wales and John Morgan-Owen always enjoyed his annual visits to Ynys Môn.

173 William Nock

B: Newtown; 1876
D: Rochdale (Eng);
  10 Nov 1931
Outside left
1 cap: (Newtown) v Ire 1897

Career: Newtown, 1894-97; West Herts, Feb 1898; Watford, Feb 1898; Finchley, 1900; Vulcans (London), Jan 1901; Newtown, 1901-02; Newtown N E, 1902-03; Newtown, 1907.

A lightly-built player with plenty of energy, Billy Nock was deceptively strong and difficult to stop in full flight. He made a speciality of accurate crosses and was described as 'a good shot and a smart player'. At Newtown, where he combined well with Dicky Morris, his only fault was noted as 'a bad trait of selfishness' which was later ironed out.

A tailor's apprentice at the age of 15, Nock moved to London in the late 1890s and took employment as a draper's assistant at Shoolbreds departmental store. He then moved to Chapel en le Frith around 1910 where he was employed as the departmental manager of a shirt factory in the town and it is likely that he remained with the company at Rochdale. Outside soccer, Nock's chief interest was music: he played the cornet in a brass band and was a member of the Rochdale Philharmonic Orchestra. His son played with the Birmingham Symphony Orchestra.

174 William Roberts Jones

B: Aberystwyth; 1870
D: Oswestry (Eng);
  13 Jul 1938
Full back
1 cap: (Aberystwyth T) v Sco 1897

Career: Aberystwyth T, 1888-1900 (173 apps, 3 gls).

W R Jones came into the Welsh side when Jim Edwards of Oswestry was unable to appear in the 1897 Scotland match. 'A safe kicker and a vigorous tackler', Jones was reckoned to be 'a thundering good player with plenty of pluck' and was a prominent member of the Aberystwyth club over many seasons, captaining the side in 1896: their first season in the Welsh League. In April 1900, Jones was one of five Welsh current or future international players who helped Aberystwyth win the Welsh Cup for the first and only time.

Articled to Aberystwyth solicitor W P Owen – a fellow Wales international player and soccer enthusiast – in 1899 he qualified and practised law for a time in Wellington, Shropshire. He then moved to Oswestry in 1909 where he opened his own firm and adopted the hyphenated name Roberts-Jones. His son, Ivor Roberts-Jones, became a figurative sculptor and his best known work is the full-length statue of Sir Winston Churchill that stands in Parliament Square. In 2006 the executors of the Ivor Roberts-Jones' estate presented 22 of his sculptures to his old school at Oswestry.

Honours:
Aberystwyth T - Welsh Cup 1900

175 John Henry Edwards

B: Ystumtuen; 29 Jan 1876
D: Ystradgynlais; 26 Nov 1958
Full back
1 cap: (Aberystwyth T) v Ire 1898

Career: Aberystwyth T, 1892-1903 (188 apps, 53 gls); West Bromwich Alb, 1895.

Jack Edwards, an Aberystwyth stalwart in the 1890s, captained the club to their greatest triumph – the capture of the Welsh Cup in April 1900, with the full back pairing of Edwards and fellow Welsh internationalist Charlie Parry playing a significant part in the success. Earlier in his career, however, he had played in the forward line and gained quite a reputation as a goalscorer, leading to a trial with Bury in 1895. Edwards also had a spell, during the 1895-96 season, as a professional with West Bromwich Albion but did not make the first XI. He did, though, score twice for Albion against Aberystwyth in their 10-1 win in September 1895.

He gained his only Welsh cap in February 1898 but was denied recognition in some record books, as his one appearance was wrongly ascribed to Jim Edwards of Oswestry. In a match against Newtown during the 1899-1900 season, Aberystwyth were leading 10-2 and Edwards, clearly believing that matters were well under control, left the field to keep an engagement at a local concert. Edwards, who worked as a carpenter in the building trade, moved to Ystradgynlais in the early 1900s.

Honours:
Aberystwyth T - Welsh Cup 1900

176 Albert Lockley
B: Cannock (Eng); 1874
D: Chirk; 26 Dec 1939
Outside left
1 cap: (Chirk) v Ire 1898

Career: Chirk, 1892-1900; Druids, Aug 1900-01; Chirk, Aug 1901-03.

Lockley moved to Chirk as a young boy and became another of the talented local footballers to be developed by village schoolmaster T E Thomas. 'A tricky and clever player', his weaknesses were described as 'a lack of energy and pluck'. Nevertheless, his display in the trial match of February 1898 convinced the FAW selectors that he was worthy of a cap.

Apart from one season with Druids, Lockley remained loyal to Chirk and ended up as club captain. In 1903, towards the end of his playing days, he was described as 'a good coach to less experienced colleagues'. A miner for 40 years and a stalwart of the local miners' federation, Lockley was a keen cricketer and a long-time member of Chirk CC who also represented Denbighshire.

Honours:
Chirk - Welsh Cup 1894

177 John Morris
B: Oswestry (Eng); 1873
D: Oswestry (Eng); 15 Jul 1914
Goalkeeper
1 cap: (Chirk) v Ire 1898

Career: Chirk, 1891-1903; Shrewsbury T, 1903-04; Chirk, 1904-07.

The eldest of the three Morris brothers – see also Charles (199) and Robert (202) – Jack was briefly reserve to Jim Trainer and later Leigh Roose. He secured his Welsh cap against Ireland when Jim Trainer was on club duty, but was unfortunate in having to compete against Roose for the goalkeeping spot after the Preston man had retired. Morris, who was Wales reserve goalkeeper in 1900 and 1903, spent the greater part of his career at Chirk, breaking his loyalty to the village club for a spell at Shrewsbury and occasional games for Northwich Vic.

Honours:
Chirk - Welsh Cup 1894; finalists 1893

178 Thomas John Thomas
B: Bangor; 8 Feb 1877
D: Bangor; 15 Jun 1957
Inside forward
2 caps (1 gl): (Bangor) v Ire, Sco 1898

Career; Friars Sch (Bangor); Bangor, 1894-1906.

'A scientific and deadly forward', Tommy Thomas was another of the international footballers produced by the Friars School in Bangor. He gained an excellent grounding in the Bangor junior side but his clever ball skills were soon seen in the first team. Lightly-built, Thomas could play at inside forward but his accurate centres made him most effective as a winger. In the 1896 Welsh Cup final, the 18-year-old scored one of the Bangor goals.

'Tom Tom', as he was known in Bangor, was a bit weak at international level but a feared opponent in the Combination League. Many years later, he was described thus: 'He excelled in this class of football by virtue of his artistic and constructive play. He could beat two or three opponents with the greatest of ease, seldom did he lose the ball and he was a deadly shot'. Thomas' uncle was Bangor FC secretary during the 1890s and his mother kept a drapery shop in the town's High Street, a business Thomas and his brother later ran.

Honours:
Bangor - Welsh Cup 1896

179 Richard Samuel Jones

B: Trelawnyd;
   Bap 14 May 1872
D: Barnsley (Eng); 1920
Half back
1 cap: (Leicester Fosse) v Sco 1898

Career: Hanley Swifts; South Shore, Mar 1896-97; Leicester Fosse, May 1897-1901 (104 FL apps, 1 gl); Burton Utd, Jul-Oct1901 (4 FL apps); Royston Utd, Sep 1902; Leeds C, Oct 1904.

Dick Jones was a durable player, cool and clever but 'not the fastest of men'. One reporter's description of him noted: 'a trier from start to finish, he seldom makes a mistake and feeds his forwards in a way which denotes judgement', while another had him as 'a hard worker, on the slow side, he is neat, pretty, never hurried or worried and outmanoeuvres the opposing forwards in a cool manner'. Although born in Flintshire, Jones moved to Hanley in the 1880s where his father found work as a miner. The high point of his career was at Leicester Fosse where he was said to have given 'stalwart displays at half back'.

On the field, Jones' one weakness was an inclination to try and do too much, while off it he was said to be 'too prone to disobedience' – a reference to his disdain for too much training. Although appointed captain of Burton United – an amalgamation of the Town and Swifts clubs – and doing a good job, he was sacked in October 1901 for 'failure to keep himself in playing condition'. The club also imposed a harsh one-year suspension that kept him out of soccer until September 1902. By 1911 Jones was working as a coal miner in Barnsley.

180 Alfred Ernest Watkins

B: Llanwnnog; 27 Sep 1878
D: Barking (Eng); 7 Dec 1957
Inside/Outside left
   (5ft 9ins, 12st 2lbs)
5 caps: (Leicester Fosse) v Sco, Eng 1898; (Aston Villa) v Sco, Eng 1900; (Millwall) v Ire 1904

Career: Ellesmere Coll; Caersws, 1893; Oswestry Utd, 1894-97; Leicester Fosse, Oct 1897-99 (31 FL apps, 12 gls); Aston Villa, Apr 1899-1901 (1 FL app); Grimsby T, Feb-May 1901 (11 FL apps, 5 gls); Millwall, 1901-06 (103 SL apps, 16 gls); Southend Utd, 1906-08.

Watkins was one of 10 children born to Thomas Watkins – one of the best known cattle dealers in mid-Wales – and brought up firstly in Caersws and then Llandyssil where his mother kept the Upper House Inn. The eldest of six brothers,

Ernie Watkins was a player who relied on skill rather than graft and had an almost languid approach to the game. A difficult player to shift off the ball, he had a productive partnership with Dick Jones at Millwall, which was seen at its best in the club's 3rd round FA Cup 1-0 win over Everton in March 1903. Although a natural inside forward, he was equally comfortable as an outside left or left half. Watkins, who gained his first cap after only one senior outing for Leicester, made his greatest impact with the Lions in the First Division of the Southern League. Earlier, he had made a handful of first team appearances for Grimsby during their Second Division championship season of 1901.

Watkins enjoyed a varied working career – furniture porter, assistant station master, and a caretaker at Rippleside Cemetery – and died in an accidental fire at his Barking home in December 1957. It is thought that his pipe set fire to the settee where he was asleep.

181 Thomas Bartley

B: Flint; 18 Aug 1874
D: Newton Le Willows (Eng); 24 Dec 1951
Inside forward (5ft 7ins)
1 cap: (Glossop N E) v Eng 1898

Career: Flint, 1890-96; Port Sunlight, 1896-97; Glossop N E, Jun 1897-99 (7 FL apps, 2 gls); Llandudno, Apr 1899-1900; Earlestown, Sep 1901-02; Ashton Wdrs, 1902-03; Earlestown, Oct 1904.

Although Tom Bartley was an original selection for the 1898 England match, he did not distinguish himself and was subsequently overlooked. He had learned his craft in the North Wales Coast League, acquiring a reputation as a goal scorer but with a tendency towards rough play. After a season with Port Sunlight in the Wirral and District League he was taken on by Glossop, an ambitious club backed by the money of chairman and owner Samuel Hill-Wood. Bartley became part of the Midland League team with a £35-a-week salary bill – an astronomical sum for those days – and at Blackpool in September 1898, he scored Glossop's first ever Football League goal. Bartley was good in the air and possessed a rasping shot and injected bite and determination into the forward line. One of his specialties was to place the ball under the cross bar from his corner kicks, a profitable tactic in the days when goalkeepers were afforded little protection. After briefly returning to north Wales, Bartley settled in Lancashire and carried on playing in the Lancashire Combination and Lancashire League for some years.

Bartley worked in a print shop before becoming a machinist in a railway wagon works, and served in the Boer War with the Royal Welsh Fusiliers. At the outbreak of the First World War he signed on for the same regiment but was discharged a few months later due to suspected heart disease.

Bartley's brother Arthur also played for Flint, as a goalkeeper, and died from injuries he received in a practice match in August 1891. While working as a labourer at a chemical works, the 23-year-old Arthur took part in a kickabout, as centre forward, during his lunch hour. He collided with another player, injured his spine, and failed to recover, becoming what was probably the first fatality in modern Welsh soccer.

Honours:
Flint - Welsh Amateur Cup finalists 1891

182 John Taylor

B: Shotton; 26 Jan 1874
D: Queensferry; Mar 1913
Half back
1 cap: (Wrexham) v Eng 1898

Career: Queensferry Ironopolis; Mancot & Pentre Utd (Queensferry), 1891-96; Queensferry Ironopolis; Wrexham, Oct 1896-98; Reading, May 1898 (4 SL apps); Crewe Alex, May 1899; Chester, 1902-03.

Taylor was playing football with Mancot at the age of 17 and turned professional with Wrexham in October 1896. He made a slow start at the Racecourse but improved steadily and turned in some sterling displays. Following his recognition by Wales he was signed by Southern League club Reading, but it turned out to be a disastrous move for both parties. Taylor was tried in several positions but his displays were 'indifferent' and, worst of all, he was labelled 'a non-trier'. His wages were cut, twice, and he was offered a free transfer and £5 to leave but, apart from an enquiry from Crewe, no club responded to Reading's circular. Taylor sought redress by appealing to the FA.

He was eventually taken on by Crewe but by 1902 was back in Flintshire. One writer described him as 'a fearless tackler' and 'one of Chester's best players', while another dubbed him 'a tower of strength'. The enigmatic Taylor, however, ended the 1902-03 season by failing to turn up for matches and the exasperated Chester club sacked him. He was then employed as an insurance agent and died in 1913 after a long illness.

Honours:
Wrexham - Welsh Cup 1897; finalists 1898

183 Robert Atherton
B: Bethesda; 29 Jul 1876
D: English Channel;
   19 Oct 1917
Outside left
   (5ft 8ins, 11st 7lbs)
9 caps (2 gls): (Hibernian) v Ire, Eng 1899; v Eng, Sco, Ire 1903; (Middlesbrough) v Sco, Eng, Ire 1904; v Ire 1905

Career: Dalry Primrose; Heart of Midlothian, Jan 1895; Hibernian, Sep 1897-1903; Middlesbrough, May 1903-06 (59 FL apps, 12 gls); Chelsea, May 1906.

Although born in the quarry village of Bethesda, Bob Atherton moved to Scotland as a child. He was educated in Edinburgh and was said to speak with a broad Scots accent. After commencing his career with Dalry Primrose, he was taken on by Hearts at the age of 17 where he developed into a capable and consistent all-round player. One of the first full-time professionals in Scotland, his brother Thomas also became a professional footballer. By 1902 he was captain of Hibs and reckoned to be: 'the most valuable forward in the Scottish League'. He also fancied himself as a vocalist, giving a rendition of 'Dolly Gray' on the balcony after being presented with the Scottish Cup that same year. It was 114 years and a further 11 finals before Hibs again claimed the trophy, with Wales international Andy Holden as assistant manager.

Bob Atherton played all of his matches for Wales as a winger and in his second game – against England – he was said, with Morris and Meredith, to be the pick of the forwards. He was also something of a utility player and made a number of appearances for Hibs at wing half and inside forward. Atherton possessed a strong shot and although 'not a sprinter, he can dart through the backs at fair speed and while he has the ball at his feet he has a very attractive way of making progress'. In 1906 Atherton joined Chelsea from Middlesbrough, where he had been captain, but in a pre-season match he aggravated a bad injury sustained during the previous season and never made the senior side.

Retired from football, he worked as assistant manager at the Market Hotel in West Hartlepool, then became a commercial traveller for a firm of office suppliers. Atherton was killed during the First World War when his ship was torpedoed by an enemy submarine. He was a member of the mercantile marine and served as an assistant steward on board the SS Britannia, a 740-ton merchant ship sailing out of Leith. On October 19th, 1917, it went down in the English Channel, south of a point between Portland Bill and the Needles, with the loss of 22 lives, the victim of enemy action. The loss is commemorated on the Tower Hill Memorial near the Tower of London.

Honours:
Hibernian - Scottish Lge 1st Div champions 1903 - Scottish Cup 1902

184 Horace Elford Blew

B: Rhostyllen; 20 Jan 1878
D: Wrexham; 1 Feb 1957
Full back (5ft 8ins, 12st 8lbs)
22 caps: (Wrexham) v Ire, Sco, Eng 1899; v Sco, Ire 1902; v Eng, Sco 1903; v Sco, Ire, Eng 1904; Sco, Ire 1905; v Sco, Eng, Ire 1906; v Sco 1907; v Sco, Eng, Ire 1908; v Sco, Eng 1909; v Eng 1910

Career: Grove Park Sch; Wrexham Old Boys, 1895-96; Rhostyllen, 1896-97; Wrexham, Aug 1897-1911, (also Bury, Jun 1904); Manchester Utd, Apr 1906 (1 FL app); Manchester C, Sep 1906 (1 FL app).

Horace Blew's earliest football influence was the Grove Park schoolmaster, and Wrexham and Wales international, Oswald Davies. Originally a centre half, Blew moved to full back after leaving school and was recommended to Wrexham – by the Rhostyllen club secretary – where he was taken on as a professional at 7/9d (38p) for a win, 6/9d (34p) for a draw and 4/9d (24p) for a defeat. He reverted to amateur status in 1902, but again turned professional for a short period six years later.

Blew was probably the finest Wrexham footballer of the pre-1914 era. His fearless tackling, accurate distribution and utter dependability made him an automatic choice for Wales for several years. He had many offers to join league clubs but appeared in the Football League on just two occasions – for both Manchester clubs. He firstly assisted United in an emergency, against Chelsea in April 1905, when they needed a single point to clinch promotion to the First Division. United got the point and Blew was presented with a special gold medal the club had struck for him. He then played one match for City in September 1906 (v Bury) having earlier been on Bury's books, but it was Manchester City who held his registration. When Wrexham sought to reward Blew with a benefit match in 1910, the FAW blocked the idea as incompatible with the player's amateur status, so he turned professional again, received due reward for his splendid service, then promptly and successfully sought reinstatement as an amateur.

Blew got his international break in March 1899 when he stood in for Smart Arridge who was unable to get his release from his club. He was retained against Scotland but for the England match Matthias got the selectors' nod. When Matthias subsequently withdrew, however, Blew was called recalled and his international exploits celebrated in piece of awful doggerel:

From the land of the leek
He's a gallant defender
His methods not meek
Are more robust than tender
And foes on the raid
Seeking goals, to annex 'em
Retire sore dismayed
From this hero of Wrexham

Blew also had short spells with Druids in 1903, Brymbo in 1910, and was capped at amateur level in 1908 and 1911. He retained a lifelong interest in football, becoming a director of Wrexham FC in the 1920s and a match reporter for the *Daily Dispatch*. Outside soccer, Blew was an auctioneer's assistant, then worked for the agents to the local Erddig estate. He later kept several hotels including the Mount Hotel in Brymbo, the Griffin Inn at Ponkey and the Bowling Green Hotel, and also dealt in livestock. He was elected to Wrexham Town Council in May 1919, was Mayor in 1923, became an

Alderman in 1927 and received the freedom of the borough in 1948. Horace's brother Lt Colonel Thomas Harry Blew served in the Boer War and in the Great War, while his son Frank played for Wrexham and Llandudno and was capped by Wales as an amateur in the early 1920s.

Honours:
Wrexham - Welsh Cup 1903, 1905, 1909; finalists 1898, 1899, 1901

185 David Charles Davies
B: Talgarth; 29 Apr 1879
D: Talgarth; 9 Sep 1956
Outside left
2 caps: (Brecon) v Ire 1899; (Hereford T) v Ire 1900

Career: Talgarth, 1897-98; Nelson; Builth T, 1898-99; Brecon, Jan-Mar 1899; Talgarth, Mar 1899; Hereford T, Apr 1899-Oct 1900; Talgarth, 1908-1913.

The unfortunate 'Chappie' Davies suffered a serious knee injury a few weeks after gaining his second cap and a promising career which might have led to league soccer was ruined. He first came to attention in March 1899, when Hereford Thistle played Builth in the Herefordshire Senior Cup. That same month, both Hereford clubs – Town and Thistle – offered him terms and Davies opted to turn professional with the former: a wise decision as Thistle collapsed a few weeks later. The *Hereford Times* commented: 'he possesses splendid control of the ball, and an ability to pass or shoot with remarkable accuracy'. Davies, who was chased by Aston Villa, Preston and QPR, aggravated a knee problem in his first Birmingham League match, against Shrewsbury, and despite several comeback attempts he quietly retired from major soccer in October 1900. Earlier, Davies had been a star forward with both Builth and Brecon, with one newspaper reporting that he was: 'A very reliable forward, quick in his movements, accurate in his passes and deadly at goal', while a later assessment was 'the features of his play were dextrous dribbling, his sangfroid and deadly shooting'. He played a few matches in 1905 but once again his knee gave way - against Elan Valley. In 1908, he was cleared by a specialist in football injuries to play and joined the village team and, showing glimpses of his old skills, he continued to play the game he loved for many years, even representing Talgarth as their goalkeeper as late as 1913. Davies, who served in France with the Royal Engineers during the First World War, was employed by the Post Office for many years, and was awarded the Imperial Service Medal for long service.

186 Edward Hughes
B: Ruabon; 11 Jul 1875
D: London (Eng); 18 Jun 1936
Centre half
(5ft 8ins, 11st 7lbs)
14 caps: (Everton) v Ire, Sco 1899; (Tottenham H) v Sco, Eng 1901; v Ire 1902; v Eng, Sco, Ire 1904; v Eng, Ire, Sco 1905; v Eng, Ire 1906; v Eng 1907

Career: Formby; Everton, 1897-99 (8 FL apps); Tottenham H, Jul 1899-1908 (148 SL apps, 8 gls).

Although born in Ruabon, in the early 1880s Teddy Hughes moved to Bootle, where his father became a rent collector. On leaving school, he worked as an office boy and played junior football locally. Not a particularly tall player, Hughes was nonetheless an excellent centre half who played very much as a stopper, anticipating by a quarter of a century the work of Herbie Roberts. He spent two seasons with Everton, and it was an ex-Evertonian – John Cameron – who secured his services for Spurs. When Jim McNaught, the Spurs captain and regular centre half, was ruled out through injury, Ted took his place and McNaught never got back into the side.

Hughes was a hardworking, intelligent and fearless centre half who was a particularly skilled header of the ball. He was reputed to be 'a keen supporter of the forwards' and 'did not hesitate to shoot for goal', while another journalist described him as 'an accurate placer and a keen worker, very consistent and shines in any half back position'. After retirement from soccer, he kept the Kings Arms in Edmonton for many years.

Honours:
Tottenham H - FA Cup 1901

187 William James Jackson

B: Flint; 27 Jan 1876
D: Flint; 1 Apr 1954
Inside forward
  (5ft 8ins, 11st 12lbs)
1 cap: (St Helens Recreation)
v Ire 1899

Career: Flint, 1894-97; Rhyl, 1897-98; Flint, 1898-99; St Helens Rec, Aug 1898-99; Newton Heath, Jul 1899-1902 (61 FL apps, 12 gls); Barrow, Oct 1902-03; Burnley, 1903-05 (22 FL apps); Flint, 1905; (also appeared for Wigan); Chester, Oct 1905-06 (15 F Comb apps, 6 gls); Flint, Jan 1910.

William Jackson was the son of a Flint publican and played in the North Wales Coast League before joining St Helens Recreation. A stockily built, hard-working player, Jackson was never a great goal scorer but always made his presence felt up front, as noted in a contemporary football handbook: 'a tricky shot, a good feeder for the outside man and an accurate shot'. He gained his one cap when Ernie Watkins pulled out of the Wales side.

Although St Helens enjoyed on-field success and won the Lancashire Junior Cup, the club failed to pay the wages owed to the players and, when the club was suspended by the FA, the players found other clubs. At Burnley, Jackson was initially a first teamer but spent most of his second season with the reserves in the North East Lancashire Combination.

Although his best playing days seemed over, having previously struggled for consistency, Jackson made his debut for Chester in October 1905, linked well with Jacky Lipsham and made an immediate impression. The club then went on an eight match unbeaten run and finished the league season as runners-up.

Employed for over 30 years as a cooper at the Aber Works in the town, Jackson's birthplace has been incorrectly stated in some reference books as Lancaster.

188 Fredrick Charles Kelly

B: Sandycroft; 23 Jan 1877
D: Flixton (Eng); 23 Jul 1957
Outside right
3 caps: (Wrexham) v Ire, Sco 1899; (Druids) v Ire 1902

Career: Mancot & Pentre Utd; Wrexham, 1897-1900; Druids, Dec 1900-02; Chester, Oct 1902-03 (23 F Comb apps, 12 gls); Barnsley; Druids, 1903-04.

Frederick, the son of FAW committeeman William Kelly, was one of several players who understudied Billy Meredith. In a preview of the 1899 Ireland match he was described as: 'One of the very best forwards in Wales. A forward who combines well and takes every opportunity of shooting for goal, in fact, a player who has to be reckoned with'.

Kelly's weakness was his inability to retain his form and he was discarded by Wrexham and Druids because of his inconsistency. At Chester he formed a useful left side partnership with former Hudson's Liverpool player, Sherman, and was second highest scorer in his only season there. Kelly appeared in three Welsh Cup finals but was on the losing side on every occasion. Kelly was an engineer by profession and worked at a nearby oil refinery.

Honours:
Wrexham - Welsh Cup finalists 1898, 1899
Druids - Welsh Cup finalists 1901

189 George Richards
B: Llansilin; 1874
D: Cefn Mawr; 28 Aug 1944
Wing half
6 caps: (Druids) v Ire, Sco, Eng 1899; (Oswestry Utd) v Ire 1903; (Shrewsbury T) v Sco 1904; v Ire 1905

Career: Druids, 1896-99; Gravesend, May 1899-1901 (24 SL apps); Oswestry Utd, 1901-03; Shrewsbury T, 1904-05; Druids, 1905-06; Oswestry Utd, 1906-08; Acrefair Utd, Jul 1908-11.

A hard working and thoughtful player, George Richards had a natural talent for ball control and followed the 'scientific approach' of working the ball skilfully out of defence. He played all of his football around the Welsh border country apart from two seasons at a higher level with Gravesend.

In the Oswestry side, Richards, who was known as 'Ike', had a good understanding with Tom Parry and the pair were regarded as the 'brains' of the team. He played on until his late 30s, closing his career with Acrefair in the Wrexham and District League. Richards was later landlord of the Grosvenor Arms Hotel in Cefn Mawr for many years.

Honours:
Druids - Welsh Cup 1898, 1899
Oswestry Utd - Welsh Cup 1901, 1907

190 Charles Edwin Thomas
B: Cefn, Ruabon; 1875
D: Cefn, Ruabon; 28 May 1935
Full back
2 caps: (Druids) v Ire 1899; v Sco 1900

Career: Druids, 1894-1902.

A reserve full back for Wales, Charlie Thomas gained both his caps as replacement for the original selections: J S Matthias in 1899 and Di Jones in 1900. He was described in 1902 as 'a good and daring back, kicks strongly, tackles very well and is altogether a first class man'. The popular Charlie also played at centre half for Druids and captained the club in 1901.

He was employed for several years at the Hafod Brickworks but emigrated to the United States in February 1906. After losing a leg in an accident, he returned to Cefn Mawr and from 1920 to 1934 was licensee of the Railway Tavern. Charlie's brother Arthur was a noted soccer administrator - secretary of the Druids FC and a vice president of the FAW.

Honours:
Druids - Welsh Cup 1898, 1899; finalists 1900, 1901

191 Ralph Stanley Jones
B: Ruabon; 23 Feb 1876
D: Wrexham; 1 May 1952
Outside left
1 cap: (Druids) v Sco 1899

Career: Druids, 1895-02; Oswestry Utd, Aug 1902-03; Druids, 1903-04.

Ralph Jones stepped up from Druids reserves to the senior XI and spent most of his career with the famous old club. A clever ball-playing craftsman, he was full of trickery but over inclined to show off his ability without any apparent advantages to his team. His dashing and lively display in the Welsh trial earned him selection as a replacement for Bob Atherton against Scotland at the Racecourse. By 1902, he was out of favour at Druids having 'lost a good deal of his old speed and judgement' and spent one season at Oswestry.

Jones served with the Royal Welsh Fusiliers in WW1 and afterwards worked in local collieries for many years.

Honours:
Druids - Welsh Cup 1898, 1899; finalists 1900

Note: In some record books R S Jones' Wales appearance was mistakenly amalgamated with those of R 'Dick' Jones (#234), the Millwall player.

192 Trevor Owen
B: Llangollen; 1873
D: Acrefair; 1 Jun 1930
Inside forward
2 caps: (Crewe Alex) v Sco, Eng 1899

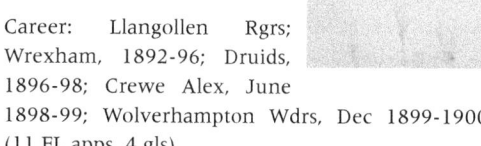

Career: Llangollen Rgrs; Wrexham, 1892-96; Druids, 1896-98; Crewe Alex, June 1898-99; Wolverhampton Wdrs, Dec 1899-1900 (11 FL apps, 4 gls).

Trevor Owen's father ran a flannel factory in Llangollen and the youngster began playing soccer with the local side. 'A scientific forward' who always gave a good account of himself, Owen excelled at close play but wasn't averse to long-range shooting. At Wrexham, he was described as 'one of the best forwards in Wales' but a knee injury in 1893 interrupted his development.

He remained with Wrexham for three seasons before moving to rivals Druids and Birmingham League football. Comparatively late in his career, Owen was given the opportunity of league football with Wolves but he was eventually forced by ill health to give up the game. Owen worked as a crane driver in Crewe and then became a machinist with a railway company in the town. He eventually returned to Llangollen but finally settled in Acrefair.

Honours:
Druids - Welsh Cup 1898
Wrexham - Welsh Cup finalists 1895, 1896

193 Thomas James Buckland
B: Bangor; Aug 1870
D: Sheffield (Eng); 29 Mar 1923
Half back
1 cap: (Bangor) v Eng 1899

Career: Hirael (Bangor), Bangor, 1888-1904; Llandegai.

Tom Buckland, the son of a ship's agent, was the strongman of the Bangor side and a stalwart for many seasons. A hard-working player, he earned a reputation with Bangor as being something of a 'war horse'. Buckland came into the Wales side to replace the injured J L Jones against Scotland. He had previously taken part in trial matches but had failed to get the nod from the FAW selectors. In his single match for Wales, Buckland had the unenviable task of facing an English forward line including Steve Bloomer and G O Smith. Although he was described in match reports as 'the pick of the half backs', it was his only appearance and in subsequent matches the selectors reverted to the more experienced Jones. This may well have been because the half back line was 'more sturdy than clever', but Buckland had acquitted himself well and according to reports, played a 'fine, aggressive game' and 'never knew when he was beaten'. His career had begun with Hirael as a youth and he joined the Bangor club when he was about 18 years old. Buckland, who captained the Bangor team in one season, was a member of the 1896 Welsh Cup winning team and won North Wales Amateur Cup medals in 1895, 1896 and 1899. Away from soccer, Buckland was employed on the railways, started his working life as an engine cleaner before progressing to engine driver based at Bangor.

Honours:
Bangor - Welsh Cup 1896

194 William Clare Harrison

B: Portsmouth (Eng); 10 Apr 1872
D: Wrexham; 22 Sep 1920
Inside forward/Wing/Half back
5 caps: (Wrexham) v Eng 1899; v Sco, Ire, Eng 1900; v Ire 1901

Career: Wrexham Gymnasium, Nov 1890-93; Wrexham, 1893-1909.

Harrison moved to Wales as a young boy and initially preferred playing cricket to soccer. He began his football career as centre forward for the Wrexham Gymnasium club, later converting to a strong tackling 'star half back'. Harrison, whom the FAW selectors erroneously thought was born in Porthmadog because of an error on his registration form, became captain of Wrexham in the 1890s and guided his team to five Welsh Cup finals, although Wrexham won only one of these - in 1897. He was noted for his 'precise corner kicks' and as a tricky player who 'drew defenders before releasing the ball to his forwards'.

Harrison's career with Wrexham continued to 1909 and after retiring he became landlord of the Turf Hotel at the Wrexham Racecourse. He was also a member of the Wrexham FC management committee, became a founder director in 1912 and was club chairman at the time of his death. Harrison once suffered the unpleasant experience of falling off the stand roof at the Racecourse while attempting to effect repairs!

Honours:
Wrexham - Welsh Cup 1897; finalists 1895, 1896, 1898, 1899
Wrexham Gymnasium - Welsh Amateur Cup finalists 1893

195 William Thomas Butler

B: Rhosymedre; 27 Jun 1872
D: Rhosymedre; 17 Feb 1953
Inside forward
2 caps (1 gl): (Druids) v Sco, Ire 1900

Career: Druids, 1889-1907.

The son of Charles Butler, secretary of the Druids in the 1880s and 1890s, Bill Butler was a diminutive inside forward possessing a clever touch. He figured prominently in the Druids' second period of dominance of Welsh soccer, appearing in four consecutive Welsh Cup finals. He never made it into league football but appeared once for West Bromwich Albion Reserves in October 1890 and a month later signed forms for Bolton Wanderers. Along with his brother Windsor, Butler was a permanent feature of the Druids team for many years. A master baker by profession, Bill later took over his father's bakery in Rhosymedre.

Honours:
Druids - Welsh Cup 1898, 1899; finalists 1900, 1901

196 Frederick John Griffiths

B: Presteigne; 13 Sep 1873
D: Westvleteren (Bel); 30 Oct 1917
Goalkeeper (6ft 2ins, 15st)
2 caps: (Blackpool) v Sco, Eng 1900

Career: South Shore, 1894-96; Clitheroe, Jan 1896-97; South Shore, 1897-1899; Blackpool, 1899-1900; Stalybridge R, 1900; Millwall Ath, 1900-01 (17 SL apps); Tottenham H, Oct 1901-02 (9 SL apps); Preston N E, Mar 1902; West Ham Utd, Sep 1902-04 (49 SL apps); New Brompton, 1904-06 (52 SL apps); Middlesbrough, Sep 1906; Shiremoore's Ath (player-coach), 1906; Shirebrook (trainer), 1911.

The sturdily built Fred Griffiths was the first Blackpool player to gain international honours, at a time when the Seasiders were a non-league club operating in the Lancashire League. With John Morris of Chirk, Fred was part of the goalkeeping interregnum between Jim Trainer and the great Roose. The son of a Presteigne coal merchant, he made a shaky start at South Shore and was released as not being 'of sufficient class'. He joined Clitheroe where his form rapidly improved, making the club mightily pleased with their 'catch of the season'. At one time Griffiths was on Sheffield United's radar as a potential 'understudy to the Leviathan Foulke', a reference to their 24-stone 'keeper. Prior to joining Spurs, Griffiths was a part-time pro and was employed as a metal worker and blacksmith.

Griffiths had a long spell in the Southern League and gained a reputation as a good shot stopper. One scribe commented: 'He repels shots from all quarters with equal ease and determination'. His commanding physical presence meant that charging held no fears for him. In a 1911 interview he recounted how in international matches the ball became the property of the player who first reached it after the final whistle blew. Griffiths 'had his eye on the leather, knowing the end was approaching, but Meredith's speed prevailed and he got possession'. Griffiths later worked as a coal miner in Shirebrook, where he coached the local Central Alliance team, and then as a barman at the Station Hotel before becoming a butcher. At the outbreak of war, he joined the Sherwood Foresters and was killed in action in October 1917, leaving a widow and six young children. At the Welsh service of remembrance in July 2017 to commemorate the 3,000 soldiers who were killed or injured at Passchendale, a delegation from the FAW joined first minister Carwyn Jones and the Prince of Wales. The FAW party, which included manager Chris Coleman who had recited the pledge, later visited the grave of Fred Griffiths at Dozinghem.

197 Richard Jones
B: Hirael, Bangor; 1879
D: Bangor; 6 Nov 1938
Centre forward
2 caps (1 gl): (Bangor) v Sco, Ire 1900

Career: Menai Bridge; Bangor, 1896-1911; Llechid Swifts, Nov 1911-14.

Dick Jones was a dogged, hard-running centre forward, at his best with the ball at his feet. A powerful shot and a prolific scorer, his one weakness was an inaccuracy in his passing. Defections from the Welsh team originally selected to face the Scots led to the front rank being 'remodelled' and Jones was one of several reserves called up. Press reports described the side as second rate but the Bangor player did well enough to hold his place for the Irish match. The selectors' confidence was rewarded when Jones gave Wales an interval lead in a 2-0 win.

Jones served on the Bangor City Council from 1926 and was elected to the Caernarvonshire County Council in 1932. He was 'a tireless champion of the poor and underprivileged' of Bangor and an energetic chairman of the housing committee from 1933, doing much to expand public sector housing in the city and playing a major part in the development of the Maesgeirchen estate. 'Dickie Town', as he was known, followed his father's trade as a house painter and at one time was in business with him and his brother.

198 Samuel Meredith

B: Trefonen (Eng);
5 Sep 1872
D: Manchester (Eng);
25 Dec 1921
Full back (5ft 8ins, 12st)
8 caps: (Chirk) v Sco 1900; v Sco, Eng, Ire 1900; (Stoke) v Eng 1902; v Ire 1903; v Eng 1904; v Eng 1907

Career: Chirk, 1894-1901; Stoke, May 1901-05 (45 FL apps); Leyton, May 1905-Apr 1910 (94 SL apps).

Long after his brother Billy had made a name for himself in the footballing world, Sam remained a player with the village team Chirk. When he eventually joined a senior club, he found himself mostly in Stoke's reserve side. In his first match for Wales, Meredith was asked to fill the unfamiliar position of right half. His merits were more fully appreciated when he proved an able deputy for Di Jones in the 1901 international against Scotland.

A splendid tackler and very reliable full back, Meredith was reckoned at one time to be one of the finest defenders in the Southern League. One writer commented: 'it matters not how the ball comes to him, he invariably gets it away neatly and does not kick it at random but disposes of it to a member of his own side', while another thought 'he would have gained more fame if he'd been in a stronger side than Leyton'. In 1909, he developed a wasting disease which curtailed his appearances and subsequently forced him to give up the game. The following year a benefit fund was opened which was bolstered by a match between Leyton Old Players and Leytonstone Old Players. Remarkably, Leyton Old Players featured a one-legged player in goal! Leyton also played a George Robey XI for the popular Meredith. The former full back became a publican and kept the Jolly Forgeman at Newbridge near Ruabon before moving to Gorton, Manchester to become a landlord for Hardy's Brewery. Meredith died at the Prince of Wales Hotel, Gorton from bronchial pneumonia and is buried in Chirk.

199 Charles Richard Morris

B: Oswestry (Eng);
29 Aug 1880
D: Chirk; 18 Jan 1952
Full back (5ft 11ins, 13st)
28 caps: (Chirk) v Sco, Ire, Eng 1900; (Derby Co) v Sco, Eng, Ire 1901; v Eng, Sco 1902; v Eng, Sco, Ire 1903; v Ire 1904; v Sco, Eng, Ire 1905; v Sco 1906; v Sco 1907; v Sco, Eng 1908; v Sco, Eng, Ire 1909; v Sco, Eng, Ire 1910; (Huddersfield T) v Ire, Sco, Eng 1911

Career: Chirk, 1897-1900; Derby Co, Apr 1900-10 (277 FL apps, 1 gl); Huddersfield T, Aug 1910-11 (16 FL apps); Wrexham, Jul 1911-12; Chirk, 1912-14.

A heavily-built full back, Charlie Morris was said to 'combine the rigidity of a stone wall with the flexibility of a rubber ball'. He worked down the mines for eight years and by the time he joined Derby during the 1900 close season to take the place of Joe Leiper, he was already a Welsh international player. The deal involved a £50 payment to Chirk FC, while Morris received a £10 signing on fee and was put on a wage of £3 a week 'all year round'.

Morris, who succeeded Archie Goodall as captain in 1903, was hardly ever out of the Derby side except for injury. One reporter commented: 'he kicks well with either foot and in almost any position, tackles promptly and clears with judgement', while another thought he showed 'masterly defence when hard pressed and knows the game from A to Z'. His greatest soccer ambition was to gain an FA Cup medal but, on his one appearance in a final, Derby lost 6-0 and he had to take over in goal from the injured Jack Fryer. Morris, who was selected by Wales on 33 occasions, had to do similar duty in 1908 against England. His long association with Derby ended in 1910 when he left because he felt he wasn't sufficiently appreciated by the club. He joined Huddersfield and took part in the newly promoted club's first game in the Second Division. Morris had a spell with Wrexham in the Birmingham and District League before becoming disillusioned with the professional game and virtually giving up serious football, being reinstated as an amateur in 1912 and playing for Chirk in the North Wales Alliance.

His greatest love was cricket and he once described his finest sporting moment as standing up to the bowling of the great Sid Barnes. Morris, who reputedly came close to playing cricket for Derbyshire, was something of an all-rounder but principally a wicket keeper. He subsequently worked as a cricket coach at several schools in the Wrexham and Oswestry areas, including Grove Park from 1933 to 1948, and was the Duke of Westminster's private cricket professional for several years. A long time member of Chirk Rural District Council and a prominent lay preacher, Morris finally retired in 1948. His brothers John and Robert were also capped by Wales.

Honours:
Derby Co - FA Cup finalists 1904

200 Thomas David Parry

B: Oswestry (Eng); 1880
D: Warrington (Eng);
   17 Aug 1946
Half back/Inside forward
7 caps (3 gls): (Oswestry Utd) v Sco, Ire, Eng 1900; v Sco, Eng, Ire 1901; v Eng 1902

Career: Oswestry Utd, 1896-1905.

Tom Parry was a brother to Maurice of Liverpool fame and they appeared together in four international matches. In his seven appearances for Wales, Tom faced England on three occasions - a sign of the FAW selectors' confidence in his abilities. While Maurice pursued a career in football, Tom turned down all offers to become a professional. His importance to the Oswestry cause was seen in the team's decline after he gave up playing. He served on the Oswestry United committee and was a batsman with Oswestry Cricket Club. Parry studied at Lamb's Leather College in London and followed his father's profession as a leather tanner. He was in business in Warrington from 1914 to his death.

Honours:
Oswestry Utd - Welsh Cup 1901

201 Samuel James Brookes

B: Llandudno; 26 Oct 1879
D: Saskatoon (Can);
   20 Jun 1938
Wing half (5ft 4ins)
2 caps: (Llandudno Swifts) v Ire, Eng 1900

Career: Llandudno Swifts, 1896-1900; London Welsh, Apr 1897; Rhyl, 1900-01; Blackpool, Jun-Oct 1901 (1 FL app); Rhyl, Oct 1901-05; Rhyl, 1910.

Sammy Brookes was one of eight children, seven of them boys, born to George Brookes, a chemist of Mostyn Street, Llandudno. His brother Alfred, who studied at Edinburgh University and played for Queens Park, became a doctor in Llanelli, while another brother became a chemist. Brookes was what would be termed in today's parlance 'a ball winner'. A strong tackler who backed up his forwards well, he applied himself diligently to the task in hand. Brookes, who turned pro' in August 1899, excelled in breaking up attacks and, 'having gained possession, opened out the play well'. His flirtation with Blackpool was short lived and he soon returned to Rhyl and the Combination. In 1900, a *North Wales Chronicle* reporter commented: 'the Rhyl team is possessed of as powerful and accomplished a set of halfs [sic] as I have ever seen in North Wales, bar none. Sammy Brookes is a little 'un, but every ounce of him is good, and despite some nasty little tricks, he plays, on the whole, a fair, straightforward, if somewhat powerful game, and never knows when he is beaten, or, if he knows it, does not admit it'. A tenacious tackler with Rhyl, he was said to be 'no favourite of the Bangor spectators', a comment that indicates how long the rivalry between the two clubs has persisted.

Brookes was employed as a draper but left Rhyl for America around 1905 and was out there for several years. One newspaper columnist, responding to a reader's query in December 1909 about Brookes' whereabouts, said: 'I do not know where Sammy Brookes is at present; but he is said to be somewhere in America. He was a great favourite with the Rhylites in its best days, and was certainly one of the very best halves to be seen in Wales. For one so small in stature, it was marvellous what performances he was able he to do. He may well be called the Wedlock of Wales'. By the following year he was back with Rhyl, 'returned home from Yankee land' as one report put it, and again working as a draper in the town. He was clearly restless and left north Wales for Canada once again, becoming a farmer in Lemberg, Saskatchewan and served with the Canadian Overseas Expeditionary force in the First World War. As late as 1935 he was living in Regina, Saskatchewan.

202 Robert Morris
B: Oswestry (Eng); 1875
D: Chirk; 23 Sep 1926
Centre half
6 caps: (Chirk) v Eng, Ire 1900; v Ire 1901; Sco 1902; (Shrewsbury T) v Eng, Ire 1903

Career: Chirk, 1893-1902; Shrewsbury T, 1902-07; Chirk, 1907-09.

An excellent defender and good leader, Bob Morris somewhat surprisingly, never made it beyond the Birmingham and District League but was briefly on Manchester City's books. A one-time Chirk captain, he was comfortable at left back or centre half and one writer called him 'unapproachable', adding 'his defence of the ball was very uncommon'.

Morris was strong in the air and was keen to go forward for corners and free kicks - an early exploiter of what is now known as the 'set piece'. A careful player, he relied on his well-developed positional sense and was 'entirely safe'. Morris, a brother to Jack and Charlie, captained Shrewsbury to a Shropshire Cup success in 1904 before returning to a Chirk club in decline. An official at Brynkinallt colliery, he was later chairman of the Chirk club.

Honours:
Shrewsbury T - Shropshire Cup 1903, 1904

203 Leigh Richmond Roose
B: Holt, Wrexham; 27 Nov 1877
D: Gueudecourt (Fra); 7 Oct 1916
Goalkeeper
(6ft 1ins, 13st 6lbs)
24 caps: (Aberystwyth T) v Ire 1900; (London Welsh) v Sco, Eng, Ire 1901; (Stoke) v Eng, Sco 1902; v Eng 1904; (Everton) v Sco, Eng 1905; (Stoke) v Sco, Eng, Ire 1906; v Ire, Sco, Eng 1907; (Sunderland) v Sco, Eng, 1908; v Sco, Eng, Ire 1909; v Sco, Eng, Ire 1910; v Sco 1911
(also 1 cap as amateur, 1911)

Career: Univ Coll Wales (Aberystwyth); Aberystwyth T, 1898-1900 (85 apps); Druids, 1900; London Welsh, Oct 1900; Stoke, Oct 1901-04 (80 FL apps); Everton, Nov 1904-05 (18 FL apps); Stoke, 1905-08 (66 FL apps); Sunderland, Jan 1908-11 (92 FL apps); Huddersfield T, Apr 1911 (5 FL apps);

Aston Villa, Aug 1911-12 (10 FL apps); Woolwich Arsenal, Dec 1911-12 (13 FL apps).

The son of a Presbyterian minister, Leigh Roose obtained his early education at the Holt Academy where he was taught for a while by H G Wells. He took a science degree at University College of Wales, Aberystwyth and it was with the town club that his extraordinary goalkeeping style and skills were first seen. A member of the town's Welsh Cup winning team, his subsequent capture by Druids was hailed as a great coup but within a short time he was appearing on a wider football stage. In October 1900 Roose moved to London to embark on a medical degree course but, unable to gain a place in that year's intake, took work as an assistant at Kings College Hospital.

His services were in demand from several top clubs and he agreed to join Stoke as an amateur, albeit an expensive one with lavish expenses. He thought nothing of travelling on the last possible train and then hiring a special for the rest of his journey and charging it to the club. It was not unusual for Roose to arrive at a ground at the reins of a horse and carriage with a band of young fans following behinds. J H Catton ('Tityrus' of the *Athletic News*) described Roose as "dexterous though daring, valiant though volatile". Another writer was more expansive – 'Few men exhibit their personality so vividly in their play as L R Roose. You cannot spend five minutes in his company without being impressed by his vivacity, his boldness, his knowledge of men and things - a clever man undoubtedly but one entirely unrestrained in word or action. On the field his whole attention is centred on the game, he rarely stands listlessly by the goalpost even when the ball is at the other end of the enclosure but is ever following the game keenly and closely. Directly his charge is threatened he is on the move, he thinks nothing of dashing out 10 or 15 yards even when the backs have a good chance of clearing as he makes himself. He will also rush along the touchline, field the ball and get in a kick, and such a kick too, to keep the ball going briskly. Equally daring though unorthodox are his methods of dealing with straight shots. He is not a model custodian by any means - he would not be L R Roose if he were'. At that time goalkeepers were allowed to handle the ball inside their own half and Roose took full advantage. It was not until 1912 that the authorities amended law 8 so that goalkeepers in future could only handle the ball in their own penalty area.

In April 1904, having suffered a loss of form, and becoming involved in a row over expenses, he decided to give up the game to concentrate of securing his medical degree. The retirement didn't last. At Everton, Roose, who was initially signed as cover, displaced Irish international keeper Billy Scott and played his part in the club's progress to the semi-final of the FA Cup and the runners-up spot in the First Division. In recognition of his services to Sunderland and his almost single handed contribution to saving them from relegation, the club were anxious to give Roose a testimonial match. The FA scotched the idea as incompatible with Roose's amateur status and he had to make do with an illuminated address, presented by the Mayor.

The superstitious Roose, who always wore his unwashed black and green Aberystwyth shirt under his Welsh jersey, was also an inveterate practical joker. He once turned up for a match in Belfast with his hand heavily bandaged, only to remove it at the start of the match before the assembled press and play a blinder. He firmly believed that sport should not be carried to excess, saying 'a pinch of salt is a good condiment but a spoonful becomes nauseating'. On goalkeeping he wrote: 'The easy confidence displayed by the goalkeeper in taking shots from all angles and positions is only equalled by the holy calm shown by the man who has just bowed his mother-in-law out of the family porch'. An erratic genius, Roose was also a generous individual, who helped his predecessor Jim

Trainer when he fell on hard times, and offered to stand down from the Wales team to allow eight-times reserve Alf Edwards an opportunity to gain his cap, but the FAW selectors would not hear of it. In January 1912, the North Wales Coast FA received a request from Ffestiniog FC to frame Roose's registration form and place it in the committee room but the club were told that it was against league rules.

The Archdeacon', as he called himself in his telegrams to friends, was thought to have joined the Royal Army Medical Corps in October 1914 and served in France and then at Gallipoli. His family lost touch with him and believed that he had become one of the many casualties of the ill-fated campaign. Extraordinarily, they later learned that he had been seen in France in 1916 but their efforts to establish his fate were unsuccessful. Lance Corporal Roose had reputedly last been seen on the battlefield by Gordon Hoare, the England amateur player. As late as 1919 newspapers were reporting that 'though he was long ago reported missing in France, there are still many who refuse to believe he has gone west'. Research has, however, shown that Roose initially served with the YMCA, providing medical and other support to soldiers in France, Malta, Lemnos and Alexandria, and indeed served at Gallipoli. It was not until July 1916, on his evacuation from Gallipoli to Egypt and his return to London, that he joined the 9th Battalion Royal Fusiliers and his surname had been misspelled as 'Rouse'. It was under that name that he was awarded the Military Medal in August 1916 for bravery in an advance of an enemy trench

Roose was lost on 7 October 1916 and his body was never found. He is commemorated in Holt Church and on the village cross. Following representations from Wales fans the Thiepval Memorial now bears his correct name after the Commonwealth War Graves Commission finally acknowledged the error. Roose was a brother-in-law to J C Jenkins, the Wales rugby union player.

Honours:
Aberystwyth T - Welsh Cup 1900
Druids - Welsh Cup finalists 1901
Everton - 1st Div runners-up 1905

204 Hugh Morgan-Owen

B: Rhyl; 15 Jan 1882
D: Repton (Eng); 6 Mar 1953
Centre forward/Winger
5 caps (2 gls): (Oxford Univ) v Eng 1900; Sco 1902; (Corinthians) v Eng, Ire 1906; v Sco 1907

Career: Colet Sch (Rhyl); Shrewsbury Sch; Hertford Coll (Oxford), 1900-04; Corinthians, 1901-09 (32 apps, 36 goals); (also Welshpool).

Hugh Morgan-Owen, the son of Timothy Morgan-Owen, H M Inspector of Schools, was one of four brothers (see also Morgan), three of whom were leading Welsh amateur footballers although Garth, the third brother, never gained international recognition. Hugh was said to be an exponent of 'pretty football' but was described as 'weak' at international level. Like his brother Morgan, he was a prominent Corinthian and a diehard amateur. While at university he appeared in four successive matches against Cambridge, scoring in 1901 and 1902 and captaining the side in 1903 and 1904. He also played for Rhyl and Welshpool where the family had homes.

Morgan-Owen entered the Nigerian Civil Service in 1909 and became a Provincial Commissioner in 1925, retiring six years later when he returned to Britain and settled in Derbyshire, near his brother Morgan. In 1939 he was responsible for arranging the billeting of evacuee children at Repton. In the latter part of his life, Morgan-Owen was Commissioner of Income Tax and Land Tax for Derbyshire and served as a magistrate on a local bench.

Morgan-Owen opted to play for Old Salopians in the 1903 Arthur Dunn Cup final and declined an invitation to appear for Wales. The Morgan-Owen family are distant kinsmen of the families of Lord Harlech and Lord Kenyon.

205 John Owen Jones

B: Bangor; 6 Sept 1871
D: Crewe (Eng); Sep 1955
Inside forward
2 caps (1 gl): (Bangor) v Sco, Ire 1901

Career: Bangor, 1890-94; Crewe Alex, Oct-Dec 1894; Chorley, Sep 1897-98; Newton Heath, May 1898 (2 FL apps); Bangor, Dec 1900-01; Earlestown; Stalybridge Rov, Nov 1901.

Younger brother of Richard Owen Jones, J O followed him to Crewe in 1894 but did not meet with the same success. For a time he played in the same team as Billy Lewis and Bob Roberts. A resilient player and a fine passer of the ball, he was said to 'work like a trojan'. Jones had to wait until his late 20s for Welsh recognition and clinched his selection with a fine performance in the trial match. He made his debut for Newton Heath in their 2-0 win over Gainsborough Trinity but was discarded two matches into the season and eventually returned to the Lancashire League. Jack Jones spent most of his working life in the locomotive works at Crewe.

206 William James Jones

B: Blaina; 8 Feb 1875
D: Aberdare; 1961
Half back (5ft 11ins, 13st)
4 caps: (Aberdare) v Sco, Eng 1901; (West Ham Utd) v Eng, Sco 1902

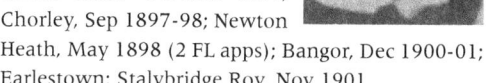

Career: Mountain Ash Excelsiors; Rogerstone; Aberdare, 1896-1901; Kettering, Aug-Dec 1901 (9 SL apps); West Ham Utd, Dec 1901-02 (16 SL apps); Aberaman, 1902-04; Rogerstone, 1904-06; Aberdare, 1907-8; Llanbradach, 1909; Penrhiwceiber Guild (captain and 'playing manager'), 1911.

Aberdare captain in the late 1890s, Bill Jones was a sound tackler who played well within himself and was 'adept at feeding the wingmen.' He was the first Welsh international soccer player to emerge from south Wales league soccer, a landmark in the development of the game in Wales. Jones, whose play was described as 'clever and resourceful', skippered Aberdare in 1900-01 and his loss to Kettering and the Southern League was much regretted in the town. Although he gave 'a particularly brilliant display' on Kettering's visit to Canning Town he failed to settle at his new club and he lost form. One press report described him as 'a complete passenger'. A swap with Peter Kyle of West Ham was arranged and he made a much better showing at the London club. In 16 outings he was only twice on the losing side but he returned to south Wales in the summer of 1902. He was subsequently a member of the first south Walian team to feature in a Welsh Cup final; a disastrous event for Aberaman but an important breakthrough nonetheless.

Jones, a coal miner from an early age, was known as 'Bill Barber' or 'Barber Jones' as his half brother George was a hairdresser and tobacconist in Mountain Ash. In the 1911-12 season he captained Penrhiwceiber Guild to the championship of Glamorgan League Third Division (Aberdare section), and Penrhiwceiber played the Cardiff & District League in a benefit match for Jones in May 1914. Once believed to have been killed in the First World War, he did not serve in the forces during the conflict and remained a miner. In later years he worked as a heavy labourer at a gas works.

Honours:
Aberdare - S Wales Lge champions 1899, 1900
Aberaman - Welsh Cup finalists 1903

207 Maurice Pryce Parry
B: Oswestry (Eng);
   7 Nov 1877
D: Bootle (Eng); 24 Mar 1935
Halfback (6ft, 13st 3lbs)
16 caps: (Liverpool) v Sco, Eng, Ire 1901; v Ire, Eng, Sco 1902; v Eng, Sco 1903; v Eng, Ire 1904; v Eng 1906; v Sco, Eng, Ire 1903; v Sco, Eng 1909

Career: Oswestry Utd, 1895-98; Long Eaton Rgrs; Leicester Fosse, Jul 1898-99 (1 FL app); Loughborough, Feb 1899; Brighton Utd, May 1899-1900 (22 SL apps); Liverpool, Mar 1900-09 (207 FL apps, 3 gls); Partick Thistle, Jun 1909-11; Wrexham 1911; Oswestry Utd, Sep 1913-14; Rotherham Co (manager), 1921-23.

In early life, Maurice Parry had been apprenticed as an engineer and once harboured thoughts of marine engineering - an idea he gave up after a rough crossing to New York. On moving to Leicester to take work, he joined Fosse and, in his own words, 'I went into it blindly as I had no intention of becoming a professional'. His employment later took him to Brighton where he gained Southern League experience with the local club. Four offers from league clubs followed and Parry opted for Liverpool as being nearest his home.

Parry was described as 'a resourceful and untiring half back who seldom plays below form'. With Alex Raisbeck and Jim Bradley, they formed the finest Liverpool half back line of the pre-First World War period. Parry had 'lengthy and loosely jointed limbs' and 'his unique methods defied explanation ... He could twist and turn and tie the opposing forward in a tangle and then steal the ball from his toe'! Parry followed Raisbeck into Scottish football but in March 1911 was reinstated as an amateur and travelled to South Africa to coach. On the outbreak of war he immediately enlisted and served as a lieutenant in the 7th Battalion Royal Welsh Fusiliers. Following war service, he managed Rotherham and was coach to Liverpool, Barcelona, Dusseldorf, Frankfurt, Cologne and finally in Jersey. Parry's coaching methods had him installed in the stand with a whistle, ready to stop the practice match to point out any fault. A keen organist, he firmly believed, like so many footballers, that 'it is essential for a football player to abstain from intoxicants'. He died in 1935 of chronic bronchitis, a legacy of his being gassed in the First World War.

Parry's 1903 view on the game is worth recording: 'The game is now played at high pressure and clubs must pay more attention to training more than they have ever done. A young man who becomes a pro footballer has many advantages. He has to live in a large town and he will find splendid facilities for improving himself. There are institutes, technical classes and many other advantages'. Parry's son Frank was an outside left on Everton's books in the early 1920s and later with Grimsby, Accrington Stanley and Nelson.

Honours:
Liverpool - FL 1st Div champions 1906
         - FL 2nd Div champions 1905

208 Ephraim Williams
B: Chirk; 13 Sep 1877
D: Chirk; 3 Nov 1954
Outside/Inside left
5 caps: (Druids) v Sco, Eng, Ire 1901; v Eng, Ire 1902

Career: Chirk, 1896-1900; Druids, 1900-03; Chirk, 1903-07.

In 1901, one newspaper described 'Eph' Williams as 'very quick, brilliant at times, a strong runner, tricky with a strong shot and hard working'. A regular goalscorer with Chirk, he spent three seasons with Druids in the Birmingham and District League and at one time was rumoured to be in Manchester City's sights but it came to nothing. Williams, the son of a coal miner, was a brother-in-law to George Williams, and worked as a collier from the age of 11 until he retired in 1950 - a staggering total of 62 years. A keen bowls player and cricketer, he was umpire in the Wrexham and Denbighshire Cricket League for some years.

Honours:
Druids - Welsh Cup 1904; finalists 1901

209 Arthur William Green

B: Aberystwyth; 28 Apr 1881
D: Nottingham (Eng); 24 Sep 1966
Centre forward
(5ft 10ins, 12st 7lbs)
8 caps (3 gls): (Aston Villa) v Ire 1901; (Notts Co) v Eng 1903; v Sco, Ire 1904; v Eng, Ire 1906; (Nottingham F) v Eng 1907; v Sco 1908

Career: Aberystwyth T, 1897-1900 (82 apps, 52 gls); Aston Villa, 1900-01; Ebbw Vale; Walsall, (Mid Lge) 1901-02; Notts Co, 1902-Jan 1907 (134 FL apps, 60 gls); Nottingham F, (£350) Jan 1907-Apr 1909 (39 FL apps, 16 gls); Brierley Hill Alliance 1911-13; Walsall, Sep 1913.

A prolific marksman for Aberystwyth, Green was described by a local journalist as 'the greatest centre forward in Wales'! He moved to Villa in the summer of 1900 but was never given a senior outing despite scoring regularly for the reserves. The Welshman knew the way to goal and was top scorer for Notts County in 1903-04 with 19 goals in 30 games and joint leading scorer in the two subsequent seasons. The *Glance Football Guide*'s verdict was: 'tall, broad and strong and a very difficult man to rob once in possession, being such a close dribbler and so exceptionally tricky. He is very cool and deliberate and shoots with wonderful accuracy and force, his only failing is that he does not exert himself to the full and is a trifle slow'. *Association Football and the Men Who Made it* (1906) had a somewhat similar view: [Green is] 'as good a shot as can be found, very rarely indeed did he miss from a penalty kick under the old rules. Green was an artist in dribbling and bewildered opposing halves and backs by his tricks. He was a little inclined to selfishness, but there was some excuse for his style of play, seeing the great command he had over the ball'. Green was not the type of player to exert himself to the full and perhaps his one fault was his reluctance to drop back once he had lost the ball. The highlight of his international career was his hat-trick against Ireland in a 4-4 draw at Wrexham in 1906.

Green's time at Notts County ended on a sour note, when relations between the player and the club were not good towards the end: he was dropped from the team, suspended and placed on the transfer list. Green, who was a draughtsman early on, was employed as a representative for a window manufacturing company for many years until his retirement in 1949. Away from work, he was a Nottinghamshire county tennis player and an expert golfer.

Honours:
Nottingham F - FL 2nd Div champions 1906
Aberystwyth T - Welsh Cup 1900

210 Robert Owen Evans

B: Wrexham; 5 Jul 1881
D: Coventry (Eng); 8 Mar 1962
Goalkeeper (5ft 10½ins, 12st)
10 caps: (Wrexham) v Ire 1902; v Eng, Sco, Ire 1903; (Blackburn Rov) v Ire 1908; (Coventry C) v Ire, Eng 1911; v Sco, Eng, Ire 1912

Career: Olympic Jnrs, 1895; Stansty Villa; Wrexham, 1898-1903; Blackburn Rov, (£150) Mar 1903-08

(105 FL apps); Croydon Common, May 1908-09 (66 apps); Coventry C, May 1909-12 (127 SL apps); Birmingham, 1912-13 (3 FL apps); Nuneaton, 1914.

Bob Evans graduated from the ranks of Wrexham Reserves and established himself in the first team during 1901-02 before Blackburn paid £150 for his services in March 1903. The best description of Evans comes from *Association Football and the Men who Made it* (1906): 'R O Evans, the captain of the team [Blackburn] gained for himself a position among the highest flight of goalkeepers. Cool, calm, collected, he is a master beneath the bar, high, low and wide shots come alike to him. Skillful to a degree, he is quickness personified and rarely indeed does his misjudge the flight of the ball; bold and daring he is one of the most fearless players that ever stepped out on the football field'.

When, at Christmas 1903, he appeared for Blackburn at Anfield, hundreds of supporters from Wrexham were there to support him. Evans continually defied the Liverpool forwards and at the end of the match the north Walians swarmed on to the pitch to carry him shoulder high to the dressing rooms. Many judges rated Evans as superior to Roose but the FAW selectors preferred the gifted but eccentric amateur. A knee injury brought the curtain down on his Blackburn career and, despite recovering well, the received opinion was that he was never quite as mobile again. After a spell with Croydon, Evans moved to the midlands and kept goal for Coventry in their FA Cup run of 1909-10 when they reached the last eight. In May 1911 he was expected to join Aston Villa but re-signed for Coventry. Evans was a brave goalkeeper and in 1902, at Cardiff, dislocated his knee while facing the Irish. 'The joint was bound up with yards of linen' and Evans saw out the remainder of the match.

In December 1915 Evans joined the Royal Garrison Artillery and served as a signaller and gunner. He was wounded and suffered shell shock. By the time he was discharged from the Army in May 1918 Evans had spent 17 months in four different institutions. His playing career was over and he retired to become a referee and an administrator in junior football, serving as chairman of Coventry and Warwickshire Football League. Prior to the First World War he had worked as a clerk in the motor industry.

Evans, whose brother Caradog played for Plymouth Argyle and Wales as an amateur, was also a county cricketer for Denbighshire.

Honours:
Wrexham – Welsh Cup 1903; finalists 1902
Croydon Common – SL 2nd Div champions 1909

211 Roger Evans

B: Porthaethwy, Ynys Môn;
    17 Nov 1879
D: Swanage (Eng);
    25 Apr 1974
Centre forward
1 cap: (Clapton) v Ire 1902

Career: Ilford, 1898-1900; Clapton, 1900-05; Queens Park Rgrs, 1899-1900 & 1901-02; Southern Utd, 1904; New Crusaders, 1905-06.

Roger Evans 'learnt his serious football at Ilford' and was the subject of an approach by Liverpool in November 1899 which caused outrage among supporters of the Essex club. Evans, an amateur and an ex-public schoolboy, was said to have no interest in professionalism. The Liverpool officials were reported to the FA, found guilty of an illegal approach and the secretary, John McKenna, was suspended for one month. Liverpool's judgement was sound but Evans never played regularly enough to develop his game. He gained his only cap at the Arms Park in Cardiff but never showed any sort of form and 'missed the easiest of chances in front of goal'. He had come late into the side for Arthur Green (Mart Watkins in some reports) and was much criticised for an inept display. However, by January the following year, the Daily Express reckoned he was back to his old form: 'The Welsh international seems to have quite recovered his best form and the manner in which he wormed his way through the opposition and shot three goals in the second half was an eye opener to the on-lookers'. Between January and March 1903 he enjoyed a good spell, scoring 13 goals in seven matches and drawing rather fanciful comparisons with the great Vivian Woodward.

During the 1904 close season Evans signed for Southern United - the brainchild of Baron von Rieffenstein (who was also associated with West Norwood) - a new club that was going to challenge the best clubs in southern England. He remained on Clapton's books but his work as an insurance manager in London, then in Sutton Coldfield, made demands on his time and increasingly football took second place. Evans was the son of a Menai Bridge corn merchant and, with his brother Christmas Evans, attended New College at Eastbourne, an establishment run by Frederick Schreiner, brother of *The Story of an African Farm* author Olive Schreiner. In the 1920s and 1930s Evans was assistant general manager of the London Guarantee & Accident Co Ltd, which was acquired by the Phoenix Assurance Company, later Royal Sun Alliance Insurance Group. His brother, Christmas Evans, was also in insurance and a qualified barrister, and was company secretary of the Commercial Union Insurance Company Ltd for 20 years. Roger Evans moved to Chorleywood in 1922 and became a leading light in the local cricket club and captain from 1930 to 1935. An excellent opening bat, he made his highest score of 106 not out against Hampstead in 1934. He is believed to have moved to live in Corfe Mullen, Dorset in 1960.

Honours:
Clapton - London Charity Cup 1901, 1902, 1903, 1904

212 Thomas Jenkins

B: Borth; 9 Jan 1877
D: Great Barrow (Eng); 24 Aug 1949
Inside forward/Half back
1 cap: (Rhyl) v Ire 1902

Career: Aberystwyth T, 1894-99 (33 apps, 20 gls); Jesus Coll (Oxford), 1897-1900; Rhyl, 1900-05 (intermittently); also Crewe Alex, 1902-03.

A Rhyl newspaper of 1901 described Jenkins as 'an intelligent player with a stinging shot, his only fault is that he waits for the ball to come to him instead of going in quest of it himself'. Another report commented 'When he has the ball at his toes, he does very clever things with it, he is a terrific shot and a good dribbler'.

Jenkins assisted Aberystwyth in his early days and was the club's leading scorer in 1897-98. His studies at St David's College, Lampeter, limited his availability, a situation not eased when, in 1897, he became a student at Jesus College, Oxford. Jenkins graduated in 1900 and was ordained that same year. He became curate of Rhyl and played as an amateur for the local XI. His duties as a cleric frequently kept him away from the football field but he had a lengthy spell with Crewe in the Birmingham and District League in 1902-03. Four years after his first Wales trial, Jenkins finally gained his cap - at Cardiff Arms Park against Ireland.

He left Rhyl in 1907, was vicar choral at St Asaph Cathedral for a year and then rector of St George, Cegidog until 1914. Jenkins was subsequently rector of Barrow, near Chester for many years until his death.

213 Hugh Jones
B: Derwen Las, Machynlleth; 1879
D: Mardy, Rhondda; 21 Oct 1930
Full back (5ft 10ins, 14st 7lbs)
1 cap: (Aberaman) v Ire 1902

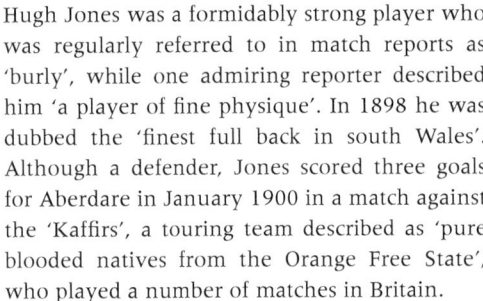

Career: Mardy Corinthians; Mardy, 1897-98; Porth, 1898; Aberdare, 1899-01; Aberaman, 1901-02; Manchester C, Feb-Apr 1902; Aberaman, 1902-03; Mardy, 1904-10.

Hugh Jones was a formidably strong player who was regularly referred to in match reports as 'burly', while one admiring reporter described him 'a player of fine physique'. In 1898 he was dubbed the 'finest full back in south Wales'. Although a defender, Jones scored three goals for Aberdare in January 1900 in a match against the 'Kaffirs', a touring team described as 'pure blooded natives from the Orange Free State', who played a number of matches in Britain.

Jones came into the Wales side as a reserve for Charlie Morris and did exceptionally well. Reports referred to him 'as the best of the backs' and 'always on hand with fine kicking'. He was offered terms by Everton but preferred to join Manchester City after a trial for a £50 transfer fee and personal terms of £3-5-0 (£3.25p) a week. Jones made six appearances for the Lancashire club's reserves and played in two friendly matches, one of which was against Blackburn Rovers at Hyde Road. One report commented: [it would be] 'unwise and unfair to say he'll never make a first class player but he is lamentably lacking in experience'. Nevertheless he was released at the end of the season and returned to south Wales where he resumed work as a miner. He settled back into the Glamorgan League and was for many seasons a stalwart of his home town club, Mardy. Jones was no stranger to the local magistrates, and in 1903 he was fined for fined for assault (broken jaw) and being drunk and refusing to leave the Royal Hotel in Mardy. When told by the bench that he had 'a very bad record', Jones replied that he had not been charged for four years.

Honours:
Aberaman - Welsh Cup finalists 1903

214 Richard Morris
B: Newtown; 16 Dec 1876
D: East Preston (Eng); 23 Oct 1957
Outside/Inside left
11 caps (1 gl): (Druids) v Eng, Sco, (Newtown) v Ire 1902; (Liverpool) v Sco, Ire 1903; v Eng, Sco, Ire 1904; (Leeds C) v Sco 1906; (Grimsby T) v Ire 1907; (Plymouth Arg) v Ire 1908

Career: Newtown; Newtown Royal Welsh Warehouse; Druids, Feb 1902; Liverpool, Mar 1902-05 (35 FL apps, 5 gls); Leeds C, May 1905-06 (27 FL apps, 5 gls); Grimsby T, Jun 1906-07 (24 FL apps, 7 gls); Plymouth A, Jun 1907-Oct 1908 (27 FL apps, 7 gls); Reading; Huddersfield T; Merthyr T, Sep 1913.

'Dicky' Morris was a player whose early career paralleled that of George Latham. Both played for Newtown in the Combination, fought in the Boer War, were members of the Newtown Royal Welsh Warehouse club and joined Liverpool as their first league club. During his service in South Africa, Morris was awarded the Queen's South Africa Medal and the King's South Africa Medal. He was a member of the 1st Battalion Royal Welsh Fusiliers and was wounded slightly when some 500 Boers attacked a convoy near Witpoortje.

'A tireless runner and a top speed dribbler', Morris had plenty of pluck and packed a 'stinging shot'. He was very much a player who could blow hot and cold and his inability to retain his form led to him playing for a string of clubs. Morris scored one of the goals in Wales' 3-2 win over Ireland in 1907 which clinched the Home International championship for the first time. Maurice Parry, the Wales international, who played in the same team as Morris, commented years later: 'Dicky, who was on the small side but very sturdy, was a box of tricks and the 'Alec James' of the side'. He was the first player from the Plymouth club to be recognized at international level.

Dicky Morris had two half brothers – Jack and Denis – both of whom played soccer. Jack was also signed by Liverpool and later went to Bradford Park Avenue. He also played football for Builth Wells, Mardy, Bargoed and Fryston Colliery, and twice appeared in Welsh amateur international trials at Wrexham. The other brother, Dennis, emigrated to Canada in 1910 and became a football legislator in Alberta. Dicky settled in Worthing, Sussex and worked as a cable hand for an electricity company.

215 Walter Martin Watkins

B: Llanwnnog; 21 Mar 1880
D: Stoke (Eng); 14 May 1942
Inside/Centre forward/
Outside left
10 caps (4 gls): (Stoke) v Eng 1902; v Eng, Sco 1903; (Aston Villa) v Eng, Sco, Ire 1904; (Sunderland) v Sco, Eng, Ire 1905; (Stoke) v Ire 1908

Career: Oswestry Utd, 1896-00; Stoke, Nov 1900-04 (106 FL apps, 48 gls); Aston Villa, Jan 1904-Oct 1904 (5 FL apps, 1 gl); Sunderland, Oct 1904-05 (14 FL apps, 8 gls); Crystal Palace, May 1905-06; Northampton, May 1906-07 (38 SL apps, 10 goals); Stoke, May 1907-08 (17 FL apps, 3 gls); Crewe Alex, Jun 1908-09; Stafford Rgrs, 1909-10; Tunstall (coach), 1910-11; Stoke, 1911-14.

Watkins and his brother Ernie were brought up on a farm in mid Wales and both gravitated to Oswestry United, one of their nearest soccer clubs. 'Mart' progressed from the reserves to the first team and was signed by Stoke during the 1900 close season. The versatile Watkins could play in almost all forward positions and the team's fortunes improved considerably after his arrival. He was the club's leading scorer in the 1901-02 and 1902-03 seasons.

In 1901, Watkins was described as a 'smart player' who 'marshalls his forces splendidly in midfield, keeps the game open and the wing men supplied with opportunities'. Another, slightly more critical, comment was: 'He shoots powerfully but is rather inclined to get too much under the ball. He keeps his wings well in hand and he is splendid for a final dash upon an opponent's goal'. Watkins was the subject of an approach by Manchester City in January 1904 and was keen to join his compatriot Meredith. Although City were asked to find £450, Watkins became an Aston Villa player when Stoke accepted their offer of £400. The move, however, was not successful: he made only a handful of appearance and in October 1904 was allowed to join Sunderland. Watkins made a sensational start, scoring two of three Sunderland goals in the defeat of league champions Sheffield United. The newspapers began wondering if Villa had been too hasty but Watkins added only a handful more goals before gravitating to the Southern League. After leaving the game he worked as a fitter on the railways and was involved in local football at Tunstall.

216 Llewellyn Griffiths

B: Ruabon; 5 Aug 1877
D: Wrexham; 15 Nov 1943
Inside forward
1 cap: (Wrexham): v Sco 1902

Career: Rhos Eagle Wdrs, 1896-99; Wrexham, May 1899-1908; Johnstown, 1908-11.

'Llew' Griffiths was a member of Rhos Eagle, a leading Wrexham amateur team and winners of the Welsh Amateur Cup in 1898, and his early career was very much linked to fellow forward Joe Owens. Both played for Rhos, joined Wrexham in 1899 and made their only international appearance in 1902 against the Scots at Greenock. Griffiths was a whole-hearted player, full of enthusiasm and drive. He was much valued by Wrexham as an accurate marksman who was always troublesome to opposing defenders. Even when out of form, his hard work and readiness to drop back and help out the defence earned him a place in the team.

His years at the Racecourse spanned an important period in the development of the Wrexham club into one of the premier clubs outside the Football League. Griffiths figured in several of the Welsh trials for the national side but his appearances were restricted by his work at a local firm where he was a clerk and later company secretary. He also helped Druids on occasions and was a leading local cricketer until the 1920s.

Honours:
Wrexham - Welsh Cup 1903, 1905; finalists 1902

217 Joseph Owens

B: Rhosllanerchrugog; 1878
D: Unknown
Outside/Inside left
1 cap: (Wrexham) v Sco 1902

Career: Rhos Eagle Wdrs, 1896-98; Wrexham, 1899-1908; Rhos Rgrs, 1908-11.

Originally an amateur with the Rhos club, Joe Owens was signed by Wrexham at the same time as his inside forward colleague Llew Griffiths. A tremendous sprinter and 'an exceptionally tricky wingman', he had a fine understanding with Griffiths, whom he regularly provided with accurate passes and centres. For years, Joe's career mirrored that of Griffiths and the pair gained their only caps when they reproduced their club partnership at international level. They went their separate ways in 1908 when Joe returned to junior level. Owens only once came close to embarking on a league career when, in August 1904, he signed for Grimsby, but it didn't work out and he was soon back in the Wrexham area, working as a coal miner. His domestic life was turbulent and by 1911 his wife and five children were in the workhouse and Owens was in Shrewsbury Prison.

Honours:
Wrexham – Welsh Cup 1905, 1909, 1910, 1914, 1915

218 Thomas Davies

B: Cefn, Ruabon; 7 Feb 1872
D: Wrexham; 10 Aug 1942
Half back
4 caps: (Druids) v Eng, Sco, Ire 1903; v Sco 1904

Career: Brookside Villa; Druids, 1890-1910.

When C B Fry saw Tommy Davies playing, he was 'astonished to find a man of such diminutive stature capable of so much effective work'. Davies was only a few inches over five feet but was a skillful and reliable half back and 'a glutton for work'. One of the Davies footballing brothers from Cefn, he was a Druids stalwart for over 20 years and later a member of the club's committee.

Throughout his career, Davies was renowned for his fitness and he never once had to leave the field through injury. He attributed the preservation of his staying powers 'the entire abstention from tobacco and alcoholic drinks'. His retirement in 1910 marked the final chapter in the Druids' decline from one of the finest Welsh teams of the 1880s and 1890s to just another village side. Davies worked as a brickmaker/clayworker at the Ruabon Brick and Terra Cotta Works, while his wife Margaret Ann, known as 'Nanny the Post', was the postmistress at Acrefair Post Office. Despite his previous abstinence, Davies was later a tobacconist at the shop.

Honours:
Druids - Welsh Cup 1898, 1899, 1904; finalists 1900, 1901

219 William Davies

B: Wrexham; 13 Apr 1882
D: Preston (Eng); 21 Jan 1966
Centre forward (5ft 7ins, 11st)
11 caps (5 gls): (Wrexham) v Ire 1903; v Ire 1905; (Blackburn Rov) v Sco, Eng 1908; v Sco, Eng, Ire 1909; v Ire, Sco, Eng 1911; v Ire 1912

Career: Wrexham National Sch; Wrexham St Giles; Wrexham Vic; Wrexham, 1902-05; Blackburn Rov, (£150) Apr 1905-13 (133 FL apps, 67 gls).

Davies joined Wrexham from Chester and District League club Wrexham Victoria, where he had a reputation as a prolific goal scorer. 'Tinker' (he got his nickname from his profession as a master tinsmith) was a short, dogged player, full of dash and determination. His habit of charging the goalkeeper frequently brought him the disfavour of referees. In one Welsh Cup match he bundled the goalkeeper into the net on no fewer than five occasions! In 1905, he joined Blackburn, largely on the advice of R O Evans, who had moved to the Lancashire club two years earlier. Liverpool were keen to secure his services but Evans' persuasion won the day. He marked his debut for Blackburn Reserves by scoring three goals in typical fashion. A reporter cabled Wrexham with the message: 'Tinker got three goals and in two of them put the goalkeeper in as well'. He twice scored four goals, - in successive away matches. On the first occasion, at Everton, the Rovers were losing 4-1 with 20 minutes remaining but Tinker's whirlwind scoring levelled matters. In 'Association Football and The Men Who Made It' (1906) Tinker was described thus: 'a snapper up of unexpected trifles, he snatched at goals with greedy delight'. He spent the second part of the 1909-10 sidelined by injury and, although approaching veteran status, came back to make 11 league appearances during Blackburn's championship season.

Davies married the daughter of Lawrence Cotton, the Blackburn chairman and head of a large fabric manufacturing business. Around 1910, probably with the proceeds of his benefit match, he went into a motor engineering/garage partnership with the England and Blackburn full back Bob Crompton and retired from football in April 1913 to concentrate on the business. During the First World War, Davies was stationed at Malta with the Mechanical Transport Corps.

Honours:
Blackburn Rov - FL 1st Div champions 1912
Wrexham - Welsh Cup 1903, 1905

220 William Wynn

B: Chirk; 1878
D: Scawthorpe (Eng); 23 Jan 1955
Forward
1 cap: (Shrewsbury T) v Ire 1903

Career: Chirk, 1898-02; Shrewsbury T, 1902-06; Chirk, Apr 1906-10.

A reserve for the 1903 trial matches, Wynn was on the fringe of the Welsh squad and was somewhat fortunate to get his Welsh cap. A right sided forward, he was long on effort and regularly on target without suggesting he was international class. Wynn, like most goalscorers, had his barren spells and was criticised for erratic shooting and a 'tendency to hang on to the ball for too long'. He gave good service to Shrewsbury, was prominent in their Shropshire Cup success of 1903 and sometimes played at half back for both Chirk and Shrewsbury. Wynn is known to have worked as a coal miner at a colliery near Doncaster in 1911, but later set up his own successful business as a haulage contractor.

NB: In some reference books, his one appearance for Wales was amalgamated with those of George Wynn.

221 Lloyd Davies
B: Cefn; 9 Aug 1877
D: Cefn Mawr; 10 Oct 1957
Full back (5ft 6ins, 10st 7lbs)
16 caps (1 gl): (Stoke) v Eng 1904; v Ire, Sco, Eng 1907; (Northampton T) v Sco 1908; v Ire 1909; v Ire 1910; v Sco, Eng 1911, Sco, Eng 1912; v Sco, Eng 1913; v Ire, Sco, Eng 1914

Career: St Johns (Rhosymedre), 1897-99; Druids, 1899-1903; Stoke, Jul 1903-04 (7 FL apps); Wellington T, 1904; Swindon T, 1904 Stoke, Nov 1905-07 (27 FL apps, 3 gls); Northampton T, (£400) Nov 1907-20 (308 SL apps); also Oldham Ath 1915.

Lloyd Davies was the youngest of the footballing Davies brothers of Cefn and displayed their typically determined and resolute approach to the game. Originally a forward, he developed into an all round defender and, despite his height, sometimes appeared at centre half. Lloyd made up for lack of inches with total commitment and effort. One report said 'he is a versatile player, no place on the field would be new to him except goal'.

In 1907, Davies became the first player ever bought by Herbert Chapman when he joined Northampton for a fee of £200 (£400 in some reports). It was a shrewd signing by Chapman, with Davies serving the club until his 40th year and becoming the first Northampton player to gain international honours. In April 1914 Northampton played a Wales XI before a crowd of 5,000 in recognition of a fine club servant.

Davies gave up his job as a brick works labourer in 1908 and used his earnings from football to buy a tobacconist shop in Cefn which his wife ran while he continued his career. He was coach to the Northampton team for their first season in the Football League before retiring to Cefn to take over the shop. Davies remained in business for many years despite one close brush with bankruptcy in the 1930s when the closure of Wynnstay Colliery affected trade. His son Ron Davies was a forward with Manchester United in the 1940s.

222 Arthur Davies
B: Wrexham; 14 Jun 1883
D: Overton; 12 Nov 1949
Outside/Inside right
2 caps: (Druids) v Sco 1904; (Middlesbrough) v Sco 1905

Career: Wrexham St Giles; Wrexham; Druids, 1903-04; West Bromwich Alb, Jun-Dec 1904 12 (FL apps, 2 gls); Middlesbrough, Feb-Apr 1905 (10 FL apps); Wrexham Nomads, 1912-13.

One of several footballers produced by Grove Park School in the early years of the 20th century, Arthur Davies, was a solid player with good acceleration and a powerful drive. Arthur and his brother, Llew (237), were the sons of Howell Davies who ran a large public contracting company. Arthur's promising career was brought to a halt by illness and he spent several years out of football. He returned to fitness through playing tennis, another of his sporting loves, and joined Wrexham Nomads. Davies never regained his previous pre-eminence and moved into the administrative side of the game.

During the 1920s, he was secretary of the Druids club and became a director of Wrexham FC for a short time in 1933 before ill-health forced him to give it up. Davies, a builder's clerk in early life, was a partner in a building firm of Davies and McCord for some years. In November

1949 he was found drowned in the River Dee. The subsequent inquest heard evidence of accumulating business problems and an open verdict was returned.

Honours:
Druids - Welsh Cup 1904

223 David Davies
B: Llanelli; 12 May 1880
D: Salford (Eng); 23 Jun 1944
Goalkeeper
 (5ft 10ins, 12st 2lbs)
3 caps: (Bolton Wdrs) v Sco, Ire 1904; v Eng (sub) 1908

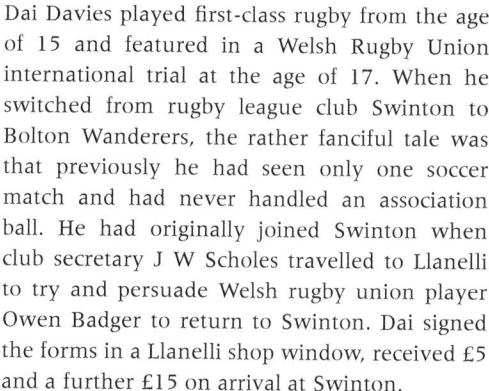

Career: Llanelli (rugby union); Swinton (rugby league), 1898-1902; Bolton Wdrs, May 1902-09 (123 FL apps); Swinton, Dec 1909-13; Leigh, Oct 1913.

Dai Davies played first-class rugby from the age of 15 and featured in a Welsh Rugby Union international trial at the age of 17. When he switched from rugby league club Swinton to Bolton Wanderers, the rather fanciful tale was that previously he had seen only one soccer match and had never handled an association ball. He had originally joined Swinton when club secretary J W Scholes travelled to Llanelli to try and persuade Welsh rugby union player Owen Badger to return to Swinton. Dai signed the forms in a Llanelli shop window, received £5 and a further £15 on arrival at Swinton.

Davies had been a school truant and started work at an early age: *'I was then 12 and large for my age and though it was against the law I had little difficulty in getting work in a tinplate mill. Not for long though – the inevitable sneak told the boss I was only 12 and I was discharged. But I would not return to school. Travelling a little further afield I got work again in a tinplate mill, earning 5s 6d a week and beginning more and more to find my feet on the football ground. Night and day thoughts were centred on a pair of football boots I had seen in a shop window marked 5s 6d, and I'd glued my nose to the window to such purpose that the shopkeeper began to suspect my motives. One day when I came home with wages burning in my pocket, I took a desperate resolve. I was determined to have those boots. They were still in the window, flaunting their charms and beckoning me. I dashed in and banged my money on the counter – six whole shillings and sixty hours of hard work. With glee, I carried off my prize. It was such a glorious game that evening, but when it was over I crept home with lingering feet and leaden conscience. Over the rest of the proceedings, I must draw a veil.'*

He was a tough individual and as a goalkeeper 'excelled in the dangerous and difficult task of diving headlong at an incoming forward's feet and whisking the ball away as he curled up and rolled to safety'. Another (later) verdict was: 'in his indifference to cuts and bruises he was characteristic of the age he was playing in'. Davies appeared for Bolton in the 1904 FA Cup final and was beaten just once, by fellow Welshman Billy Meredith. Despite being on the losing side, he had a good match and made a number of fine saves. Dai won his single cap, against England, in unusual circumstances. L R Roose had to leave the field through injury and Charlie Morris took over in goal until half time. Dai was watching the game from the stand and the England captain Vivian Woodward and FA officials sportingly agreed to allow him to fill the position for the remainder of the match.

When his soccer career came to an end, Davies returned to Swinton to captain the rugby league side before moving to Leigh, where he was forced to retire through injury in 1913. His brother Dan was also a rugby league player with the club but was unsuccessful in his efforts to break into soccer. Dai won a rugby league Challenge Cup medal in 1900 and, with Dan, represented Wales at rugby league against England in 1910. During the First World War, Davies and his brother Dan served in the 2nd Salford Battalion (Swinton Pals) of the 19th Lancashire Fusiliers, and it was Davies who organised the sporting activities of the Pals at their training camp in north Wales. After the war, Davies assisted Swinton Park amateur RLFC. He remains, to this day, the only man who has appeared in the final of both the FA Cup and RL Challenge Cup. He is believed to have worked in the 1930s as a club steward.

Honours:
Bolton Wdrs - FA Cup finalists 1904

224 John Hughes
B: Liscard (Eng); 10 Feb 1876
D: Wallasey (Eng); 5 Jul 1950
Wing half (5ft 8ins, 11st 7lbs)
3 caps: (Liverpool) v Sco, Eng, Ire 1905

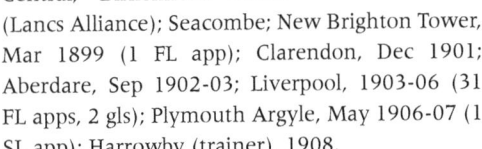

Career: Liscard Young Men's Friendly Society; Liscard Central; Birkenhead Locos (Lancs Alliance); Seacombe; New Brighton Tower, Mar 1899 (1 FL app); Clarendon, Dec 1901; Aberdare, Sep 1902-03; Liverpool, 1903-06 (31 FL apps, 2 gls); Plymouth Argyle, May 1906-07 (1 SL app); Harrowby (trainer), 1908.

According to a 1902 profile, 'as a half-back Hughes is a great success at Aberdare and he has gained a reputation through the judgement he displays in passing to his forwards and by the soundness of his tackling. Hughes is a total abstainer and a great believer in daily training. He is never out of condition, and a good future is before him'. Jack `Geezer' Hughes gained his early soccer experience in Wallasey, assisting New Brighton Tower to the Liverpool and District Combination championship, the Cheshire Cup and the Liverpool Cup. He had turned professional with Birkenhead Locos in the Lancashire Alliance but was signed by Liverpool from south Wales league club Aberdare. He was recommended for a try out in the league side by Maurice Parry and he clearly impressed. A report in January 1904 commented: 'Hughes is about the hardest working player at present figuring in league football. He never tires and is seldom beaten. One thing he lacks, however, is judgement and just a little more of this and Hughes could be classed among the best 'middies' in the country'. Hughes, who according to one report was at one-time lightweight boxing champion of England, crowded all of his senior Liverpool appearances into the 1903-04 season, but was a useful man to have in reserve.

He moved to Southern League Plymouth during the 1906 close season but was already carrying the injury which would cut short his career. His time at Plymouth was a disappointment for all concerned and he managed only one senior appearance before retiring in 1907. Hughes became the trainer of West Cheshire League club Harrowby in 1908 and retained the post for many years. In 1927 the popular coach, who worked as a bricklayer's labourer, was given a benefit by the club. Before the Irish match in April 1905 a dispute arose about which side Hughes should play for but he satisfied both associations that he was eligible for Wales. It now appears that, under the rules current at that time, he was not eligible for either side, having been born on the Wirral not Flint, which was his wife's birthplace.

225 George Latham
B: Newtown; Dec 1880
D: Newtown; 9 Jul 1939
Wing half/Full back
  (5ft 8ins, 12st 4lbs)
10 caps: (Liverpool) v Sco, Eng 1905; v Sco 1906; v Ire, Sco, Eng 1907; v Eng 1908; v Ire 1909; (Southport Central) v Eng 1910; (Cardiff C) v Ire 1913

Career: New Rd Sch; Newtown, 1897-98 and 1901-02; Liverpool, 1902-09 (18 FL apps); Southport Central, Jun 1909-11; Cardiff C, Mar 1911-32 (1 FL app) (player-coach in 1911); Chester, (trainer) 1932-34; Cardiff C (trainer).

George Latham's name is now perhaps associated only with Latham Park, home of Newtown FC, but in the inter-war years he was one of the great characters of Welsh soccer. A popular individual, George acted as trainer to the national side and was usually to be found alongside FAW secretary Ted Robbins. A volunteer with the South Wales Borderers at the age of 17, it was not until Latham returned from the Boer War that he took up soccer seriously, originally as a forward, then wing half. A trial with Everton had ended with the match being abandoned because of snow and Latham, who worked as a tailor, returned to South Africa. He first signed for Liverpool in 1902 as an amateur, turning pro' in February 1903. In his six seasons at Anfield he was never a regular first teamer but was thought good enough to play for Wales on eight occasions. His final appearance for Wales saw him make an unexpected return to international football in 1913 when the national side were a man short and 'poor old George played the full 90 minutes and must have lost pounds in weight'. Strangely, Latham found himself in similar circumstances in 1922 when he had to turn out for the Bluebirds in a First Division match at Blackburn, making him Cardiff's oldest Football League debutant.

Latham was commissioned in August 1915 and stationed at Park Hall Camp, Oswestry before being sent to the front in July 1916. He served as a captain in the 7th Battalion Royal Welsh Fusiliers on the Turkish front, winning the Military Cross. In the first battle of Gaza in March 1917, Latham's party of 40 men were successful in overcoming the Turkish line, only to learn that HQ had, the previous midnight, ordered a withdrawal on the basis of reports that 7,000 Turkish re-enforcements were on their way. The line was abandoned and reoccupied by the Turks only for the RWF to be ordered to retake the position once again. In November 1917 he was recommended for the Victoria Cross.

Throughout the 1920s, Latham enjoyed a reputation as a trainer of rare skill; he acted as manager to the Great Britain Olympic team of 1924 and played an important part in Cardiff's preparation for the 1927 FA Cup final. In 1932, he left Cardiff for Chester but returned two years later to resume his old position. Latham was badly injured in a bicycle accident in the mid-1930s and ill health, said to be the result of war service, later forced him to retire to his beloved Newtown, where he died a few months before the outbreak of war. Outside football, Latham did much charitable work, regularly raising money for the Newtown hospital where his mother was matron. It is said that during his many years at Cardiff 'Gentleman George' never failed to send a telegram to his mother after the match giving her the score.

Honours:
Cardiff C - Welsh Cup 1912

226 Alfred Oliver
B: Eccles (Eng); 15 Sep 1882
D: Glyn Garth, Ynys Môn;
    29 Mar 1963
Outside left
2 caps: (Bangor) v Sco 1905;
(Blackburn Rov) v Eng 1905

Career: Beaumaris T; Bangor, Sep 1903-05; Blackburn Rov, (£200) Mar 1905-06; Bangor, 1906-14; Llandegfan.

For years, Alf Oliver was invariably referred to as the only full international soccer player produced by Ynys Môn but it has not been possible to establish conclusively that he was born on the island. In some accounts he was born in Bangor and only moved to Ynys Môn at age of 11 or 12. The evidence from the census returns suggests he was born in Eccles in Lancashire and moved to Bangor as a young boy. Oliver later lived at Min y Don with his grandfather - a Trinity House pilot on the Menai Straits - and attended Beaumaris Grammar School as a day pupil. At the school, Madoc Jones, a young master, encouraged Oliver's footballing talent and he played for the school XI and Beaumaris Town before joining Bangor in September 1903.

His participation in the first Welsh win over Scotland, in 1905, led to a move to Ewood Park, but he refused terms for the 1906-07 season and returned to Bangor. Oliver was known for his 'sprints along the touchline, inimitable feints and well-judged passes', and was 'alert, fleet of foot, diplomatic and level headed'. A pro' throughout his career, he tried a comeback with Bangor after the First World War but 'anno domini would not be thwarted'. Oliver continued playing soccer until his mid-40s with Llandegfan, and for some years worked in the building industry, principally as a joiner. His son, Glyn, worked as an aerospace designer in the US and was involved in the Apollo moon landing project, being responsible for designing the docking hatch through which Neil Armstrong and Buzz Aldrin passed from the command module into the lunar lander to make their way to the surface of the Moon. Oliver's great grandson, Ben Heald, was a goalkeeper in the 1990s for Rhyl, Bangor and Caernarfon Town, has represented Ynys Môn in the Island Games, and played for Holyhead Hotspur, and Glantraeth in the Welsh Alliance.

227 Albert Thomas Jones

B: Talgarth; 6 Feb 1883
D: Belper (Eng); 28 Jul 1963
Full back (5ft 10½ins, 12st)
2 caps: (Nottingham F) v Eng 1905; (Notts Co) v Eng 1906

Career: Builth Jnrs; Builth T, 1900-02; Talgarth; Harbone Lynwood; Swindon T, 1902-03 (21 SL apps); Nottingham F, Sep 1903-04 (13 FL apps); Notts Co, Dec 1905-07 (30 FL apps); Norwich C, May 1907-08 (6 SL apps); Wellington T, 1908-Sep 1909; Swansea T, 1913.

The son of John Peace Jones, a Builth chemist, Albert Jones captained the local club and was given a trial by Aston Villa but not taken on. In October 1902, he was persuaded to go to Swindon, where he was 'given a severe test against Southampton from which he emerged with flying colours'. Jones, who may have faced parental opposition to his footballing activities, submitted to pressure to turn professional and was soon chased by several league clubs.

Spells at the two Nottingham clubs ended in a return to Southern League football and in 1908 he was described as 'the young full back who promised such great things when he came out of Swindon'. Jones 'followed the example of so many footballers and took up a hotel' in Wellington. He then left the Bucks Head Hotel in 1910 to become the proprietor of the Barley Mow Hotel in Broad Street, Builth. Jones made an unexpected returned to the Welsh scene three years later when, as a reinstated amateur on Swansea's books, he was capped by Wales at that level. At one time he had a gentleman's hairdressing business and then worked as a pharmacist's assistant. He was a brother to Gordon Peace Jones.

228 William `Lot' Jones

B: Chirk; 28 Jun 1882
D: Chirk; 13 Jul 1941
Inside right
(5ft 6ins, 10st 2lbs)
20 caps (6 gls): (Manchester C) v Eng, Ire 1905; v Sco, Eng, Ire 1906; v Ire, Sco, Eng 1907; v Sco 1908; v Sco, Eng, Ire 1909; v Eng 1910; v Eng 1911; v Sco, Eng 1913; v Ire, Sco 1914; (Southend Utd) v Ire, Eng 1920

Career: Chirk National Sch; Chirk, 1901-02; Druids, 1902-03; Manchester C, Jan 1903-19 (281 FL apps, 69 gls); Southend Utd, Aug 1919-20 (35 FL apps, 7 gls); Aberdare Ath, (player-manager) May 1920-Feb 1922 (18 FL apps); Wrexham, Mar-Apr 1922 (7 FL apps, 2 gls); Oswestry T, 1922-23; Chirk, 1923-26.

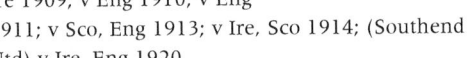

'Like Billy Meredith, Lot Jones owed much of his skill to the instruction he received when a boy from his school master, T E Thomas. Whilst the boys were playing football in the school year, Mr Thomas would be giving instructions and in this way young Jones learned, not only how to dribble but much of his game'. A collier in early life, Jones, who was rejected by Bolton as too small, joined Manchester City from Druids in 1903 but it was not until the 1904-05 season that he began to make an impact. One scribe remarked on 'his cleverness in control of the ball, his awareness, bigness of heart, making one oblivious to the smallness of his stature'.

Jones, a nephew of Bolton and Manchester City full back Di Jones, was an extremely gifted footballer, often described as 'the brainiest forward in the league', but he was also a grafter, prepared to do his share of defensive work. Despite his 'wizardry with the ball' and 'uncanny skill in drawing the defence before delivering a pass', he was reputed to be an erratic shot.

After the First World War, during which he served in France with the 'Sportsman's Battalion', Jones spent a season with Southend before becoming player-manager at Southern League Aberdare. There, he built a side good enough to gain election to the Third Division, but a disappointing run early in 1922 and the desire to move closer to home led to his resignation. He signed for Wrexham and great things were expected of him but he was touching 40 years of age and the expectations were unrealistic. Jones, who was known as 'Lot' after his grandfather, completed his playing career back at Chirk and ran a greengrocery business in Chirk and Oswestry until his early death in 1941.

Honours:
Manchester C - FL 2nd Div champions 1910

229 William Mathews

B: Rhyl; 1883
D: Christleton (Eng);
    29 Apr 1921
Outside right/Wing half
    (5ft 4½ins)
2 caps: (Chester) v Ire 1905; v Eng 1908

Career: Rhyl, 1900-03; Chester, Aug 1903-06 (69 F Comb apps, 29 gls); Rhyl, Aug 1906; Heart of Midlothian, Nov-Dec 1906; Rhyl, Dec 1906-07; Chester, Apr 1907-15 (75 F Comb apps, 30 gls), (33 Lancs Comb Div II apps, 3 gls), (60 Lancs Comb Div I apps, 15 gls).

Billy Mathews spent all of his footballing career with Rhyl and Chester, apart from a brief and unsuccessful sortie to Scotland. He made the Wales squad in 1902, at the age of 19, but had to be content to act as a reserve. Mathews made his two international appearances at outside right, although he often played at half back for his club. One match report described him as 'a host in himself and more than a match for his opponent'.

Mathews was ever present for Chester in 1904-05 and in his first four seasons with the club (both spells) the club were runners-up each time. They finally became Combination champions in 1909, with Mathews one of the backbones of their team. At the start of March 1913 Chester's league match against Hyde was treated as a benefit match for Mathews and Jacky Lipsham, raising a sum of £82-10-0 to be shared between the two players. A great favourite with their crowd, Mathews was singled out in one match for playing to the gallery instead of scoring goals, seemingly harsh criticism considering his goals ratio.

He worked as an engine driver for Chester Corporation, but in May 1915 joined up and served as fitter and shoesmith with the Royal Field Artillery. He suffered badly during the hostilities and his health never recovered. Mathews was demobbed in March 1919 and he died in 1921 aged only 38.

Honours:
Chester - Welsh Cup 1908; finalists 1909, 1910

230 John Tracey Morgan

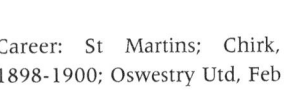

B: Llandysilio; 24 Aug 1874
D: Unknown
Goalkeeper
1 cap: (Wrexham) v Ire 1905

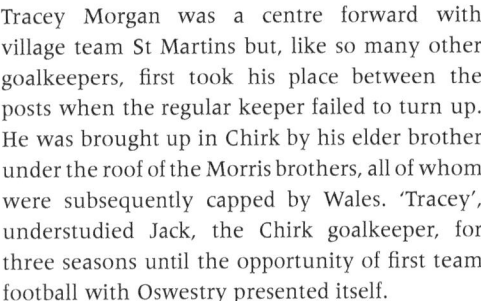

Career: St Martins; Chirk, 1898-1900; Oswestry Utd, Feb 1900-02; Druids, Jun 1902-04; Wrexham, 1904-06 (retired); Chirk, 1908-09; Chester, 1910-11.

Tracey Morgan was a centre forward with village team St Martins but, like so many other goalkeepers, first took his place between the posts when the regular keeper failed to turn up. He was brought up in Chirk by his elder brother under the roof of the Morris brothers, all of whom were subsequently capped by Wales. 'Tracey', understudied Jack, the Chirk goalkeeper, for three seasons until the opportunity of first team football with Oswestry presented itself.

In his first season with Druids, the stockily built goalkeeper stopped 12 out of 18 penalty kicks, and the following year added a second Welsh Cup medal to the one he gained with Oswestry. He subsequently won a third medal when he kept goal for the finest Wrexham team of the pre-War era. A broken wrist interrupted his career in 1906 and for a while he contemplated retirement. His period as a Shropshire FA councillor ended when he was disqualified from office as a professional footballer.

Tracey, who took the surname Morgan from his uncle, worked as a colliery under-manager at Brynkinallt Colliery, Chirk, and had a spell in the coal mines at Jammein-Sen in China during 1907. He left coal mining in 1911 to work briefly as a commercial traveller, securing a job in Glasgow, but was then employed in Germany for a time. Morgan returned to coal mining and in 1912 posed as a single man, but his wife caught up with him in Bamfurlong, Wigan, where he was lodging with the father of a young lady he had met. When his wife turned up, the father commented, 'The game is up, you'd better go home with your wife'. Mrs Tracey Morgan then brought a complaint of desertion at Llangollen Petty Session. In his defence Morgan described his relationship with the young lady as a 'passing lark' and that he was willing to make a home for his wife but she refused to leave Chirk. The charge of desertion was found to be proved and Morgan was ordered to pay his wife £1 a week and meet the cost of the hearing. Earlier, Jack Tracey, as he was known, played cricket for Chirk, as a wicket keeper.

Honours:
Oswestry Utd - Welsh Cup 1901
Druids - Welsh Cup 1904
Wrexham - Welsh Cup 1905

231 Robert Ernest Evans

B: Chester; 19 Oct 1885
D: Chester; 28 Nov 1965
Winger (5ft 10ins, 10st 9lbs)
10 caps (2 gls): (Wrexham) v Sco, Eng, (Aston Villa) v Ire 1906; v Eng 1907; v Sco, Eng 1908; (Sheffield Utd) v Sco 1909; v Sco, Eng, Ire 1910

Career: Saltney Ferry; Bretton, 1900; Saltney Carriage and Wagon Works, 1902-05; Wrexham, 1905-06; Aston Villa, (£300) Apr 1906-08 (16 FL apps, 5 gls); Sheffield Utd, (£1,100 + Peter Kyle), Oct 1908-19 (205 FL apps, 37 gls); (also Tranmere

Rov & Sandycroft during WW1); Crichtons Ath (Saltney); Saltney Ferry; Brook Hirst.

After turning out in friendlies for Saltney Ferry, Evans joined Bretton and in lieu of travelling expenses was given two turnips a week! He won several trophies with Saltney Works and an invitation to play for Chester followed but he was released after just two games - one of which was against Wrexham in the Welsh Cup. Evans was given a trial at the Racecourse and after scoring on his debut was signed on for 10s (50p) a week. A brilliant display against Villa Reserves led to his transfer to the midlands for a £30 fee, and Bob's wages went up to £4 a week, riches in comparison to the 6s (30p) he had been earning as an apprentice plus the money from football.

Evans was unusually tall for a winger; he covered the ground with a long, raking stride and packed a stinging shot. In 1908, he joined a Sheffield United side which was desperate for points and his debut coincided with their first win. Evans had appeared for Wales on 10 occasions when the English FA discovered, after a tip off from the Sheffield United secretary John Nicholson, that he had been born in Chester, although his parents moved to Wales when he was three weeks old. The English FA caused great controversy in Welsh football circles in 1910 by objecting to his qualification, and he was subsequently selected to play for England on four occasions. Evans played for England v Wales at Wrexham where four years earlier he had appeared for Wales against England! This led to him being described as 'the best winger England and Wales ever had'.

During the First World War he worked for a petroleum company and guested for Tranmere and Sandycroft. He played his last match for Sheffield United a few weeks after the end of the Great War and a broken leg the following year marked the end of his league career. In 1921 he became manager of Brook Hirst and two months later, in his first appearance for the club, again sustained a broken leg, this time finally ending his playing career. Evans subsequently worked as a welfare supervisor for Shell Mex at Ellesmere Port and acted as trainer to a works team that included a young Joe Mercer.

One of only two men to play for both England and Wales at full international level (see also John Hawley Edwards)

Honours:
Sheffield Utd - FA Cup 1915

232 Edwin Hughes
B: Wrexham; 18 Oct 1886
D: Montgomery; 17 Apr 1949
Half back (5ft 7ins, 10st 3lbs)
16 caps: (Wrexham) v Sco, (Nottingham F) v Ire 1906; v Sco, Eng 1908; v Sco, Eng, Ire 1910; v Ire, Sco, Eng 1911; (Wrexham) v Sco, Eng, Ire 1912; (Manchester C) v Sco, Eng 1913; v Ire 1914

Career: Wrexham National Sch; Wrexham St Giles (Chester & Dist League); Wrexham Vic, (Wirral Lge) 1902-03; Wrexham, 1903-06; Nottingham F, Apr 1906-11 (163 FL apps, 5 gls); Wrexham, Apr 1911-12; Manchester C, Oct 1912-15 (71 FL apps, 2 gls), 1915-19 FL Lancs section, 1919-20 (6 FL apps); Aberdare Ath, Jun 1920-23 (34 FL apps); Colwyn Bay Utd; Llandudno T, (player-coach) Aug 1923-24.

Apprentice joiner Teddy Hughes followed his former Wrexham St Giles colleague 'Tinker' Davies into Wrexham's Combination side. By the time he signed for Forest in April 1906 as a 19-year-old he'd had three years experience with Wrexham and been well schooled by Horace Blew, Tom Gordon and 'Mac' Robinson. Hughes reckoned he owed a great deal to the three Wrexham men, particularly for the rapid progress he made. According to one assessment, Hughes was 'a stylish wing half who could feed his forwards and knew how to supply his colleagues with precise passes that produced results'. A sturdy player, he was said to 'stand any amount of work' and was an early exponent of the long throw in. Originally a reserve for Maurice Parry, Hughes quickly established himself in the Welsh team and was later captain.

He returned to Wrexham in 1911 and took over a public house before moving back into league soccer. After a lengthy career at Manchester City, he joined Lot Jones at Aberdare, where the pair were the backbone of the side that gained election to the Football League. Hughes, who had a largely unsuccessful spell as player-coach of Llandudno in the Welsh National League, was subsequently a publican in Wrexham and then in business as an artificial stone manufacturer. He died during a weekend break: while staying at the Dragon Hotel, Montgomery he went for a short walk, collapsed and died. Hughes' brother Dick played for Wrexham and Bury and was capped by Wales as an amateur; another brother, Len, was a winger with Llandudno.

Honours:
Wrexham - Welsh Cup 1905
Wrexham Vic - Welsh Amateur Cup 1903

233 John Love Jones
B: Rhyl; 1885
D: Rhyl; 21 Dec 1913
Forward (5ft 8ins, 10st 8lbs)
2 caps (1 gl): (Stoke) v Sco 1906; (Middlesbrough) v Ire 1910

Career: Rhyl Amateurs; Rhyl, 1902-05; Stoke, Nov 1905-07 (13 FL apps, 3 gls); Crewe Alex, Nov 1907-08; Middlesbrough, Aug 1908-11 (14 FL apps); Portsmouth, Jun 1911-13 (41 SL apps, 19 gls).

When the Stoke secretary saw Love Jones playing for Rhyl against Birkenhead, he was so impressed that he persuaded the club's committee to call a meeting after the match so he could sign the player before leaving town. The 19-year-old subsequently made his debut against Newcastle on 16 December 1905 and drew the description 'favours the open game by long swinging passes to the wing men and has the good positional sense to receive the centres'. When Arthur Green was unavailable, Love Jones was called into the Wales side, but thereafter his career faltered and he spent much of his time in the reserves at Stoke and Crewe. A second cap followed in 1910, this time when Lot Jones was unable to appear. After a largely unproductive spell at Middlesbrough, Jones began to re-establish himself with Portsmouth, where he was converted to a winger and scored some crucial goals in the 1911-12 season to help the club gain promotion to the first division of the Southern League. Jones fell ill with tuberculosis in the summer of 1913 and returned to Rhyl where he died a few months later.

Early in his career, Jones was the centre of a bizarre dispute. In January 1904, Rhyl Reserves were expected to play Flint U.A.C at Shotton in the semi-final of the Chester and District Senior Cup. When the other members of the team became aware of the decision of the committee, that Love Jones had been selected to assist the first team in the Combination match against Middlewich, the players 'resolved that they would not go to Shotton without him'. The Rhyl committee decided that, rather than be dictated to by the team, the club should scratch from the competition.

Honours:
Portsmouth - SL 2nd Div runners-up 1912

234 Richard Jones
B: Burton (Eng); 1881
D: Lambeth (Eng); 8 Nov 1943
Inside forward
  (5ft 8ins, 11st 10lbs)
2 caps: (Millwall Ath) v Sco, Ire 1906

Career: Millwall Ath, 1899-01; Manchester C, May 1901-02 (9 FL apps, 2 gls); Millwall, 1902-12 (328 apps, 85 gls).

Although Dick Jones was described in *Men Famous in Football* as 'Welsh by birth, Millwall by training', he was actually born in Burton-upon-Trent. His family hailed from Llanbrynmair and moved to Burton before settling in London around 1885. After attending Glengall School on the Isle of Dogs, Jones was one of a number of boys from the school who went on to play for Millwall. The school was always a strong contender in both the Poplar and the Tower Hamlets FAs' competitions. At the end of the 1900-01 season, Millwall almost went out of existence, with the loss of their ground at East Ferry Road, and Jones, along with their brightest stars Sammy Frost and Fred Bevan, was recruited by Manchester City. He returned to the London club and their new ground at North Greenwich in 1902 and struck up a useful partnership with Ernie Watkins. The pair played a large part in Millwall's defeat of Everton in the 1902-03 FA Cup and the club's progress to the semi-final.

Jones was the first Millwall player, since J W Sutcliffe kept goal for England in 1895, to get an international cap. 'He had to wait longer for the honour than many thought he would', and would also have faced England in 1906 had he not been injured. A Southern League player for almost the whole of his career, Jones was 'a vigorous forward with rare dribbling powers' but ever prepared to get back to defend. One report described him as 'always troublesome to defences, an artistic dribbler, neat passer and a dangerous worker near the net', while another had him as 'a shot of splendid precision and accuracy'. After retirement he became Millwall's assistant trainer and remained in post until July 1935, completing many years of devoted service to the London club. His brothers Edward and Will were also Millwall players; Will died on the football field at Ryde.

235 John Lewis

B: Birmingham (Eng); 1879
D: Unknown
Inside forward (5ft 8ins, 11st)
1 cap: (Bristol Rov) v Eng 1906

Career: Bristol Rov, Sep 1899-00 (25 SL apps, 5 gls); Portsmouth, May 1900-01 (21 apps, 7 gls); Burton Utd, Jul 1901-04 (73 FL apps, 24 gls); Bristol Rov, May 1904-06 (56 FL apps, 25 gls); Brighton & H A, 1906-07; Southampton, May 1907-08 (24 SL apps, 10 gls); Croydon Common, Sep 1908-09 (60 apps, 40 gls); Burton Utd, Sep 1909.

The son of a draper from Aberystwyth who settled in Handsworth, Jack Lewis learnt his football at Birmingham where he first appeared for a City XI against Glasgow in a representative match. He was introduced into Southern League football by Bristol Rovers while still in his teens and in his second spell at the club became the first Rovers player to win a full international cap. A plucky little forward, Lewis was said to be 'small but robust and able to create goal scoring opportunities from seemingly nothing'. His lack of stature, though, was a handicap against 'burly opponents' despite his extreme cleverness. Nevertheless, he usually ended up as leading scorer at each of his clubs, was particularly influential in Bristol Rovers' Southern League title win and had very impressive strike rate for Croydon Common, once scoring five goals in an FA Cup match in September 1908. Lewis gained his only Welsh cap at Cardiff Arms Park as a deputy for the injured Dick Jones (Millwall). He was later employed in the motor engineering trade and in the mid-1940s was living in Handsworth.

Honours:
Bristol Rov - SL 1st Div champions 1905
Croydon Common - SL 2nd Div champions 1909

236 James Roberts

B: Chirk; 10 Apr 1876
D: Shipley (Eng); 27 Oct 1944
Full back
2 caps: (Bradford C) v Ire 1906; v Ire 1907

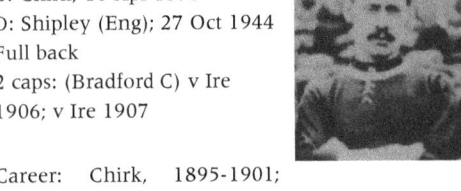

Career: Chirk, 1895-1901; Crewe Alex, Jul 1901-04; Bradford C, May 1904-09 (23 FL apps); Huddersfield T, Jun 1909-10.

Jimmy Roberts was said to have a 'grand physique' and was a difficult player to get past. He 'kicked well and with judgement' and tackled crisply. After a long and thorough grounding at Chirk, he moved into a higher class of soccer, firstly with Crewe, where he was appointed captain, and then Bradford City.

Bradford considered Roberts to be a good acquisition but he was signed as a reserve and not expected to displace either Halliday or Wilson, the regular full backs, yet in early 1906 he had a spell in the Second Division side which clinched his selection for Wales. Roberts joined Huddersfield in 1909 but his form was beginning to become erratic. He subsequently lived in Shipley and returned to Valley Parade, where he was trainer for some years before becoming a wool warehouseman.

Roberts was the first Bradford City player to earn international honours, beating Jimmy Conlin of England by one week. His brother Matthew also played for Chirk, while another, Harry, appeared for Aberdare.

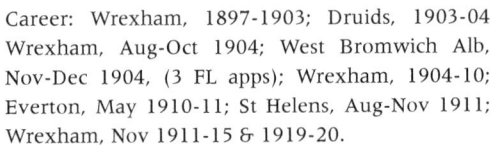

Career: Wrexham, 1897-1903; Druids, 1903-04 Wrexham, Aug-Oct 1904; West Bromwich Alb, Nov-Dec 1904, (3 FL apps); Wrexham, 1904-10; Everton, May 1910-11; St Helens, Aug-Nov 1911; Wrexham, Nov 1911-15 & 1919-20.

A brother to Arthur Davies (222), Llew was an extremely versatile player, appearing for Wales at full back, left half and outside left. He gave Wrexham great service in four spells before the First World War, but the relationship between player and club was not always smooth. Davies, an amateur throughout his career, was once stung by criticism by the committee and refused to turn out until he received an apology. 'A most enthusiastic defender and a very effective tackler, the only criticism of his play could be in his feeding of the forwards', was how one reporter described him. Davies had a short spell at West Brom and earned a niche in the club's history by being the only player to be preferred to the great Jesse Pennington.

Davies served with the Royal Welsh Fusiliers during the First World War, enlisting as private and ended the conflict as a lieutenant. A Wrexham XI, including Billy Meredith, played Everton in November 1919 for Llew's benefit game and one paper commented accurately, 'Wrexham never had a better defence man than Llew Davies'. An excellent tennis player, he represented North Wales and Shropshire, and worked as a clerk at a brickworks, then as a commercial traveller and later as a clerk of works in Ealing.

Honours;
Wrexham – Welsh Cup 1905, 1909, 1910, 1914, 1915

237 Llewellyn Davies

B: Wrexham; 28 Jan 1881
D: Ealing (Eng); 10 Feb 1961
Full back/Wing half
    (5ft 6ins, 11st 6lbs)
13 caps: (Wrexham) v Ire 1907; v Sco, Eng, Ire 1910; v Ire, Sco 1911; v Sco, Eng, Ire 1912; v Ire, Sco, Eng 1913; v Ire 1914

238 Arthur Howell Hughes

B: Llangollen; 14 Jul 1883
D: Llangollen; 5 Aug 1970
Forward
1 cap: (Chirk) v Ire 1907

Career: Chirk, 1906-07; Wrexham, 1907-09; Whitchurch, 1909; Llangollen, 1911.

The son of a Llangollen jeweller and watchmaker, he worked in London for a while before joining the family firm in Wrexham with his two brothers. Arthur Hughes took part in the 3-2 win over Ireland in Belfast which clinched the 1907 Home International championship for Wales and, together with his brother T H Hughes, Arthur designed the gold medal which was awarded to all of the Welsh players who took part in the championship.

An amateur throughout his career, Hughes was quick on the ball, showed deft touches and good distributive qualities. Like so many players he had a tendency to hold onto the ball for too long and try and overdo it, when a cross would suffice. Hughes, who was capped at amateur level by Wales in 1908, 1909 and 1911, was signed by West Brom in August 1907 and played one friendly at outside left.

Honours:
Wrexham - Welsh Cup 1909

239 Gordon Peace Jones

B: Talgarth; 23 Oct 1886
D: Llandrindod; 6 Mar 1977
Outside left
(5ft 5ins, 10st 5lbs)
2 caps: (Wrexham) v Ire, Sco 1907

Career: Builth T; Wellington T; Wrexham, 1906-07; Shrewsbury T, 1907-08; Wellington T, Sep 1908-10; Accrington S, 1910-11; Shrewsbury T, 1911-14; Ebbw Vale, May 1914.

Gordon Jones moved to Builth at a young age and later took up soccer for the local side. He played alongside Gren Morris, Walter Evans and Ned Howell but the team was short of regular competitive matches, which 'did nothing for his game'. He followed his elder brother Albert to Swindon, but turned down their offer of terms 'for family reasons'. At Wrexham, Jones was known as 'a very attractive player to watch, fast in his runs and accurate in his centres'. He was called into the reckoning for the Welsh side as understudy to Bob Evans and took part in two of the three matches in the 1907 Home International championship.

Jones linked up with Albert at Wellington and remained in the area until the outbreak of war, apart from one season in the Lancashire Combination. In 1913, Jones was described as one of the best wingers in the Birmingham and District League. One writer commented of the Shrewsbury favourite, 'He scores more goals than any outside man in the league. He does not believe in running to the flag to centre, but makes the short cut for goal, and is fond of beating his man by nipping into the centre of the field and having a slug at goal'. After retiring from soccer, he became a well-known referee and followed his father's profession as a chemist in Builth, then at Talgarth. During the First World War Jones was lance corporal with the Montgomeryshire Yeomanry, serving in Egypt, and was commissioned in 1917 as a lieutenant in the Machine Gun Corps. The Gordon Jones Cup, which he donated, was a schools tournament for youngsters in Builth.

240 George Owen Williams

B: Wednesbury (Eng);
  15 Oct 1878
D: Wednesbury (Eng);
  24 Apr 1927
Centre half
  (5ft 10ins, 10st 8lbs)
1 cap: (Wrexham) v Ire 1907

Career: Kings Hill Sch; Monway; Worcester Rov, Jul 1896; Oldbury, Jan 1898; Wednesbury Old Ath, 1898; West Bromwich Alb, Oct 1900-Apr 1902

(15 FL apps); Brierley Hill Alliance; Kidderminster Harriers, 1903; Shrewsbury T, 1905; Wrexham, 1906-08; Stafford Rgrs, Sep 1908-10; Willenhall Swifts, 1911; Walsall, 1912.

A centre half in the traditional mould, George Williams was 'a great stumbling block to forwards' and 'particularly useful with head and feet'. He gained early experience with West Brom but spent most of his career in the Birmingham and District League.

In 1907, he was described as: 'a most consistent player, although he does not always feed his forwards with judgement; but he has compensative qualities, is the backbone of the defence and is always in the thickest of the fight'. There is some mystery why Williams was selected for Wales as Wrexham officials were aware of his birthplace. The player's family believe it was his surname that prompted the call-up and that the mischievous Williams may have hoodwinked the selectors when asked to confirm his birthplace. Alternatively, it may simply have suited the FAW to include him in the team to face Ireland. Whatever the reason, his family were astounded when he was selected. In early 1908, he lost his place in the Wrexham team through injury and, with Pryce Williams playing so well, the directors were happy to allow him to seek out another club. Injury ended his career and he died at a young age from complications arising from influenza.

241 Ioan Hayden Price

B: Mardy, Rhondda;
 1 Mar 1883
D: Portsmouth (Eng);
 7 Mar 1964
Wing half/Forward
 (5ft 8ins, 11st 6lbs)
5 caps: (Aston Villa) v Sco 1907; (Burton Utd) v Ire 1908; (Wrexham) v Sco, Eng, Ire 1909

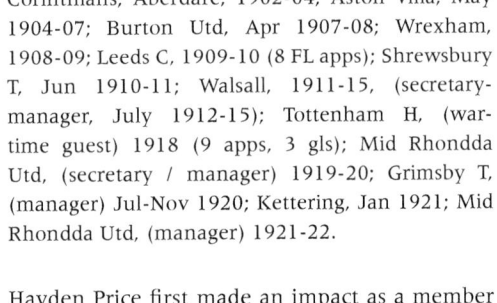

Career: Porth Co Sch; Mardy Thistles; Mardy Corinthians; Aberdare, 1902-04; Aston Villa, May 1904-07; Burton Utd, Apr 1907-08; Wrexham, 1908-09; Leeds C, 1909-10 (8 FL apps); Shrewsbury T, Jun 1910-11; Walsall, 1911-15, (secretary-manager, July 1912-15); Tottenham H, (war-time guest) 1918 (9 apps, 3 gls); Mid Rhondda Utd, (secretary / manager) 1919-20; Grimsby T, (manager) Jul-Nov 1920; Kettering, Jan 1921; Mid Rhondda Utd, (manager) 1921-22.

Hayden Price first made an impact as a member of the Aberdare side which ran Druids so close in the 1904 Welsh Cup final. At Porth County School he had played rugby but became an outside right with Mardy Thistles. Price attended Porth Pupil Teachers Centre and played some matches for Cardiff Association, in pre-Cardiff City days, at centre half but declined an offer to join Porth. An elementary school teacher at Mardy Boys School, he was signed by Aston Villa for £3 a week and fixed up with a second wage with an assistant schoolmaster's post in Birmingham. Several large clubs had wanted him, including Notts Forest, Luton, Bradford, Stoke, Wrexham and Northampton but Villa won the race. The midlands club had a large playing staff and Price rarely made the reserves; he was in fact selected for Wales from Villa's third team. Price then moved to Burton where he had the dubious distinction of making his debut for the club in their last game in the Football League. A strong sprinter with good distributive ability, Price was let down by faulty shooting. He was also a versatile player, at Wrexham he occupied three positions in the space of a month - wing half, left wing and centre forward.

Price spent three years as secretary-manager of Walsall and in 1920 became Grimsby's first manager. In what was then a novel departure for the club, he was given responsibility for signing players and team selection. When things went wrong and results were poor, the directors knew who to blame. Price resigned in a most public fashion by writing a letter to a local newspaper. The club's view was that he had lost the confidence of the public, the directors and the players. He returned to Mid-Rhondda where he was later hit by more controversy: the club failed to pay the players and honour other debts and were suspended by the FAW as allegations of mismanagement, and the organising of sweepstakes and lotteries contrary to FAW regulations, surfaced. The FAW were unable to confirm the allegations but Price was suspended until 1924. The 'Birmingham school master', as he was dubbed, was no mean judge of a player; he discovered Welsh international forward Dai Collier and launched Jimmy Seed on his career from Mid-Rhondda. He later lived at Tonyrefail and was employed as an elementary school teacher while continuing to scout for several clubs.

Honours:
Wrexham - Welsh Cup 1909
Aberdare - Welsh Cup finalists 1904

242 William Charles Davies

B: Newtown; 28 Feb 1881
D: Leominster (Eng); 18 Aug 1962
Winger (5ft 7ins, 11st 4lbs)
4 caps: (Crystal Palace) v Sco 1908; (West Bromwich Alb) v Eng 1909; v Sco 1910; (Crystal Palace) v Eng 1914

Career: Rhayader & Llandrindod Schs; Knighton, 1900; Shrewsbury T, 1903-05; Stoke, Dec 1905-07 (26 FL apps, 3 gls); Crystal Palace, May 1907-08 (30 SL apps); West Bromwich Alb, May 1908-10; Crystal Palace, May 1910-15 (162 SL apps, 18 gls).

Although Davies was born in Newtown he moved to Knighton as a child and later followed his father's trade of bricklayer/stone mason before becoming a professional footballer. He was one of the first players to emerge from the newly formed Mid-Wales League and came to prominence with Shrewsbury, attracting a number of clubs. When Davies played against Stoke Reserves in a Birmingham and District League match, the club's officials liked what they saw and beat off competition from Aston Villa for his signature. A fleet-footed winger with good control, he excelled at pin-point centres. He also knew where the goal was and showed no reluctance to unleash his strong shot. His style was best summed-up by the following description: 'an exceptionally fine wingman and a most dangerous goal getter for a man who does the bulk of his play near the touchline. R E Evans is more polished but Davies is stronger and bolder'.

Davies gained his first cap as replacement for Billy Meredith, but against Scotland in 1910 he played inside right to the great man. During his second period at Crystal Palace he linked up with J W Williams to form 'the only Welsh left wing in first-class football'. Davies would have added another cap to his total but the invitation to deputise for Ted Vizard against England in 1913 arrived too late. He was the first Crystal Palace player to gain international honours and he retired from professional football at the outbreak of the First World War. Davies worked in a munitions factory during the war before setting up the building contractors Keely and Davies, in Wigmore, Herefordshire in 1920 and continued in the business until his retirement in 1956.

243 Albert Victor Hodgkinson

B: Pembroke Dock; 4 Aug 1884
D: Stone (Eng); 1 Nov 1959
Outside left (5ft 7ins, 11st 3lbs)
1 cap: (Southampton) v Ire 1908

Career: Old Normanton; Hinckley T, 1902-03; Derby Co, May 1903; Grimsby T, Oct 1903-04 (13 FL apps, 3 gls); Plymouth A, May 1904-05 (16 SL apps, 4 gls); Leicester Fosse, May 1905-06 (33 FL apps, 5 gls); Bury, Jun 1906-07 (25 FL apps); Southampton, May 1907-09 (56 SL apps, 19 gls); Croydon Common, 1909-11 (38 SL apps, 6 gls); Southend, Mar-May 1911 (10 SL apps, 2 gls); Ilkeston Utd, Nov 1911 (Central Alliance).

'Hodgkinson's parents moved to Derby when he was a lad and he learnt his football there'. His father had been a musketry instructor with the 95th Regiment who were stationed at Pembrokeshire at one time. In October 1903, Hodgkinson left Derby for Grimsby and played his first game for his new club, ironically, against a Derby reserve side which included his brother William. The following season he moved to Plymouth Argyle but found the travelling too onerous and returned to the midlands at the earliest opportunity.

One description of Hodgkinson was: 'a mercurial player who will suddenly achieve the sensational and then disappear from prominence for a time', while another had him as: 'very speedy with a keen inclination to close in towards goal during his remarkable dashes down the wing'. He gained his one Welsh cap while with Southern League Southampton, who reached the semi-finals of the FA Cup the same season but drew the comment, 'he did fairly well but was the weakest of the forwards'. He was then one of several players signed by Southend in March 1911 in an unsuccessful bid to avoid relegation from the first division of the Southern League. Hodgkinson was also a good baseball player and gained two gold, winners medals at the National Baseball Association's annual tournament. From 1911 to 1932 he was the owner and licensee of the Rose and Crown Inn at Chellaston, Derby, while his brother William, the Derby County forward, also kept wicket for Burton Gentlemen and Chellaston.

244 Jeffrey Woodward Jones

B: Llandrindod; 27 Feb 1886
D: Bridgend; 29 Feb 1976
Full back (5ft 9ins, 11st 10lbs)
3 caps: (Llandrindod) v Ire 1908; v Ire 1909; v Sco 1910

Career: Llandrindod Jnrs; Llandrindod Wells, 1904-06; Aston Villa, 1906-07; Northern Nomads, 1908-11; (also Llandrindod Wells 1910-11).

Jeff Jones, who also played for Wales at amateur level in 1908 and 1910, made a nervous start in his first full international but gained in certainty as the game progressed. Although not quite up to international class and lacking the competitive edge from not playing regular league soccer, Jones was looked upon by the FAW selectors as a reserve and deputised for Charlie Morris in 1908 and Horace Blew in 1909 and 1910.

He had learned the game with Llandrindod Juniors and left school at 16 to study engineering at Manchester Technical College. During the 1906-07 season he played for Aston Villa reserves but had little interest in becoming a professional and was more at home with Northern Nomads. Jeff Jones gained a BSc in engineering in 1913 and then headed to the university in Swansea to become a lecturer. He turned to medicine and enrolled at the university in Cardiff but, in September 1914, joined the Royal Army Medical Corps giving his occupation as 'medical student and engineering lecturer'. With the government concerned about a shortage of doctors, they were keen to see medical students qualify and Jones was discharged, in line with War Office instructions, in April 1915. He was later allowed to rejoin the RAMC as a lieutenant, attached to the Rifle Brigade, and was posted missing in June 1918. The following month, his father, who ran the Brynawel Hotel in Llandrindod, received a postcard from his son to say that he had been captured and was a prisoner of war in Germany. On demob, Jones worked at the Middlesex Hospital, then at Cardiff's Edward VII Hospital before becoming medical superintendent at the Mid Glamorgan County Hospital in Bridgend. An excellent golfer, he was at one time Glamorgan County champion.

245 Thomas Daniel Jones
B: Aberaman; 2 Jun 1884
D: Porthcawl; 8 Feb 1958
Centre forward/Left wing
(5ft 7ins, 10st)
1 cap: (Aberdare) v Ire 1908

Career: Aberaman Corinthians; Aberdare, 1903-04; Nottingham F, Mar 1904-05 (3 FL apps); Cwmaman, 1906-07; Aberdare, 1907; Leicester Nomads, May 1908; Aberdare.

An amateur throughout his career, 'Tommy' Daniel Jones was one of the finest players in south Wales before the First World War. Jones was described as 'the star forward' of the south Wales valleys, while one reporter's verdict was 'a brilliant runner and a tricky dribbler'. At Forest he was understudy to Gren Morris but a back injury put him out of the game for a while. As with so many of the leading exponents of the game in England before the First World War, he came from a comfortable background; his father was Constable of Higher Miskin and chairman of both the Pontypridd Water Company and the Aberdare Gas Company. In January 1913 Jones took a break from the game to study for his final law exams and was admitted as a solicitor later that year but decided to sign amateur forms for Cardiff City. During the First World War Jones served as an aircraftsman with the Royal Naval Air Service after which he practised as a solicitor in Aberdare for many years. He was secretary-manager of Merthyr during the 1923-24 season and later scouted for Cardiff City.

Honours:
Aberaman - Welsh Cup finalists 1903
Aberdare - Welsh Cup 1904, 1905

246 Ernest Peake
B: Aberystwyth; Oct 1888
D: Bridgend, Bridgend;
   19 Nov 1931
Wing half (5ft 8ins, 11st)
11 caps (1 gl): (Aberystwyth T) v Ire 1908; (Liverpool) v Sco, Eng, Ire 1909; v Sco, Ire 1910; v Ire 1911; v Eng 1912; v Eng, Ire 1913; v Ire 1914

Career: Aberystwyth T, 1904-08 (96 apps, 30 gls); Liverpool, May 1908-14 (51 FL apps, 5 gls); Third Lanark, May 1914; Blyth Spartans (manager), 1919-20; Aberaman (manager), Jun 1920-22; Caerphilly (manager), Jun 1922.

'The dark haired and clever youth of Aberystwyth', as *Athletic News* described Ernie Peake, began his career with Aberystwyth Barbarians. Together with his brother Bob, Peake rendered excellent service for the town club and developed into 'a most useful half, quick at intercepting, and with considerable trickiness'. The brothers were capped in Wales' first ever amateur international and Ernie was soon sought after. He made one appearance for Blackburn Reserves, prompting an official to comment 'Yon Peake is a right good lad', but opted to join Liverpool.

Peake was an excellent squad member for Liverpool and in January 1909 earned praise as being 'particularly prominent with his clever dribbling and accurate workmanship'. He would undoubtedly have found regular first team football if he had decided to accept one of the many offers to leave Anfield, although he did get a regular run in 1912-13. The FAW selectors were sufficiently impressed to appoint him as captain against Scotland in February 1913 but injury prevented him from claiming the honour. In 1920, Peake settled in south Wales and was secretary-manager of Aberaman from 1920 to February 1922 before taking a similar post with Caerphilly. He later worked as a fitter in Aberdare and scouted for Liverpool. Peake's brother, Bob, was a professional with Cardiff and played for City in their very first Southern League match.

Honours:
Aberystwyth T - Welsh Amateur Cup finalists 1907

247 George Arthur Wynn

B: Treflach (Eng); 14 Oct 1886
D: Abergele; 28 Oct 1966
Inside forward (5ft 6ins, 10st)
10 caps (1 gl): (Wrexham) v Sco, Eng, Ire 1909; (Manchester C) v Eng 1910; v Ire 1911; v Sco, Eng 1912; v Sco, Eng 1913; v Eng, Sco 1914

Career: Holy Trinity Sch (Oswestry); Trinity Guild; Pant Glas, 1904; Oswestry Utd, Apr 1906-08; Wrexham, May 1908-09; Manchester C, (£250) Apr 1909-19 (119 FL apps, 54 gls); Coventry C, (£300) Nov 1919-22 (25 FL apps, 4 gls); Halifax T, Jan 1922 (1 FL app); Mossley, (Cheshire League) 1923-24.

George Wynn worked as a telegram boy for Oswestry Post Office on leaving school and played for Trinity Guild Reserves for a couple of seasons before his employment prevented him from playing much football. He then got an apprenticeship as a carpenter on Lord Harlech's estate and during this time he played a part in the formation of Pantglas FC, becoming vice-captain. A hat-trick in Pantglas' 6-3 Gedrid Cup win at Oswestry impressed the watching officials and he was persuaded to sign for Oswestry Reserves for a weekly wage of 5s (25p). Wynn figured consistently in the Wrexham and District League and in October 1906 was called up for the Combination side, settling easily into an Oswestry side which went on to win the Welsh Cup. In the final, he scored a spectacular goal and within weeks had been signed by Wrexham, then playing in the Combination League. Wynn formed a very productive partnership with Arthur Berry in a very successful side. One reporter commented: 'Though somewhat lacking in inches when compared with his colleagues, he is blessed with plenty of pluck and perseverance. These attributes, couple with cleverness in controlling the ball make for success, and he is particularly dangerous in the shooting area, as opponents have found to their cost'.

Several league clubs chased Wynn and he decided to join his compatriot Meredith at Maine Road, where he crowned a remarkable three years since becoming a pro' footballer by helping City gain promotion to the First Division in 1910. Wynn drew the descriptions: 'a more spirited, daring and dauntless player can hardly be found in the English League' and 'when in the right mood, Wynn is a rare forager at inside right and a capital shot'. During the war, he joined the Lincolnshire Regiment and saw action in France. It is said that he sustained a serious leg injury and would have suffered an amputation but for his protests to the surgeon. Nevertheless, on demob Wynn successfully resumed his footballing career for a few years, before assisting in his brother's coal merchant's business and managing Abergele Athletic in the 1930s.

Honours:
Manchester C - FL 2nd Div champions 1910
Oswestry Utd - Welsh Cup 1908, 1909
Wrexham - Welsh Cup 1909

248 Evan Jones

B: Trehafod; 20 Oct 1888
D: Bedwellty; 1972
Inside/Centre forward
(5ft 9ins, 12st)
7 caps (1 gl): (Chelsea) v Sco, Ire 1910; (Oldham Ath) v Sco, Eng 1911; v Sco, Eng 1912; (Bolton Wdrs) v Ire 1914

Career: Trehafod, 1904; Treharris; Cwmparc; Aberdare, Jul 1908-09; Chelsea, Sep 1909-11 (21 FL apps, 4 gls); Oldham Ath, Feb 1911-12 (50 FL apps, 25 gls); Bolton Wdrs, (£750) May 1912-15 (90 FL apps, 24 gls); Newport Co, 1918-19; Swansea T, Aug 1919-20 (24 SL apps, 8 goals); Pontypridd, Jul 1920; Porth, Aug 1921-23.

Evan Jones was signed by Chelsea from Aberdare, where he scored 51 goals in 1908-09 for the Rhymney Valley champions, as understudy to George Hilsdon. On his London League debut he hit a hat-trick but found the going tough in the First Division. David Ashworth, Oldham's shrewd manager, took him to Boundary Park where his robust, fearless style and power in the air quickly brought dividends. Jones set the pattern with netting twice in his first match and became Oldham's top scorer in 1911-12 with 17 goals. His acquisition by Bolton was considered by the club to be a 'neat bit of business' and, in 1913, Jones was reckoned to be 'improving with each season that passes'. The intervention of the war stopped that development and his decision to refuse Bolton's terms after the war and remain in south Wales effectively ended his career in the top flight. Unfortunately, he had never reproduced his club form for Wales. He resumed playing with Swansea in the Southern League and his play was once described in a piece of journalistic embroidery as: 'With dazzling decision he manoeuvres the ball at will through the opposition and when confronted with a number of players grouped together, his weird wizardry was brought into action and out of the tangle the ex-Bolton Wanderer would pursue his course towards the home citadel'.

By 1920 the competition from emerging young players at Swansea was too great and 'Ianto', as he was known, played out the remainder of his career with Rhondda club, Porth, and his experience was invaluable to the Welsh League club and in 1922 they were promoted to the Southern League. An effervescent character, he was known for his singing as well as his football prowess. On retiring from the game, Jones worked in the Trefor Pit at Lewis Merthyr Colliery in Trehafod. He continued as a collier throughout the 1931 strike, despite sustaining a double compound fracture of his right leg in a mining accident and was later employed in the nearby Maritime Washery, in Maesycoed, then on the railways, but ended his working life with the Western Welsh Bus Company at Caerwent. When his nephew was born, Evan persuaded his sister to name him Vivian after his great pal at Chelsea, Vivian Woodward, the English international player.

Asked in 1912 about the best goal he ever scored, 'Ianto' explained: 'I can't call it a good one but it was certainly a funny one. I was on the West Brom ground when I was playing for Chelsea in the 1910-11 season. We were leading by two goals to one but the Albion were playing well. They were in our goal area in the second half and we had all our work cut out to stop them from scoring. At last one of our players got in a big kick and I ran up the field. The ball somehow passed Pennington but he turned round and, instead of putting it out of play, passed back to the goalkeeper. I kept pressing Pennington. The goalkeeper got there first and I knew about it for he let go a flying kick and I was a yard off him and he hit me in the -------, that's all I remember about it. When I came round, I was on the 18-yard line where I dropped but they told me it was a fine goal'.

In January 1922 Jones found himself in Pontypridd Police Court after trying to catch the 6.10pm train from Trehafod to Barry without attempting to purchase a ticket. He was charged with using indecent language and in court explained that he had played football for 16 years, captained several clubs and 'had never heard any indecent language and had never been sent off the field'. Fining him 20 shillings, J W John, the magistrate, commented 'if you have played football for 16 years and never used bad language you must be a saint'.

249 Thomas John Hewitt

B: Connah's Quay;
  26 Apr 1889
D: Cardiff; 12 Dec 1980
Full back (5ft 9ins, 11st 7lbs)
8 caps: (Wrexham) v Ire, Sco, Eng 1911; (Chelsea) v Ire, Sco, Eng 1913; (S Liverpool) v Sco, Eng 1914

Career: Hawarden County Sch; Sandycroft, 1906-07; Connah's Quay Utd, 1907-1908; Saltney, Jul 1908-10; Wrexham, 1910-11; Chelsea, Mar 1911-13 (8 FL apps); South Liverpool, 1913-14; Swansea T, May 1914-20 (12 SL apps); Aberaman Ath, (manager) Jun 1920.

Described in 1911 as 'a young player of great promise', Hewitt looked set for a successful league career when he was transferred to Chelsea for £350 (£500 in some reports). The London club had some eight full backs on their books and competition for places was intense. One reporter dubbed him 'a capital tackler, sound throughout but lacking a little pace', while another described him as 'reliable under pressure and prompt in his clearances'. After only a few outings, the luckless Hewitt was badly injured at Northampton in January 1912, suffering a serious injury to his kidneys in a South Eastern League game. He was sidelined for some time and then Chelsea placed a hefty transfer fee on him which deterred another league club from signing him. The rules at the time meant that a player could sign for a non-league club, without a transfer fee, while his registration was retained by the league club, and this enabled Hewitt to move to Lancashire Combination club South Liverpool. Chelsea eventually reduced the asking price for Hewitt and Swansea stepped in to acquire him.

Earlier, Hewitt had studied engineering at Sandycroft and helped the local side to the Chester and District League title. The following season he gained a second Chester League medal with Connah's Quay Victoria. He had turned professional with Saltney but came to prominence in Wrexham's Birmingham League team. Hewitt then became manager of Aberaman in June 1920 while also continuing to work as an engineer for Messrs Fitt Brothers and Davies but an accident in January 1921 ended his footballing career. Hewitt, a director of the company, had travelled to Newport to carry out urgent repairs on the *War Soldier*, a Union Castle steamer and, upon leaving the ship in darkness, he slipped and fell into the dock. Hewitt was unconscious for two days and had sustained sufficiently serious injuries to force him to give up the game, for which Union Castle paid him £750 damages in compensation. Hewitt was later employed as a commercial traveller for Schweppes for over 30 years. His brother Charles was manager of Mold Town, Connah's Quay, and Shotton in the 1920s and boss at Milllwall from 1948 to 1956.

Honours:
Swansea T - Welsh Cup finalists 1915

250 Edward Thomas Vizard

B: Cogan, Penarth;
  7 Jun 1889
D: Wolverhampton (Eng);
  25 Dec 1973
Outside left
  (5ft 10ins, 11st 6lbs)
22 caps (1 gl): (Bolton Wdrs) v Ire, Sco, Eng 1911; v Sco, Eng 1912; v Sco 1913; v Ire, Eng 1914; v Eng 1920; v Sco, Eng, Ire 1921; v Sco, Eng 1922; v Eng, Ire 1923; v Sco, Eng, Ire 1924; v Sco, Eng 1926; v Sco 1927

Career: Cogan Old Boys (Cardiff & Dist Lge); Penarth RFC; Barry & Dist; Bolton Wdrs, Nov 1910-31 (434 lge apps, 64 gls), ('A' team coach 1931-33); (also Chelsea in WW1 as a guest); Swindon T, (manager) Apr 1933-39; Queens Park Rgrs, (manager) May 1939-44; Wolverhampton Wdrs, (manager) Apr 1944-May 1948; Cradley Heath, (manager) Feb 1949.

In his youth Ted Vizard divided his time between soccer for Cogan Old Boys, and rugby for Penarth. At the age of 19 he was invited to play for Cardiff RFC while, in 1916, the Leeds rugby league side sought his services, and although soccer came first, Ted was an accomplished rugby three-quarter. He was recommended to Bristol Rovers but was not engaged and then signed as an amateur for Aston Villa, but again was not called upon. Vizard offered his services to Cardiff City for 30 shillings a week only to be told by two of the directors that he should be ashamed of himself for asking for such a sum: 'they could get first-class players for that amount'. It was his mentor, R A Lewis, principal of Barry Secondary and Commercial School, who then drew Bolton's attention to the player. Vizard joined Bolton at the relatively late age of 21, on a month's trial, but did not play a senior match until November 1910. By the following January, though, he was a full international and in this first season helped his new club secure promotion to the First Division. The *Athletic News* was moved to verse in 1913 and described the Welshman thus:

Clever and fast is Vizard
With energy all a-glow
As dexterous as a wizard
When the leather's at his toe

The 'poetry' continued for a further seven verses.

His emergence helped ease the Welsh disappointment at the loss of regular left winger Bob Evans to England. Vizard, who served with the Royal Field Artillery during the war, went on to play for Bolton for 16 seasons and his left wing partnership with Joe Smith was described as one of the finest in the history of the game. In February 1919, while still a prominent first team player, Vizard also took over as temporary team boss at Burnden Park.

A subtle dribbler who could tie a defence in knots, Vizard showed great loyalty to the Lancashire club and earned three benefits in his time there. He remains the oldest Bolton player to appear in a league match, playing against Derby County in March 1931 at the age of 41 years 287 days, his first First Division appearance since 1928. By 1931 his playing career was drawing to a close, and he became 'A' team coach but two years later he left Burnden Park, and ended his 23-year connection with the club. Vizard became manager of Swindon Town and turned a £2,000 club debt into a substantial credit balance at the end of his first season. After five years at QPR, he moved to Molineux where he laid the foundation of a good side for Stan Cullis to inherit in 1948. Vizard, who successfully completed a BA degree course while playing football, was later an hotelier in Wolverhampton.

Fellow Wales international player Evan Jones' assessment of Vizard was: 'I have seen him play some sheer dazzling football, beating man after man with wonderful trickery and also putting the ball across to the centre in a way which made splendid openings for the inside men'.

Honours:
Bolton Wdrs - FA Cup 1923, 1926
- FL 2nd Div runners-up 1911

251 Joseph Thomas Jones

B: Rhosymedre, Wrexham; 9 Jan 1887
D: Stoke (Eng); 23 July 1941
Half back (5ft 11ins, 11st)
15 caps: (Stoke) v Sco, Eng, Ire 1912; v Ire, Eng, 1913; v Ire, Sco 1914; v Ire, Sco, Eng 1920; (Crystal Palace) v Sco, Eng 1921; v Sco, Eng, Ire 1922

Career: Rhosymedre Church Guild, Acrefair Utd; Druids; Treharris; Cefn Alb; Wrexham, Jul1910; Stoke, Sep 1910-20 (60 SL apps, 1 gl) (16 FL apps, 3 gls); Crystal Palace, Jun 1920-22 (61 FL apps, 6 gls); Coventry C, Jul 1922-24 (50 FL apps, 1 gl); Crewe Alex, May 1924-25 (15 FL apps, 1 gl).

'Jos' Jones made his international debut a short time after joining Stoke from junior football and was something of a surprise selection for his first international. A strong, bustling defender, he was particularly good in the air but early in his career was said to lack distributive qualities. Jones was a very consistent player, excellent in the air and a 'tower of enthusiasm'. Somewhat gangling in style, he was once described as 'all arms and legs and a rare stumbling block to opposing forwards'. A later verdict was: 'His height and his headwork usually caused great discomfiture to the opposing forwards and his clever ball control was a delight to watch'.

After trial matches, he went straight into the Stoke first team and almost continuously maintained his place in the Southern League, Birmingham League and eventually the Football League sides. Outside of football, Jones worked as a coalface miner and during the war sacrificed a day's pay each Saturday to play for Stoke. On leaving Stoke he proved a good investment for Crystal Palace, where he scored their first goal after promotion to Division One, and then Coventry. He was recruited by Crewe to captain their Third Division side but was forced to retire from soccer in 1925 when he sustained an eye injury. At one time Jones ran a billiards hall near Stoke but in the years before his death he worked in a bookshop for the blind.

Honours:
Stoke - FL Lancashire Section champions 1918; runners-up 1919

252 Moses Richard Russell

B: Tredegar; 20 May 1888
D: Chepstow; 18 Dec 1946
Full back (5ft 9ins, 13st)
23 caps (1 gl): (Merthyr T)
v Sco, Ire 1912; v Eng 1914;

(Plymouth Arg) v Ire, Eng, Sco 1920; v Sco, Eng, Ire 1921; v Eng, Ire 1922; v Eng, Sco, Ire 1933; v Sco, Eng, Ire 1924; v Sco, Eng 1925; v Sco, Eng, 1926; v Sco 1928; v Eng 1929

Career: Ton Pentre, 1911; Merthyr T; Southport Central, c/season 1912-13; Merthyr T, Feb 1913-14; Plymouth A, (£400) 1914-30 (314 FL apps, 5 gls); Thames Association, Jun 1930-31 (13 FL apps); Llanelli, 1931.

Moses Russell left school to work down the pits but spent his leisure time playing football and rugby. He also boxed and swam, once rescuing a drowning child from a river. He was discovered by Albert Fisher, Merthyr's first manager, but only gave up working in the pits when he was selected at left half by Wales in 1912 to face the Scots. Earlier, Russell had left Wales to join Southport but when the club hit financial problems, he accepted a free transfer rather than take a cut in wages. A bout of rheumatic fever had left Moses 'thinly thatched' and his bald head made him appear years older than his age. Several clubs supposedly rejected him as a veteran but, shortly before the outbreak of the First World War, Plymouth paid a then club record fee of £400 for him. Bob Jack, the Plymouth manager, thought that Moses looked older than his stated age so he travelled to Tredegar to check his birth certificate before signing him.

After service with the Royal Army Service Corps, Russell resumed his footballing career with Plymouth. His unquenchable enthusiasm and gritty determination were an inspiration throughout the 1920s to his colleagues at club and country level. A big, strong defender, he was quick, had good positional sense and was of inestimable value to Argyle. He was said to be absolutely fearless and would kick and tackle with great determination. Plymouth finished as runners-up for six successive seasons - in those days, only the Third Division champions were promoted - and Moses was dubbed 'the unluckiest captain in soccer'. The club finally made it to the Second Division in 1930 but Moses played in only seven senior matches during the season and never realised his ambition to play in the top flight.

Russell played many fine games for his country and in 1924 converted the penalty in Belfast that gave Wales a 1-0 win over Ireland and the 'triple crown'. He also toured South America with Plymouth Argyle in the summer of 1924, playing exhibition matches in Uruguay and Argentina. Russell, who was captain for all nine matches, was accorded the following tribute in a Buenos Aires newspaper: 'The visit of Plymouth Argyle will be best remembered by the outstanding personality and genius of Moses Russell. His effective style, precise judgment, accurate and timely clearances, powerful kicking and no less useful work with his head ... one of the most wonderful backs and one of the brainiest players ever seen on the football field'. Russell was a member of the Welsh party that toured Canada in 1929 and was involved in a disturbing incident at Hamilton, Ontario. The match against the local XI got a little rough and the crowd invaded the pitch and surrounded Russell. The unflappable Moses remained calm until one of the crowd drew a pistol. Fortunately, the Mounties got their man before he could get to Moses.

During his playing career he kept a public house in Plymouth but subsequently returned to Wales and joined Southern League side Llanelli. His powers were, unfortunately, on the wane and the association lasted only a matter of weeks. At the outbreak of war, he joined the Territorial Army and it was while working at the Royal Propellant Factory in Chepstow that he died soon after the end of hostilities. Russell, who at one time was known as the 'The Plymouth Rock', served on the Players' Union management committee in the 1920s.

253 John William Williams
B: Burntwood, Buckley; 15 Feb 1885
D: France; 5 Jun 1916
Inside forward
(5ft 8½ins, 11st, 10lbs)
2 caps: (Crystal Palace) v Sco, Ire 1912

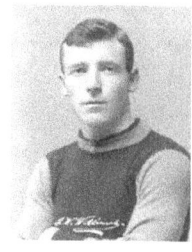

Career: Buckley Engineers; Bury; Accrington, Oct 1907; Birmingham, May 1908-09 (12 FL apps, 3 gls); Accrington, Feb 1909-c/season 1909; Crystal Palace, c/season 1909-14 (142 SL apps, 56 gls); Millwall, Feb 1914-15 (50 SL apps, 12 gls)

'Ginger' Williams was brought into the Wales side for his first cap in place of Ted Vizard and was retained against the Irish as Meredith's deputy. 'A very smart forward', he struggled a little at international level and had 'difficulty in coping with the inside berth'. His form at club level was good and one report commented: 'he has a conspicuously bright head of hair, he is plucky, fearless and clever, while near goal he is a terror'. Another said: 'he is full of fire and dash, while his shooting is generally good'.

Williams, who was known in the Buckley area as 'John Will Farm', had two spells at Accrington and a short stint in the Second Division before turning to Southern League football in 1909. His five goals for Crystal Palace against Southend in September 1909 got his Southern League career off to the best possible start. When Williams joined Millwall in February 1914, the *Daily Express* commented (he) 'can play in almost any forward position but is best at centre or an inside position ... he is a clever dribbler and a player whose speed and judgement have made him a footballer of merit'. In November 1915, he joined the 17th Battalion of the Middlesex Regiment - 'the Footballers' Battalion' - later transferring to the Royal Engineers and was killed in a mine explosion in June 1916 in the Souchez area of northern France. He left a wife and three-month old son, has no known grave and is commemorated on the Arras Memorial.

254 David Walter Davies

B: Treharris; 1 Oct 1888
D: Treharris; Jan 1967
Inside forward
   (5ft 7ins, 11st, 4lbs)
2 caps (1 gl): (Treharris) v Ire 1912; (Oldham Ath) v Ire 1913

Career: Merthyr T, 1909; Treharris; Oldham Ath, (£175) May 1912-13 (12 FL apps, 3 gls); Stockport Co, Jan-Apr 1913 (10 FL apps, 2 gls); Sheffield Utd, Apr 1913-15 (50 FL apps, 14 gls); Cardiff C; Millwall, 1919; Merthyr T, 1919-20 (2 SL apps); Treharris Alb; Fleur de Lys, 1922.

Coal miner Davies was discovered by Oldham manager David Ashworth while playing in the South Wales League. Lightly built with a clever ball-playing style, in his final season before entering league soccer he had hit 37 goals for Treharris. Davies made an immediate impact at Oldham, scoring in the first minute of his first appearance in September 1912 at Sheffield United - Davies had been signed to replace Welsh international Evan Jones who had been transferred to Bolton - but thereafter he did not show his best form. His display in the 1912 trial match impressed the FAW selectors and persuaded them to pick him for the Irish match. He made his second appearance for Wales for the unavailable George Wynn.

Davies had played only 10 league games when he got injured, and soon after regaining fitness he was transferred to Stockport for a small profit. A player of excellent ball control, his tricky, mazy runs made him popular with the crowds. He enjoyed the best of his league career at Sheffield United but the war put paid to his ambitions. He was on Millwall Athletic's books in 1919 and then had one season back at Merthyr before returning to junior soccer with his home town club. Davies was a colliery labourer at the age of 14 and returned to the pits once his league career ended, working at the Ocean Colliery for 50 years.

Honours:
Treharris – S Wales & Monmouthshire Cup 1911

255 John Evans

B: Bala; 31 Jan 1889
D: Cardiff; 24 Sep 1971
Winger (5ft 11ins, 12st)
8 caps (1 gl): (Cardiff C) v Ire 1912; v Ire 1913; v Sco 1914; v Ire, Sco 1920; v Ire 1922; v Eng, Ire 1923

Career: Bala Wdrs; Welshpool, 1907-08; Wrexham, Mar 1908-09; Cwmparc Wdrs; Treorchy Utd; Cardiff City, Jul 1910-25 (183 FL apps, 6 gls) (war-time football - Cardiff C in 1915, Stockport Co in 1916); Bristol Rov, Jun 1926-28 (64 FL apps, 7 gls).

As a youngster, apprentice printer Jack Evans turned out for Bala Wanderers in preference to Bala Press, for whom his three older brothers played. After sustaining a serious shoulder injury while playing for Wrexham in a Combination match, he was reputedly told that his football career was at an end. Another version has it that Jack was sacked for failing to turn up for work on Monday after playing for Wrexham and staying over the weekend. A friend from the Rhondda area suggested he could find work as a printer in the south so he migrated to Treorchy. The shoulder improved and while competing in junior football he came to the notice of Cardiff City. Evans, described as a 'raw-boned youth', became the first ever professional signed by Cardiff when he accepted a 6s (30p) signing on fee. In his first season he scored his side's first goal in the friendly against Aston Villa to mark the opening of Ninian Park on 1 September 1910, and was the subject of an unsuccessful £300 bid by Bradford City. Two years later, he was the first Cardiff player to be capped when he was called up as a late substitute for Ted Vizard. It is said that when he returned to Bala in 1912, having made his international debut, he presented his mother with four gold sovereigns and his cap. His mother responded 'Did you get these for kicking wind'?

Following Army service, Evans returned to the Cardiff club that had gained election to the Football League in 1920. Inevitably, he marked his league debut against Stockport with a goal. Nicknamed the 'Bala Bang' on account of his fearsome shooting power, Evans broke the wrist of one goalkeeper and once knocked Manchester City's Sharpe out cold. The speedy winger was rarely off form and his crosses from the left wing were pinpoint in accuracy, a skill, it was said, which was due in part to Billy Meredith's coaching. Jack's career at Ninian Park ended in 1925, by which time he was beginning to take on Meredith's mantle as the 'Peter Pan of Soccer'. He linked up with Joe Clennell, his former Cardiff colleague, at Bristol Rovers before finally bringing a great career to an end in May 1928 and retiring to become a full-time printing compositor for the *Western Mail* newspaper.

On Evans' retirement, Len Davies wrote: 'What a great outside left he was. He began playing for Cardiff City before some of us had left our mother's apron strings. But after years of loyal service to the City club he could still hold his own with the best when Cardiff City became a First Division club. Jack was in my opinion one of the greatest players Wales produced. I certainly cannot recall a player who could middle the ball with uncanny precision he could. And what a wonderful shot he was. I doubt if there was a player who could hit a ball harder. I do recall very distinctly that on one occasion he broke a goalkeeper's finger'.

Honours:
Cardiff C – Welsh Cup 1920, 1922, 1923

256 Leonard Frank Newton

B: Halifax (NS, Can);
    23 Apr 1888
D: Cardiff; 7 Feb 1939
Centre forward/Centre half
1 cap: (Cardiff Corinthians) v Ire 1912

Career: St Vincent's 1904; Cardiff Post Office; Cardiff C, 1912-14 (4 SL apps - also on Cardiff Corinthians' books in this period).

Newton began work at Cardiff Post Office in 1903 as a sorting clerk and telegraphist and eventually rose to become superintendent. From the early years of the twentieth century the young centre forward was an integral part of the Cardiff Post Office team, a club he helped formed and which played in the Cardiff Wednesday League. Newton created a good impression on the selectors with his performance at centre half in the amateur international in February 1912. Facing the prolific England goalscorer Vivian Woodward, the Cardiff man acquitted himself well. With the senior international scheduled for Ninian Park a few weeks later, the FAW cannily called upon two Cardiff players in Newton and Jack Evans.

Although he was on Cardiff City's books for three seasons he had difficulty in securing a first team place and made only four appearances in the Southern league. He played mostly for the Post Office and Cardiff Corinthians and was reckoned to be 'a rare worker and tackler'.

257 William Ellis Bailiff

B: Ruabon; 19 Mar 1882
D: Aberdare; 12 Apr 1972
Goalkeeper (6ft 1in, 11st 4lbs)
4 caps: (Llanelli) v Ire, Sco, Eng 1913; v Ire 1920

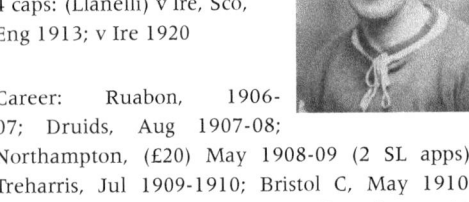

Career: Ruabon, 1906-07; Druids, Aug 1907-08; Northampton, (£20) May 1908-09 (2 SL apps); Treharris, Jul 1909-1910; Bristol C, May 1910-11; Treharris, Oct 1911-12; Llanelli, Jul 1912-20; Bargoed, 1920-21; Llanelli, Mar 1924.

Bailiff was the son of a Ruabon hairdresser and his first job was as a labourer in a local brickworks. He was a late starter and followed Lloyd Davies - another Druids player - to Northampton, but eventually settled in southern Wales. Bailiff was an unorthodox goalkeeper, 'quick, agile with a safe pair of hands', but inclined to hot-headedness on occasions.

Cardiff City were keen to sign him in 1912 but Llanelli beat them to his signature. Treharris were loath to part with him but 'were not in strong financial circumstances'. While at Llanelli, he was employed at a steel works, where an industrial accident in 1913 almost ended his career prematurely. He was surprisingly preferred to R O Evans for the 1913 internationals by a majority of two among the FAW selectors, but justified his selection. In March the same year a First Division club, thought to be Everton, were said to be 'prepared to offer to offer a sum approaching four figures' for Bailiff but the negotiations came to nothing.

Bailiff was unexpectedly recalled to international duty in 1920 when his great rival Ted Peers was unable to secure his release from Port Vale. He retired from soccer at the age of 39 to work as a platelayer on the railways but wasn't quite done with the game. Llanelli were unable to find what they called a 'competent goalkeeper' and Billy Bailiff, as he was known to the club's supporters, had been retired for a couple of season when in March 1924 he was recruited by the Southern League side.

In 1912 Bailiff scored a penalty in Llanelli's record win 17-1 win against Treharris at Halfway Park, while wearing a mackintosh and holding an umbrella. Bailiff was granted a benefit match by Llanelli in early March 1920, for which Billy Meredith assembled a Wales XI team of mostly Cardiff City players plus Ivor Jones and Meredith himself.

Honours:
Llanelli - Welsh Cup finalists 1914

258 Walter Otto Davies

B: Bistre, Buckley; 29 Sep 1888
D: London (Eng); 20 May 1937
Centre forward (5ft 7ins, 11st, 4lbs)
5 caps (1 gl): (Millwall) v Ire, Sco, Eng 1913; v Ire, Sco 1914

Career: Army football; Metrogas; Millwall, Oct 1911-20 (113 SL apps, 65 gls).

One of six brothers, Davies was born in Bistre in Flintshire but brought up in London where his father, Alderman D J Davies, became Mayor of West Ham in 1920-21. When one of his brothers died at Leytonstone in a junior football match, his parents ordered him to stop playing. Walter (his second name came from a German army general friend of his father) joined the Army and, now no longer under his parents' watchful eye, began playing for the 2nd Bedfordshire Regiment while stationed in Gibraltar. On demob, he joined Metrogas (Old Kent Road) but soon turned professional with Millwall and was in their first team within three weeks.

Davies emerged as the goalscoring sensation of the 1912-13 season and 'almost fabulous offers' were made for his services. A deadly finisher, he had balance, speed and extraordinary ball control. Wally would leave defenders flat footed in his 'amazing dashes for goal' and was 'quite untiring'. Another report commented: 'he traps the ball nicely, turns on it when tackled, slips through with the ball after making an opening. Nearing goal he plays hard on to the backs. Whenever he is in the vicinity of the goal, the 'keeper has an anxious time'. Davies scored from 30 yards against England at Bristol, and his solo effort for Millwall against Bradford in 1914 was reckoned by many to be the best ever scored at the Den.

During the war, Davies was a pioneer with the Royal Engineers and served in Italy. He once turned out for Millwall in a war-time match against Clapton Orient, scoring a hat-trick wearing Army boots. After the war a knee injury ended his career and he became groundsman at Chelmsford. By the 1930s, he was working as a docks labourer and was found drowned in Bow Creek in 1937: the coroner's jury returning an open verdict. His birth certificate, acquired by Millwall historians, shows that his surname at birth was Davies, not Davis.

259 Edward James Roberts

B: Mold; 7 Jan 1891
D: Mold; 1961
Outside left
   (5ft 8ins, 11st, 2lbs)
2 caps (1 gl): (Wrexham) v Ire, Sco 1913

Career: Mold Villa, 1905-07; Mold T, 1907-10; Wrexham, c/season 1910-13; Crewe Alex, May 1913-14; Everton, Apr 1914-16 (1 FL app); Tranmere Rov, 1920-21; Crewe Alex, 1921-22; Wrexham, 1922-23 (6 FL apps); Mold T, 1924.

An early starter, Roberts joined Mold Villa at 14 but was progressed to Mold Town who played in the Liverpool County Combination. He was the club's top scorer in their Chester League championship season of 1907-08. 'A spirited player', he was reckoned to be 'a very effective forward' but was sometimes criticised for holding onto the ball for too long.

In 1910, Roberts joined Wrexham, then competing in the Birmingham League, and crowned his first season at the Racecourse with an amateur cap. Two years later he came into the Wales senior side in place of Lot Jones and scored on his debut. Roberts was recruited by Crewe along with Irish international forward Cunningham and one newspaper commented approvingly on his displays: '(his) clever manipulation of the ball, coupled with his shooting makes him a thorn in the side of his opponents'. His good form at Crewe suggested that he was well able to cope with a higher standard of football but he was unfortunate to arrive at Everton a few months before the outbreak of war and made only one First Division appearance. Roberts ended his career back with Mold Town where he also worked as shoe repairer.

Honours:
Wrexham - Welsh Cup 1911

260 Edward John Peers

B: Connah's Quay;
   31 Dec 1886
D: Wolverhampton (Eng);
   20 Sep 1935
Goalkeeper
   (5ft 10ins, 12st, 5lbs)
12 caps: (Wolverhampton Wdrs) v Ire, Sco, Eng 1914; v Sco, Eng 1920; v Sco, Eng, Ire 1921; (Port Vale) v Sco, Eng, Ire 1922; v Eng 1923

Career: Connah's Quay Jnrs, 1906-07; Connah's Quay Vic, 1907-08; Connah's Quay, Jul 1908-11; Wolverhampton Wdrs, (£50) Apr 1911-21 (186 FL apps); also Stoke in the war-time Victory League; Hednesford T, Aug 1921; Port Vale, 1921-23 (57 FL apps); Hednesford T; also Buckley and Connah's Quay Twenties.

The only son of master mariner, Captain Edward J Peers, young 'Teddy' gained early honours with junior clubs - a Chester League championship medal with Connah's Quay Vics and a Welsh Cup finalist's medal with the town's premier club. He was granted a trial with Wolves after giving an outstanding display for Connah's Quay against Northern Nomads in a Welsh Cup tie (won 3-1) and it was mostly due to his display that his side beat Nomads. Peers played so well in the trial – the final match of the 1910-11 season – that he was selected for Wolves' first team and he proved to be a loyal servant to the club, making 245 appearances including cup ties. Like so many goalkeepers, Peers began as an outfielder, at outside right, but later at full back. An agile and consistent custodian between the posts, Peers made full use of his enormous hands and was very safe.

He made his last FA Cup appearance for Wolves in the 1920-21 season during which they faced Spurs in the final. Peers did not feature in the final, having lost his place to Noel George after the FA Cup second round replay, and had to watch the 1921 final from the sidelines. Another disappointment for Peers was that he would have added to his Welsh appearances if Port Vale had been more amenable to his release. After retiring, he kept a succession of public houses in Wolverhampton, including the White Rose, the Horse and Jockey, the New Inn and, from 1932 until his early death, Peers was the landlord at the Swan Garden Tavern. One tribute after his death read: 'Peers was a brilliant, reliable goalkeeper, and when he retired the game lost one of the best players it ever saw. He was the perfect gentleman on and off the football field and not once did I see him play a poor game'. His fellow Welsh international player Evan Jones reckoned Peers was one of the best goalkeepers he had played against.

Honours:
Stoke - FL Lancashire Section champions 1918
Connah's Quay - Welsh Cup finalists 1911

261 William Jennings

B: Barry; 25 Feb 1893
D: Penarth; 12 Nov 1968
Full/Half back
(5ft 9ins, 11st 9lbs)
11 caps: (Bolton Wdrs) v Sco Eng 1914; v Sco 1920; v Eng, Ire 1923; v Sco, Eng, Ire 1924; v Sco, Ire 1927; v Sco 1929

Career: Romilly Rd Sch (Barry); Romilly Old Boys; Wales Schoolboys; Bethel Baptists; Barry W E; Bolton Wdrs, Aug 1912-31 (258 FL apps, 2 gls); Notts Co, (coach/manager) Oct 1931–May 1934; Cardiff C, (coach) Jan 1934, (manager) Apr 1937-39; Barry T, (general adviser) May 1948-Jan 1949.

Bill Jennings was first capped by Wales in the very first schoolboy international, in April 1907 at Walsall, and subsequently joined Bethel Baptists in the Cardiff and District League, winning the Cardiff and District League second division championship. He moved to Bolton from the West End club and began an association, initially playing at full back before 'he found his proper place at left half', that was to last 19 years. Jennings, who overcame two serious injuries during his career, remained with the Trotters for so long that he earned three benefits. During the First World War he enlisted in November 1915 and served with the mechanical transport repair unit, then in the Royal Flying Corps.

A loyal clubman, Jennings was a real artist, capable of brilliance at full back or half back. His calm assurance lent great steadiness to many a Bolton defence. He played in the first FA Cup final at Wembley, and the shirt he wore in that famous final sold in 2014 for £6,000, along with a gold watch for winning the match (£1,000) and his winner's medal from 1926 (£4,000). Towards the end of his playing career Jennings took to coaching the younger players at Burnden Park and, on retirement, moved to Notts County where he became coach and part-time scout, then manager. A further move followed in 1934, to Cardiff City, where he initially worked as a coach before being appointed manager in 1937, succeeding Watts-Jones. The Cardiff chairman had publicly expressed his disappointment at the quality of the applications for the manager's post so the directors decided to appoint Jennings for the following 12 months. It was hardly the most confident backing, but the appointment was nevertheless a popular one. His period in charge at Ninian Park was, however, largely unsuccessful and a few months before the outbreak of the Second World War he was replaced by Cyril Spiers. Jennings then took a job as a motor mechanic before working for Glamorgan County Council until his retirement in 1958. His sole soccer connection after the war was in assisting in the administration of Barry Town FC.

Honours:
Bolton Wdrs - FA Cup 1923, 1926

262 Thomas James Matthias

B: Broughton; 7 Nov 1890
D: Towradgi (NSW, Aus); Jun 1965
Wing half (5ft 6ins, 10st 8lbs)
12 caps (Wrexham) v Sco, Eng 1914; Ire, Sco, Eng 1920; Sco, Eng, Ire 1921; v Sco, Eng, Ire 1922; v Sco 1923

Career: Pentre Broughton; Mold; Saltney; Summerhill; Shrewsbury T, 1910-11; Chester, 1911-12 (26 apps, 2 gls); Wrexham, 1912-28 (150 FL apps, 7 gls); Whitchurch; Oak Alyn, Feb 1929-30.

Tommy Matthias was one of the finest Wrexham players of the interwar era and a loyal servant to the club. His career at the Racecourse began in Birmingham League football and lasted well into the 1920s during the club's formative years in the Third Division. He played in Wrexham's first ever Football League match (against Hartlepool) and made 390 appearances, of all descriptions, for the club, scoring 28 goals. When Matthias first joined Wrexham, he was little more than a raw and vigorous half-back but he developed quickly and soon acquired a knowledge of the finer points of the game. A whole hearted and tenacious defender with a never-say-die spirit, Matthias was a player of skill and certainty and was once described as 'the human representation of a Welsh terrier ... he tackles big and small alike and generally comes out on top'.

Although on the small side (he was rejected for the Welsh amateur team because of his size), he was strong in the air, could outjump most forwards and always gave good value for Wales on the international stage. Towards the end of his time at Wrexham he stepped down to the reserves, where his experience and encouragement were invaluable to the younger players. During his playing career Matthias worked as a coal miner, keeping himself fit by skipping while underground. He was subsequently landlord of the Old Swan Inn at Wrexham for several years, in parallel with his footballing career, and scouted for the Racecourse club. He later took work as an office caretaker but, in 1964 at the age of 74, emigrated to Australia with his daughter Betty, who was married to former Wrexham and Rhyl goalkeeper Bert Jones. Matthias's grandson Alan was selected for Australia's Olympic basketball team but was unable to play because of problems with his nationality papers, not once but twice.

Honours:
Wrexham - Welsh Cup 1914, 1915, 1921, 1925; finalists 1920

263 Alfred Stanley Rowlands

B: Wem (Eng); 12 Jan 1889
D: Barnstaple (Eng);
   7 Oct 1974
Centre forward
   (5ft 11ins, 11st 4lbs)
1 cap: (Tranmere Rov) v Eng 1914

Career: Snailbeach White Stars, 1905; Abbey Jnrs; Montgomery; Welshpool; Wellington T, c/season 1909; Birkenhead N E, 1909-10; Nottingham F, Feb-Apr 1910 (1 FL app); South Liverpool; Liverpool, Dec 1910-11; South Liverpool; Wrexham, Jun 1912-13 (21 goals); Tranmere Rov, Jun 1913-14; Reading, May 1914; Crewe Alex, 1918-22 (23 FL apps, 10 gls); Wrexham, Jun 1922-Aug 1923 (9 FL apps); Oswestry T, Aug 1923-24; South Molton, (player-manager) Aug 1924-26; Bideford T, (player-coach) 1926-27; Ilfracombe, 1927; Barnstaple T, (player-coach) Sep 1930.

Stan Rowland began his career in the Shropshire and District League as a 16-year-old and later played in the Montgomery side that won the Montgomeryshire Challenge Cup. In 1909, after a few games with Welshpool in the Combination, he moved to Birkenhead to take work on the railways and began playing for North End. Rowlands hit 38 goals in six months with the club and was invited to spend a few weeks at Forest, but refused the Second Division club's terms and returned to the Wirral. A second opportunity of league football presented itself at Anfield, but Rowlands sustained a knee injury in his first match and was out of action for a long spell during which Liverpool decided he was 'unsound' and released him.

Rowlands made a cracking start at Wrexham but lost form in the second part of the season and was allowed to leave to join Tranmere. His 32 goals during the 1913-14 season, including a hat-trick against South Liverpool, helped the Cheshire club to the Lancashire Combination championship. Rowlands earned his selection by Wales on the strength of those 32 goals for Tranmere and, despite the gulf between the Lancashire Combination and international level, he was far from outclassed. Although he was born in Wem, in Shropshire, he had spent some years in Welshpool, where his father was a tailor, and the selectors clearly thought he was qualified to stand in for Walter Davies who was unable to play against England

After the war, during which he served in France, Rowlands spent three seasons with Crewe in the Central League and was with the club during the 1921-22 season: their first in the Third Division (North). Rowlands was a robust leader who was a continual worry to defenders. He had an excellent shot, made good use of his head and 'lost few opportunities into opening out the game and giving the wing men plenty to do', and hit 43 goals in 44 matches during the 1923-24 season to help Oswestry Town to the Welsh National League championship. A master tailor by profession, he weighed anchor in Ilfracombe, Devon and assisted a number of clubs in the East Devon League until retiring from playing.

Honours:
Tranmere Rov - Lancashire Comb champions 1914
Oswestry T - Welsh National League (N Section) champions 1924

264 Stanley Davies

B: Chirk; 14 Apr 1895
D: Chatham (Eng);
   3 Jan 1972
Centre/Inside forward
   (5ft 11ins, 12st)
18 caps (5 gls): (Preston N E) v Ire, Sco, Eng 1920; (Everton) v Sco, Eng, Ire 1921; (West Bromwich Alb) v Sco, Eng, Ire 1922; v Sco 1923; v Sco, Ire 1925; v Sco, Ire, Eng 1926; v Sco 1927; v Sco 1928; (Rotherham Utd) v Ire 1930

Career: Chirk; Rochdale, Jan 1919; Man Utd, (trial) Apr 1919; Preston N E, Apr 1919-21 (24 FL apps, 11 gls); Everton, (£4,000) Jan-Nov 1921 (20 FL apps, 9 gls); West Bromwich Alb, (£3,300) Nov 1921-27 (147 FL apps, 78 gls); Birmingham, (£1,500) Nov 1927-28 (14 FL apps, 2 gls); Cardiff C, May 1928-29 (27 FL apps, 10 gls); Rotherham Utd, Mar 1929-30 (1 FL app); Barnsley, Aug-Oct 1930 (1 FL app); Manchester Central, Oct 1930-33; Dudley T, Sep 1933; Chelmsford C, (trainer) Apr 1938-Jul 1939; Shorts Sports Club, Rochester, (manager) Jul 1939-46; Chatham T, (manager) Oct 1949.

Stan Davies worked in the coal mines in Chirk for 12 months before he began playing for the local club. He was assigned to a goalkeeping role for Chirk Reserves, in the Oswestry and District League, on the basis that he couldn't do much damage there and might stop a few shots! When war broke out, Davies joined the Volunteers at Aberystwyth, was immediately sent for training, and by November 1914 found himself on the Western Front in France with the 4th Battalion Royal Welsh Fusiliers. He was wounded at Cambrai and on discharge from hospital joined the Army Signalling School at Dunstable. Davies ended the war with the Military Medal and the Belgium Croix de Guerre.

He resumed football during war time when invited to play for Rochdale, and joined Preston after the cessation of hostilities. A big, strong player, Stan Davies had loads of stamina and could hit a ball hard and true. He failed to settle at Deepdale, the club were not prepared to persist with him and he was transferred to Everton for £4,000. Although a forward, Davies earned a reputation for adaptability and could give a good account of himself in any position. In 18 matches for Wales he played in two different forward positions, and at right and left back. He was emergency full back when the ten men of Wales beat England in 1920, and two seasons later took over in goal from the injured Ted Peers against Scotland, leading to him becoming known as 'Mr Versatility'. Supposedly, before a match, he always asked 'where do I play tomorrow' because the FAW kept in him reserve for any place left vacant.

In March 1929, he became player-manager at troubled Rotherham but found that there was no cash for players and had to rely on young talent. Lack of success turned a section of the supporters against him and he resigned in March 1930. Remaining convinced that he could still play football good enough for the Football League he managed only one further such appearance, at Barnsley. Davies later played for Manchester Central in the Lancashire Combination but, in 1933, was reinstated as an amateur and joined Dudley Town. During the Second World War, he managed Shorts of Rochester, twice winners of the Kent Senior Cup.

265 Ivor Jones
B: Merthyr Tydfil; 31 Jul 1899
D: Swansea; 24 Nov 1974
Inside right
(5ft 6ins, 10st 10lbs)
10 caps (1 gl): (Swansea T) v Ire, Sco 1920; v Eng, Ire 1921; v Sco, Ire 1922; (West Bromwich Alb) v Eng, Ire 1923; v Sco 1924; v Ire 1926

Career: Merthyr Schs; Wales Schoolboys, 1913; Merthyr T; Caerphilly, 1918-19; Swansea T, (£50) Nov 1919-20 (21 SL apps, 8 goals), 1920-22 (66 FL apps, 14 gls); West Bromwich Alb, (£2,500) Apr 1922-26 (61 FL apps, 8 gls); Swansea T, May 1926; Aberystwyth T, (coach) 1927-28 (16 apps, 8 gls); Aldershot, Jun 1928; Thames Association, Nov 1928; Eastside, Feb 1930; Aberavon Harlequins, Apr 1933.

The first star of the Jones footballing family of Merthyr, Ivor initially followed his father and four brothers down the pits but, to their father's delight, the brothers found their escape from coal mining through football. Ivor was just old enough to be called up in 1917, but ran home after a week and was given a good hiding by his father and sent back to the forces. On return from France in 1918 he joined Caerphilly but, in a few weeks, had been signed by Swansea after a brilliant display against their reserves. One report noted: 'His play is very fine and his passing almost perfect. Here is a player the Swans want'.

Jones, who started out as a centre half, played in Swansea's final season in the Southern League and was capped by Wales for the first time the following year, making him the first Swansea player to gain such recognition. By March 1920, Swansea were said to have had 25 offers for the young forward. Together with Billy Hole he formed an outstanding right wing partnership for the Swans, although one reporter described Jones as 'unusually clever but holds the ball too much', while another had him as 'a clever forward who has a tendency to attempt more than he can hope to achieve single handedly'. Nevertheless, the West Brom approach suited his ball playing style perfectly.

In addition to Bryn, he had three other footballing brothers - William (Merthyr, Aberdare and Ton Pentre), Emlyn (Merthyr, Bournemouth, Barrow, Everton and Southend) and Bert (Southend and Wolves), and was the father of Cliff Jones. For 50 years, until Cliff Jones retired in 1968, there was at least one member of the Jones family playing professional football.

266 Frederick Charles Keenor

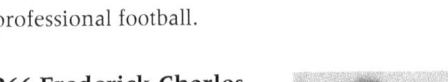

B: Cardiff; 31 Jul 1894
D: Cardiff; 19 Oct 1972
Half back (5ft 7½ins, 11st 7lbs)
32 caps (3 gls): (Cardiff C) v Ire, Eng 1920; v Sco, Eng, Ire 1921; v Ire 1922, v Eng, Sco, Ire 1923; v Sco, Eng, Ire 1924; v Sco, Eng, Ire 1925; v Sco 1926; v Sco, Eng, Ire 1927; v Sco, Eng, Ire 1928; v Sco, Eng, Ire 1929; v Sco, Eng, Ire 1930; v Sco, Eng, Ire 1931; (Crewe Alex) v Sco 1933

Career: Albany Rd Sch (Cardiff); Stacey Rd Sch (Cardiff); Wales Schoolboys; Roath Wed; Cardiff C, 1912-31 (369 FL apps, 10 gls); Crewe Alex, May 1931-34 (116 FL apps, 5 gls); Oswestry T, Aug 1934-35 (player-manager); Tunbridge Wells Rgrs, (player-manager, then secretary-manager) 1935-37; The Weald, Apr 1938.

Fred Keenor joined Cardiff City in their pre-First World War, Southern League days as an amateur inside forward, having been capped at outside right in 1907 in the first schoolboy international between Wales and England. He made his Southern League debut against Plymouth Argyle in December 1913, but competition for places in Cardiff's first team was stiff and it was not until January 1915 that he got a long run out. The following month he enlisted in the 'Footballers' Battalion' (17th Middlesex) but still managed to play a few games for the battalion while training. His unit embarked for France in November 1915 and in July 1916 were involved in the Battle of the Somme where Keenor was twice wounded in action. He was hit by shrapnel above the knee in Delville Wood and also badly wounded in the shoulder, being fortunate to survive - his leg wound was so serious that he might have undergone an amputation - and spent six months recovering in a Dublin hospital. It was remarkable that he was ever able to play football after the war

On demob, he returned to Cardiff but with the Southern League yet to recommence took temporary work. Once back with the Southern League club he quickly established himself in the Cardiff side and made his first appearance in a Wales senior shirt at right half in the Victory internationals in March 1920. Throughout the 1920s, Fred was 'a remarkable rallying force' for both club and country, with his uncompromising tackling, terrific will to win and inspirational captaincy. He led Wales to the Home International championship in 1924, took Cardiff to an unsuccessful FA Cup final the following year and returned to Wembley in 1927 as victorious captain. Charles Buchan, the Arsenal captain, later recalled: 'I can still remember Fred's great display on that occasion, he marshalled his men magnificently ... his store of energy seemed inexhaustible in defending his goal and supplying his forwards with crisp passes'.

In 1928, Keenor was described as: 'a leader in every sense of the word, he commands respect of colleagues and sets an inspiring example by his whole-hearted enthusiasm. He might not be a stylish player but his doggedness and determination makes him one of the most effective centre halves in the country'. He captained the 'Unknowns' in October 1930 when the bookmakers were prepared to offer odds on Scotland, after allowing Wales a five goal start. Keenor's spirit and enthusiasm guided the no-hopers to a surprise 1-1 draw. It was said that the FAW never troubled to think of choosing a captain whilst 'Freddie' was in the side; secretary Ted Robbins told him 'well, Fred, you look after the boys as usual'. After 19 years at Ninian Park, and 505 first-team appearances, he moved to Crewe and, in his late 30s, notched up another century of league appearances before going into non-league soccer. To his surprise he was also called up for one last match for Wales and signed off his international career with a 5-2 win against Scotland at Hampden Park. Keenor became player-manager at Oswestry Town - then playing in the Birmingham and District League - but after one season moved to Lamberhurst in Kent where he took a similar post with Southern League club Tunbridge Wells Rangers. Outside football he had a small poultry business and at one time worked as a builder's labourer, getting up at 4.30am to get a lift in a newspaper delivery van and then walking the remaining five miles to the site. Keenor resigned from Tunbridge Wells in February 1937 but was then felled by serious illness, and spent time in hospital being treated for diabetes. Thankfully, by March 1938 he had recovered and with the lure of the game still strong, he turned out the following month for The Weald in the Tunbridge Wells League.

In later years Keenor returned to live in the Cardiff area, where his son Graham was secretary of the Cardiff City for a long period in the 1950s and 60s, and worked for the local authority. In 2007 the Cardiff City Trust set up an appeal to erect a statue of Keenor at the new Cardiff City Stadium, after the fans voted him their best ever player. Fellow Cardiffian and one-time Bluebirds captain Craig Bellamy agreed to become patron of the appeal committee. The £85,000 target was reached and the figure of Keenor, the man who had become a legend in Welsh soccer, now stands proudly outside the stadium.

Honours:
Cardiff C - FA Cup 1927; finalists 1925
- 1st Div runners-up 1924
- Welsh Cup 1920, 1921, 1923, 1927, 1928, 1930; finalists 1929
- FA Charity Shield 1927

267 Harry Millership
B: Chirk; 27 Aug 1889
D: Blackpool (Eng); 1959
Full back
6 caps: (Rotherham Co) v Ire, Sco, Eng 1920; v Sco, Eng, Ire 1921

Career: Chirk; Fryston Colliery; Castleford T, 1908; Barnsley; Blackpool, 1912-15 (30 FL apps); Leeds C, 1917-Oct 1919 (8 FL apps); Rotherham Co, Sep 1919-22 (82 FL apps, 7 gls); Barnsley, Sep 1922-23 (5 FL apps); Castleford T, 1923-24.

Millership's aptitude for football was spotted at the age of nine by Chirk schoolmaster T E Thomas, who reckoned that if he stuck at the game he would become a leading player. The family later moved to Staffordshire where his father found work and, in 1913, Millership was described as 'a solid, stalwart full back and an accurate ground passer'. His career was interrupted by the war and in the early weeks of the 1919-20 season he became a casualty of the Leeds City scandal when the club was closed down following an illegal payments investigation. Leeds were expelled from the Football League and the team quickly dispersed. Millership's transfer to Rotherham County for £1,000 was a minor sensation and one newspaper commented 'never in the history of Rotherham football has anything approaching such a sum as £1,000 been either given or received for the transfer of a player'. Millership didn't receive a share of the transfer fee as he'd only been with Leeds a short time and initially continued to work in the pits while with Rotherham.

'A sound player with 'timely interventions', Millership gave good service to the Yorkshire club in their first few seasons in the Football League, with some of his displays being described as 'faultless'. A mooted transfer to Fulham fell through and by the time he joined Barnsley it was likely that he was carrying the injury that ended his career. After retiring from the game, Millership ran the Castle Hotel in Castleford but later settled in Blackpool. At one time he worked as an attendant at the Winter Gardens but later took employment as a general labourer with a firm of building contractors.

268 Richard William Richards

B: Runcorn (Eng); 1892
D: Salford (Eng); 29 Jan 1934
Inside left/Winger
   (5ft 8ins, 11st 6lbs)
9 caps (1 gl): (Wolverhampton Wdrs) v Sco, Eng 1920; v Ire 1921; v Sco, Eng 1922; (West Ham Utd) v Sco, Eng, Ire 1924; (Mold T) v Sco 1926

Career: Bronygarth; Chirk; Oswestry Utd; Wolverhampton Wdrs, 1913-22 (86 FL apps, 22 gls, WW1 intervening); West Ham Utd, Jun 1922-24 (43 FL apps, 5 gls); Fulham, 1924-25 (21 FL apps, 2 gls); Mold T, Sep 1925-27; Colwyn Bay Utd, Jul 1927-28.

Long thought to have been born in Chirk, Richards was born in Cheshire and moved at a young age to Glyn Ceiriog, about six miles from Chirk. An eager-beaver type of player who had great on-the-ball ability, Richards created many match winning goals for Wolves and West Ham. At one time Wolves had Welsh internationals Richards, Peers and Vizard in the same side. Originally an outside left with Wolves, he was converted to the other flank at West Ham and appeared in that position in the 1923 FA Cup final against Bolton Wanderers. In 1924, Richards took part in all three Welsh victories over the Home International sides. One report noted that Richards could 'take the ball nicely and knows when to pass and shoot'. Unfortunately, his time at Fulham was dogged by illness and injury and in 1925 he returned to north Wales for domestic reasons, spending one season with Mold Town, the pioneers of the policy of high-spending professionalism in the Welsh National League, before concluding his career at Colwyn Bay. In 1933 Richards left the Glyn Ceiriog district to take a job with the Mid Cheshire Electric Light Company and it was while unloading electric light poles that he suffered the serious back injury that led to his death. He was taken to Salford Infirmary but failed to survive an operation and died at the age of only 42. Richards is the only player from a Mold club to be capped by Wales.

Honours:
West Ham Utd - FA Cup finalists 1923

269 David John Collier

B: Llwynypia, Rhondda;
   12 Apr 1894
D: Barry; 21 Feb 1973
Inside right (5ft 4ins, 11st)
1 cap (1 gl): (Grimsby T) v Sco 1921

Career: St Cynon's; Mid Rhondda Utd, Oct 1913-20; Grimsby T, Jul 1920-22 (44 FL apps, 13 gls); Llanelli, Jun 1922-23; Mid Rhondda Utd, Jul 1923-24; Barry T, Nov 1924-29.

Dai Collier began playing soccer in the Rhondda League for St Cynon's, a church team which was later taken over by the Mid Rhondda club to serve as a reserve side. In his first outing for the Mushrooms he netted three goals, drawing the comments: 'a smart, all-round youngster who was a pillar of strength to St Cynons last season'. Following war service with the 16th Welsh Regiment, during which he served at Ypres and the Somme and was awarded the Military Medal, Collier emerged as a first team player noted for his skill at opening up stubborn defences. When Hayden Price, the Mid Rhondda manager, took over at Grimsby, Collier was one of four players who joined him at the Second Division club in a £200 transfer deal.

The diminutive inside man gained his single cap on the strength of his performance in a trial match. He scored against the Scots but failed to live up to expectations, as although Collier was quick, fearless and a real trier, at international level his lack of height was marked and his passes were over-hit and lacking their usual accuracy. In 1922, he returned to Wales and operated successfully in the Welsh League (South) with several clubs before retiring. Collier was rated as one of the greatest opportunists in the league and at Llanelli he was reckoned to be particularly effective on heavy ground. Outside soccer, he was a leading batsman and prolific run scorer in local cricket during the 1920s. A miner in early life, he became an electrical fitter at St Athan after moving to Barry in 1938.

270 Francis Hoddinott*
B: Brecon; 27 Nov 1894
D: Southend (Eng); Nov 1980
Inside/Centre forward
  (5ft 8ins, 10st 8lbs)
2 caps: (Watford) v Sco, Eng 1921

Career: Brecon Sports Club; Aberdare Ath, 1913-14; Watford, Jul 1919-21 (39 FL apps, 22 gls); Chelsea, Jun 1921-23 (31 FL apps, 4 gls); Crystal Palace, May 1923-26 (78 FL apps, 20 gls); Rhyl Ath, Jul 1926-27 (62 apps, 31 goals); New Brighton, May 1927-28 (24 FL apps, 6 goals); Newark, Aug 1928-31; Grantham T, (player-manager) Jun 1931; Ilkeston Utd, Feb 1932.

Sergeant Major Tom Hoddinott served in India with the 1st Brecknockshire Battalion of the South Wales Borderers, and towards the end of the First World War was a member of the Mesopotamia Expeditionary Force in Baghdad. He showed great potential in the Army as a boxer, winning a welterweight championship in India, and might have made a career as a professional boxer or footballer. He opted for football but boxed professionally while on Watford's books. Hoddinott, who came late into the Football League, was an arch schemer who could baffle defences. His displays for Watford persuaded Chelsea to pay £3,500 for him, a large sum in those days which broke the transfer record of the Hertfordshire club. Hoddinott moved to Stamford Bridge with quite a goalscoring reputation but never lived up to expectation. Similarly, he disappointed on his two appearances for Wales.

Hoddinott was a player of rare cunning, invariably described in match reports as 'crafty', and although successful at centre forward - from which position he once scored a hat-trick for Crystal Palace in the space of 20 minutes - his creative flair made him a natural inside man. His capture by Rhyl caused a minor sensation in 1926 and had the fans wondering how on earth his services were going to be paid for. The signing was a shrewd one and Rhyl were one of the giantkillers of the FA Cup in the 1926-27 season. After two drawn first round matches with Stoke City, Rhyl found themselves a goal down in less than a minute in the second replay at neutral Old Trafford, but recovered to defeat the League side. Rhyl then beat Wrexham in the next round but went out to Darlington in the third. Sadly for the Rhyl fans, Hoddinott moved back into league football with New Brighton after just the one memorable season. He returned to non-league as player-manager of Newark where he enjoyed further FA Cup glory in 1930, and concluded his playing career in the Midland League with Grantham before becoming trainer at Chelmsford City. In the 1930s, Hoddinott plied pleasure boats at Southend.

Honours:
Rhyl Ath - Welsh Cup finalists 1927
[*Hoddinott's birth was registered as Francis and his death as Thomas Francis. In a letter to a Milford Haven fishermen's charity, dated May 1923, he signed as 'Tommy'.]

271 David Rees Williams

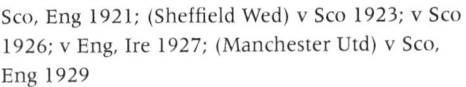

B: Abercanaid, Merthyr Tydfil; 1900
D: Merthyr Tydfil; 30 Dec 1963
Outside right/left
8 caps (2 gls): (Merthyr T) v Sco, Eng 1921; (Sheffield Wed) v Sco 1923; v Sco 1926; v Eng, Ire 1927; (Manchester Utd) v Sco, Eng 1929

Career: Pentrebach; Merthyr T, Apr 1919-22 (65 FL apps, 5 gls); Sheffield W, Jun 1922-27 (160 FL apps, 8 gls); Manchester Utd, Oct 1927-29 (31 FL apps, 2 gls); Thames Association, Aug 1929; Merthyr T, Aug 1931; Glenavon, 1933.

Rees Williams, whose parents kept a public house and was known in Merthyr as 'Rhysi tavern', had to carry the heavy burden of being looked upon in Welsh footballing circles as the successor to Billy Meredith. The expectation clearly affected the winger's performance on his debut for Wales and his display was described as disappointing. College studies had meant that his career at Merthyr did not properly get underway until 1920, but he was considered 'too small and not strong enough for Southern League football', and kept in the reserves for a while. However, his clever wing play and brilliant ball control soon had a number of clubs clamouring for his services and there was talk of clubs approaching Merthyr with blank cheques. Manchester United, Aston Villa and Sunderland made unsuccessful approaches before Williams decided to join Second Division Sheffield Wednesday.

A former Wales schoolboy player, Williams was described as 'a master of every trick' who 'fears no foe and has high speed and rare ball control': his best time for 100 yards was said to be 10.2 seconds. A natural wing man, he created numerous chances for his colleagues and, during the 1925-26 season, Williams was absent from Wednesday's championship side on just one occasion. He lost his place in 1927 and was transferred to Old Trafford but could not reproduce the form that earlier had made him such a feared opponent. Williams was an accomplished batsman with Hill's Plymouth, and Abercanaid cricket clubs and once scored 154 not out. Sadly, Williams, who worked for the Hoover company in Merthyr and coached the factory team, took his own life in December 1963 while concerned about his health.

Honours:
Sheffield Wed - FL 2nd Div champions 1926

272 William James Hole

B: Swansea; 1 Nov 1897
D: Swansea; 7 Dec 1983
Outside right
  (5ft 6ins, 10st 3lbs)
9 caps (1 gl): (Swansea T) v Ire 1921; v Eng 1922; v Eng, Ire 1923; v Sco, Eng, Ire 1928; v Sco, Eng 1929

Career: Hillside; Swansea T, Aug 1919-20 (19 SL apps, 3 goals), 1920-31 (341 FL apps, 40 gls); Llanelli, Jun 1931-32.

Billy Hole was one of the first league stars produced by Swansea and a great favourite at the Vetch Field in the 1920s. He had served in the Royal Navy during the First World War and took part in the Battle of Jutland. On demob, he joined Hillside FC where he was seen by Swansea and was signed on amateur forms in April 1919, making his Southern League debut in October 1919 against Brighton as a part-time professional, earning £3 a week. Hole quickly became an established feature of the side and by November 1920 it was reported that he was the subject of an 'offer from an east coast club nearer £2,000 than £1,000'. He formed a formidable right wing partnership with Ivor Jones and the pair reproduced their partnership at international level in April 1921 against Ireland at the Vetch. The previous month he had missed out on his first cap, against England, when the selectors decided against him by one vote. He remained a Swansea player throughout, but a collision with Moses Russell in 1923 left him badly injured and almost ended his career. Hole, who was 'always a source of danger' and 'a thorn in defences', was a leading light in Swansea's FA Cup run of 1925-26 which took them to the semi-final of the competition.

Appropriately, Hole was first selected to face Ireland at the Vetch Field and scored the first international goal seen at the ground. In October 1927, he opened a newsagent, confectionery and tobacco shop in Swansea which became his full-time occupation after retiring from soccer. Hole remained in business until the 1980s.

Honours:
Swansea T - FL 3rd Div (S) champions 1925
- Welsh Cup finalists 1926

273 Robert William Matthews
B: Plas Bennion, Ruabon; 14 Apr 1897
D: Wrexham; 18 Dec 1987
Centre half (6ft 2ins, 13st)

3 caps: (Liverpool) v Ire 1921; (Bristol C) v Eng 1923; (Bradford P A) v Ire 1926

Career: Colwyn Bay; Liverpool, 1916-22 (9 FL apps, 4 gls); Bristol C, Mar 1922-23 (42 FL apps, 1 gl); Wrexham, Nov 1923-25 (63 FL apps, 2 gls); Northwich Vic, May 1925; Barrow, Nov 1925-26 (9 FL apps); Bradford PA, Jan 1926-30 (112 FL apps, 5 gls); Stockport Co, May 1930 (5 FL apps); New Brighton, Oct 1930-32 (41 FL apps, 1 gl); Chester, Jan 1932; Oswestry T, Jun 1932; Witton Alb, Sep 1932; Sandbach Ramblers, Nov 1932; Colwyn Bay Utd, 1932-33; Rossendale Utd, 1933-34; Llangollen (manager).

Billy Matthews was a tall, cultured defender who believed in positional play, ball control and intelligent distribution. He had many clubs but enjoyed his greatest success with Bristol City and Bradford PA. After Army service, during which he fought in the Battle of the Somme, he joined Liverpool as a centre forward but, when he was unable to secure his place, he followed Alex Raisbeck to Bristol in a £750 deal. Matthews was outstanding at centre half in City's championship side, but was keen to return to Ruabon and Wrexham secured him for a £350 transfer fee and a job in the town. Racecourse opinions were divided as to his abilities: some reckoned he was the most constructive centre half in the Third Division (North), while others criticised his inconsistency and lack of sharpness in the tackle. In 1925, Matthews declined Wrexham's terms and he was released to join non-league Northwich who had also arranged employment for him and, according to the rules at that time, Wrexham did not receive a transfer fee because he had moved outside of the Football League. Journalist George Lerry, a one-time FAW member, wrote: 'In my opinion Matthews was one of the best constructive centre half backs in the Third Division (North). He was a little inconsistent last season and with his physical advantages one often expected more successful tackling and it was in this respect that he was sometimes disappointing. His wing passes and constructive work, however, pleased every keen observer'.

The resilient defender disproved the critics by going on to win a further Welsh cap and a championship medal with Bradford before concluding his league career at New Brighton in 1932, seven years after being written off. Matthews, who was mentioned as a candidate for the post of Wrexham boss in 1936, subsequently managed Llangollen FC, which then served as a nursery team for Nottingham Forest and later, as scout for Blackpool, discovered Glyn James. In 1937, Matthews was again mentioned as possible candidate for the Wrexham manager's post but the job went to 'Captain' James Logan. At one time a general labourer, Matthews was a fitness fanatic throughout his life and a keen cyclist until he was almost 80 years of age, with his distinctive headgear, visible above the hedgerows as he rode by, led to him being known as 'Billy White Hat'.

Honours:
Bristol C - FL 3rd Div (S) champions 1923
Bradford P A - FL 3rd Div (N) champions 1928
Wrexham - Welsh Cup 1924

274 Leonard Stephen Davies

B: Splott, Cardiff; 28 Apr 1899
D: Prescot (Eng); 25 Nov 1945
Centre forward/Inside left
 (5ft 8ins, 10st 8lbs)
23 caps (6 gls): (Cardiff C)
v Sco, Eng, Ire 1922; v Eng, Sco, Ire 1923; v Sco, Eng, Ire 1924; v Sco, Ire 1925; v Ire, Eng 1926; v Eng, Ire 1927; v Sco, Eng, Ire 1928; v Sco, Ire, Eng 1929; v Sco, Eng 1930

Career: Radnor Rd Sch (Cardiff); Gladstone Rd Sch (Cardiff); Cardiff Teilo; Canton Vic Ath; Cardiff C, 1917-18 & 1919-31 (304 FL apps, 129 gls); Thames Association, Jul 1931-32 (27 FL apps, 12 gls); Bangor C, Aug 1932-35 (player-manager 1932-33).

Writing in 1928, Len Davies paid tribute to his mentor Jack Richards who gave him great encouragement in his early days at Radnor Road School. His brother was his main rival and there was apparently little to choose between them as players. However, the only available pair of football boots was too small for the brother but fitted Len perfectly. He then played for Gladstone Road for three years, appeared twice for Cardiff Schools and in 1913 represented Wales Schoolboys against England at Merthyr before a crowd of 14,000.

In 1917 Davies joined Cardiff Teilo and, when they disbanded, Canton Victoria. It was while with Canton Vic that he first came to Cardiff City's attention. His club decided not to play him in a benefit match between Canton Vic and Cardiff City because he was 'considered too small for such an ordeal'. Instead, Cardiff City secretary Bart Wilson asked him to play for City and he scored twice. Davies, a qualified marine engineer, decided to go to sea in May 1918 and while on leave the following New Year's Day, was fixed up as an amateur by City manager Fred Stewart. Mostly used initially as a Welsh League player, Davies decided to turn pro in November 1919 after a game at Aberaman.

At Ninian Park, Davies enjoyed a long and illustrious career and was part of the 1927 FA Cup final team. He had earlier suffered the disappointment of being left out of the 1925 FA Cup final team which faced Sheffield Utd. He had suffered a kick on the knee while playing for Wales against Scotland and although he had recovered in time for the final, the directors decided to take no risks so Nicholson led the attack. Throughout the 1920s Len Davies was a great Cardiff favourite and he remains the only player to score over 100 league goals for the club. Ironically, he is perhaps best remembered for the goal he missed rather than those he scored. In 1924, the Bluebirds required two points from their match against Birmingham to take the First

Division title and were awarded a penalty which no-one was anxious to take. Len stepped up, but missed, and the match ended goalless, leaving Cardiff as runners-up to Huddersfield Town: the closest a Welsh club has come to winning the First Division (or Premier League). After the match Davies was inconsolable, and he was haunted by the penalty miss for the rest of his life. Poor Len left his own account of the incident: '[it was 0-0 when] Jimmy Gill got his head to the ball. The Birmingham goalkeeper was hopelessly out of position, another Birmingham player made a full-length dive and dragged it back with his hands. A spot kick was awarded and Jimmy Blair beckoned to me. I fully realised what it meant. I shouldered the responsibility and took the kick. Imagine my utter chagrin when I saw the ball go almost straight to Tremmelly who gathered and cleared. I shall always look back on that penalty kick as the most tragic miss of my career. The match ended goalless and Huddersfield won the championship by something like 0.04 of a goal'.

In 1929, Davies toured Canada with the FAW party and in one match at Vancouver he hit seven goals against a Lower Mainland XI. His final match for Cardiff, against Spurs in April 1931, also marked the end of Fred Keenor's career with the Bluebirds. Davies captained Thames Association in their final Football League season and played in their 9-2 defeat by Cardiff which was City's record league win at Ninian Park. Davies was a strong supporter of the Players' Union and served on the management committee for some 10 years from the mid-1920s. He moved from league soccer to join Bangor City as player-manager for their first season in the Birmingham League but thereafter opted to continue as a player only, leaving Bangor City in 1935 to become coach at Mostyn House School at Parkgate on the Wirral. Davies later worked as a fitter in war-time aircraft production at Speke, Liverpool. It is said that Davies, during the 1930s, always sent FAW secretary Ted Robbins a good luck telegram before each international to say that his boots were still oiled if he was wanted!

Outside football, he listed rabbit shooting among his interests and if his goalscoring was any guide he must have been a pretty deadly shot. He died of pneumonia at a young age not long after the end of the Second World War.

Honours:
Cardiff C - FA Cup 1927
- FA Charity Shield 1927

275 Herbert Price Evans
B: Llandaf, Cardiff;
30 Aug 1894
D: Dinas Powys; 19 Nov 1982
Right half
(5ft 7ins, 10st 10lbs)
6 caps: (Cardiff C) v Sco, Eng, Ire 1922; v Sco, Eng, Ire 1924

Career: Radnor Rd Sch; Cardiff Corinthians; Cardiff C, Aug 1920-26 (95 FL apps, 2 gls); Tranmere Rov, May 1926-27 (44 FL apps); retired c/season 1928.

Herbie Evans, who was capped as a schoolboy in 1908, was signed by Cardiff City from Cardiff Corries as an amateur inside forward and converted to play wing half, and remained an amateur with City long enough to win an amateur cap against England in 1922. Evans, who turned professional in March 1922, was 'sturdily built' and, in the words of one scribe: 'determined to succeed; more than a spoiler, he is a constructive half back capable of initiating and joining in combined attacking movements'.

In March 1924, Herbie sustained a double fracture of his left leg at Blackburn and a difficult recovery meant a two-year absence from first class football. He moved to Tranmere in 1926 but fate struck again the following year when he broke his right leg, a cruel blow that ended his career. As one newspaper noted, 'A brilliantly successful career has been prematurely cut short and the game has lost one of the most charming personalities that has ever graced it'. Evans was also a golfer and boxer and played cricket for Cardiff and St Fagans. He spent two seasons with Glamorgan CC from 1920 to 1922 and had eight first-class innings to his name. Awarded the Distinguished Conduct Medal, in August 1917, for conspicuous gallantry, Evans was later employed as a Post Office worker.

Honours:
Cardiff C - Welsh Cup 1922, 1923

276 James Henry Evans
B: Rhyl; 29 Dec 1894
D: Rhyl; 25 Apr 1975
Full back (5ft 6ins, 10st 7lbs)
4 caps: (Southend Utd) v Sco, Eng, Ire 1922; v Sco 1923

Career: Rhyl Ath; Ton Pentre; Southend Utd, Aug 1919-23 (98 FL apps, 14 gls - also 25 SL apps); Burnley, Apr 1923-25 (19 FL apps); Swansea T, Jul 1925-26 (7 FL apps); Rhyl Ath, Oct 1926-27; Kinmel Bay Utd, 1931.

Jimmy Evans was a sturdy full back who packed a powerful shot and could really shift a football. His parents kept the Birmingham Arms in Rhyl, and later the Victoria Hotel. Although he enlisted in the Army Service Corps in December 1915, there is no indication that he served abroad before being discharged from the Forces in July 1919. Evans embarked on a league career at a relatively late age, but was soon appointed captain of Southend.

Evans was a sound defensive player with good timing and judgement, but was vulnerable to a fast and direct winger. Despite Southend's parlous league position and desperate need for points, the club's directors released him to play for Wales. Evans made a competent international debut and 'Tityrus' of the *Athletic News* described him as 'a strong volleyer of a snow-laden ball.' In the 1921-22 season, Evans was Southend's leading scorer, converting 10 out of 11 penalty attempts. He enjoyed his reputation as a penalty taker and relied on blasting the ball past the goalkeeper. A nephew of Harry E Stafford, the Manchester United player, Evans was the Rhyl trainer in the mid 1930s and worked in the club's social club for many years afterwards until his retirement. His earlier employments had included periods as a joiner and then as a fitter/turner.

277 Edward Parry
B: Colwyn Bay; 8 Dec 1892
D: Rhos-on-Sea; 18 Nov 1976
Full back
(5ft 9½ins, 11st 3lbs)
5 caps: (Liverpool) v Sco 1922; v Eng, Ire 1923; v Ire 1925; v Ire 1926

Career: Colwyn Bay Celts, 1910; Colwyn Bay Utd, 1919-21; Liverpool, Feb 1921-26 (13 FL apps); Walsall, 1926-27 (29 FL apps); Colwyn Bay Utd, Jul 1927-28; Llandudno T, 1928-31; Colwyn Bay Utd, Sep 1931-33.

After war service with the 16th Battalion Royal Welsh Fusiliers, alongside several other north Wales footballers, Ted Parry signed amateur forms for Colwyn Bay and, by 1920, had earned the description 'the finest full back on the coast'. Trials with Bury and Oldham followed but he was not thought good enough and was allowed to return to Colwyn Bay. It was, however, his participation in the first victory by the Wales amateur side over England in 1921 that led to him turning professional with Liverpool.

At Anfield he was unable to get a regular first team place due to the club having three other international full backs on their books, and despite receiving offers to go elsewhere Parry remained with Liverpool until 1926. A fast, stylish defender, Ted continued playing as a pro' with Walsall and then in the Welsh National League well into his 40s. Outside of soccer, Ted's love was golf and later bowls. He became captain of Colwyn Bay Golf Club, while his brothers held the same position at the golf clubs in Abergele and Rhos on Sea, earning a living through a painting and decorating business he ran with a brother. In 1948 he acted as trainer to the North Wales Coast FA XI.

278 Robert Idwal Davies

B: Ewloe; 17 Aug 1899
D: Durban (SA); 7 Jun 1980
Centre forward
1 cap: (Bolton Wdrs) v Sco 1923

Career: Abergele Co Sch; 1st Battalion Gordon Highlanders; London Scottish; Conwy, 1919; Buckley Utd, 1921-22; West Bromwich Alb (trial); Southport, Dec 1920; Liverpool Marine; Rhyl Ath, Jun 1923-24; Liverpool, Aug 1923; Bolton Wdrs, Dec 1924 (3 FL apps); Rhyl Ath, 1925-27; Welsh Dragons, 1926.

The son of a Presbyterian minister, Idwal Davies played football in the Army for the London Scottish Battalion, and later the Gordon Highlanders. On demob he joined Conway in the North Wales Coast League, but it was while playing in the West Cheshire League with Buckley that his talents began to be recognised. West Bromwich Albion were keen to sign him but Davies, an amateur, felt that travelling to the Midlands to play would be too onerous. When he took a bank appointment in Southport, Davies joined the local club, then in the Central League but shortly to become a Third Division (North) club.

A clever forward, Davies was said to 'lead the line with spirit and tact' and was 'equally adept at the short passing game or swinging the ball out to the wings'. One scribe called him: 'a pertinacious player with deft and neat touches'. His three goals for Wales against England in an amateur international in January 1923 had impressed the FAW selectors, and he was called into the full Wales team when previously selected players became unavailable. Davies worked for the National Provincial Bank in Southport and then joined Hartleys Jam Company of Aintree. From 1930 onwards he played little, preferring to concentrate on his employment with Hartley's as north west representative and later south of England area manager.

279 George Alfred Godding

B: Caergwrle; 3 May 1896
D: Caergwrle; 18 Nov 1960
Goalkeeper (5ft 10ins, 11st)
2 caps: (Wrexham) v Sco, Ire 1923

Career: Caergwrle; Crichton's Ath, 1920-21; Wrexham, May 1921-26 (160 FL apps); Llandudno T, Jun 1926-28; Oak Alyn Rov, Jan 1929-30.

From junior team Caergwrle, George Godding was given a successful trial by Cheshire League club Crichton's Athletic, and was on Wrexham's books from April 1920, but his big break came the following year when he was called up to play in an FA Cup tie as a stand in for the unavailable Fred Boxley. Godding was said to have a safe pair of hands and 'good judgement'. A contemporary report commented: 'he never gets flurried, is a good kicker, can hold his own in a struggle and understands his backs'. He was selected to play for Wales because of non-availability of Ted Peers and did so well that he was retained for the Irish match.

After leaving Wrexham, Godding wound down his career in the Welsh National League with Llandudno. He was secretary to Caergwrle FC in the 1930s and worked as a lorry driver, subsequently owning a garage/petrol station in Caergwrle. Godding's son, Earl, was a goalkeeper with Wrexham in the 1950s.

Honours:
Wrexham - Welsh Cup 1924, 1925

280 Robert Frederick John

B: Barry; 3 Feb 1899
D: Barry; 17 Jul 1982
Left half (5ft 11ins, 10st 6lbs)
15 caps: (Arsenal) v Sco, Ire 1923; v Ire 1925; v Eng 1926; v Eng 1927; v Eng, Ire 1928; v Sco, Eng, 1930; v Eng 1932; v Ire, Fra 1933; v Ire 1935; v Sco 1936; v Eng 1937

Career: Hannah Str Sch; Barry T; Caerphilly T; Arsenal, (£750) Jan 1922-38, (421 FL apps, 12 gls); West Ham Utd, (coach) Jul 1938; Torquay Utd, (trainer, manager) 1945-47; Crystal Palace, (trainer) May 1947-49; Cardiff C, (chief coach/scout).

Ted Drake, the Arsenal and England centre forward of the 1930s said of Bob John: 'he must go down as one of the all-time Welsh greats. He was everything you want a professional footballer to be'. John had left school when he was 14½ to start work in a grocer's shop and then secured employment in the docks as an apprentice blacksmith, when he was about 19 or 20. 'Bobbie', as he was always known by the local newspaper, started playing for Barry Town earning £1 as a part-time pro who, due to his superstition, always ran out last when the teams took the field.

After he had completed his apprenticeship, John wrote to Cardiff City for a trial but didn't receive a reply to his letter so instead joined Caerphilly for an extra 10s (50p) a week. The Caerphilly trainer Bob Chatt then alerted Arsenal to the stocky wing half who was 'unspectacular but whose brain and technique gave him a cool, classical perfection'. Arsenal manager Les Knighton travelled to Cardiff, met John at the Criterion Hotel, ironically owned by a Cardiff director, and offered him a contract. Bob John won his first cap while still a reserve at Highbury but didn't make his first-team debut until October 1922, against Newcastle United. He went on to make 421 league appearances for the Gunners, a club record that stood until 1974, and during his years at Arsenal, John appeared in three cup finals, scoring in the 1932 FA Cup final but ending on the losing side. Eddie Hapgood rated Bob John as the best wing half he had played behind, but John also played many games for Arsenal at full back and he appeared in the 1932 Cup Final at outside left. John spent the 1937-38 season in the reserves, retiring at the end of the campaign to become trainer at West Ham. He was employed at Barry Docks during the war but returned to soccer in peace time, acting as trainer or coach and was Wales trainer at one time.

Honours:
Arsenal - FL 1st Div champions 1931, 1933, 1934
 - FA Cup 1930; finalists 1927, 1932
 - FA Charity Shield 1930, 1933, 1934

281 David Sidney Nicholas

B: Aberdare; 12 Aug 1897
D: Aberdare; 7 Apr 1982
Outside left
 (5ft 9ins, 11st 4lbs)
3 caps: (Stoke) v Sco 1923;
(Swansea T) v Eng, Ire 1927

Career: Aberdare Int Sch; Aberdare G Sch; Wales Schoolboys, 1911; Swansea T (am); Crystal Palace (London Comb); Merthyr T, 1918-21; Stoke, (£1,000) Mar 1922-24 (55 FL apps, 3 gls); Swansea T, Nov 1924-30 (150 FL apps, 13 gls); retired c/ season 1930.

Dai Nicholas was capped by Wales schoolboys in 1911 and was invited for trials at Southern League Merthyr Town at the age of only 15. The First World War intervened and he joined the Royal Navy, serving for three years. In December 1918 his performance for an *HMS Lancaster* XI in the Canadian competition, the Brown Service Cup, drew the following comment from the *Victoria Daily Times*: 'The fair head sailor boy is a hard customer when once he gets the ball and he has a knack of getting it very often and he shows a burst of speed down the left wing'. When hostilities were over, he played several games for Swansea but it was with Merthyr that he turned professional in October 1918. That same month, he entered Carmarthen Training College to train as a teacher.

Nicholas was 'a very speedy left wing' who had splendid ball control, an ability to centre 'with judgement' and possessed 'an elusive swerve'. He formed a productive partnership with Rees Williams and the pair were dubbed 'Merthyr's sparkling wingers'. A bid for Nicholas from Birmingham in March 1922 was turned down by Merthyr directors as it did not meet their valuation.

A serious motor cycle accident in 1923, in which he fractured his skull, sidelined him at Stoke and when he later secured a teaching appointment in Aberdare he was transferred to Swansea. Although Nicholas could operate in several positions he was happiest on the flanks, using his pace to get to the by line and cross the ball for his colleagues. During the 1925-26 season, he played a prominent role in the Swansea team which reached the semi-final of the FA Cup. In later years, he was headmaster of Abernant School in Aberdare, and was involved in the administration of schoolboy football, serving on the Welsh Schools FA.

Honours:
Swansea T - FL 3rd Div (S) champions 1925
 - Welsh Cup finalists 1926

282 Albert Gray

B: Tredegar; 23 Sep 1900
D: Blackpool (Eng);
   16 Dec 1969
Goalkeeper
(6ft 3ins, 12st 7lbs)
24 caps: (Oldham Ath) v Sco, Eng, Ire 1924; v Sco, Eng, Ire 1925; v Sco, Eng 1926; v Sco 1927; (Manchester C) v Sco, Eng 1928; v Sco, Eng, Ire 1929; (Manchester Central) v Sco 1930; (Tranmere Rov) v Sco, Eng, Ire 1932; (Chester) v Eng, Sco, Ire 1937; v Sco, Eng, Ire 1938

Career: Rhyd Welfare, Rhyd Ath, 1919; Ebbw Vale, 1921-23; Oldham Ath, May 1923-27 (100 FL apps); Manchester C, (£2,250) Jan 1927-30 (68 FL apps); Manchester Central, (loan) Aug 1929; Coventry C, Aug 1930-31; Tranmere Rov, Jun 1931-36 (192 FL apps); Chester, Jun 1936-38 (73 FL apps); Waterford, Sep 1938; Congleton T, Oct 1938-39.

Bert Gray's career as a goalkeeper took off when he deputised for the injured custodian of a local colliery team. Jack Peart, the Ebbw Vale manager, persuaded him to turn out for the club and he made his debut in long trousers. Gray soon attracted the league clubs and in May 1923 he joined Oldham Athletic in a move necessitated by financial problems but nevertheless unpopular with the fans. At 6ft 3ins, he was one of the tallest players in the game and he used his height to great advantage. A very capable goalkeeper, Gray was cool and safe and inspired confidence in his defenders.

His career was a lengthy one and he was awarded his final cap when he was getting on for 38 years of age. Gray was a good tennis player and a very keen golfer at Fleetwood Golf Club, winning the Merseyside Footballers' championship in 1933, 1934 and 1936. He applied for the manager's post at Tranmere in 1936 but was passed over and joined Chester. After winding up his career at Congleton in the Cheshire League, he became a sergeant-instructor during the Second World War, and later a bookmaker in Cleveleys, near Blackpool.

Honours:
Tranmere Rov - Welsh Cup 1935; finalists 1934

283 William Davies

B: Troedrhiwfuwch, Rhymney;
  16 Feb 1900
D: Llandeilo; 6 Aug 1953
Outside right
  (5ft 7ins, 10st 10lbs)
17 caps (6 gls): (Swansea T) v Sco, Eng, Ire 1924; v Sco, Eng, Ire 1926; v Sco 1927; v Ire 1928; (Notts Co) v Sco, Eng, Ire 1929; v Sco, Eng, Ire 1930

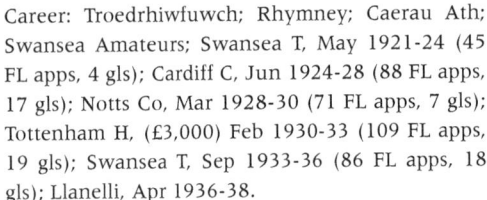

Career: Troedrhiwfuwch; Rhymney; Caerau Ath; Swansea Amateurs; Swansea T, May 1921-24 (45 FL apps, 4 gls); Cardiff C, Jun 1924-28 (88 FL apps, 17 gls); Notts Co, Mar 1928-30 (71 FL apps, 7 gls); Tottenham H, (£3,000) Feb 1930-33 (109 FL apps, 19 gls); Swansea T, Sep 1933-36 (86 FL apps, 18 gls); Llanelli, Apr 1936-38.

Willie Davies played for school and village teams in Troedrhiwfuwch, Glamorgan, before joining Rhymney, for whom he hit 61 goals in a single season. He was signed by Swansea for the grand sum of 10/6d (52½p), filling every forward position before settling down on the right wing, and by the time he was sold to Cardiff his value had increased to £25. A very tricky and clever player, one report described him as 'wonderfully speedy, perfect ball control and the power to beat the cleverest of half backs'.

Davies made his international debut against Scotland at Cardiff in 1924 and scored one of the Welsh goals in a 2-0 win. The following year, he was part of Cardiff's FA Cup side and scored a vital goal directly from a corner kick in the quarter-final against Leicester to win the match in the dying seconds. A serious chest illness interrupted his career at Ninian Park and he was out of action for 12 months, missing the 1927 Cup final, but he came back to be a great success with Spurs. At White Hart Lane, he was described as: 'Davies, the speedy, orthodox Welshman who played many good games and never any bad'.

He wound down his career with Swansea and as captain of Llanelli before taking charge of the caretaking department of Pontarddulais schools in 1938. He died in Llandeilo whilst visiting his brother-in-law.

Honours:
Tottenham H - FL 2nd Div runners-up 1933
Cardiff C - FA Cup finalists 1925

284 John Jenkins

B: Gwersyllt, Wrexham;
  17 Mar 1892
D: Brighton; 16 Apr 1946
Full back
  (5ft 10ins, 11st 10lbs)
8 caps: (Brighton & H A) v Sco, Eng, Ire 1924; v Sco, Ire 1925; v Sco, Eng 1926; v Sco 1927

Career: Mold T, 1907-10; Wrexham, Jul 1910; Gwersyllt; Pontypridd, 1913-14; Mardy, 1919-22; Brighton & H A, May 1922-29 (216 FL apps, 1 gl), retired May 1929.

Jack Jenkins was a cool, purposeful player and a great tactician. His worth went largely unrecognised until he migrated south to seek work in the pits at Mardy, Rhondda. He was beginning to make a name for himself when the First World War broke out, but gained valuable experience in war-time soccer with Cardiff, Portsmouth and Brighton Reserves.

In 1919 he joined Mardy, a club that was to produce several fine players in the 1920s but, in July 1922, was persuaded in to move to nearby Pontypridd. He finally got into league football at Brighton and went on to give splendid service to the club at an age when many footballers wind down towards retirement. Strong as an ox, Jenkins captained the south coast club for several seasons and was a steadying influence on his fellow defenders. He had been recommended to Charlie Webb, the Brighton manager, by F

Osbourne, a former Brighton player who had taken over the running of Pontypridd FC. Webb travelled to Wales to watch Jenkins but arrived late and, failing to gain entry to the ground, had to view the proceedings through a hole in the fence. Fortunately, Webb was able to see that part of the field where Jenkins was in action and liked what he saw. Webb told Osbourne that he would be making an approach to Jenkins on the Monday following the last day of the season, and the expiration of his contract. Leeds United were also tracking Jenkins but Webb got wind of this development and whisked the Welshman to Osbourne's home in Birmingham until the player's agreement with Pontypridd ran out. Jenkins captained the south coast club for several seasons before retiring to become a licensee in Brighton. He was granted a benefit match against Merthyr in 1928.

285 John Barry Lewis Nicholls

B: Cardiff; 14 Feb 1898
D: Cardiff; 1970
Inside forward
   (5ft 10ins, 11st 10lbs)
4 caps: (Newport Co) v Eng, Ire 1924; (Cardiff C) v Eng, Sco 1925
Corinthians, 1925-30. Also **Welsh League** v Irish League 1928; retired 1930.

Career: Cardiff Corinthians, 1920-22; Bridgend, 1922-23; Newport Co, Jun 1923-24 (10 FL apps, 4 gls); Cardiff C, Apr 1924-25 (2 FL apps); Cardiff Corinthians, 1925-30; retired 1930.

Jack Nicholls was the son of Syd Nicholls, a rugby footballer with Wales and Cardiff RFC and a one-time Cardiff City chairman and FAW vice-president. Both his father and his uncle, Erith Gwyn Nicholls, played rugby for Wales but Jack chose to follow the association code. During the 1923-24 season, he enjoyed a startling rise, making his league debut for Newport and then becoming the club's first Welsh international player. He had earlier been capped at amateur level against England and went on to make a further nine appearances for the Wales amateur side.

Nicholls was employed by the Cardiff City Water Board and work commitments limited his league appearances for Newport. As he was generally unable to travel to away matches Nicholls was released by the club at the end of the 1923-24 season. On the international front, Nicholls was reserve to Fred Cook for the 1924 Scottish match and came into the Wales side against England to take the place of Ivor Jones. Although he was a regular goal scorer at club level and an entirely adequate performer for the amateur side, his selection for Wales was a surprise and carried a hint of nepotism. Nicholls served for many years on the Cardiff Corinthians committee and was manager of the club when it agreed, in 1939, to become City's nursery club. A keen water polo player outside soccer, Nicholls at one time kept a public house in Cardiff.

Honours:
Cardiff Corinthians - Welsh Amateur Cup 1929

286 George Harold Beadles

B: Llanllwchaiarn, Newtown;
   28 Sep 1897
D: Sychdyn, Mold;
   29 Aug 1958
Inside left (5ft 6ins, 11st 7lbs)
2 caps: (Cardiff C) v Sco, Eng 1925

Career: Newtown Royal Welsh Warehouse, 1912-14; Newtown, 1919; Graysons (Garstang); Liverpool, Jun 1921-24 (17 FL apps, 6 gls); Cardiff C, May 1924-25 (31 FL apps, 14 gls); Sheffield W, (£200) Nov 1925-26; Southport, Aug 1926-29 (93 FL apps, 60 gls); Workington, (trial) Jul 1929; Dundalk, (player-coach) Jul 1929-30.

One of six boys, on leaving school at the age of 12 Harry Beadles went into employment with the Royal Welsh Warehouse, Newtown, as a furrier and hosier and played for one of the local teams. On the outbreak of war, Beadles, then aged 16, and two his brothers immediately joined up. He was initially a bugle boy with the Royal Welsh Fusiliers but then served as a rifleman at Gallipoli in 1915 and later in Turkey and Palestine. During the conflict Beadles was awarded the Serbian Gold Medal in 1917 for saving the life of a Serbian observer officer who had been hit in no-man's land and was unable to return to the line. The youngster had bravely rescued the officer despite coming under heavy artillery fire and getting his cap shot off. Beadles was involved in all three battles for Gaza and the push by General Allenby to capture Jerusalem. His regiment remained in Palestine until mid-1919 and, under the influence of his fellow Newtownian and great friend, Captain George Latham, the 7th Battalion RWF won the British Forces (Egypt) Football League Cup.

Beadles returned to Newtown in 1919 and played for the local club, but soon moved to Merseyside, linking up with amateur side Grayson's of Garston in Liverpool, a well-known local shipping company. In June 1921 he signed as a professional with Liverpool and started well, scoring six goals in his first 11 appearances for the club. Although he was not a regular starter for the first team Beadles was a member of the squad which twice won the league championship. Adding to his frustration, he was not released to play for Wales but was required to cover for other players who were selected for the England team. In 1924 Beadles was given the opportunity to sign for Cardiff City, where his life-long friend George Latham was trainer, and he played in the 1925 FA Cup final against Sheffield United and finally gained his Welsh cap. In late 1925 the Cardiff City board decided to sell the Welshman to Sheffield Wednesday where he never actually appeared for the first team.

In May 1926 the Southport directors embarked on a plan to rebuild their team around an international player and decided that Beadles was their man. He was a prolific goal-getter for the Sandgrounders and topped the club's scoring charts in each of his three seasons at Haig Avenue. He was reputed to have been the best header of a ball Southport ever had and did much to foster the younger players. His club record of scoring in six successive games stood until 1957. In 1929 he moved to Dundalk FC but his family didn't settle and he opted to retire, a decision that was influenced by an old injury to his right knee. Beadles found employment as a prison officer at Walton Jail, then ran a sports out-fitters before joining Bents Brewery as a pub manager. He kept a succession of premises including the brewery's flagship hotel, the Hillside in Huyton, which was opened in 1939. A decline in his health in the early 1950s led Beadles to retire to Flintshire, where he died in 1958.

Honours:
Liverpool – FL 1st Div champions 1922, 1923
Cardiff C - FA Cup finalists 1925

287 Frederick Cook

B: Aberdare; 20 Jan 1902
D: Leicester (Eng);
   25 Mar 1966
Outside left (5ft 11ins, 11st)
8 caps: (Newport Co) v Sco, Eng 1925; (Portsmouth) v Sco, Eng 1928; v Sco, Eng, Ire 1930; v Eng 1932

Career: Albions; Aberdare Ath, May 1922-23 (6 FL apps, 1 gl); Newport Co, May 1923-26 (119 FL apps, 10 gls); Portsmouth, (£900) Apr 1926-May 1933 (247 FL apps, 41 gls); Southampton, Aug 1933; Waterford.

A pocket-sized left winger, Fred Cook's signature move was the long penetrating dribble followed by an accurate cross, and he preferred to beat the full back on the left side and accelerate past him. Cook was a consistent player and missed only four matches in his time at Newport. His acquisition by County also saw an upswing in the team's fortunes. He had been allowed to leave Aberdare on a free transfer and was said to have never made a finer move. When Pompey paid £900 for him, one newspaper commented: 'He is the type of left winger to make the forward line work with precision'. A shrewd signing by manager John McCartney, he scored on his debut in a 4-0 win over Chelsea.

Cook remained with Portsmouth for seven seasons and was judged their best player in the 1929 FA Cup final against Bolton. Idolized by the Fratton Park crowd, who dubbed him 'Little Cookie', he was an ever present in the 1926-27 and 1928-29 seasons but his remarkable 11-season injury-free run ended in 1932 when he had to undergo a cartilage operation. Released by Pompey and signed by Southampton as a free transfer, the move was seen as a gamble with one newspaper posing the question: 'will his knee stand the strain?' It didn't, and he retired from first-class football. Cook served as a physical training instructor with the RAF during the Second World War and, after the end of hostilities, settled in Leicester where he worked for a number of companies: the British United Shoe Machinery company, Bostik Ltd, and finally the Dunlop company.

Honours:
Portsmouth – FA Cup finalists 1929

288 William Williams
B: Llantwit Fardre; c. 1896
D: Unknown
Wing half
1 cap (1 gl): (Northampton T)
v Sco 1925

Career: Pontypridd, 1919; Cardiff C, 1919-21; Northampton T, 1921-27 (187 FL apps, 4 gls); Newport Co, Aug 1927-28 (6 FL apps).

Billy Williams first played football in the Army for the Royal Field Artillery after signing on at the age of 18. He joined Pontypridd on demobilisation and his promising form in friendly games led to an approach by Cardiff. At Ninian Park, Williams played full back for the reserves but didn't get an opportunity to show his paces in the first team. Nevertheless he helped the reserves to win the Welsh League (South) and finish runners-up in the Western League.

Williams, a Welsh speaker, then moved to Northampton on the recommendation of the former Cobblers full back Charlie Britten. He made his debut for his new club in August 1921 but the following month sustained an ankle injury which put him out for several weeks. More suited to wing half, Williams became a regular with Northampton and was described thus: 'can kick a good length, is a sound and reliable tackler and kicks well under pressure, has good judgement and a cool head'. Another report said 'Williams possesses wonderful ball control and some of his tricks of juggling the leather border on the marvellous'. His light, almost frail, build masked his considerable reserves of stamina, but he suffered an injury in October 1926 which required an operation on his damaged knee and kept him out of the game for some time. In August 1927, Williams joined Newport but was already carrying the ligament injury which had caused him to miss most of the 1926-27 campaign. He aggravated the leg injury in October 1927, against Walsall, and was forced into premature retirement.

289 Jack Fowler
B: Cardiff; 3 Dec 1899
D: Swansea; 26 Jan 1975
Centre forward
   (5ft 10ins, 12st)
6 caps (3 gls): (Swansea T) v Eng 1925; v Ire, Eng 1926; v Sco 1927; v Sco 1928; v Eng 1929

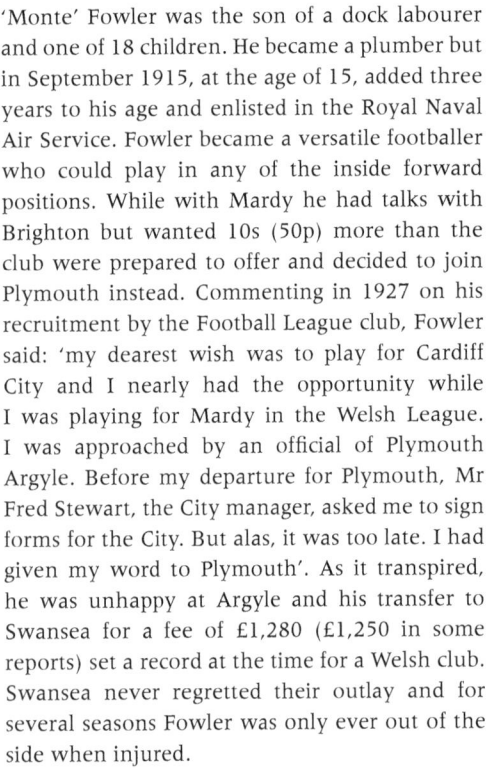

Career: Mardy, 1919-21; Plymouth Argyle, May 1921-24 (37 FL apps, 25 gls); Swansea T, (£1,280) Feb 1924-29 (167 FL apps, 100 gls); Clapton Orient, Jun 1930-32 (75 FL apps, 14 gls); retired.

'Monte' Fowler was the son of a dock labourer and one of 18 children. He became a plumber but in September 1915, at the age of 15, added three years to his age and enlisted in the Royal Naval Air Service. Fowler became a versatile footballer who could play in any of the inside forward positions. While with Mardy he had talks with Brighton but wanted 10s (50p) more than the club were prepared to offer and decided to join Plymouth instead. Commenting in 1927 on his recruitment by the Football League club, Fowler said: 'my dearest wish was to play for Cardiff City and I nearly had the opportunity while I was playing for Mardy in the Welsh League. I was approached by an official of Plymouth Argyle. Before my departure for Plymouth, Mr Fred Stewart, the City manager, asked me to sign forms for the City. But alas, it was too late. I had given my word to Plymouth'. As it transpired, he was unhappy at Argyle and his transfer to Swansea for a fee of £1,280 (£1,250 in some reports) set a record at the time for a Welsh club. Swansea never regretted their outlay and for several seasons Fowler was only ever out of the side when injured.

He was known as a 'player of strength and brain' and was a shrewd and determined leader of the Swansea forward line. The crowd at the Vetch Field would urge him on with the cry of 'Fow Fow Fowler, score a goal for me', the fans' version of the popular song of the time, 'Chick chick chicken, lay a little egg for me'! During the 1924-25 season, Fowler's 28 goals played a large part in the club's promotion to the Second Division, and his displays brought a first Welsh cap in February 1925 when Len Davies was injured. Despite the greater demands of Second Division football, he maintained a high standard of marksmanship and, between 1924 and 1929, scored nine hat-tricks for Swansea. Fowler's club record of five goals in a match (v Charlton in September 1924) still stands. He played only one first team game during 1929-30 and, with other Swans, was transferred to Clapton Orient. Fowler got off to a furious start, scoring five goals in his first three appearances and he holds the unusual distinction of having scored a brace at Wembley in a Football League match. His Clapton Orient club had been deprived of their ground and in November 1930 were given special dispensation by the FA to play at Wembley where, in December 1930, Fowler put two goals past Southend. Injury ended his playing career and he returned to Swansea where he kept the Rhyddings Hotel in Brynmill for 35 years. Fowler was something of an entrepreneur and promoted amateur boxing contests and benefit concerts during which he often performed his own monologues on stage.

Honours:
Swansea T - FL 3rd Div (S) champions 1925

290 Edwin Samuel Jenkins
B: Cardiff; 6 Jul 1895
D: Porthcawl; 4 Jul 1976
Wing half (5ft 9ins, 11st 6lbs)
1 cap: (Lovell's Ath) v Eng 1925

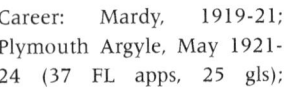

Career: Cardiff Boys; Cardiff Corinthians, 1913-14, 1920-21; Cardiff C, (am) Aug 1921-24 (12 FL apps, also 1 SL app in 1919-20);

Lovell's Ath, Jun 1924-25; Cardiff C, Aug 1925-26; Bristol C, 1926; Lovell's Ath, 1926-33, retired, (then manager to 1939).

Eddie Jenkins, whose father kept the Boar's Head in Canton, was the most accomplished Welsh amateur of the 1920s and described thus: 'built on good lines, acquired his knowledge of the game in a good school and never tires in a fast game'. Although Jenkins was called into the senior international side on only one occasion, he was a virtual ever-present for the Welsh amateur XI for over a decade, usually skippering the side. In all, he totted up 14 amateur appearances in 11 years, rarely missing a game.

One scribe said of Jenkins: 'he is a real artist at half back play, his low swift passes are the acme of judgement, while he can also shoot'. A player of intelligence and 'wonderful generalship', he had a short run in the Cardiff City first XI and was briefly on Bristol City's books in 1926 during which he overcame a bad illness and returned to play at Rexville for Lovell's Athletic, the sweets and confectionery works team. He went on to manage the team for most of the 1930s, vacating the post shortly before the outbreak of war, but continued to work for the company as a distribution and warehouse manager.

Honours:
Lovell's Ath - Welsh Amateur Cup 1926, 1927, 1928
Cardiff Corinthians - Welsh Amateur Cup finalists 1921

291 Ernest James Morley
B: Sketty; 11 Sep 1901
D: Swansea; 26 Jan 1975
Full back (5ft 8ins, 11st 2lbs)
4 caps: (Swansea T) v Eng 1925, (Clapton Orient) v Sco, Eng, Ire 1929

Career: Sketty; Swansea T, 1921-28 (123 FL apps); Clapton Orient, Jun 1928-31 (71 FL apps); Aberavon Quins, Apr 1933.

Morley and Willie Davies were signed by Swansea in the close season of 1921 where Morley quickly built up a splendid full back partnership with Wilfred Milne, and the pair were a notable feature of Swansea's 1924-25 promotion side. Morley, who was quick and had excellent positional sense, was known for his 'strong and judicious clearances', but at the start of the 1927-28 season he lost his place to Ben Williams. Despite his outstanding displays for the reserve side he was unable to displace Williams and made only a couple of appearances that season. In April 1928, Swansea recognised that he fully merited a place in a league side and, with some regret, transferred him to Clapton Orient. A leg injury kept Morley out of action for a long period in 1929-30 and when he broke a leg against Watford in February 1931 his league career was at an end. He later worked as a fitter in a local hospital.

Honours:
Swansea T - FL 3rd Div (S) champions 1925

292 Daniel Edgar Thomas
B: Cardiff; 19 May 1895
D: Cardiff; 9 Dec 1960
Wing half (5ft 8ins, 11st 4lbs)
1 cap: (Cardiff Corinthians) v Eng 1925

Career: Cardiff Alb, 1919 & 1921-23; Bridgend, Feb-Apr 1923; Cardiff Alb; Cardiff Camerons; Cardiff Corinthians, (also Cardiff C) 1923-26; Lovell's Ath, 1926-27; Cardiff C.

A leading amateur in the 1920s, Edgar Thomas appeared in ten amateur internationals for Wales and was 'a consistent performer'. He had suffered a setback in 1919 when he broke his leg and the long and difficult recovery kept him out of soccer for over two years. A methodical defender who was more than willing to shoulder his share of the work, Thomas gained his one full cap as a stand in for John Moulsdale who had been injured in a school match. Although outstanding in amateur internationals and the 'mainstay of the back division', he was a surprising choice for full honours but 'with clever forwards against him, stuck to his task'.

Thomas was on Cardiff City's books for several seasons but never played a league match for the senior side. Competition for places was stiff - the club had 17 full international players on their books - and Thomas had business commitments which limited his availability. Along with Eddie Jenkins and other top Welsh amateurs, he toured Germany during the 1924 close season with the Welsh Wanderers. In later years, Thomas worked in the Cardiff area for the Spillers flour company.

293 James Jones
B: Treorchy, Rhondda; c.1895
D: Unknown
Centre forward
(5ft 10ins, 11st 7lbs)
1 cap: (Wrexham) v Ire 1925

Career: Ton Pentre, 1913; Portsmouth & Cardiff C (both war-time); Ton Pentre, 1919-22; Cardiff C, May 1922-24 (13 FL apps, 2 gls); Wrexham, Nov 1924-26 (41 FL apps, 24 gls); Aberdare Ath, Sep 1926-27 (31 FL apps, 19 gls); Torquay Utd, Jun 1927-29 (20 FL apps, 7 gls); Worcester C, Jan 1929-30 (2 apps), retired.

Jimmy Jones had begun his career with Ton Pentre before the First World War and was something of a latecomer to the Football League. When Cardiff played Ton Pentre in the 1922 Welsh Cup final, Jimmy Jones gave such an outstanding display for the underdogs that the City directors laid out £1,000 for the clever forward. Although he showed excellent form for Cardiff Reserves, his first-team action was limited to a handful of appearances towards the end of the 1923-24 season when the club finished as First Division runners-up.

Jones and his reserve team partner, Jack Nock, were taken to the Racecourse by the newly appointed Wrexham manager Charles Hewitt, where both players got among the goals and in April 1925 Jones was called up by Wales. The following month he was transfer listed by Wrexham, an action that was described as 'hard to understand'. He moved back to south Wales the following year, but when Aberdare lost their league status Jones joined their replacements, Torquay United. He managed only two matches for Worcester on trial but was released when the club signed the ex-England man Jimmy Moore. By April 1930 Jones was said to have given up football and was playing cricket for Ton Pentre CC as a wicket keeper and 'very sound batsman'. He worked as a steward at the Mid-Rhondda Professional and Businessmen's Club in Tonypandy, but was later reported to be employed as a baker in Cardiff.

Honours:
Wrexham - Welsh Cup 1925
Ton Pentre - Welsh Cup finalists 1922

294 John Reginald Blackwall Moulsdale
B: Llanrwst; 21 Aug 1899
D: Birchington (Eng);
  4 Jul 1982
Wing half
1 cap: (Corinthians) v Ire 1925

Career: Llanrwst; Friends Sch (York); Emmanuel Coll, Cambridge (soccer blue 1922); Corinthians, 1921- 27 (76 apps, 3 gls); Cambridge T.

John Moulsdale was one of the leading amateur players of the 1920s, a strong, skilful wing half and resolute in the tackle. He was a member of the Cambridge University side of 1921-22, considered by many at the time to be their best ever. After graduating, he became an assistant master at Bradfield College, Reading, and a member of the Corinthians. Moulsdale took part in several important matches with the Corinthians, particularly in the FA Cup. Exempt until the competition proper, the Corinthians defeated Blackburn Rovers 1-0 and drew 3-3 with Manchester City in 1926. The following year, they lost 3-2 to Newcastle United, then leaders of the First Division, watched by a crowd of 56,000.

Moulsdale was capped by Wales at amateur level on nine occasions and the FAW selectors were determined to award him his full cap. In February 1925 he received a letter from Ted Robbins at the FAW that stated: 'My dear Moulsdale, we have so much faith in you that we have chosen you to represent your country in the above match (v England). I do hope you can play. The English team travel down on Friday arriving Swansea 10.10. Then leave for London after 6pm. They return to London on Saturday night. Do your best'. He was also selected for the Scotland match and although he told them not to consider him because of his teaching duties, the FAW got its way by playing him against Ireland during the Easter vacation. The match report described him as 'a tall, fair-haired young man who plays the game according to the textbook and was a pleasing success'.

Moulsdale was a housemaster at Bradfield College from 1924 to 1950 where he became a teacher of history to the College's university scholarship candidates - including Richard Adams, author of *Watership Down* - and was considered 'a fine football coach' and a 'splendid teacher of history'. In the mid-1960s he retired to Shrewsbury, where he wrote and published a history of the King's Shropshire Light Infantry.

295 Jesse Thomas Williams

B: Cefn y Bedd, Wrexham;
  16 Mar 1903
D: Toronto (Can); 20 Oct 1972
Outside left (5ft 5ins, 9st)
1 cap: (Middlesbrough) v Ire 1925

Career: Caergwrle; Oak Alyn Rov; Wrexham, Jun 1923-24 (35 FL apps, 3 gls); Middlesbrough, (£600) May 1924-28 (37 FL apps, 8 gls); Clapton Orient, Jan 1928-29 (32 FL apps, 3 gls); Rhyl Ath, Jul 1929-30; Ashton National Gas, Jun 1930-31; Shrewsbury T, Aug 1931-33; Wellington T, Jul 1933-34; Colwyn Bay Utd, Oct 1934-37.

'A diminutive yet mercurial winger', Jesse Williams was discovered by Wrexham in junior football and recruited for their first campaign in the Football League. He made his debut in September 1923 at Darlington and kept his place in the side that went on to win the Welsh Cup by defeating Merthyr Town. His busy, non-stop approach and delicate footwork made him a popular player with the crowds and he was aptly described as 'a 5ft 5ins bundle of energy'. His excellent form was rewarded with his single Welsh international cap at senior level against Ireland.

Williams was at Ayresome Park when Middlesbrough won the Second Division championship in 1926-27 but he was mainly a reserve and played only four senior matches during the campaign. He helped Clapton narrowly avoid the drop in 1928, but the following season the club were relegated and Williams left senior football. He moved to Rhyl and the Welsh National League and, with his brother Frank, a former league player with Wrexham, helped the club reach the Welsh Cup final. The brothers moved to Ashton during the 1930 close season and were later familiar figures on the Birmingham League circuit. In July 1933, Williams was at the centre of a dispute between Shrewsbury and Wellington, having signed for the latter club while still a retained player with the former. He was, however, able to show that his agreement with Shrewsbury allowed him a free transfer at the end of the 1932-33 season and was exonerated. He maintained his contact with the game after retirement by becoming a referee and, with his wife, acting as a fervent fund raiser for the Rhyl club. Williams was employed in a rayon factory and then he ran a guest house in Rhyl where he also worked as an undertaker. He emigrated to Canada in 1959 to be reunited with his two sons and was employed at Toronto General Hospital until his retirement

He named his son Frank Arthur Williams so his initials would read FAW.

Honours:
Wrexham - Welsh Cup 1924
Rhyl - Welsh Cup finalists 1930

296 Samuel Raymond Bennion

B: Gwersyllt, Wrexham; 1 Sep 1896
D: Burnley (Eng); 12 Mar 1968
Right half (5ft 9ins, 11st 2lbs)
10 caps: (Manchester Utd) v Sco 1926; v Sco 1927; v Sco, Eng, Ire 1928; v Sco, Eng, Ire 1929; v Sco 1930; v Ire 1932

Career: Gwersyllt Sch; Ragtimes; Crichton's Ath (Saltney), 1919-20; Manchester Utd, (£250) Apr 1920-May 1932 (286 FL apps, 2 gls); Burnley, Oct 1932-34 (31 FL apps); Burnley, (coach/trainer) Aug 1934-63.

Ray Bennion was signed by Manchester United from Cheshire League club Crichton's Athletic as a reserve to Clarence Hilditch but ended up playing alongside him. He had written to United for a trial and the club were so impressed with his display that he went straight into the reserves and helped them take the Central League title. He made his senior debut during the 1921-22 season and quickly acquired a name as a good, bustling half back. A 90-minute player, he always gave his best, making him a popular individual with the Old Trafford crowd, with *Athletic News* aptly describing him as: 'a toiler and a spoiler'. He remained a regular in United's side for almost 11 years and, in 1932, joined Burnley on a free transfer, becoming one of the club's most astute acquisitions.

Bennion's playing career quickly drew to a close and in 1934 became club coach at Turf Moor. He was later assistant coach and first team trainer, remaining with the club until retirement in 1963. He was highly regarded by Tommy Lawton whose progress at Burnley was due in no small part to the efforts of the former Wales player. When Cliff Britton, the former Everton and England left half, became Burnley manager in the first season after the Second World War, the experience of men like trainers Bennion and Billy Dougal proved to be a splendid combination and culminated in Burnley winning promotion back to the old First Division for the time in 17 years, and losing FA Cup finalists against Charlton Athletic in 1947. Bennion was also first team trainer at Turf Moor when Burnley won the First Division championship in 1960. His son Jack was a league player with Hull in the 1950s.

Honours:
Manchester Utd - FL 2nd Div runners-up 1925

297 James John Lewis

B: Newport; c.1902
D: Unknown
Wing half (5ft 8ins, 11st 7lbs)
1 cap: (Cardiff C) v Sco 1926

Career: Newport Co, May 1922-24 (26 FL apps); Cardiff C, Jan 1924-26 (1 FL app); Tranmere Rov, Mar 1926-34 (277 FL apps, 9 gls).

'Ginger' Lewis won his only full cap in October 1925 against Scotland at Ninian Park in unusual circumstances. He had joined Cardiff City from his home town club in 1924, but had made only one appearance when the call came. Lewis was waiting on a Newport station platform for a train to Birmingham, where he was due to play for Cardiff, when he was told to report to Ninian Park instead to solve a Welsh selection problem.

Lewis, who would not normally have been considered for international duty, was a forceful and enthusiastic player who became known on every ground in the Third Division (North). Mostly a ball winner, he was a loyal servant to Tranmere, earning the following tribute: 'the half back position suits him down to the ground ... he has sureness of tackle and no matter who blocks the ball in opposition to this stockily built Welshman, the betting is always odds on his coming through with it. Off the field he is the life of the party, on it he is as serious as a judge and nothing will disturb his complacency. There was never a more wholehearted servant, he treated reserve matches as first team games and gave every ounce of effort'. It is said that in 1927, after Tranmere's 7-3 win at Darlington, Lewis gave a full-blooded rendition of *Cwm Rhondda* followed by *Hen Wlad fy Nhadau*. He started off solo and invited everyone to join in and was still singing by the time the train reached Liverpool. Lewis was brought out of the reserves in 1934 to face Liverpool in an FA Cup match at Anfield and gave a typical battling performance in what turned out to be his swansong. As he had served only eight years with Tranmere he did not qualify for a testimonial match, merely a parting handshake from secretary-manager Bert Cooke.

298 Arthur Ivor Brown

B: Aberdare; 10 Oct 1903
D: Aberdare; 3 Apr 1971
Goalkeeper (5ft 11ins, 11st 4lbs)
1 cap: (Aberdare Ath) v Ire 1926

Career: Abercwmboi Mush; Aberdare Ath, Aug 1925-27 (45 FL apps); Reading, May 1927-29 (14 FL apps); Port Vale, Jun 1929 (1 FL app); Crewe Alex, Oct 1929-33 (120 FL apps); Merthyr T, c/season 1933-34.

Arthur Brown, the son of a coal miner, joined Aberdare from a church football team and enjoyed a remarkable first season in league football. He made 40 league appearances and gained an international cap - replacing Bert Gray - when English Football League clubs refused to release the selected Welsh players. Ireland and Wales were 'at the mercy of the English league clubs and a Swansea newspaper deplored the situation: 'Something must be done if the international games are to be genuine criterions of the merits of the competing countries'.

During the 1926-27 season Brown competed for the first-team spot with Len Evans, but was eventually sold to Reading when cash-strapped Aberdare lost their Football League status. At Elm Park he faced stiff competition against Joe Duckworth who had also joined the club from Aberdare. A competent goalkeeper, Brown was then bought by Crewe, for a small fee plus a player, and earned a reputation at Gresty Road for consistency and reliability. Towards the end of his time at Crewe he lost his first team place to Foster and was not retained at the end of the 1932-33 season. Brown worked as a door-to-door meat delivery salesman in Aberdare and Abercwmboi after retirement from football.

299 David Evans

B: Abercanaid, Merthyr Tydfil; 28 Jan 1902
D: Sully; 15 Dec 1951
Wing half (5ft 9ins, 11st 2lbs)
4 caps: (Reading) v Ire 1926; v Eng, Ire 1927; (Huddersfield T) v Sco 1929

Career: Troedyrhiw Stars; Merthyr T, 1922; Nelson, Oct 1923; Bolton Wdrs, Oct 1923-24; Reading, (exchanged for Cockerell) Aug 1924-28 (123 FL apps, 10 gls); Huddersfield T, (£6,200) Jun 1928-29 (18 FL apps); Bury, (£5,300) May 1929-30 (19 FL apps); Merthyr T, Aug 1931-32; Burton T, Feb 1932-33, (player-manager from Aug) retired; Bangor C, Aug-Nov 1935.

'Dai' Evans was a stylish wing half who played some fine, constructive football but was not altogether consistent. He was signed by Bolton from Merthyr but couldn't break into the first team and was later given a free transfer. He resurrected his career at Reading where his clever play at wing half and inside forward made him a popular individual with the Elm Park crowd. An expert penalty taker, Evans approached the task coolly and had a high success ratio.

Evans was a versatile player and also had a spell at centre forward for the Third Division club. An affable individual, who was a member of the Reading side which in 1927 reached the FA Cup semi-final only to be knocked out by eventual winners Cardiff City, he always had time to stop and chat to the crowd before taking the field. However, when he joined Huddersfield for a record fee, he found himself as part of a large squad, all competing for first team football, and never managed to establish himself. Evans gave up soccer after one season of managing Burton Albion but was lured back to the game by former Merthyr manager, Harry Hadley, who had taken over at Bangor City. He made a handful of promising appearances for the Birmingham and District League club in August and September 1935, but then failed to agree terms and decided to leave. Thereafter, he returned to Merthyr and worked at the Hoover factory, involving himself little in soccer. Known as Dai `Gethin', after his parents' public house, his brother Danny also played league football, for Watford and Brighton and Hove Albion.

Honours:
Reading - FL 3rd Div (S) champions 1926

300 Thomas Jones
B: Penycae, Wrexham;
  6 Dec 1899
D: Cefn, Wrexham;
  20 Feb 1978
Full back (5ft 8ins, 10st)

4 caps: (Manchester Utd) v Ire 1926; v Eng, Ire 1927; v Ire 1930

Career: Rhosymedre; Acrefair, 1921-22; Oswestry T, 1922-24; Manchester Utd, May 1924-37 (189 FL apps, 4 gls); Scunthorpe Utd, Jul 1937-39; Chirk (during WW2).

Tom Jones graduated from junior football to Oswestry in the Birmingham League where, after an unsuccessful trial at Burnley, he was discovered by Manchester United. At Old Trafford he proved a loyal player, and was a member of the United team who were Second Division runners-up in 1924-25, but only became a first team regular in 1933-34. Jones concentrated on defence and was never inclined to wander upfield, with the result that in a 14-year league career his name never appeared on the scoresheet. He then became player manager of Midlands League Scunthorpe, leading the club to the league championship in 1939, and when war broke out, Jones returned to Wrexham. Known as 'Tom Delft', he was later employed by the Monsanto Chemical Company as a process worker and acted as coach to Druids in his spare time.

Honours:
Manchester Utd - FL 2nd Div runners-up 1925
Scunthorpe Utd - Midland Lge champions 1939

301 John Newnes
B: Trefnant, St. Asaph;
  4 Jun 1895
D: Salford (Eng); 3 Feb 1969
Half back (5ft 9ins, 11st 6lbs)
1 cap: (Nelson) v Ire 1926

Career: Wales Schoolboys, 1909; Whitchurch; Brymbo Inst, 1919-22; Bolton Wdrs, 1922-23 (8 FL apps); Nelson, Sep 1923-26 (113 FL apps, 6 gls); Southport, Oct 1926-28 (37 FL apps, 2 gls); Mossley, Jul 1928; Manchester N E; Winsford Utd, 1931; Glossop, 1932; Altrincham, 1933.

'A very sturdy half back', Jack Newnes came late into league football when he was signed by Bolton from Welsh National League club Brymbo. He was equally at home at centre half or right half and one writer described him as, 'a rare distributor of the ball who can also score goals'. Newnes only occasionally made the Bolton first team but became a regular at Nelson and gave good service to the Third Division side.

A neat, dependable player who went about his work quietly, Newnes lost form after being capped by Wales and his club identified the weakness in their 1925-26 side. He was out of favour at the start of the 1926-27 season and, after a few games in the reserves, he was transferred to Southport. On completing his league career, Newnes became a familiar face in the Cheshire League, appearing with various clubs. One report from the latter part of his career described him as 'a valiant defender and an inspiration to the forwards'. In later years he was employed as a wholesale fruit salesman in the Manchester fruit and vegetable market.

302 Charles Jones

B: Troedyrhiw, Merthyr Tydfil;
   12 Dec 1900
D: Liverpool; 8 Jun 1969
Outside left/Right half
   (5ft 6ins, 11st 5lbs)
8 caps: (Nottingham F) v Eng 1926; v Sco Ire 1927; v Eng 1928; (Arsenal) v Sco, Eng 1930; v Eng 1932; v Fra 1933

Career: Troedyrhiw Sch; Wales Schoolboys, 1915; Cardiff C, 1919-21 (3 SL apps, 1 FL app); Stockport Co, Aug 1921-23 (48 FL apps, 14 gls); Oldham Ath, (£1,000) Mar 1923-25 (56 FL apps, 6 gls); Nottingham F, (£750) Sep 1925-28 (100 FL apps, 22 gls); Arsenal, (£4,800) May 1928-34 (176 FL apps, 8 gls); Notts Co, (manager) May-Dec 1934; Crittall's Ath, (secretary-manager)1935-Nov 1941.

Charlie Jones had made only one league appearance for Cardiff before being injured and, with Grimshaw and Jack Evans playing so well, he was unable to regain his place. However, his exceptional displays for Stockport after being transferred - such as when he scored the vital goal in the Third Division championship decider against Darlington - led to much recrimination in Cardiff about the decision to release him. Now on an upward curve, his consistent play for Oldham prompted another move, this time to Nottingham Forest, where he produced some brilliant form. One reporter commented: '[he is the] directing genius of the Forest attack. He is a most cunning dribbler and never is he seen telegraphing his next move'. Charlie, who was a partner in a hosiery and underclothing company while at Nottingham, was instrumental in the 1926 defeat of England at Selhurst Park, and caught the eye of several leading clubs but it was not until two years later that he moved to Highbury. Arsenal manager Herbert Chapman moved Jones to wing half to solve a selection problem and the Welshman responded in fine style. His tenacious play - he tackled strongly and never knew when he was beaten - was an inspiration to his team mates. Jones was also very much a thinking player, always keen to try out new tactical ideas, and an integral part of the Gunners' success in the early 1930s.

After winning three league championship medals with the club and an FA Cup final loser's medal in 1932, he moved to Notts County as manager. The appointment caused controversy and Arsenal successfully moved an amendment to the Football League rules so that no approach to a player to act for a club as manager or coach could be made without the consent of his club. Jones had an unhappy time at County and, after the team gained only one win in 17 attempts, he resigned in December 1934 following a difference of opinion with the directors. He was later secretary-manager to the Essex works side Crittall Athletic (now Braintree Town FC), playing in the Eastern Counties League - it is said that he coached his players wearing a pair of carpet slippers! - before leaving in November 1941 to join the staff of Napier Motors in Liverpool.

Honours:
Arsenal - FL 1st Div champions 1931, 1933, 1934;
   runners-up 1932
   - FA Cup finalists 1932
   - FA Charity Shield 1931
Stockport Co - FL 3rd Div (N) champions 1922

303 William John Pullen

B: Ebbw Vale; 1 Nov 1901
D: Bedwellty; 1969
Centre half (6ft, 12st 10lbs)
1 cap: (Plymouth Arg) v Eng 1926

Career: Victoria Cross; Ebbw Vale; Plymouth Argyle, c/season 1924-35 (194 FL apps, 17 gls); retired.

There are two versions as to how Jack Pullen got his only Welsh cap. According to one account he was travelling up to London with Plymouth team mate and Welsh international, Moses Russell, when the selected centre half had to cry off. The alternative story is that he was called up by telephone and Plymouth manager Bob Jack willingly released him to play. A splendidly-built defender, he had played soccer as an amateur with Ebbw Vale, turning professional when Bob Jack took him to the Devon club. Some of his early time at Home Park was marred by injuries but Pullen occupied the centre half spot for most of Plymouth's championship season of 1929-30.

A reporter in 1930 described Pullen thus: 'his headwork is always valuable and he is just the man in a hurly burly sort of game, where the judicious application of a little weight is required. His physical advantages are invaluable and he is good in heavy conditions'. Another scribe commented 'he is a sure tackler with a gift for disrupting opponents' best movements - he is likely to be of greatest value in hard hitting games', suggesting that Pullen was a good man to have on one's side. He later worked in an Ebbw Vale steelworks.

Honours:
Plymouth Arg - FL 3rd Div (S) champions 1930

304 Thomas John Evans

B: Mardy, Rhondda;
   17 Apr 1902
D: Hackney (London, Eng);
   31 Aug 1983
Full back (6ft, 11st 4lbs)
4 caps: (Clapton Orient) v Sco 1927; v Sco, Eng, (Newcastle Utd) v Ire 1928

Career: Mardy; Clapton Orient, Jul 1924-27 (54 FL apps, 1 gl); Newcastle Utd, Dec 1927-30 (14 FL apps, 1 gl); Clapton Orient, Jun 1930-32 (26 FL apps).

'Con' Evans was a cousin to Arsenal's Dan Lewis and, like the goalkeeper, worked in the pits before embarking on the career of a professional footballer. The pair were to join Clapton Orient club in 1924, but a problem arose with Lewis' registration and he was instead signed by the Highbury-based club. Evans, though, made his debut for Clapton Orient in place of the injured Bertie Rozier, a player with whom he was later to form a useful full back partnership: Evans was one of the tallest backs in the Football League, and Rozier one of the smallest. He was once described as a 'clean limbed athlete who possesses the style and polish of a top notcher'.

Evans made an unpromising start at Newcastle, after joining the north east England club for £3,650. He was rushed into the first team and 'failed to do justice to his international reputation', as the First Division side lost three matches in succession. One newspaper commented: 'his play resembles the taste for tomatoes, it has to be cultivated'. Once he had settled in, Evans did much to 'repair the unfavourable impression' created by his inauspicious start, but his selection to face Northern Ireland in February 1928 divided footballing opinion on Tyneside. A tall, battling defender, Evans was dogged by injuries at Newcastle, and he was just hitting a rich seam of form when he was forced to retire from the game after a knee injury suffered at Sheffield United. Unfortunately, Evans' Welsh caps were destroyed during the Blitz. He later worked as a night watchman.

305 Tom Percival Griffiths

B: Moss, Wrexham; 21 Feb 1906
D: Moss, Wrexham; 25 Dec 1981
Centre half
(5ft 11ins, 11st 10lbs)
21 caps (3 gls): (Everton) v Eng, Ire 1927; v Eng 1929; v Eng 1930; v Ire 1931; v Sco, Eng, Ire 1932; (Bolton Wdrs) v Sco, Eng, Ire, Fra 1933; (Middlesbrough) v Sco, Eng 1934; v Eng, Ire 1935; v Sco, (Aston Villa) v Ire 1934; v Eng, Sco, Ire 1937

Career: Frith Valley; Wrexham Boys' Club; Cross St; Wrexham, (am) Dec 1922, (pro) Jul 1923-27 (36 FL apps, 2 gls); Everton, (£1,750) Dec 1926-31 (76 FL apps, 9 gls); Bolton Wdrs, (£7,000) Dec 1931-33 (48 FL apps, 6 gls); Middlesbrough, (£6,500) Mar 1933-35 (92 FL apps, 1 gl); Aston Villa, (£5,000) Nov 1935-38 (65 FL apps, 1 gl); Wrexham, (player-coach) Aug 1938-Jul 1939 (10 FL apps); retired.

Tommy 'TP' Griffiths began his soccer career as a centre forward and would have been selected for Wrexham and District Schoolboys in that position but, by tradition, only a boy from Wrexham itself could lead the forward line so, much to his indignation, he was thrown in at centre half. The Wrexham and Wales full back Tom Matthias introduced Griffiths to Wrexham after he had scored eight goals at centre forward in a match for a local club. Griffiths, a cabinet-maker, was tried out by Wrexham at inside right against Flint and was retained for the season as an amateur. The 17-year old was offered professional terms by several clubs but turned them down, however, when Wrexham Reserves were short of a player to fill the right half position, Tom found himself filling the breach. An indifferent performance by his full back colleague - a youngster on trial - necessitated a reshuffle of the team and Tom was moved to centre half. Later that season, his progress in his new position led to inter-league and junior international caps.

A near-£2,000 signing, Griffiths played his first game for Everton behind Dixie Dean, who faced him as an opponent the following Saturday when Wales played England, and when Griffiths subsequently moved to Bolton, Dean was once again in the opposing side. Griffiths was a most stylish centre half and a great header of the ball, who wasted little time in clearing the ball out of defence. One newspaper commented: 'though his value is chiefly in his defensive capabilities, Griffiths does not stick purely to such work, and can turn defence into attack with his swift passes to his forwards. He is especially good with his head, he has scored seven goals for Bolton this season – an unusual number for a centre half'. Griffiths took over the Wales centre half position from Fred Keenor and held it for most of the 1930s, captaining his country on several occasions. His career ran into injury problems at Aston Villa and he was forced to give up playing because of rheumatic trouble. Griffiths then returned to Wrexham and by August 1938 had improved sufficiently to make a comeback with Wrexham. He was club coach for two brief spells, and in the early 1950s became a trainer for Wales. A one-time Wrexham director, he was successively landlord of the Turf Hotel, the Hand Hotel and finally the Red Lion in Marchwiel, and was an excellent cello player who performed in local concerts.

Honours:
Everton - FL 2nd Div champions 1931
Wrexham - Welsh Cup 1925

306 Daniel Lewis

B: Mardy, Rhondda;
  4 Dec 1902
D: Scarborough (Eng);
  17 Jul 1965
Goalkeeper (6ft, 11st 7lbs)
3 caps: (Arsenal) v Eng 1927;
v Ire 1928; v Eng 1930

Career: Mardy, 1922-24: Arsenal, Aug 1924-31 (141 FL apps); Gillingham, May 1931-32 (6 FL apps).

Dan Lewis is forever associated with the 1927 FA Cup final, and his unfortunate error in failing to cleanly gather Hughie Ferguson's ordinary shot, allowing it to bounce off his body for the only goal of the match. There was added piquancy in the fact that the Welshman's slip up meant that the FA Cup was taken out of England for the first and only time. Lewis, who remarked 'I am surely the most disappointed man in the world', was not the same man after his dismal experience. Some observers blamed his shiny goalkeeper's jersey and Arsenal were believed to have, thereafter, banned goalkeepers from wearing a new jersey without it having been washed. Lewis, though, had the full backing of Arsenal manager Herbert Chapman who commented: 'If we had to play the game all over again tomorrow Lewis would still be our goalkeeper'.

A former coal miner, Lewis had moved to London from Mardy in July 1924 to supposedly play for Clapton Orient, but 'something went wrong with his registration and he became an Arsenal player', much to the annoyance of the Clapton Orient officials. He broke into Arsenal's senior side in his first season after displacing the Scottish international keeper Harper and retained the position through to the famous Wembley appearance against Cardiff. Arsenal were again FA Cup finalists in 1930 and Lewis hoped to make amends for his earlier mistake but was sidelined by injury. He later worked for the Kodak film company in Harrow and died while on holiday in Yorkshire.

Honours:
Arsenal - FA Cup finalists 1927

307 Wilfred Leslie Lewis

B: Swansea; 1 Jul 1903
D: Swansea; Nov 1979
Centre forward/Outside left
  (5ft 8ins, 10st 12lbs)
6 caps (3 gls): (Swansea T)
v Eng, Ire 1927; v Eng, Ire 1928; v Sco 1929; (Huddersfield T) v Eng 1930

Career: Baldwins Welfare; Swansea Amateurs; Swansea T, Mar 1924-28 (64 FL apps, 43 gls); Huddersfield T, (£7,000) Nov 1928-31 (15 FL apps, 7 gls); Derby Co, Apr 1931-32 (8 FL apps, 3 gls); Yeovil & Petters Utd, Jul 1932-33 (73 apps, 85 gls); Bath C, Dec 1933-34; Altrincham, Jul 1934; Cardiff C, Aug 1934-36 (33 FL apps, 6 gls); Haverfordwest Ath, Sep 1936.

Wilf Lewis was another of Swansea's local discoveries during the 1920s who went on to play for Wales. It looked at one stage as if he would not fulfil his early promise but, after development in the London Combination, he settled into the side as Jack Fowler's goalscoring left wing partner and, whenever Fowler was absent, Lewis took over the centre forward berth. He had a reputation as a 'clever worker' who was always ready to drop back to help out his defence, and for being 'deadly accurate in the air'. Another report noted him as 'a rare schemer with a deadly shot', but at times he was faulted by some for trying to do too much with his head.

A methodical and thoughtful player, Lewis was tracked by Manchester United in March 1926 but the clubs failed to agree terms. The expected move came some 18 months later when First Division Huddersfield bought Lewis for £5,000: at the time a record fee involving a Welsh club. Although he marked his debut against Burnley with two goals, a few days later, at Cardiff, he sustained a knee injury which troubled him for the remainder of his career. Huddersfield had denied Lewis his release to play for Wales on the same day, and Wilf always believed that if the club had released him to play for Wales the course of his career would have been very different.

He recovered sufficiently to help Huddersfield to the 1930 FA Cup final but a few days before the match he slipped in training and aggravated his knee injury. Lewis missed the final and the following year, after further surgery on the knee, he was released. A comeback with Derby was unsuccessful and he joined Southern League Yeovil. Lewis hit 65 goals in a season but the club were short of cash and his transfer to Bath was controversial. Wilf returned to league soccer in 1934 but continued to be hampered by his injury problem. Nevertheless, he still managed to score 48 Welsh League Division 2 goals for Haverfordwest Athletic in the 1936-37 season. Lewis later worked in the stores department of a rubber and asbestos company in the Swansea area.

308 Harry Thomas
B: Swansea; 28 Feb 1901
D: Swansea; 17 Sep 1964
Outside left (5ft 6ins, 10st)
1 cap: (Manchester Utd) v Eng 1927

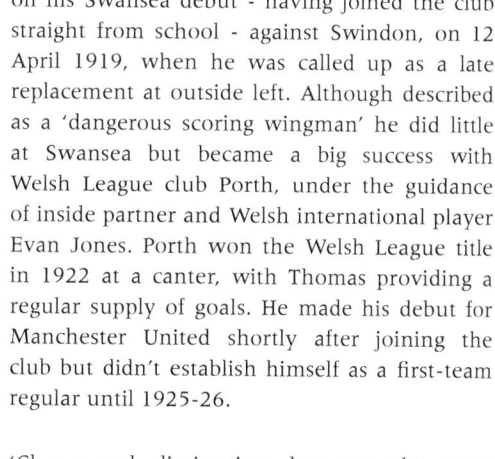

Career: Swansea T, 1919-20 (3 SL apps); Porth, 1920-22; Manchester Utd, Apr 1922-30 (128 FL apps, 12 gls); Waterford, Sep 1930; Merthyr T, Oct 1930-Mar 1931; Abercarn, Apr 1932-33; Aberavon Harlequins, Mar 1934.

A 'fleet-footed winger', Harry Thomas scored on his Swansea debut - having joined the club straight from school - against Swindon, on 12 April 1919, when he was called up as a late replacement at outside left. Although described as a 'dangerous scoring wingman' he did little at Swansea but became a big success with Welsh League club Porth, under the guidance of inside partner and Welsh international player Evan Jones. Porth won the Welsh League title in 1922 at a canter, with Thomas providing a regular supply of goals. He made his debut for Manchester United shortly after joining the club but didn't establish himself as a first-team regular until 1925-26.

'Clever and diminutive, but not the most consistent of players', Thomas was much more of a creator than scorer for United. He returned to Wales in 1930 and was evidently putting on weight, as one scribe commented: 'he is a creator of chances, not renowned for scoring and an unlikely shape for a winger - `big' around the middle'. He was employed as a crane driver after retiring from soccer.

309 Sidney John Vivian Leonard Evans
B: Llandaf, Cardiff;
  20 May 1903
D: Bournemouth (Eng);
  26 Dec 1977
Goalkeeper (6ft, 13st)
4 caps: (Aberdare Ath) v Ire 1927; (Cardiff C) v Sco, Eng 1931; (Birmingham) v Ire 1934

Career: Cardiff Corinthians, 1922-26; Aberdare Ath, Oct 1926-27 (24 FL apps); Lovell's Ath, Oct 1927; Merthyr T, Jul-Oct 1927 (5 FL apps); Cardiff Corinthians, Oct 1927; Lovell's Ath, 1927-28; Barry T, 1928-29; Cardiff C, Jan 1930-32 (7 FL apps); Birmingham, Sep 1933 (2 FL apps); Svenborg (Denmark); Birmingham, (trainer) May 1934-May 1936; Blackburn R, (trainer) 1937-39.

In early life, Len Evans had sung in a church choir and harboured ambitions to become a clergyman, but as a goalkeeper, he was something of a latter day Roose: cool, unorthodox and with 'a disregard for the canons of sound goalkeeping'. He was known as a risk-taker who made simple shots look difficult, but was a classy and reliable custodian, whose one weakness was a tendency to be haphazard when clearing the ball. Evans, a Wales Schoolboy player, remained an amateur almost throughout, turning pro' only in the last six months of his career. Between 1925 and 1933 he won 12 amateur caps - a record at the time - and made his first full international appearance when Dan Lewis of Arsenal was unable to play. When, in 1930, Ted Robbins was struggling to recruit a team to play the Scots, Len Evans was a natural choice in goal. One match report said he was 'cool under the severest of pressure, there were repeated occasions when the Scottish forwards swarmed around his goal - he saved shot after shot'.

During the 1920s, Evans was a member of Glamorgan Police Force, stationed at one time at Barry Docks, and in November 1931 he decided to give up soccer in order, he said, to put his career first. In fact, his police duties were restricting his availability. Colonel Lionel Lindsay, chief constable of Glamorgan, quickly arranged for Evans to be released from duty on Saturdays and his 'retirement' lasted one week. In 1932 Evans decided to become a physical training instructor, undergoing a course of 'physical culture' in Denmark and, having secured his diploma, he resigned from the police with the intention of securing an appointment as a physical culture instructor. Evans participated in many sports including swimming, boxing, cricket, baseball and gymnastics, and was one of the first Welshmen to play soccer on the Continent, and the first in Scandinavia, when he guested for Svenborg, Denmark, while training at Ollerup. In later years he lived in Mudeford in Dorset.

310 Ernest Robert Curtis

B: Cardiff; 1 Jun 1907
D: Cardiff; 21 Nov 1992
Winger (5ft 9ins, 12st)
3 caps (3 gls): (Cardiff C) v Sco 1928; (Birmingham) v Sco 1932; (Cardiff C) v Ire 1934

Career: Severn Rd Old Boys; Cardiff Corinthians; Cardiff C, Nov 1925-28 (46 FL apps, 8 gls); Birmingham, (£3,000) Mar 1928-33 (163 FL apps, 44 gls); Cardiff C, Nov 1933-34 (17 FL apps, 7 gls); retired; Coventry C, Feb 1935-37 (21 FL apps, 2 gls); Hartlepool Utd, Jul 1937-38 (16 FL apps, 1 gl).

After representing Cardiff Boys, and Wales, as a schoolboy in 1921, Ernie Curtis became an electrician with Cardiff City Corporation, playing amateur soccer in his spare time. He was taken on by Cardiff City and within weeks was capped by Wales at amateur level. During the 1926 close season, Curtis turned professional and began a highly successful year at Ninian Park, culminating in his appearance for Cardiff in the 1927 FA Cup final. He was selected in place of Billy Thirlaway, who was ineligible, and the injured Harry Wake. At the age of 19 years 317 days, Curtis was - at the time - the youngest player to take part in an FA Cup final, but was far from overawed by the occasion. Birmingham showed an interest in Curtis and it was with some reluctance that he left Ninian Park for St Andrews. His time at the club was a happy one, but tempered by the club's unwillingness to release him for international matches, and Birmingham's opposition meant that he didn't feature in the Wales side as often as he might have done. He moved back to Cardiff in November 1933, but soon found himself in a wages dispute with the club and left the game to become a licensee in Birmingham. Coventry obtained his release from contract, resurrecting his career, first as a player and later as player-coach.

At the outbreak of war, Curtis joined the Royal Artillery and was sent to the Far East, where he was captured by the Japanese and, from 1941 to 1945, endured great hardship as a prisoner of war. After the war, he returned to the licensed trade, in Cardiff and, from the late 1940s, took on first the post of Cardiff City trainer, before occupying various positions at the club until he decided to retire when Jimmy Scoular became manager.

In August 1930, Curtis played in a match between Welsh and English Baseball League sides at Liverpool. The English League side included rugby league star Jim Sullivan and England footballer Louis Page, while Wales had Cardiff's Curtis and Jack McJennet among their team.

Honours:
Cardiff C - FA Cup 1927
- Welsh Cup 1927
- FA Charity Shield 1927
Birmingham - FA Cup finalists 1931

311 Benjamin David Williams

B: Penrhiwceiber; 29 Oct 1900
D: Bridgend; Jan 1968
Full back
(5ft 9½ins, 11st 5lbs)
10 caps: (Swansea T) v Eng, Ire 1928; v Sco, Eng 1930; (Everton) v Ire 1931; v Eng 1932; v Sco, Eng, Ire 1933; v Ire 1935

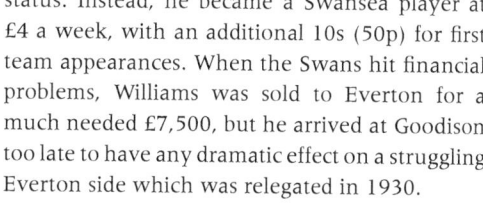

Career: Penrhiwceiber; Swansea T, (£25) Feb 1925-30 (102 FL apps); Everton Dec 1929-35 (131 FL apps); Newport Co, 1935-38 (18 FL apps); retired.

A coal miner who played for a junior side in the Welsh League, Ben Williams might have begun his league career at Cardiff but he was not willing to accept City's initial offer of amateur status. Instead, he became a Swansea player at £4 a week, with an additional 10s (50p) for first team appearances. When the Swans hit financial problems, Williams was sold to Everton for a much needed £7,500, but he arrived at Goodison too late to have any dramatic effect on a struggling Everton side which was relegated in 1930.

This disappointment was a prelude to a period of remarkable success for Everton. Williams was appointed captain and, at the end of the 1930-31 season, the club were promoted back to the First Division club as champions. The following season, Everton went one better and were crowned Football League champions. It's worth noting Williams' remuneration from Everton – wages of £8 a week, and a bonus of £2 a win, £1 for a draw. A feature of the successful team was Ben's defensive partnership with Warney Cresswell. Williams was described as 'a big, hefty fellow who stands off rather than rushes in and has superb judgement on when to tackle', while another writer's verdict was: 'a sound and sturdy tackler and possesses a deceiving turn of speed'.

A cartilage operation in January 1933 kept him sidelined for months and he never regained his former pre-eminence. He was released in 1935 and returned to Wales to join Newport, firstly as a player and then player coach. Williams retired from soccer in 1938 and returned to the colliery where he had begun his working life. Sadly, his health seriously deteriorated in the 1960s and he was afflicted by senile dementia, which some thought had been exacerbated by heading a heavy leather ball.

Honours:
Everton - FL 1st Div champions 1932
- FL 2nd Div champions 1931

312 Hywel Davies

B: Llanddulas; 20 Nov 1902
D: Denbigh; 16 Aug 1976
Outside left/Centre forward
(5ft 9ins, 11st 6lbs)
1 cap: (Wrexham) v Ire 1928

Career: Abergele G Sch; Jesus Coll (Oxford); Abergele; Llanddulas; Wrexham, Dec 1924-26 (13 FL apps); Chesterfield (on loan), 1926 (1 FL app), Corinthians, 1926 (1 app, 2 gls); Wrexham, 1927-31 (2 FL apps); Chirk 1928; Brynford, 1931.

Hywel Davies, the son of a blacksmith, was, with Tom Jenkins, only the second clergyman to appear for Wales at soccer. He was educated at St David's College, Lampeter, where he was a brilliant scholar, and took a second degree, in theology, at Jesus College, Oxford, where he became a soccer blue in 1924. Davies was a winger of some pace but his forte was ball control. He toured Canada and the United States of America in 1924 with the Corinthians, where *The Vancouver Sun* dubbed him 'a youngster of great promise' and commented 'Davies is a Welsh international (amateur), youthful, tall, clean cut like all his fellows and easy to look at'. Between 1928 and 1931 he made five appearances for Wales at amateur level but, from 1929 onwards, his ecclesiastical duties largely kept him away from the football field although he continued to act as secretary to the Welsh Dragons: an amateur side modelled on the Corinthians. Davies later played for Brynford in the Dyserth Area League and held several honorary posts in soccer, including President of the North Wales Coast FA and the Dyserth Area League. He was always keen to help out youngsters at church school kick-arounds and frequently took the field in clerical garb to play and do some coaching. Davies maintained a close involvement with the Dyserth League and North Wales soccer generally for many years and was chairman of Brynford FC in the late 1940s. Ordained in 1925, he served as Curate of Wrexham until 1934 when he became Rector of Brynford, and from 1947 until 1973 he was Rector of Denbigh.

During the reverend's Wrexham days, a league scout turned up at the Racecourse and, liking the look of the outside left, suggested a transfer fee to a Wrexham director. It was refused and the scout upped the figure. When a third, very substantial offer, was refused, the scout enquired 'why ever not', to which the director replied 'because he a ****** parson, that's why, and he'll be working tomorrow'. 'Well, I'll be at the church' said the scout, and he was.

313 Stanley James Bowsher

B: Newport; 3 Oct 1899
D: Newport; 14 Dec 1968
Half back (5ft 9ins, 10st 9lbs)
1 cap: (Burnley) v Ire 1929

Career: Lovell's Ath, 1923; Newport Co, Aug 1925-29 (119 FL apps, 3 gls); Burnley, (£500) Jan 1929-33 (82 FL apps, 2 gls); Rochdale, Mar 1933 (10 FL apps); Newport Co, Jun 1933-34 (5 FL apps) & (trainer) Sep 1937-38.

Bowsher was signed by Newport from Lovell's Athletic, a local toffee factory side and leading amateur club in south Wales. He broke into the league side in the early part of the 1925-26 season and developed a reputation as a tireless worker with bags of stamina. In April 1927, Bowsher appeared for the Welsh League against Ireland and several big clubs began to take an interest in him. Sunderland's enquiries came to nothing but two years later the hard-up Newport club accepted Burnley's £500 offer for the versatile half back, and Bowsher made his international debut a couple of days after leaving Newport. At Turf Moor, he was used mostly as a defender but had an unsuccessful try out at centre forward.

Bowsher later returned to Somerton Park and took over as trainer when his playing days were over, but resigned in 1938. After the war, he returned to the post but the association was short lived and in 1946 he took work outside football, first in the haulage department of a local authority and later as a steward in a gentlemen's club. Bowsher also captained Wales at baseball.

Honours:
Lovell's Ath - Welsh Amateur Cup 1926

314 Arthur Albert Lumberg

B: Connah's Quay; 20 May 1901
D: Wrexham; 16 Feb 1986
Full back (5ft 8ins, 11st 4lbs)
4 caps: (Wrexham) v Ire 1929; v Sco, Eng 1930; (Wolverhampton Wdrs) v Sco 1932

Career: Connah's Quay & Shotton; Mold T, 1924; Wrexham, Nov 1924-30 (169 FL apps); Wolverhampton Wdrs, May 1930-33 (20 FL apps); Brighton & H A, (£250) Jun 1933-34 (21 FL apps); Stockport Co, May 1934-35 (2 FL apps); Clapton Orient, Jan-May 1935; Lytham, c/season 1935; New Brighton, Nov 1935-36 (2 FL apps); Winsford Utd (Cheshire League), July 1936; Newry T (player-manager), Nov 1937; Rhyl 1938; Newry T (manager), Jan-May 1939.

Lumberg spent his formative soccer years in the Welsh National League with Connah's Quay and Mold, mostly as a full back and occasionally at inside right. He joined Wrexham in November 1924, despite stiff competition from Hull City, and once at the Racecourse, Lumberg formed a great defensive partnership with the long-serving Alf Jones. A resolute defender, he was equally at home in either full back slot and never gave less than 100 per cent.

He impressed Wolves while playing for Wrexham Reserves in the Birmingham and District League and was sold to the Second Division club for £650. Wolves were intent on building a promotion-winning side and liked Lumberg's positional play and his 'out of the ordinary' defensive work. However, he never became a regular member of the first team and was eventually sold to Brighton. Lumberg was player manager of Newry Town FC in the late 1930s, Wrexham `A' team trainer in 1950 and later coached Wrexham Old Boys. Before embarking on his league career, he had worked for a firm of furniture removers.

Honours:
Wrexham - Welsh Cup 1925

315 Albert William Mays

B: Ynyshir, Rhondda; 18 Jul 1902
D: Derby (Eng); 3 Nov 1959
Centre forward (5ft 9ins, 11st 4lbs)
1 cap (1 gl): (Wrexham) v Ire 1929

Career: Ynyshir Swallows; Porth; Wattstown; Bristol C, Sep 1923-26 (19 FL apps, 4 gls); Plymouth Argyle, Jun 1926-27; Merthyr T, Jun 1927-28 (34 FL apps, 14 gls); Wrexham, Aug 1928-30 (54 FL apps, 41 gls); Notts Co, (£650) Mar 1930 (8 FL apps, 5 gls); Burnley, May 1930 (2 FL apps); Walsall, Jan 1931 (17 FL apps, 11 gls); Halifax T, Jun 1931-32 (25 FL apps, 8 gls); Margate T, Jul 1932.

Albert Mays had learned his football with Ynyshir Swallows (154 goals in two seasons!) and his career as a pro' footballer got underway when Mog Benjamin, an Ynyshir man, persuaded Bristol City to give him a trial. It took a further two run-outs, though, before City manager Archie Annan was convinced. Merthyr were keen to sign him in 1926 but Mays opted for Plymouth, although Albert Lindon, the Merthyr manager, finally secured his services the following year. Mays worked in the pits for a time while with Merthyr but then found himself surplus to first-team requirements. Opinions on his play were divided although the Wrexham directors had no doubts and were impressed by his Welsh Cup hat-trick against them at the Racecourse, and he reached a standard of marksmanship he was never to repeat at any of his many other clubs. In a purple patch he hit 32 goals in 34 matches and was dubbed 'the amazing Mays'. Such goal scoring made it difficult for the FAW selectors to overlook him and although he scored on his one appearance he didn't do enough to merit further selection. Notts County paid £650 for

Mays in an unsuccessful bid to avoid relegation and thereafter his career meandered to a close in 1932.

Mays was a dashing centre forward with a fine shot and good passing skills, but dogged by a lack of consistency. One description was 'a bustling type of centre forward with a knack for swift shooting and slick heading'. After concluding his nomadic career at Margate through injury, Mays had several employments: as an artificial silk finisher, in the NAAFI offices and then on the maintenance staff at Derby police station. Outside work Mays did a lot of charity work, organising boxing matches and other sporting events. His son, also Albert, was a Derby County wing half between 1949 and 1959.

316 Eugene O'Callaghan

B: Ebbw Vale; 6 Oct 1906
D: Hammersmith (Eng);
   4 Jul 1956
Inside right (5ft 9ins, 11st)
11 caps (3 gls): (Tottenham H) v Ire 1929; v Sco 1930; v Sco, Eng 1932; v Sco, Eng, Ire 1933; v Sco, Ire, Eng 1934; v Eng 1935

Career: Victoria Sch; Ebbw Vale Schoolboys; Wales Schoolboys; Victoria Utd; Ebbw Vale Corries, 1923; Ebbw Vale; Tottenham H, 1924, Barnet (loan), Northfleet (loan); Tottenham H, (pro) Dec 1926-35 (252 FL apps, 94 gls); Leicester C, Mar 1935-37 (84 FL apps, 30 gls); Fulham, Sep 1937-45 (41 FL apps, 6 gls); Tottenham H (war-time guest); Fulham, (reserve team trainer) 1945-56.

O'Callaghan, the son of an Irish soldier who served in Wales, joined Ebbw Vale Corries from school and was soon invited for trials with Newcastle, Everton and Spurs, and while awaiting the outcome he played for Ebbw Vale. After opting for Spurs, O'Callaghan initially impressed at White Hart Lane but was then thought to be too small and, being too young to turn professional, he was found employment in London and farmed out to Barnet where his precocious footballing skills made him a great favourite with the crowd and he was dubbed the 'Boy Wonder'. On the strength of his performances he was selected to play for London against Birmingham and then against Denmark.

After two season at Barnet, he turned pro' with Spurs, making his debut against Everton in January 1927 and, 12 months later, he marked the anniversary of his debut with four goals - against Everton. 'An individual and original player', O'Callaghan was a master of positional play and one writer commented: 'he is extraordinarily fast in his stride and darts through the middle, gets into position to shoot before anyone realises the danger'. Although he was one of the leading Spurs players of the inter-war years, there was a feeling that he never quite lived up to his early promise.

O'Callaghan was reunited with his boyhood mentor when Jack Peart, the Fulham manager and player-coach at Ebbw Vale in the 1920s, signed him for the west London club. O'Callaghan, who was known as 'Taffy', captained Wales in a number of matches and was always an inspiration to his colleagues. He played an important part in Wales' Home Championship wins in 1932-33 and 1933-34. After the Second World War, O'Callaghan was reserve team trainer at Craven Cottage until his early death.

Honours:
Leicester C - FL 2nd Div champions 1937
Tottenham H - FL 2nd Div runners-up 1933

317 Frederick Windsor Warren

B: Cardiff; 23 Dec 1907
D: Milton Keynes (Eng);
   Jul 1986
Outside left (5ft 7ins, 10st)
6 caps (3 gls): (Cardiff C) v Ire 1929; (Middlesbrough) v Ire

1931; v Eng, Fra 1933; (Heart of Midlothian) v Ire 1937; v Ire 1938

Career: Cardiff C, Jan 1927-30 (38 FL apps, 7 gls); Middlesbrough, Jan 1930-36 (162 FL apps, 50 gls); Heart of Midlothian, (£650) May 1936-39 (142 Scot L & cup apps, 46 gls); Barry T (war-time).

Freddie Warren's first team career at Ninian Park got underway in April 1928 and the following season he had several outings in the senior side, culminating in his selection for Wales. During the 1929 close season he toured Canada with the FAW party and made the most of his appearances in the unfamiliar right wing position. 'Fleet of foot with a delightful elusive quality', Warren was controversially allowed to leave Cardiff for Ayresome Park in an £8,000 transfer that also involved Jack Jennings and Joe Hilliar. In his first full season for Middlesbrough, Warren scored 20 goals from the outside left position, and was described in 1929 as: 'quick off the mark, fearless and of sound judgement'. However, he had some detractors who preferred to see Charlie Phillips in the Welsh squad. While acknowledging his liveliness and very accurate centres, some criticised Warren for being 'prone to dispose of the ball too hurriedly'.

After six seasons at Ayresome Park, he moved to Scotland to join an attractive Hearts side where he played alongside the gifted inside forwards Tommy Walker and Andy Black. At the outbreak of war he was allowed to return to Wales to assist Barry Town and work for a brewery company.

Honours:
Hearts - Scottish Lge runners-up 1938

318 Richard Prytherch Finnegan

B: Wrexham; 16 May 1904
D: Halton (Eng); 4 Nov 1979
Goalkeeper (6ft 11st, 4lbs)
1 cap: (Wrexham) v Ire 1930

Career: Oswestry T; Holyhead; Connah's Quay & Shotton; Wrexham, Aug 1922-24 (3 FL apps); Holyhead T, Sep 1924-25; Connah's Quay & Shotton, Aug 1925-26; Manchester C, May 1926-27 (8 FL apps); Accrington Stanley, May 1927-28 (42 FL apps); Connah's Quay & Shotton, Sep 1928-29; Wrexham, May 1929-32 (98 FL apps); Colwyn Bay Utd, Aug 1932-33; Chester, Feb 1933-34 (13 FL apps); Stockport Co, Mar 1934-36 (26 FL apps); Winsford Utd, 1936-37; Bala T, Mar 1939.

Dick Finnegan was of Irish extraction and was reputedly discovered by Wrexham working in a circus. He had a lengthy career, alternating between the lower divisions of the Football League and non-league, and his form could vary from brilliant to erratic, but it was in his second spell at the Racecourse that he achieved his greatest consistency. Wrexham had re-signed Finnegan from Connah's Quay after his fine display for the Welsh National League side in their victory over First Division Cardiff in the 1929 Welsh Cup final.

Finnegan's form began to suffer towards the end of 1932 and after some comically inept performances, he joined Colwyn Bay in the Birmingham and District League. He rebuilt his confidence sufficiently to make a comeback with Chester in February 1933, but three months later, he was given a free transfer only to be re-signed by the club in June 1933. Finnegan, who lived in Ruthin, was later employed by the Post Office Engineering Department as a linesman.

Honours:
Connah's Quay & Shotton - Welsh Cup 1929
Wrexham - Welsh Cup 1931

319 Arthur Ronald Hugh

B: Rogerstone; 5 Aug 1909
D: Newport; 2000
Full back (5ft 11ins, 11st 7lbs)
1 cap: (Newport Co) v Ire 1930

Career: Rogerstone Night Sch (Newport & Dist Lge); Newport YMCA; Newport Co, Aug 1929-31 (14 FL apps), 1931-32 (13 SL apps), Sep 1932-34 (43 FL apps); Lovell's Ath.

Ron Hugh, then an amateur, was given a trial by Newport County at centre forward at the beginning of the 1929-30 season, scoring a hat-trick and convincing the club that he should be taken on permanently. When regular defender Anderson got injured, Hugh was tried out at full back and did so well that he kept his place, making his debut against Exeter in December 1929 although not becoming a part-time professional until 1932. Unusually, Hugh was selected to play for the Wales amateur side in February 1930, one week after appearing in the senior side.

Hugh had an unusual style, best encapsulated in this 1930 description of him: 'his long limbs give him extraordinary reach in tackling; his style conveys the idea of a kind of deft clumsiness but really is not clumsy. Hugh reaches out his long right leg, hooks the ball and, in a manner that is not quite clear to those who look on, a forward raid is crumbled up'. He remained a first team regular until the 1933-34 season when an injury resulted in a very long lay-off. He returned to the reserve side shortly before the outbreak of war but played no serious football thereafter. Hugh found employment with a seed and corn merchant but later had a horticultural business at Newport market.

320 Edward Lawrence

B: Cefn Mawr, Ruabon;
  24 Aug 1907
D: Nottingham (Eng);
  20 Jul 1989
Left half (5ft 7ins, 11st 6lbs)
2 caps: (Clapton Orient) v Ire 1930; (Notts Co) v Sco 1932

Career: Druids; Wrexham, 1925-28 (22 FL apps); Clapton Orient, Aug 1928-31 (10 FL apps); Notts Co, (£275) May 1931-36 (139 FL apps, 2 gls); Bournemouth, Aug 1936-37 (39 FL apps, 1 gl); Clapton Orient, May 1937-38 (21 FL apps); Notts Co, 1939.

An amateur signing from Druids, Eddie Lawrence spent three seasons at the Racecourse before turning professional with Clapton Orient. He was a 'scientific' wing half, and was 'never content to kick the ball and hope for the best' but always tried to be constructive. Lawrence 'followed the first rule of his job and drew an opponent before passing', leading him to him being described as 'one of the best wing half backs Notts County have had for years'. Despite his modest height he was strong in the air and 'capable of rising to seemingly impossible heights', gaining his first cap when he replaced T P Griffiths. Another reporter noted that: 'He is never content to kick the ball and hope for the best. As a wing half back he was always trying to do something with the ball'.

During the close season in 1936, County decided on a change of policy and Lawrence became a casualty of the wholesale clear out of players, joining Bournemouth. He returned to Meadow Lane three years later and took employment with the John Player cigarette company before joining the RAF in 1940 and spending three years of the war in North Africa. Afterwards, he scouted for Notts County until the late 1970s.

321 Tudor James Martin

B: Caerau, Bridgend;
  20 Apr 1904
D: Newport; 6 Sep 1979
Centre forward
  (5ft 10ins, 11st 8lbs)
1 cap: (Newport Co) v Ire 1930

Career: Caerau Harlequins; Bridgend T; West Bromwich Alb, (am) Feb 1925, (pro) May 1926-29; Newport Co, Jul 1929-30 (27 FL apps, 34 gls);

Wolverhampton Wdrs, May 1930-32 (15 FL apps, 9 gls); Swansea T, Jul 1932-36 (116 FL apps, 45 gls); West Ham Utd, Jun 1936-37 (11 FL apps, 7 gls); Southend Utd, Feb 1937-39 (59 FL apps, 29 gls), retired.

Young Tudor Martin was an out of work miner when, in October 1926, he was offered a contract by West Bromwich Albion. He had come to the attention of the midlands club when seen playing for Caerau, his home town club. Martin spent three years at the Hawthorns without getting a first team game and at the end of the 1928-29 season had a cartilage operation. West Brom thought his career was over but Newport manager Jimmy Hindmarsh heard about Tudor and took him on. When the 1929-30 season opened, Martin could not command a first team place but, after two months in 'the obscurity of the Southern League', he suddenly leapt to fame and became 'one of the most discussed centre forwards in Britain'. In his third match he hit a hat-trick against QPR, followed by hat-tricks against Gillingham and Coventry City. In April 1930 he scored five goals against Merthyr, in County's record 10-0 win, and then a fifth hat-trick v Exeter. His 30 goals in 24 games beat Archie Waterman's 1927-28 record of 27 goals in 30 matches.

Once described as 'County's greatest forward', Martin scored more goals in a season than any other Newport player, is the only Newport player to score five in a match, and holds the County record for the most hat-tricks in a season, yet he only spent one season at Somerton Park, playing in 29 Football League matches and two FA Cup ties. County received several tempting offers for Martin's transfer but although desperately short of cash – they once had to borrow money to pay the train fares to Watford – they refused to sell him until they had completed their fixtures. By then the financial position was so critical that they had no option but to sell Martin, and Major Buckley took him to Wolves for £1,500 plus Cyril Pearce in part exchange. Martin never became a regular at Molineux but a move to Swansea in 1932 brought a change of fortune and a return to the 'goal standard'.

After moving to West Ham in June 1936 Martin was sent off in a match for retaliation and suspended. It transpired that he was the first West Ham player to get his marching orders in 25 years. Nothing was said to him but he never played for the Hammers again and was transferred to Southend. After retirement from football, Tudor Martin returned to Wales where, for many years, he found employment at a tube works and enjoyed regularly watching his local club Newport County.

322 John Pugsley

B: Grangetown, Cardiff;
   1 Apr 1900
D: Neath; 1 Aug 1976
Left half (5ft 6ins, 11st 6lbs)
1 cap: (Charlton Ath) v Ire 1930

Career: local soccer in Cardiff; Grangetown YMCA; Cardiff C, Apr 1922-25; Grimsby T, May 1925-27 (80 FL apps, 6 gls); Bristol C, May 1927-28 (16 FL apps); Charlton Ath, May 1928-34 (214 FL apps, 8 gls); Lovell's Ath, Aug 1935; Bostall Heath, (manager) Jul 1938; Clapton Orient, (asst trainer) 1939.

A full back with Cardiff City Reserves in the early 1920s, Pugsley later formed part of the half back line in Grimsby's championship-winning side. MacLachlan, Hardy and Pugsley were 'a half back line and driving force of Grimsby Town' and 'destructive of the opposing attack and shone as a feeding line'. The well-built Pugsley was 'a polished and effective footballer' with good leadership qualities. He rarely found the target, though, scoring his first goal in league football in his 55th game, a 1-6 defeat at Port Vale.

He left Grimsby because his wife didn't take to the east coast of England so moved closer to home by joining Bristol City. Unusually, he had signed for Grimsby on the understanding that he would be given a free transfer when he indicated he wanted a move, but the club were reluctant to let him go in 1927 despite knowing they had little choice. However, Pugsley was completely out of form at Ashton Gate and was released in May 1928, with one journalist commenting that the Welshman's form had been so poor he didn't expect to hear of him again; he was later surprised to see Pugsley doing so well in the Charlton team and gaining a Welsh cap. The defender was a tough individual and suffered a broken jaw and broken nose in the early part of the 1930-31 season but still did not miss a match. On leaving the game, Pugsley worked as boilermaker/riveter in a shipyard but after the war was on the coaching staff at Ninian Park and kept a public house in the city.

Jack's brother Joe was capped by Wales at rugby union in 1910 and 1911 and another brother, Tommy, played soccer for the amateur side Cardiff Albion and was on Cardiff City's books.

Honours:
Grimsby T - FL 3rd Div (N) champions 1926
Charlton Ath - FL 3rd Div (S) champions 1929

323 Bertie Williams
B: Merthyr Tydfil; 4 Mar 1907
D: Sheffield (Eng); 5 Jan 1968
Outside left/Inside forward
   (5ft 6½ins, 10st 6lbs)
1 cap: (Bristol C) v Ire 1930

Career: Castle Sch (Merthyr); Georgetown Sch; Georgetown Stars; Cyfartha Stars; Merthyr T; Bristol C, 1927-32 (97 FL apps, 26 gls); Sheffield Utd, (£1,400) Jan 1932-37 (108 FL apps, 16 gls).

Bertie Williams joined Bristol City as 'a slip of a lad' and was subsequently described by one of the City directors as: 'that clever little beggar we got from Merthyr. You never saw such a box of tricks, the way he beat his man sometimes would have made a cat laugh'.

Despite playing well in the reserves, he had to wait a long time for his senior debut as he was thought to be too small. By February 1930, he was 'City's little box of tricks' and one writer commented: 'For sheer cleverness he is easily the best soccer player in Bristol at the present moment', while another noted, 'He isn't big but he is tenacious and daring in the way he refuses to be knocked off the ball'.

Although he possessed terrific ball control, Williams could be erratic and his performance against Derby into the FA Cup clinched his selection for Wales. Unfortunately, the team were thumped 7-0 in Belfast and he was discarded. Financial pressure in 1930 forced City to put all of their players on the transfer list but Williams, the club's top scorer, remained with Bristol until 1932, when he moved to Bramall Lane. At Sheffield United, he was in and out of the first team and spent long periods in their Central League side. Best at outside right, he filled most of the forward positions in his time at United and was called up for FA Cup final duty in 1936 when he was controversially preferred to Bird. He spent the following season almost exclusively in the reserves and left the club during the 1937 close season, over a dispute about terms, to take employment with a tool company.

Honours:
Sheffield Utd - FA Cup finalists 1936

324 Thomas Bamford
B: Port Talbot; 4 Sep 1905
D: Wrexham; 12 Dec 1967
Centre forward
   (5ft 9ins, 11st 11lbs)
5 caps (1 gl): (Wrexham) v Sco, Eng, Ire 1931; v Ire 1932; v Fra 1933

Career: Dock Stars; Cardiff Docks XI; Cardiff Wed; Bridgend T; Wrexham, April 1929-34 (204 FL apps, 175 gls); Manchester Utd, Oct 1934-38 (98 FL apps, 53 gls); Swansea T, Jun 1938-39 (FL 36 apps, 14 gls); Wrexham, (17 war-time apps, 8 gls); Hartlepool Utd, 1943-44 (13 war-time guest apps, 6 gls).

Bamford's football career never really got going until he signed amateur forms for Wrexham in April 1929, at the age of 23, and scored six goals in his first seven games. He had moved north in search of work after previously playing in local leagues around south Wales. The Brylcream-haired centre forward was soon put on pro' forms and he took over the centre forward berth from Albert Mays. His goals enabled the Racecourse club to reach their highest pre-war position, as Third Division (North) runners-up to Hull City, in 1932-33, and went on to become the club's most successful goal scorer. He still holds the Wrexham record for the most goals in a season, with 44 in 1933-34, and the club aggregate total of 175. In all competitions, including the Welsh Cup, he scored 207 goals in 245 Wrexham appearances, guaranteeing his place in the club's 'hall of fame'. Bamford's exploits attracted attention from Birmingham and Sheffield United and when Second Division Manchester United played a friendly at Wrexham in 1934, for the Gresford Colliery disaster fund, Bamford impressed and a move to Old Trafford quickly followed. His Racecourse colleague Bill Bryant moved with him as part of the club record transfer deal, with Jimmy Rice, a United reserve player, joining Wrexham.

An opportunist striker of the first order, he made his United debut at Newcastle in October 1934, scored the only goal of the game and finished the season as joint second highest scorer. In United's Second Division championship season of 1935-36, Bamford found the net on 16 occasions in 27 league appearances. The following campaign started well for Bamford, bagged eight goals in the first seven matches and finished the season as top scorer with 14 goals but couldn't save United from relegation. He moved back to Wales in 1938, where he continued to find the target on a regular basis for Swansea Town and, after retirement from football soon after the war, he settled in Wrexham where he worked at a local steel works. On the international scene, the prolific goalscorer had gained his first call-up for the 'Unknowns' in 1930 and found the net after six minutes, beating the Scottish goalkeeper, Jock Thomson, who died tragically a year later during an 'Old Firm' match. Bamford held the record for the most goals scored in the Football League by a Welsh player until overtaken by Ivor Allchurch. His brother Walter made one Football League appearance for Wrexham and later joined Carlisle United.

Honours:
Manchester Utd - FL 2nd Div champions 1936; runners-up 1938
Wrexham - Welsh Cup 1931; finalists 1932, 1933
Swansea T - Welsh Cup finalists 1938, 1940

325 William Elvet Collins

B: Rhymney; 16 Oct 1902
D: Blackwood; 23 Jan 1977
Outside right
    (5ft 7ins, 10st 10lbs)
1 cap: (Llanelli) v Sco 1931

Career: Rhymney T, 1922-23; Cardiff C, Aug 1923-27 (13 FL apps); Clapton Orient, May 1927-29 (40 FL apps, 1 gl); Lovell's Ath, Aug-Oct 1929; Rhymney, Oct 1929-30; Llanelli, 1930-32; Newport Co, Aug 1932-34 (6 FL apps, 1 gl); Oakdale Utd, 1934-37.

Elvet Collins was the type of winger who on his day could devastate a defence with his 'spectacular dashes' and 'splendid dribbles'. While never really able to reproduce his skill with the regularity to firmly establish himself in a league side, Collins was one of the most dangerous wingmen in Welsh soccer. He was 'fleet of foot', 'difficult to hold' and created plenty of chances for his colleagues. Collins was originally set to sign for Merthyr but was whisked away by Cardiff City yet, at Ninian Park, he faced stiff competitions for places and he made few first team appearances. He did play in every round of the 1927 FA Cup up to the final but was disappointed at being left out, as 12th man, at Wembley.

Collins was reckoned to be the greatest match winner Llanelli ever had: 'many games, in which they were badly outplayed, were won because he had broken away on his own and scored great goals'. When the English League clubs were unwilling to release players, Ted Robbins, the FAW secretary, raised a team from Welsh League and non-league clubs who did not have a right of veto over their players. In this way, Collins was called up for the team later dubbed the 'Unknowns'. Their battling performance against the Scots led to the team being selected *en bloc* for a second match (v England), but Collins cried off because of a knee injury he had suffered playing for Llanelli against Ebbw Vale. In April 1931, he again attracted the attention of several league clubs, including Sunderland and Everton, but remained in south Wales for the rest of his career, ultimately in the Tredegar and District League. From 1934 until his retirement Collins worked at Oakdale Colliery.

Honours:
Llanelli - Welsh National Lge (S) champions 1930
         - Welsh League Cup 1930

326 Wynne Crompton

B: Cefn y Bedd, Wrexham;
   11 Feb 1907
D: Wrexham; 28 May 1988
Full back (5ft 8ins, 11st 6lbs)
3 caps: (Wrexham) v Sco,
Eng, Ire 1931

Career: Oak Alyn Rov, 1926-27; Wrexham, Sep 1927-32 (64 FL apps); Tunbridge Wells Rang, Jun 1932-33; Clapton Orient, Jul 1933-35 (79 FL apps); Crystal Palace, May-Oct 1935; Exeter C, Oct 1935-36 (7 FL apps); Oswestry T, Sep 1936-37; Cross Street, Dec 1938-39.

Wynne Crompton was snapped up by Wrexham from Oak Alyn, where he was an ever present during the 1926-27 season. He made his league debut on 22 October 1927 against Doncaster and showed a neat, methodical approach to his work and a keenness in the tackle. Crompton developed a fine understanding with his full back partner Alf Jones and became noted for his excellent covering, tenacious tackling and reliability under pressure.

Although unlikely to have been considered if the Football League players from English clubs had been available, Crompton came to the aid of Ted Robbins in October 1930 when the selectors were having difficulty raising a side. Crompton was recruited to the 'Unknowns', came through his international test well and remained for all of the Home International Championship matches. He brought a much needed steadiness to Oswestry's Birmingham League team in 1936, but two years later a knee injury virtually ended his career. Crompton worked as a miner in Llay near Wrexham and later at the Shotton Steel Works until retirement. He was grandfather of Steve Crompton, the former Wolves and Hereford United player.

Honours:
Wrexham - Welsh Cup 1931

327 Frederick Thomas Dewey

B: Cardiff; 11 Oct 1898
D: Cardiff; 18 Jan 1980
Full back (5ft 8ins, 11st 6lbs)
2 caps: (Cardiff Corinthians) v Sco, Eng 1931

Career: Cardiff Corinthians, 1922-35.

Fred Dewey was the doyen of Welsh amateur players in the 1920s, and between 1928 and 1933 won 11 caps at that level. A hard working and safe defender, he was a splendid tackler and his whole-hearted approach made him a very popular player in south Wales soccer circles. Dewey received an unexpected call to the full Welsh side in October 1930 when Ted Robbins was unable to raise a team from the English Football League clubs. He was awarded a second cap when the 'Unknowns', were selected *en bloc* for the England match.

Dewey retired in January 1935 after giving the Corries years of dedicated service. He remained a committee member for a period and was later an FAW councillor for five years. At one time he served as a member of the FAW selection committee but resigned in August 1960 commenting; 'It is simply ridiculous that 11 men should be appointed to pick 11 players in international football, and very often Herbert Powell [FAW secretary] stands in as 12th man. They are out of step with public opinion but it is doubtful whether the Council of the FAW will listen to reason. They are a law unto themselves'. Dewey was chairman of Cardiff City for ten years from 1962, eventually becoming president. In February 1967, as Cardiff chairman, he had another clash with the FAW when he asked to watch the draw for the Welsh Cup, only to have his request turned down on the grounds that 'the draw is made in private'. Outside soccer, he was a successful businessman and had extensive interests in travel and shipping.

Dewey, who was the son of a law clerk from Somerset and an American mother, also represented Wales at junior international level in 1927. His brother, Cyril, played for Cardiff Corinthians and died in January 1933 at the age of 29.

Honours:
Cardiff Corinthians - Welsh Amateur Cup 1929, 1930, 1934; finalists 1932

328 Emrys Ellis

B: Plas Bennion, Ruabon;
   29 Jun 1904
D: Rhostyllen, Wrexham;
   24 Jun 1981
Wing half (5ft 5ins, 10st 4lbs)
3 caps: (Nunhead) v Sco, Eng 1931; (Oswestry T) v Ire 1932

Career: UCNW Bangor, 1923-27; Rhos, 1923-24; Caernarvon Ath, 1926-27; Nunhead, 1927-30; Oswestry T, Nov 1930-33; Blaenau Ffestiniog, 1933-34; Oswestry T, Aug 1934.

Emrys Ellis, the son of a miner, was an outstanding footballer and cricketer at Ruabon Grammar School, where the soccer XI were undefeated in 1921 under his captaincy. At Bangor University he gained a soccer blue in 1923-24 and was a member of the Welsh Universities championship team. While at University, Ellis also played for Rhos in the Welsh National League and then Caernarvon Athletic.

Ellis graduated in 1927 and took a teaching post in London. After playing in friendlies for Merton and Tooting, he joined Nunhead of the Isthmian League, but in late 1930, he secured a post at Oswestry Grammar School and began playing for the local club in the Birmingham League. Small of stature, Ellis was a keen tackler, very speedy and made good use of the ball. One of the 'Unknowns' who put up such a redoubtable show against the Scots in October 1930, he was known as 'Emie', and eventually became headmaster at Weston Rhyn School near Oswestry.

329 John Edward Neal

B: Llandudno; 29 Nov 1899
D: Rhos on Sea; 14 Jan 1965
Centre forward/Inside left
   (5ft 7ins, 11st 8lbs)
2 caps: (Colwyn Bay Utd) v Sco, Eng 1931

Career: UCNW Bangor, 1919-21; Llandudno T, 1921-24; Colwyn Bay Utd, Jan 1924-29; Wrexham, (£100) Mar 1929-30 (17 FL apps, 3 gls); Colwyn Bay Utd, Jan 1930-31, retired.

John Neal, the son of a Llandudno butcher and cattle dealer, spent two years at Bangor University but left without a degree. While a student, he was reserve right half for the Wales amateur XI in 1920, although later in his career he was to become far better known as a prolific goal scorer. Neal regularly found the target for Llandudno and a 13-goal spell in eight matches in October 1922 prompted Sheffield United to make an offer of £750 for him. In retrospect, Neal's failure to move was regrettable and when he did finally taste league football, at Wrexham, he was almost 30 and his powers were in decline.

Neal had signed for Colwyn Bay in January 1924, preferring a local club to an offer from Derby, and later became the club's player-manager, piling up the goals in the Welsh National League, with 42 in 1928-29: including 22 goals in seven matches between 22 December 1928 and 26 January 1929! He gained his first international cap as a member of the 'Unknowns' - a Wales side of mostly non-leaguers who were written off by the press - with one poster wondering whether the Scots would stop at 24 goals!

After retiring from the game Neal became entertainments and publicity manager for Colwyn Bay Corporation for many years and, in that capacity, he had much to do with the development of the town's Eirias Park. A one-time chairman of Colwyn Bay FC, Neal was also a keen cricketer, golfer, and a crown green bowler to county standard.

330 Walter William Robbins

B: Cardiff; 24 Nov 1910
D: Swansea; 7 Feb 1979
Outside/Inside left/Centre forward (5ft 11ins, 12st 7lbs)
11 caps (4 gls): (Cardiff C) v Sco, Eng 1931; v Sco, Eng, Ire 1932; (West Bromwich Alb) v Eng, Sco, Ire, Fra 1933; v Sco 1934; v Sco 1936

Career: Ely Central Sch; Cardiff Senior Schs; Cardiff Boys; Ely Brewery; Ely Utd (Cardiff & Dist Lge); Cardiff C, 1926-32 (88 FL apps, 38 gls); West Bromwich Alb, (£3,000) Apr 1932-39 (85 FL apps, 28 gls); Newport Co, c/season 1939-40; Cardiff C, (trainer) 1945; Swansea T, (chief scout) 1958, (trainer) Jul 1960, (asst manager) Jun 1968-71.

A forceful front runner, Robbins was a member of the Cardiff Boys team who were finalists in the 1925 Welsh Schools Shield. He worked for a local brewery in Cardiff before taking a motor engineering apprenticeship, but made a name for himself by hitting 70 goals in one season for Ely United. Robbins joined Cardiff as a 16-year-old amateur and was taken under George Latham's wing. He made a scoring debut for the Bluebirds and his invitation to join the FAW tourists to Canada in 1929 marked him out as a future international player. Robbins scored all of his first 37 goals for Cardiff at Ninian Park; his first goal in an away game came at Brentford in February 1932, a couple of months before he joined West Brom.

Robbins was a well built winger, who packed a powerful shot and once scored five goals from the outside left position against Thames FC. He spent seven seasons at West Brom but faced stiff competition for senior places and was in and out of the first team. During the Second World War, he was a trainer at Cardiff City but a long association with Swansea began in 1946. At the Vetch, Robbins filled a variety of jobs over the years and on one occasion turned down the opportunity to manage the Swans, preferring to remain one of the back-room boys. When manager Trevor Morris ran the club, Robbins was the track-suited coach who oversaw the training sessions, but he did have one spell as caretaker manager, winning five out of nine games and losing a two-legged Welsh Cup final to Cardiff. A familiar sight as Wales trainer in the 1950s, including the overseas tours, Robbins retired in 1971 but continued to scout, mostly for Swansea and Manchester United.

Honours:
Cardiff C - Welsh Cup 1930

331 William Rogers

B: Summerhill, Wrexham; 1905
D: Penyffordd, Wrexham; 14 Jan 1936
Right half/inside right
(5ft 6ins, 10st 6lbs)
2 caps: (Wrexham) v Sco, Eng 1931

Career: Summerhill; Oak Alyn Rov, Flint T (both Welsh National Lge); Tranmere Rov, (trial) 1925; Bury (am) Aug 1925; Flint T; Wrexham, Jul 1926-32 (171 FL apps, 23 gls); Newport Co, Aug 1932-33 (22 FL apps, 3 gls); Bristol Rov, 1933; Clapton Orient, Nov 1933-34 (3 FL apps); Bangor C, Sep 1934-35; Oswestry T, Jul 1936; retired.

A Wrexham stalwart for five seasons, 'Billie' Rogers spent the best years of his career at the Racecourse, during which time he appeared in virtually every position. The Wrexham chairman offered the following description of Rogers: 'He is a wholehearted player and more than that he is a utility player who can play anywhere. His love is in the game and he fears nothing. All he knows when he is on the field is that he is playing for Wrexham'. Although his all-out style of play was not universally admired, Rogers was one of the most popular players at the Racecourse with both the crowd and his colleagues.

In 1929 Billie was selected to tour North America with a Welsh FA XI and made six appearances which eventually led to him gaining two caps in 1931. When Wales were short-handed for the Scotland match, FAW secretary Ted Robbins called up the hard-working Rogers for the Wales 'Unknowns', and during his final season with the Robins he was awarded a benefit match against Everton. After leaving Wrexham, his league career quickly drew to a close and he spent one season with Bangor in the Birmingham and District League and then signed for Oswestry before retiring from football to open a billiards hall in Gwersyllt, near Wrexham. However, he soon fell ill with tuberculosis and, after a long illness, died at the early age of 30, leaving a wife and two month old child, passing away within a couple of days of his father-in-law.

Honours:
Wrexham - Welsh Cup finalists 1932

332 William Rees Thomas

B: Port Talbot; 20 Aug 1903
D: Port Talbot; Jul 1992
Outside left
(5ft 5ins, 10st 6lbs)
2 caps: (Newport Co) v Sco, Eng 1931

Career: Port Talbot Steelworks, 1921-22; Bridgend T, 1922-26; Lovell's Ath, 1926-27; Newport Co, 1927-31 (131 FL apps, 22 gls), 1931-32 (24 SL apps, 5 gls), 1932-36 (150 FL apps, 30 gls); Barry T; Aberdare Ath, 1937-39; Port Talbot Steelworks.

After starting his career with the under-19s at Port Talbot steelworks, Billy Thomas joined

Bridgend Town in the Welsh League and gained representative honours against the Irish. An exceptionally clever winger with neat footwork and a strong shot, Thomas, like many Newport County players, was signed from Lovell's Athletic, and after serving his apprenticeship with County's reserves he soon made the senior XI.

Thomas remained with Newport for ten seasons during which time the club lost and regained Football League status. A consistent player, his forceful dashes down the wing and accurate centres earned him the description 'the shining light of the Newport attack'. The wheel turned full circle for Billy when, after spells with Barry and Aberdare, he returned to play for Port Talbot steelworks during the war. Thomas, who was employed as a steel worker, was at one time the oldest living Welsh international player.

333 Leslie Williams
B: Wrexham; 16 Apr 1908
D: Wrexham; 8 Mar 1985
Outside right/Inside forward
 (5ft 8ins, 11st)
1 cap: (Wrexham) v Eng 1931

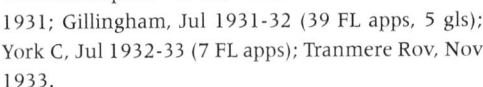

Career: Chester; Wrexham, 1929-31 (24 FL apps, 4 gls); Wolverhampton Wdrs, Feb 1931; Gillingham, Jul 1931-32 (39 FL apps, 5 gls); York C, Jul 1932-33 (7 FL apps); Tranmere Rov, Nov 1933.

Les Williams was one of 13 children and attended the National School at Wrexham. Although his brother Harold was considered to be the better footballer, Oldham Athletic were keen to sign Les but he remained at home to help look after the large family. Initially an amateur, Williams first joined non-league Chester before moving back home to Wrexham in the 1929 close season, and made his Football League debut in November 1929 at outside right in a 4-2 defeat at Doncaster Rovers. Selected to replace George Wynn, with Archie Longmuir switching wings to accommodate Williams, the following season - having turned pro in April 1930 - he began to make a name for himself as first-choice outside right and bigger clubs started to show an interest. In November 1930, Williams was called into the Wales team at the 11th hour to take the position vacated by the injured Elvet Collins after previews of the match had A N Other at outside right: perhaps the only time this ubiquitous name has featured in a Wales squad. After their performance against Scotland, the FAW selectors had been intent on fielding the 'Unknowns' *en bloc* against England, with Williams the only change, but he 'found the proposition with which he was faced too much'. Subsequently, Williams also lost his place in the Wrexham side and Wolves stepped in to sign him. His time at Molineux was short lived and he was allowed to join Gillingham without playing a first team match for the west midlands club.

'A dangerous raider and marksman', Williams could lead defenders a merry dance but the received opinion was that he lacked pace and polish and was in need of coaching. He enjoyed a good season with the Kent club but moved back north in 1932 to sign for York City. A report of a pre-season trial match stated: 'All the new men were impressive especially Williams who would appear to have solved the long-standing wing problem'. However, the assessment was premature, it turned out to be a disappointing period for the winger and after just seven league outings he was released in the summer of 1933. Williams was invited to join Glentoran in Belfast and then had a month's trial at Tranmere Rovers in November 1933 at £3 10s a week. Williams worked as a fitter's mate during in the late 1930s, before taking employment at a Wrexham leather works and then for Maelor District Council.

334 David John Astley

B: Dowlais, Merthyr Tydfil; 11 Oct 1909
D: Birchington (Eng); 7 Nov 1989
Inside forward
(5ft 11ins, 11st 11lbs)
13 caps (12 gls): (Charlton Ath) v Ire 1931; (Aston Villa) v Eng 1932; v Sco, Ire, Eng 1933; v Sco, Eng 1934; v Sco 1935; v Eng, Ire 1936; (Derby Co) v Eng, Sco, (Blackpool) v Fra 1939

Career: Dowlais Central Sch; Wales Schoolboys, 1923; New Rd Amateurs; Dowlais Welfare; Merthyr T, (am) Jul 1927, (pro) Aug 1927-28 (5 FL apps, 3 gls); Charlton Ath, (£100) Dec 1927-31 (95 FL apps, 26 gls); Aston Villa, Jun 1931-36 (165 FL apps, 92 gls); Derby Co, (£5,250) Nov 1936-39 (93 FL apps, 45 gls); Blackpool, Jan-May 1939 (18 FL apps, 6 gls); (Blackpool, Charlton Ath and Clapton in wartime); FC Metz, 1945; Inter Milan, 1948; Genoa, 1949-50; Djurgardens IF, 1950-54; Sandvikens IF, 1954-57.

Dai Astley was a coal miner who joined Merthyr from Dowlais Welfare, a Merthyr League club. Albert Lindon, the player-manager of Charlton and a former Merthyr boss, was a man who knew the Welsh soccer scene well and took him to the Valley in 1927. A slenderly-built, skilful player, he had superb positional sense and could shoot with either foot. Although naturally right-footed, Astley was said to have a 'mustard left peg' that had been perfected by hours of practice with a tennis ball. He preferred to keep the ball on the ground and was a master at deceiving defenders with his body swerve. Astley proved to be one of the most astute signings made by Aston Villa, as his prolific goal scoring record indicates, and once scored four goals for the midlands club in an FA Cup match against Swansea: not a bad achievement for a player considered by some to be lazy.

In 1936, Astley preferred a move to Derby rather than a return to Charlton and he maintained his goal-getting reputation at the Baseball Ground in an all-international forward line, but without the prospect of regular first team appearances he reluctantly left Derby to join Blackpool. At the international level, Astley found the net on a regular basis for Wales and his 12 goals in 13 matches demonstrated his uncanny knack for goals. He retired not long after the 1939-45 war and coached in Italy (Inter Milan and Genoa), France and Sweden (Djurgardens IF and Sandvikens IF) before returning the Britain to become landlord of the White Horse in Ramsgate, Kent, and in July 1957 served as president of Thanet Football League. Outside football, Astley worked for while for Rolls Royce in Derby and was uncle to Len Astley who was with Charlton Ath from 1955 to 1960.

Honours:
Charlton Ath - FL 3rd Div (S) champions 1929

335 Wilfred Bernard James

B: Newport; 17 Jan 1907
D: Sydney (Aus); 16 Aug 1976
Inside forward
(5ft 10ins, 11st 10lbs)
2 caps: (West Ham Utd) v Ire 1931; v Ire 1932

Career: Cross Keys Sch; Abercarn Welfare; Ynysddu Crusaders; Newport Co, Oct 1925-27 (20 FL apps, 8 gls); Thorne Colliery; Owston Park Rgrs, 1927-28; Notts Co, Oct 1928-30 (16 league apps, 6 goals); West Ham Utd, May 1930-32 (40 league apps, 7 goals); Charlton Ath, Feb 1932-33 (28 league apps, 3 goals); Workington, 1933-35; Carlisle Utd, Sep 1935-April 1937 (39 league apps, 4 goals).

Wilf James, the son of a bricklayer, had spells with Cross Keys, Abercarn Welfare and Ynysddu

Crusaders before signing for Newport County. A useful and clever inside forward, James had a reputation for 'good distributive work' but was himself seldom on target. Another description was 'fast, with good ball control and a splendid centre'. He left Newport for a Yorkshire colliery team and later resumed his league career at Notts County before West Ham manager, Alex MacFarlane, personally financed Wilf's move to the London club: he was later reimbursed.

In 1933, Wilf moved to Cumbria but took some time to win a place in the Workington first eleven. Carlisle then offered him a trial period in September 1935 and he was finally signed on some six weeks later. James played most of his football with Carlisle, for the reserves in the North Eastern League, and at the close of the 1936-37 season was given a free transfer. While at West Ham, James was said to have had a deep affection for his bowler hat, which was the first article of clothing he donned after emerging from the after match bath! In the late 1930s he worked as a coppersmith for the Great Western Railway Company before emigrating to Australia with his family in October 1956.

336 William Ronald John

B: Briton Ferry; 29 Jan 1911
D: Port Talbot; 12 Jul 1973
Goalkeeper
 (5ft 11ins, 11st 10lbs)
14 caps: (Walsall) v Ire 1931; (Stoke C) v Sco, Eng, Ire, Fra 1933; v Sco, Eng 1934; v Eng, Sco 1935; (Sheffield Utd) v Sco, Eng, Ire 1936; (Swansea T) v Eng, Sco 1939

Career: Neath Rd Sch; Briton Ferry Schoolboys; Briton Ferry Ath; Swansea T, 1927-28; Cwmtillery Utd, Middlesbrough (trial); Manchester Utd, 1928 (trial); Walsall, May 1928-32 (88 FL apps); Stoke C, April 1932-34 (71 FL apps); Preston N E, c/season 1934; Sheffield Utd, (£1,250) Dec 1934-36 (28 FL apps); Manchester Utd, (£600) Jun 1936-37 (15 FL apps); Newport Co, Mar-July 1937 (10 FL apps); Swansea T, Jul 1937-39 (40 FL apps); Southport (war-time guest).

Unusually for a goalkeeper, John's career had begun as an outfielder at a league club when he first went between the posts. He was a reserve half back with Walsall, but the transfer of Biddlestone and an injury to the reserve goalkeeper left the club short of cover. He did so well in a practice match that he was given the custodian's job and within months was selected for Wales. As a goalkeeper, he was 'dashing and daring - a gay cavalier who laughs fortune in the face', as one writer put it.

Earlier in his career, 'Roy' John spent three seasons with Briton Ferry Athletic and was described as a 'resolute tackler with a useful kick'. He then joined Swansea in 1927 as a full back but 'was not greatly appreciated in that position'. John was a superstitious man, to the point of never shaving on the morning of a match, and also loved playing cricket: he was, unsurprisingly, considered a talented wicket keeper. John officially retired on 11 November 1939 to become an hotel manager, playing his last match against England in the Red Cross international, but re-appeared to don Southport's colours in war-time and, in September 1942, played for a Wales XI v RAF.

Honours:
Stoke C - FL 2nd Div champions 1933
Swansea T - Welsh Cup finalist 1938

337 Cuthbert Phillips

B: Ebbw Vale; 23 Jun 1910
D: Lichfield (Eng); 21 Oct 1969
Inside forward/Winger
 (5ft 8ins, 11st)
13 caps (5 gls): (Wolverhampton Wdrs) v Ire 1931; v Eng 1932; v Sco 1933; v Sco, Ire,

Eng 1934; v Eng, Sco, Ire 1935; v Sco, (Aston Villa) v Eng, Ire 1936; v Sco 1938

Career: Victoria Sch; Wales Schoolboys, 1924; Ebbw Vale; Wolverhampton Wdrs, Oct 1929-36 (191 FL apps, 59 gls); Aston Villa, (£9,000) Jan 1936-38 (22 FL apps, 5 gls); Birmingham, Mar 1938-39 (24 FL apps, 9 gls); Chelmsford C, Jun 1939; war-time soccer; retired 1945.

'Charlie' Phillips was working as a boilerman and playing part-time football for Ebbw Vale in the Welsh League when he was chased by several clubs including Cardiff, Plymouth, and Torquay, but he opted for Wolves and headed to Molineux. An exciting winger, Phillips was fast, could centre the ball accurately and scored goals regularly. He was equally at home in the inside forward berth, was full of enthusiasm and had a large appetite for work.

In 1936, a struggling Aston Villa paid £9,000 for his services, as part of a £35,000 transfer spree over a two month period, in an attempt to stave off relegation. Phillips scored on his debut but couldn't succeed in pulling the club from the foot of the First Division and, during the 1937-38 season when Villa took the Second Division championship, he managed just a handful of games. Charlie marked his Wales debut in 1931 at the Racecourse with a goal. During the war he worked as a fitter in Bristol and retired from the game in 1945, at the age of 37, to keep a public house in Bushbury, and later in Lichfield. His son-in-law was Noel Dwyer, the Wolves, West Ham, Swansea Town and Republic of Ireland player, while his granddaughter married the former England player Frank Worthington.

Honours:
Wolverhampton Wdrs - FL 2nd Div champions 1932

338 David Thomas Richards

B: Abercanaid;
  31 Oct 1906
D: Birmingham (Eng);
  1 Oct 1969
Left half/Inside forward
  (5ft 8ins, 10st 8lbs)
21 caps: (Wolverhampton Wdrs) v Ire 1931; v Sco, Eng, Ire 1933; v Sco, Ire, Eng 1934; v Eng, Sco, Ire 1935; v Sco, (Brentford) v Eng, Ire 1936; v Eng, Sco, (Birmingham) v Ire 1937; v Sco, Eng, Ire 1938; v Eng, Sco 1939

Career: Abercanaid Schs XI; Riverfield; Bedlinog; Merthyr T, 1925-27; Wolverhampton Wdrs, (£300) Aug 1927-35 (218 FL apps, 6 gls); Brentford, (£3,500) Nov 1935-37 (29 FL apps); Birmingham C, (£3,500) Mar 1937-39 (61 FL apps, 2 gls); Walsall, Jul 1939-40 (31 FL apps); Sedgley, 1945; retired.

'Dai' Richards was a strong player, full of ability and with a keen eye for an opening. Originally a full back, he was converted by Wolves to the half back position where his distributional skills were far more effective. The versatile Richards spent nine years at Molineux, helping Wolves to promotion to the First Division in 1932, and was described as: 'one of the few players who considered it important, early in their career, to develop two good feet ... he plies the ball well and is not content with a defensive role, often seen backing up his forwards in hot attacks'. He joined Brentford, for their first season in top flight, following a £3,500 transfer, forming a highly effective half back line with McKenzie and James. He failed to settle in the English capital but the nature of his transfer to Birmingham was a surprise, and highly unusual. He was supposed to appear for Brentford against the Blues but on the morning of the match was transferred and instead found himself facing his former colleagues. As war approached, Richards was transfer listed by Birmingham for £1,500 and was signed by Walsall, although it was unlikely that they paid what would have been a club record fee. A keen cricketer in the off season, Richards later had a building contracting business.

Honours:
Wolverhampton Wdrs - FL 2nd Div champions 1932

339 Thomas Edwards
B: Aberfan: 9 Apr 1906
D: Belfast; 16 Nov 1980
Wing half/Inside forward
1 cap: (Linfield) v Sco 1931

Career: Llanelli; Fordsons (later Cork C); Portadown, c/season 1929-31; Linfield, Jun 1931-38; Coleraine, c/season 1938-39; Cliftonville, (coach) 1939-40.

One of nine children, Edwards was something of a rarity – a Welshman playing in Northern Ireland. He was originally a half back and left Llanelli to join Cork club, Fordsons, where he switched to the forward line and his career flourished. In September 1930 he was invited for a trial at Spurs but failed to agree terms and returned to Northern Ireland where, in 1931, he was described as: 'a polished forward who knows the shortest way of drawing off a defence and leaving an opening for a club mate'. At the end of the 1930-31 season he was again chased by several clubs and eventually opted for Linfield. A magnificent tackler, Edwards was also a fine attacking player and had a particularly good game against the Football League at Windsor Park. Later, he reverted to half back and acquired a reputation for consistent but unflashy play. Edwards, who also interested Blackpool in the early 1930s, married a local girl – the nurse who looked after him when he was in Belfast City Hospital with a septic throat – and settled in Ulster, working at the Harland and Wolfe shipyard until being made redundant, after which he took an office job until his retirement in 1979. Edwards, who remains the only player capped by Wales at full level while with an Irish club, missed the 1932 Irish Cup final because his father had been killed in a pit accident and he returned home for the funeral.

Honours:
Linfield - Irish Lge champions 1932, 1934, 1935
         - Irish Cup 1934, 1936

340 Ernest Matthew Glover
B: Swansea; 9 Sep 1910
D: Tamerton Foliot (Eng); 9 Sep 1971
Centre forward (6ft, 12st 9lbs)
7 caps (7 gls): (Grimsby T) v Sco 1932; v Ire 1934; v Sco 1936; v Eng, Sco, Ire 1937; v Ire 1939

Career: Glanmôr Sch (Swansea); Swansea Schoolboys; Wales Schoolboys, 1925; Forward Movement; Swansea T; Grimsby T, Dec 1928-39 (227 FL apps, 180 gls); Plymouth Argyle, May 1939-40 (3 FL apps, 1 gl).

At school, 'Pat' Glover was a splendid athlete but on the soccer field he, 'neglected his skill because of his size'. Remarkably, when the school's sports master resigned, mid-term, Glover took over the job until a successor was found! He won schoolboy honours for Wales but didn't turn professional on leaving school, opting to play for Swansea while working as a machinery dismantler and later a railway porter. When, aged 18, Grimsby offered him an opportunity he moved to England and he joined the club where he developed quickly and, in 1929-30, set a Midland League record with 71 goals for Grimsby Reserves. When the club's first team centre forward, Coleman, joined Arsenal, Glover was promoted to the senior side.

'Pat' was a deadly shot around goal but was also a creative player. He topped the Second Division scoring charts in 1933-34 with 42 goals and, in 1934-35, netted 34 in the First Division. In contemporary reports he was described as 'a handsome Welshman with a leonine head capped by luxuriant black hair' and 'a centre forward of popular imagination'. Grimsby refused an offer of £12,000 for his transfer, but at the beginning of the 1937-38 season a knee injury seriously interrupted his career. Out of the first team and unable to regain his place, Glover was transferred to Plymouth but the war prevented him from re-establishing his league career. He served with the Marine Police during the war and then kept the Kings Arms in Tiverton for 28 years until his death.

Glover also played in Inter-League matches and made one appearance in goal for Grimsby when they were short-handed in March 1939; the two first choice goalkeepers Tweedy and Moulson were injured and Pat was selected to stand in.

Honours:
Grimsby T - FL 2nd Div champions 1934

341 Philip Henry Griffiths

B: Tylorstown, Rhondda;
  25 Oct 1905
D: Stoke (Eng); 14 May 1978
Outside right
  (5ft 9ins, 10st 6lbs)
1 cap: (Everton) v Sco 1932

Career: Tylorstown; Wattstown; Stoke C, (trial) Apr 1926; Port Vale, Aug 1926-31 (85 FL apps, 32 gls); Everton, May 1931-33 (8 FL apps, 3 gls); West Bromwich Alb, May 1933-34; Cardiff C, Jun 1934-35 (13 FL apps, 2 gls); Folkestone T, Aug 1935; London Paper Mills, Oct 1936; Dunkerque, (player-coach) c/season 1937-39; Folkestone T, Aug 1939; Port Vale, 1939-46.

A prolific goal scorer for Wattstown - 79 goals during the 1925-26 season - Phil Griffiths was invited to Stoke for a trial but ended up signing for neighbours Port Vale. At the Potteries club, he was switched to the right wing and played a leading part in the club's championship success of 1930. Griffiths moved to Everton for what was described as 'a heavy fee' but did not live up to expectation, although while at Goodison he gained his only cap - a fact inexplicably omitted from several record books. His international debut was not a success as one report commented: 'he only came into the picture by reason of an occasional flash and missed a gilt-edged chance'. Griffiths, whose wife was a French teacher, was player-coach for Dunkerque in the late 1930s. A well-known tenor and keen badminton player, he was for more than 21 years a PT instructor at Bagnall Youth Club.

Honours:
Port Vale - FL 3rd Div (N) champions 1930
West Bromwich Alb - Central Lge champions 1934

342 Aneurin Glyndŵr Richards

B: Mardy, Rhondda;
  24 Aug 1902
D: Barnsley (Eng); 4 Jan 1976
Full back
  (5ft 8½ins, 11st 6lbs)
1 cap: (Barnsley) v Sco 1932

Career: Mardy Alb; Mardy, Aug 1922; Pontypridd; Tylorstown, Mar 1925; Bridgend, Dec 1926; Hull C, Aug 1927; Barnsley, 1927-34 (122 FL apps); Southport, Feb 1935 (1 FL app); Bexhill 1935-36.

Richards, a coal miner, played for several clubs in the south of Wales before the opportunity of a trial at Hull City presented itself. He was turned down but Barnsley secretary-manager J J Commins stepped in and Richards made his

Football League debut in December 1927 at, ironically, Hull City. An eye injury in January 1928 interrupted his progress and it was not until September 1930 that he gained a regular place in the Barnsley side.

A skilful and polished defender, Richards was called up by Wales when neither Ben Williams nor Sid Lawrence was available for selection, thus becoming the first Barnsley player to be called up for international duty since George Utley in 1913. The popular full back was, according to one scribe, 'an intrepid type of defender and not one to be intimidated by shock tactics or a mere display of brawn where brain was lacking', and 'a fearless tackler and a resourceful player'.

A badly broken leg at Tranmere in October 1933 was the turning point of his career and a blow from which he never really recovered. Richards sustained a compound fracture of the left leg below the knee and his recovery was long and difficult. Barnsley took some time to adjust to his loss but eventually went on to take the Third Division (North) championship. Richards, who had played only nine league matches in the 1933-34 campaign when injury struck, tried a comeback at Southport for his former Barnsley manager J J Commins but could no longer cope with the demands of Third Division football.

His brief period as Bexhill player-coach ended when they were knocked out of the FA Cup and 'Nye', as he was known, went into business for a time before spending 18 years in the Barnsley Borough Police Force, retiring at 55 to become an ambulance attendant at Barnsley Colliery.

343 Benjamin Ellis
B: Aberbargoed; 11 Apr 1906
D: Motherwell (Sco);
   11 Jan 1968
Full back (5ft 9ins, 10st 10lbs)
6 caps: (Motherwell) v Eng 1932; v Sco, Eng 1933; v Sco 1934; v Eng 1936; v Sco 1937

Career: Aberbargoed; Bargoed; New Tredegar; Bargoed Ath; Bangor (N Ireland), 1928-30; Motherwell, (£400) Oct 1930-39.

Ben Ellis was one of five sons of an Ipswich-born colliery worker. He initially joined Bangor on trial but the Irish club's executive decided to offer him terms before the end of his probation. He was said to have 'displayed capital form from the start', with one scribe commenting: '[Ellis] does not stand on ceremony when the enemy is knocking at the door, but gets right in and sends them about their business. He is not rash because in his speed to put his own side on the attack he uses method and brains. A splendid kicker with both feet, Ellis is a good positional player and can accommodate himself on either flank'.

In October 1930, Ellis switched to the Scottish League and his solid and steadfast performances for Motherwell marked him out as one of the best full backs in the league. Club officials had travelled to Northern Ireland especially to see him play and were authorised to spend £500 on the player: they got their man for £350 plus another £50 after 12 senior appearances. Ellis remained north of Hadrian's Wall for so long that he almost came to be regarded as a naturalised Scotsman and, in 1939, he toured the United States of America and Canada with the Scottish Football Association squad. On the occasion of his benefit match in 1937 against Huddersfield he was described thus: 'Ben Ellis, whose skill, courage and enthusiasm stamps him as one of the greatest players ever to wear the Firs Park claret and amber'. Motherwell won the Scottish League championship in 1932, their first such championship, which broke the dominance of league championship wins by Rangers and Celtic that had lasted since 1904, when Third Lanark had taken the title. Ellis was selected by Wales on 16 occasions but Motherwell were riding the crest of the wave in Scotland and would not release him.

On retiring from the game following an accident at an engineering works in 1943, he joined the Motherwell staff as groundsman and coach and held the posts until 1955 when a new management team was appointed. Subsequently, Ellis earned a living with his own masseur business near Firs Park, was later a machine operator and, at the time of his death, a factory inspector with Anderson Boyes Ltd. Ben is probably the only Welsh international player to have a road named after him, outside Wales – Ellis Way in Motherwell – which is in sight of Firs Park and Ben's own home. It was opened by his daughter Nita in 1990.

Ellis was also an excellent snooker player and competed in exhibition matches against some of the country's leading players, including Joe Davis. His brother William also played in the Irish League.

Honours:
Motherwell - Scottish Lge champions 1932;
runners-up 1933
- Scottish Cup finalists 1933, 1939

344 Hugh Edward Foulkes

B: Llandudno; 13 Apr 1909
D: Birmingham (Eng);
16 Dec 1981
Full back (5ft 9ins, 11st 4lbs)
1 cap: (West Bromwich Alb) v Ire 1932

Career: Wales Schoolboys; Llandudno T, 1928-30; Manchester C, (trial) Jan 1929; West Bromwich Alb, Mar 1930-37 (15 FL apps); Guildford C, (SL) May 1937-38; Darlington, Jun 1938-39 (35 FL apps, 1 gl).

Foulkes was one of several players who came to notice in the amateur international trials. His performances for Llandudno in the Welsh League were monitored by a number of clubs and, in March 1930, he was signed by West Brom on amateur forms. Foulkes remained with Llandudno until the end of the season but failed to gain the expected amateur cap.

He moved to the Hawthorns at the start of the 1930-31 season but found his first team prospects were limited and he made only a handful of league appearances in seven years with the club. Nevertheless, during that time he gained three Central League championship medals with the reserves. Hughie was a thoughtful, polished player who packed a powerful shot and cleared his lines neatly. He returned to league action with Darlington after a spell with Guildford and retired during the war. Before turning professional, Foulkes had worked as a plumber.

345 Sidney Wilfred Lawrence

B: Penrhiwceiber;
16 Mar 1909
D: Swansea; 10 Jun 1949
Right back (5ft 9ins, 12st)
8 caps: (Swansea T) v Ire 1932; v Fra 1933; v Sco, Ire, Eng 1934; v Eng, Sco 1935; v Sco 1936

Career: Penrhiwceiber Rgrs; Swansea T, Jul 1930-39 (312 FL apps, 11 gls); Swindon T, Jun 1939-40 (1 FL app); Haverfordwest, 1946-47.

Swansea discovered Sid Lawrence with Penrhiwceiber Rangers and he was invited to join the Vetch Field club following a successful trial where he replaced Ben Williams, the Swans' accomplished defender, who had been transferred to Everton. An early assessment of Lawrence was: 'he has a splendid physique and with additional speed should be the equal to the demands of all opponents'.

Lawrence went on to become one of the strongest defenders in the Second Division and a splendid servant to the Vetch Field club but, when former Swans manager Neil Harris took over at Swindon, Lawrence and Bill Irvine joined him at the Wiltshire club. The full back played in 10 of Swindon's matches in the South-West section of the regional league in 1939-40 and in one game, against Swansea, 14 of the 22 players on the pitch were Welsh. The link with Swansea continued when he became a licensee in Swansea, but that resulted in Sid's appearances for Swindon becoming fewer. The *Swindon Advertiser* bemoaned the absence of the Lawrence and Emanuel full-back partnership, noting that every time the pair played together Swindon had been victorious. Interestingly, Hitler's invasion of The Netherlands and Belgium caused disruption to Swindon's preparations for the match with several servicemen on standby and half-an-hour before the game there were only seven players in their dressing room. A full side was eventually mustered with a player under the prosaic name of 'Smith' emerging as the hero by scoring two goals to earn a draw. Assumed names were common in war-time matches as players would often swap duties unbeknown to their officers.

Lawrence, whose career at Swindon came to an end when the club's ground was requisitioned by the War Department until late 1945, continued as landlord of the Ye Olde Red Cow, Swansea, but died at a young age. His son David played league football with Swansea between 1967 and 1971, and was capped by Wales at an amateur level.

Honours:
Swansea T - Welsh Cup 1932; finalists 1938

346 Thomas John Jones

B: Tonypandy, Rhondda;
11 Aug 1908
D: West Bromwich (Eng);
20 Aug 1971
Outside right (5ft 8½ins, 11st)
2 caps: (Sheffield Wed) v Ire 1932; v Fra 1933

Career: Mid-Rhondda; Tranmere Rov, Mar 1926-29 (89 FL apps, 30 gls); Sheffield Wed, Jun 1929-34 (29 FL apps, 6 gls); Manchester Utd, Jun 1934-35 (20 FL apps, 4 gls); Watford, May 1935-46 (122 FL apps, 22 gls); Guildford C, (free) Jun 1946; Tranmere Rov, (trainer/coach) Aug 1946; Workington, (trainer/coach) 1953; Birmingham C, (asst trainer) Aug 1958; West Bromwich Alb, (asst trainer) Dec 1965-68.

When Bert Cooke, the Tranmere manager, arrived in Tonypandy to sign Jones he was buttonholed by the young footballer's father who commented, 'yes, my boy can play football and fight too. Whenever anyone is in trouble off comes his coat and up come his sleeves'. Much to the embarrassment of Jones, by no means a pugnacious player, the story became folklore in Tranmere circles. Originally an inside left, Jones had also interested Dundee but preferred to join the Cheshire club.

After a few seasons on the Wirral, Jones moved on to Sheffield Wednesday, where a bright future was predicted for him, but the consistent form of teammate Hooper largely kept him out. Jones moved on to Watford, where he settled in well after a good start, scoring a hat-trick in a trial match. A strongly-built winger with a habit of cutting inside the defence, the industrious Jones became a popular figure at Vicarage Road. He retired from playing soon after leaving Watford, lived in Rickmansworth and was employed in a paper mill. Subsequently he worked as a trainer/coach at various clubs until 1968.

347 John Edward Parris

B: Pwllmeyric, Chepstow;
31 Jan 1911
D: Sedbury (Eng); 1971
Outside left
(5ft 10ins, 12st 4lbs)
1 cap: (Bradford P A) v Ire 1932

Career: Chepstow T; Bradford P A, Aug 1928-34 (132 FL apps, 38 gls); Bournemouth, Jun 1934-36 (104 FL apps, 23 gls); Luton T, Feb 1936-37 (7 FL apps,

2 gls); Northampton T, Nov 1937-39 (25 FL apps, 7 gls); Bath C (war-time); Cheltenham T; Gloucester C.

The first black player to appear in a full international match for Wales, Ted Parris was born in Wales of parents who, according to census returns, had emigrated from Canada. However, when his father enlisted in the Army during the First World War he gave his birthplace as Barbados. Parris joined Bradford PA from Chepstow as a 17-year-old trialist and immediately pleased the Third Division (North) club with his displays, scoring 14 goals during the 1931-32 season - the club's leading scorer - in the Second Division. Well-respected Bolton referee J T Howcroft welcomed the emergence of Parris with the admirable, if possibly not wholly accepted, view: 'There is rather too much of this colour bar and I should not like to think that it will have any effect against Parris. If merit is anything to go by he has certainly come to stay in the Bradford team'.

An exceptionally quick player, Parris was said to 'provide plenty of opportunities for his colleagues' and packed a tremendous shot in both feet. One scribe wrote: 'he is a dangerous winger who has given many full backs an uncomfortable afternoon and needs close marking', while another commented 'he has speed and cleverness, his unselfishness is an excellent trait but he should shoot more'. Parris was signed for Luton in 1937 by manager Warney Cresswell, to solve his 'urgent left wing problem', but made only a handful of appearances in two seasons. He was later employed in an aircraft factory.

348 David Jenkin Lewis

B: Merthyr Tydfil; 2 Nov 1912
D: Llanharan; 4 Aug 1997
Outside left (5ft 5ins, 9st 6lbs)
2 caps: (Swansea T) v Sco, Eng 1933

Career: Gellyfaelog Amateurs; Swansea T, 1929-36 (109 FL apps, 5 gls); Bury, May 1936-37 (8 FL apps); Crystal Palace, 1937-38; Bristol Rov; Bath C; Llanelli; Aberaman.

The diminutive winger had joined Gellyfaelog Amateurs on leaving school and tasted early success in the Aberdare and Merthyr leagues. Lewis' performances soon caught the attention of Swansea where he made a rapid entry into league football, playing in the first team a mere six weeks after joining the club.

Lewis did well on his league debut against Burnley but never got an extended run in the first team. Although something of a lightweight, and liable to be put off his game by hard tackling full backs, he was a tricky individual who packed a rasping shot. 'Jinky', as he was known, suffered from knee trouble throughout his career and was released by Bury after only one season. He made no senior appearances at Crystal Palace or Bristol Rovers and then had a short spell with Bath while working in industry with ICI. Lewis spent the war as a physical training instructor with the Welch Regiment and played for Blyth Shipyard FC, the war-time equivalent of Blyth Spartans. Following the War he continued to work for ICI until 1952 after which, for many years until his retirement in 1979, he was employed as a postman in Sketty.

Honours:
Swansea T - Welsh Cup 1932

349 James Patrick Murphy

B: Pentre, Rhondda;
  8 Aug 1910
D: Manchester (Eng);
  14 Nov 1989
Right half (5ft 8ins, 10st 5lbs)
15 caps: (West Bromwich Alb) v Eng, Ire, Fra 1933; v Sco, Eng 1934; v Eng, Sco, Ire

1935; v Sco, Eng, Ire 1936; v Sco, Ire 1937; v Sco, Eng 1938

Career: Ton Pentre Sch; Wales Schoolboys, 1924; Ton Pentre Boys; Treorchy Thurs; Treorchy Jnrs; Mid-Rhondda Utd; West Bromwich Alb, Feb 1928-Mar 1939 (204 FL apps); Swindon T, Mar-May 1939 (4 FL apps); Morris Commercial, 1939-40.

Although Jimmy Murphy spent 11 years at the Hawthorns and made over 200 league appearances for West Brom, his club career is forever associated with Manchester United and the era of the Busby Babes. It was Murphy who took over the reins at Old Trafford after the Munich air crash of 1958 while Matt Busby lay injured in a German hospital, and guided United to the FA Cup final on a wave of popular public sentiment.

A schoolboy international, Murphy was the son of Irish parents and played the church organ as a youth. On leaving school, he became an errand boy and played for local junior sides. However, sport and work didn't mix and he lost his job for taking too much time off. The out-of-work Murphy was recruited by West Brom as an outside left but was converted to an attacking wing half with a reputation as a sharp tackler and a huge appetite for work. Having gained his first cap in November 1932 when Fred Keenor was 'rested', Murphy remained a regular for Wales for most of the 1930s.

He served with the Eighth Army during the war and fought in the North African campaign before being moved to Italy where he spent the last 18 months of the war in charge of sports services for his regiment. Murphy's team included seven internationals, including Bryn Jones, and it was while he was out in Italy that he met Matt Busby. Over a cup of tea in the NAAFI they discussed Manchester's prospects and decided to get together after the war. In 1945, he was duly invited by Busby to join United as chief coach, becoming assistant manager some ten years later. The United boss later described him as: 'my first and most important signing'. It has been widely recognised, and especially by those involved with Manchester United at the time, including players and coaching staff, that Murphy had more than a little influence in bringing players through to first team level. Although Matt Busby had the courage to play what became the famous Busby Babes, it was Jimmy Murphy who coached them and turned them into stars. Many in the football world felt that Murphy never received the proper recognition that was due to him.

In October 1956, Murphy took on the additional job of Welsh team manager, succeeding Walley Barnes but, as one newspaper commented: 'as a manager, all Jimmy Murphy does at the moment is advise on tactics after the team has been chosen [by the FAW selectors]'. A great coach and an excellent motivator, he guided Wales to their only appearance, to date, in the World Cup finals held in Sweden in 1958. The pressure of running the two jobs became too much and in 1964 he gave up the Wales post. Murphy continued as assistant manager at Old Trafford until 1971 and then scouted for the club. Jimmy's son was one of those involved, with others from Welsh football and Manchester United, who unveiled a plaque outside the house where Murphy was born, and options for a statue of Murphy at Old Trafford are being explored to recognise his importance to the success of Manchester United.

Honours:
West Bromwich Alb - FA Cup finalists 1935

350 William Evans

B: Waunllwyd, Ebbw Vale; 7 Nov 1912
D: Ponders End (London, Eng); 22 Jul 1976
Outside left (5ft 6ins, 13st)
6 caps (1 gl): (Tottenham H)
v Ire 1933; v Sco, Eng 1934; v Eng 1935; v Eng, Ire 1936

Career: Ebbw Vale ex-schoolboys; Cardiff C, (am); Tottenham H, (am, with Hayward Sports and

Northfleet) May 1929, (pro) May 1931-36 (178 FL apps, 78 gls); Fulham, May 1937.

'Willie' Evans attended the same school as Eugene O'Callaghan and Bill Whateley who also both joined Spurs, but before moving to the London club as a young amateur he had worked as a pit lad. Willie was firstly given a football apprenticeship at Hayward Sports and Northfleet - Tottenham's nursery clubs - before turning professional in May 1931. He made his debut for the north London club as a teenager in November 1931 and scored twice in a 6-2 victory over Swansea.

Evans had superb ball control, perfect timing and a cannon shot in each foot, but more importantly he never seemed to have an off day. Every time he made tracks for goal there was a buzz of anticipation from the Spurs crowd and his reputation and accuracy as a penalty taker was second to none. In his first full season - 1932-33 - he helped the club gain promotion to the First Division, scoring a remarkable total of 28 goals in 42 games. However, a collision with Harry Hibbs in the England match in September 1934 left him badly injured and led to a loss of confidence. Evans came back successfully enough, but in 1936 a serious knee injury ended his bright career at White Hart Lane. At the age of 24, he retired and joined Fulham on a free transfer to take up coaching duties. In later years, he reported on youth football for the *Daily Mirror*.

Honours:
Tottenham H - FL 2nd Div runners-up 1933
[Also won a London Challenge Cup medal and Sheriff of London's Shield medal]

351 William Edward Richards

B: Abercanaid, Merthyr Tydfil; 11 Aug 1905
D: Wolverhampton (Eng); 30 Sep 1956
Outside right
 (5ft 8ins, 11st 4lbs)

1 cap: (Fulham) v Ire 1933

Career: Troedyrhiw Carltons; Mid Rhondda Utd, Jul 1923; Merthyr T, 1926 (1 FL app); Wolverhampton Wdrs, May 1926-28 (30 FL apps, 2 gls); Coventry C, Dec 1928-31 (77 FL apps, 11 gls); Fulham, Jun 1931-34 (76 FL apps, 13 gls); Brighton & H A, Aug 1935-37 (44 FL apps, 8 goals); Bristol Rov, Oct-Dec 1937 (4 FL apps); Folkestone T, Aug 1938.

Bill Richards was a product of the many pit teams of industrial south Wales, and joined Wolves with his brother Dai, initially as an amateur. He made his debut in December 1927 when regular winger Coundon went down with diphtheria, but his career failed to take off at Molineux and he enjoyed his best periods at Coventry and then, after a £100 transfer, at Fulham where Richards helped The Cottagers to the Third Division (South) championship in 1931-32. He was noted as a fast, raiding winger who supplied an endless supply of crosses for Fulham's big central attackers, and his recognition by the FAW selectors made him the first Fulham player to win a Welsh cap when - in his only international appearance - he made a useful contribution to a 4-1 win. Richards left Craven Cottage when John Arnold's signing meant increased competition for places and found life more congenial at Brighton, before concluding his career at Southern League Folkestone. Richards was also a good cricketer and golfer. After leaving soccer he was employed in the construction industry.

Honours:
Fulham - FL 3rd Div (S) champions 1932

352 Leslie Jenkin Jones

B: Aberdare; 1 Jul 1911
D: Llanfyrnach; 11 Jan 1981
Inside left
 (5ft 7ins, 10st 12lbs)
11 caps (1 gl): (Cardiff C) v Fra 1933; (Coventry C) v Ire 1935; v Sco 1936; v Eng, Sco,

Ire 1937; (Arsenal) v Sco, Eng, Ire 1938; v Eng, Sco 1939

Career: Wales Schoolboys 1925; Aberdare Ath; Cardiff C, Aug 1928-34 (140 FL apps, 31 gls); Coventry C, Jan 1934-37 (139 FL apps, 69 gls); Arsenal, Nov 1937-45 (46 FL apps, 3 gls); Swansea T, (guest) 1944-45, (player-coach) Jun 1946-47 (2 FL apps); Barry T, (manager/coach) Jun 1947-48; Brighton & H A, Aug 1948 (3 FL apps); Scunthorpe Utd, (manager) Jun 1950-51; Barry T, (manager) Jul 1963-Mar 1964.

Les Jones joined Cardiff in 1928 from his home town club Aberdare where he had combined his playing career with an apprenticeship for his father - also the president of the Aberdare Valley League - in the family's butcher shop. At Ninian Park, Jones formed a formidable left wing partnership with Walter Robbins and soon attracted the interest, and an offer, from Charlton Athletic which was rejected by Cardiff's directors. However, they couldn't prevent the inevitable and, in 1934, the forward moved to Coventry City where he was the club's leading scorer in the 1934-35 season with 27 goals and earning the glowing comment: 'Quicksilver, he is always on the move, has sound ball control, an uncanny sense of position and a non-stop urge to keep on the move'.

Jones was controversially transferred to Arsenal in 1937 - in exchange for £1,500 plus Davidson, after Coventry had turned down a £6,000 bid from Spurs a year earlier - and in his first season with the Gunners, Jones won a First Division Championship medal. Along with other members of the Gunners' squad, the Welshman also appeared in the 1939 film *The Arsenal Stadium Mystery*. During the late 1930s, Les was an automatic choice for his country but the outbreak of war badly affected his career and, by the time hostilities ended, he was 34 years old and he never really re-established himself as a player. He turned to management at Swansea and then at Scunthorpe United, leading them into the Football League in 1950. He was later secretary of the British Timken social club in Northampton, where he was in charge of sporting activities, but after several years out of the game he returned to manage Port Talbot. When, after a few weeks, he saw the post of Barry manager advertised, he applied and was appointed. It was not an entirely happy time; the team struggled and when Barry lost 10-1 at Ashford in February 1964 the writing was on the wall. Jones resigned in March 1964 and returned to Northampton.

Honours:
Arsenal - FL 1st Div champions 1938
 - FL War Cup finalists 1941
 - London Lge champions 1942
Cardiff C - Welsh Cup 1930
Coventry C - 3rd Div (S) champions 1935

353 Alfred Day

B: Ebbw Vale; 2 Oct 1907
D: Harringey (London, Eng); Nov 1997
Right half
 (5ft 9ins, 10st 10lbs)
1 cap: (Tottenham H) v Ire 1934

Career: Pontygof Sch; Ebbw Vale; Cheshunt; Northfleet (Spurs' nursery side); Tottenham H, May 1931-36 (13 FL apps); Millwall, May 1936-37 (5 FL apps); Southampton, (free) May 1937-38 (22 FL apps); Tranmere Rov, May 1938-39 (32 FL apps); Swindon T, Jun 1939 (1 app); Brighton & H A, 1939-40; Bournemouth, 1940-41; Lincoln C, Nov 1941; Reading, Sep 1945.

Remarkably, Alf Day played for Wales before making his debut in first-class football. FAW secretary Ted Robbins rang Arthur Turner, his counterpart at Spurs, to ask him if he knew of anyone who could turn out for the much-depleted Wales team. Turner mentioned a promising reserve half back whom he thought might be Welsh, checked with the player, and Day was capped far quicker than he could have imagined.

He had joined Spurs as an amateur along with Eugene Callaghan, another Ebbw Vale player, and the two were considered to be 'Spurs future men'. However, Day never made his mark at White Hart Lane, possibly because his style did not fit in with the Spurs method of the time. Nevertheless, he appeared in 139 London Combination matches before eventually being released on a free transfer.

At Southampton, Day showed solid defensive qualities, was an excellent long passer but had a tendency to dwell on the ball, and his thoughtful distribution was sometimes marred by his being caught in possession. His subsequent transfer to Tranmere Rovers not only prolonged his professional career but also meant that he had played in all the divisions of the Football League. During the Second World War, Day was telephone operator with the RAF and later worked at Brimstown power station in Edmonton.

354 Harry Hanford

B: Blaengwynfi; 9 Oct 1908
D: Melbourne (Aus);
  26 Nov 1995
Centre half (5ft 10ins, 11st)
7 caps: (Swansea T) v Ire 1934; v Sco 1935; v Eng, (Sheffield Wed) v Ire 1936; v Sco, Eng 1938; v Fra 1939

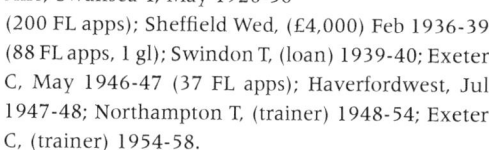

Career: Wales Schoolboys, 1922; Ton Pentre; Blaengwynfi Jnrs; Swansea T, May 1926-36 (200 FL apps); Sheffield Wed, (£4,000) Feb 1936-39 (88 FL apps, 1 gl); Swindon T, (loan) 1939-40; Exeter C, May 1946-47 (37 FL apps); Haverfordwest, Jul 1947-48; Northampton T, (trainer) 1948-54; Exeter C, (trainer) 1954-58.

Harry Hanford joined Swansea as a groundstaff boy, quickly demonstrated the qualities to make the grade in league football and spent nine years at the Vetch Field, eventually becoming club captain. Hanford was a centre half of the stopper variety, 'tough as teak', 'cool and clever' and a good distributor of the ball. He didn't believe in running about but relied on his positional play.

This quiet but effective player made a lasting impression at Sheffield Wednesday and helped the Hillsborough club get back on its feet. Despite having his league career with Wednesday cut short by the war, when he had guested for Swansea while serving in the Police War Reserve, his services were recognised by the Yorkshire club on 26 August 1946. He was, by then, an Exeter player, but was invited as a guest of honour to a dinner held at the Grand Hotel, Sheffield, to recognise those players who had given the club loyal service. Hanford retired from league football in 1947 to captain Haverfordwest in the Welsh League (South) but the following year ended his playing career to become trainer for Northampton Town. A qualified physiotherapist, he was subsequently trainer at Exeter City before opening a private physiotherapy practice in Swansea. Hanford later emigrated to Australia and worked for the MEB Power Station. On his death in Melbourne, he was cremated and his ashes returned to Swansea and scattered on the Vetch Field.

355 David Owen Jones

B: Cardiff; 28 Oct 1910
D: Leicester (Eng);
  20 May 1971
Full back (5ft 11ins, 11st 7lbs)
7 caps: (Leicester C) v Ire, Eng 1934; v Eng, Sco 1935; v Eng, Ire 1936; v Ire 1937

Career: Ely Utd (Cardiff); Ebbw Vale, 1929; Charlton Ath (trial); Ebbw Vale; Millwall (trial); Clapton Orient, Aug 1931-33 (56 FL apps); Leicester C, (£200) May 1933-47 (230 FL apps, 4 gls), (war-time guest for Notts Co and West Ham Utd); Mansfield T, Oct 1947-49 (74 FL apps); Hinckley Ath, (player-manager) c/season 1949.

'Dai Osmond' was seen by Millwall scouts while playing for Ebbw Vale and spent one season at the Den - exclusively as a reserve - having earlier been an unsuccessful trialist at Charlton. Jones, who began work as a sawyer and later worked on the fishing trawlers operating out of Cardiff before turning pro', made his name with Clapton Orient and became noted for his 'pace, power and fine judgement'.

He moved to Leicester in May 1933 and at £200 proved a bargain buy. A strong defender, described as 'a steady player with skilful clearances and a sure kick', Jones was an ever-present in Leicester's promotion side of 1937. When Mansfield decided on a 'major reconstruction' in October 1947, Jones, who was reckoned to 'still have a lot of good football in him', was one of three Leicester players to join the Third Division (North) club. From 1968 to his death, he worked as a sales executive in the shoe trade but was previously in business as Day and Jones, leather factors of Leicester.

Honours:
Leicester C - FL 2nd Div champions 1937

356 Thomas James Edward Mills

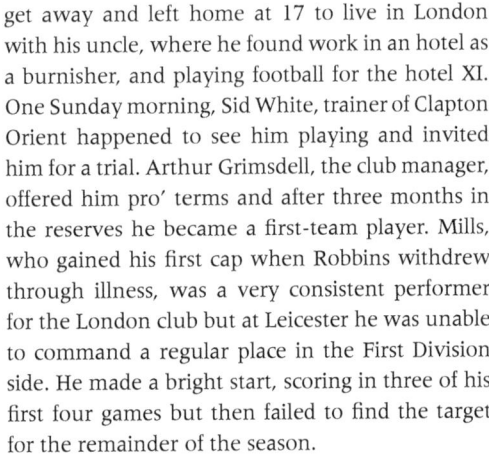

B: Pentre, Rhondda;
   28 Dec 1911
D: Bristol; 15 May 1979
Inside forward (5ft 7ins, 11st)
4 caps: (1 gl): (Clapton Orient) v Ire, Eng 1934; (Leicester C) v Eng, Sco 1935

Career: Wales Schoolboys, 1926; Ton Pentre Boys' Club; Trocadero Restaurant; Clapton Orient, c/season 1929-34 (120 FL apps, 21 gls); Leicester C, May 1934-36 (17 FL apps, 5 gls); Bristol Rov, May 1936-39 (99 FL apps, 17 gls).

Tommy Mills was twice capped by Wales at schoolboy level and harboured thoughts of becoming a pro' but left school to become a miner. 'The dream faded away' but he was determined to get away and left home at 17 to live in London with his uncle, where he found work in an hotel as a burnisher, and playing football for the hotel XI. One Sunday morning, Sid White, trainer of Clapton Orient happened to see him playing and invited him for a trial. Arthur Grimsdell, the club manager, offered him pro' terms and after three months in the reserves he became a first-team player. Mills, who gained his first cap when Robbins withdrew through illness, was a very consistent performer for the London club but at Leicester he was unable to command a regular place in the First Division side. He made a bright start, scoring in three of his first four games but then failed to find the target for the remainder of the season.

Captain Prince-Cox, the Bristol Rovers manager and an admirer of Mills since his Orient days, took him back to the Third Division (South) in a deal involving £375 for the Welshman and winger David Bruce. An intelligent schemer, Mills, together with Houghton formed the 'engine room' of the Rovers team and the pair kept their colleagues supplied with nicely weighted passes. Tommy Mills died tragically in a road accident when he was knocked down by a lorry.

357 Ronald Williams

B: Llansamlet, Swansea;
   23 Jan 1907
D: Swansea; 30 Mar 1987
Centre forward
   (5ft 7ins, 10st 8lbs)
2 caps: (Newcastle Utd) v Eng, Sco 1935

Career: National Oil Refinery (Skewen); Bethel Jnrs; Swansea T, 1928-33 (137 FL apps, 46 gls); Llanelli, (loan) 1929; Newcastle Utd, (£1,500) Nov 1933-35 (35 FL apps, 15 gls); Chester, (£800) April 1935-36 (24 FL apps, 15 gls); Swansea T, May 1936-39 (50 FL apps, 5 gls); Chester, c/season 1939; Swansea T, (war-time); Llanelli.

'Ronnie' Williams, who played rugby at school, was a strong, bustling type of centre forward who was extremely difficult to force off the ball. After joining Swansea in 1928 he spent a short time in the A team before being 'put into action earlier than planned because of the sorry state of the team'. He made his league debut on Christmas Day 1929, against Notts County, and scored a hat-trick. One report commented: 'He has a pronounced aptitude for leadership, his quick, well-judged distribution of the ball affords the wings a chance to give of their best'. However, a warning note was sounded: 'his fondness for a vigorous tilt at opposing defenders is bringing him too often to the attention of referees and is a failing'. This robust style resulted in a catalogue of injuries, including a broken jaw, wrist, ribs, ankle, collar bone and a burst blood vessel.

He scored on his debut for Newcastle and hit a Boxing Day hat-trick against Everton, but was unable to maintain this form and spent his second season with the club in the reserves. While at Newcastle, he was released by the club to play for Wales and help FAW secretary Ted Robbins out of a tight spot. One Saturday he was playing in the Newcastle A team against Reyrolle, a works team, yet the following week he was making his international debut. Williams served in the War Reserve Police and was subsequently employed by the housing department of Swansea Corporation. A one-time fast bowler for Swansea Cricket Club in the South Wales and Monmouthshire League, he was in later life a keen rugby fan. Uniquely, Williams was also capped by Wales at bowls in 1976.

Honours:
Swansea T - Welsh Cup 1932

358 Idris Morgan Hopkins
B: Merthyr Tydfil;
 11 Oct 1910
D: Widmer End (Eng);
 9 Oct 1994
Outside right
 (5ft 6ins, 11st 4lbs)

12 caps (2 gls): (Brentford) v Sco, Ire 1935; v Eng, Ire 1936; v Eng, Sco, Ire 1937; v Eng, Ire 1938; v Eng, Sco, Ire 1939

Career: Georgetown Sch; New Road Amateurs (Merthyr); Gellyfaelog Amateurs; Merthyr T; Sheffield Wed, Aug 1930; Dartford (also Ramsgate Ath); Crystal Palace, May-Nov 1932 (4 FL apps); Brentford, (£200) Nov 1932-May 1947 (290 FL apps, 77 goals); Bristol C, May 1947-48 (24 FL apps); IEK Norrkoping (coach); FK Sleipner (coach); Ramsgate, (manager); Portadown, (manager) Jan-Aug 1952; Sutton Utd, 1953; coach in Turkey.

Idris Hopkins came to the fore at Merthyr Town as a centre forward alongside fellow miner Dai Astley. The pair, who shared the same birthday, were also born in the same street. Hopkins was converted to outside left after moving to Hillsborough but was not a success, confined to the reserves and passed out of league football to assist Kent League club Dartford. There, he developed into a capable winger and Crystal Palace paid a small fee to take him back into league football. Hopkins again struggled but one of his four first-team games for Palace was against Brentford. The Bees manager Harry Curtis was looking to sign Alec Harry but was more impressed with Hopkins' display and signed him for £200, with Bill Berry moving to Palace.

Hopkins really found his feet at Brentford, scoring six times in 21 appearances as the Bees took the Third Division (South) title, and a lot of Brentford's success in the 1930s was down to the skilful persistency of the small and dapper winger. Dai, as he was inevitably known, was said to 'threaten danger to the defence every time he got the ball' and his clever wing play and ability to take scoring chances - 16 goals in 1934-35 - helped Brentford make a remarkable rise from Third to First Division in three years. In his first three seasons he did not miss a game, featuring in 155 league games and three FA Cup matches: a sequence only broken by his selection for Wales. During the war years, Hopkins, who was proficient at bowls and billiards, worked as a steeplejack and then in an aeroplane factory. On retirement from playing, he coached in Norway and Sweden before becoming manager/coach of Portadown in Northern Ireland. Hopkins subsequently kept a confectionery/tobacconist shop and, appropriately for a former miner, was a breeder of canaries.

Honours:
Brentford - FL 2nd Div champions 1935
 - FL 3rd Div (S) champions 1933
 - London War Cup 1942

359 John Iorwerth Hughes

B: Rhosllanerchrugog; 29 Jan 1913
D: Harrowden (Eng); 26 Sep 1993
Goalkeeper
(5ft 9ins, 13st 4lbs)
1 cap: (Blackburn Rov) v Ire 1935

Career: Rhos National Sch; Plas Bennion; Llanerch Celts; Aberystwyth T, 1929-30; Afongoch; Druids, 1931-32; Blackburn Rov, Aug, 1932-37 (pro from Jan 1933) (47 FL apps), 'Dick, Kerr XI', (loan) Jan 1933; Mansfield T, (£500) Jun 1937-39 (76 FL apps); Nelson; Bacup Borough, 1946-47; Rossendale Utd, 1947-48; Darwen, 1948-49; Third Lanark.

Jack Hughes began his career in the Wrexham Amateur League but had to leave Plas Bennion when he reached the age of 18 because the club operated an age limit for players. He moved to Llanerch Celts and then joined Aberystwyth Town where he gained a championship medal for winning the Mid Wales section of the Welsh National League. The introduction of a FAW rule making it compulsory for players to live within a radius of 20 miles from the club's ground brought his connection with the mid-Wales club to an end. Aberystwyth offered him a job in the area but after careful consideration he turned it down. He returned to the Wrexham and District Amateur League with Afongoch and given a trial by Oswestry, only to be rejected as they felt he was not good enough for the Birmingham and District League. However, Hughes' form with a Druids team that went through the season unbeaten in winning the Wrexham Amateur League impressed Blackburn sufficiently to offer him amateur terms in September 1932. During the later part of the 1932-33 season he spent some time with 'Dick, Kerr XI' in the Lancashire Combination, then stepped up to the Central League side but ended the campaign in style, gaining his Welsh amateur cap and making his league debut. In the amateur international against England at Torquay in January 1933, Hughes was the star performer and one newspaper commented: 'The honours of the day must go to Hughes for the best display of goalkeeping seen on the Torquay ground'. Despite the English team bombarding the Welsh goal it was only in the last 30 seconds of the match that they scored the only goal. After the match Hughes was personally congratulated by Sir Frederick Wall, the FA secretary. The following Saturday he made his first team debut for Blackburn in their 2-0 success over Birmingham.

Welsh-speaking Hughes, a former brickworks employee, turned professional in March 1933 but found first team football at Ewood Park hard to come by. A collision with a goal post on Good Friday 1936 left him with a fractured spine and, after a three-week hospital stay, he was out of the game for some months. Hughes had a good run in the Blackburn team towards the end of the 1936-37 season but had the misfortune to be beaten five times in the same week as the club announced their retained list, and was released. A brave goalkeeper, Hughes had good anticipation and was 'quick thinking in crises and flawless in his fielding of the ball'. He was a consistent performer during his two seasons at Mansfield, for whom 'his positioning was uncanny and his fearlessness in dashing out was a feature of his exhibition'. At the start of the 1939-40 season he sustained a serious leg injury in a practice match which put him out until Christmas, but in February 1940 was advised to retire from league soccer. Hughes was later invited to play in war-time internationals for Wales at Wrexham and Cardiff but refused on account of his injury.

After the war, Hughes played Lancashire Combination soccer for various clubs and took employment with the Philips Radio Company. He remained with the company as a stores manager until his retirement at 60, but he then worked for a further five years as a stock controller for the Open University. His grandson John Gareth Hughes was a county cricketer with Northamptonshire in the 1990s.

360 Brynmor Jones

B: Penyard, Merthyr Tydfil;
   14 Feb 1912
D: Wood Green (London, Eng);
   18 Oct 1985
Inside left (5ft 6ins, 10st 6lbs)
17 caps (5 gls): (Wolverhampton Wdrs) v Ire 1935; v Sco, Eng, Ire 1936; v Eng, Sco, Ire 1937; v Sco, Eng, Ire 1938; (Arsenal) v Eng, Sco, Ire 1939; v Sco, Ire 1947; v Eng 1948; v Sco 1949

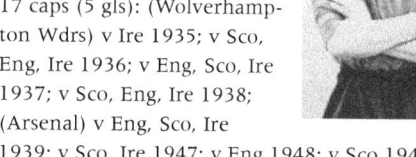

Career: Queen's Rd Sch; Merthyr Amateurs; Plymouth Utd (Merthyr & Dist Lge); Glenavon, 1932; Aberaman, Aug 1933; Wolverhampton Wdrs, Nov 1933-38 (163 FL apps, 52 gls); Arsenal, Aug 1938-49 (71 FL apps, 7 gls), (also over 100 war-time apps); Norwich C, Jun 1949-Feb 1951 (23 FL apps, 1 gl).

For a player who was to become the most expensive footballer in Britain, Bryn Jones had a remarkably circuitous entry into league soccer. From local football in Merthyr he was given a trial by Southend, where his brother Emlyn played, and then by Swansea. Unsuccessful in both, Jones joined Glenavon in the Irish League before returning to Wales to play for Aberaman.

He was seen by a Wolves scout and moved to the midlands club for a fee of £1,500. In a matter of weeks he had made his league debut and his brilliant displays earned him headline notices in the sporting press.

Jones was a splendid ball player, lithe and elusive and with the ability to turn defences inside out. He excelled at creating openings, seemingly out of nothing, and could open up a defence with his long penetrating passes. In 1938, he became the sporting sensation of the year when he joined Arsenal for the then record fee of £14,000. The fact that Jones was one of the few players to stand up to Wolves manager Major Buckley may well have been a contributory factor in the club's decision to sell. Nonetheless, the size of the fee staggered the sporting world. The attendant publicity proved a heavy burden for Jones and affected his play. Arsenal manager George Allison thought a spell in the second string might help Bryn but there was no respite from the publicity and 33,000 turned up to see his debut for the reserves! It was not until Arsenal's Scandinavian tour of 1939 that he began to recover his form.

During the war, Jones served in the 34th Light AA Regiment in North Africa and Italy but continued to play soccer regularly. He returned to Arsenal in peacetime but his best years had been lost to the war, and in 1949 he joined Norwich as player-coach. Forced to retire 18 months later on medical grounds due to a serious chest condition, Jones ended his connection with the game which had promised him so much and he took a newsagent and confectionery business in Stoke Newington, north London. Bryn was an uncle to Cliff Jones of Spurs and Wales fame, and brother to Emlyn (Everton, Bournemouth, Southend and Barrow), William (Merthyr, Aberdare and Ton Pentre), Bert (Southend and Wolves) and 'Shoni' (Aberdare and Ton Pentre).

Honours:
Arsenal - FL 1st Div champions 1948
      - FA Charity Shield 1938, 1948

361 Charles Wilson Jones

B: Pentre Broughton;
  29 Apr 1914
D: Birmingham (Eng);
  Jan 1986
Centre forward
  (5ft 10ins, 10st 10lbs)
2 caps (1 gl): (Birmingham) v Ire 1935; v Fra 1939.

Career: Brymbo Chums; Brymbo Green, 1930-32; Wrexham, (amt) May 1932, (pro) Sep 1932-34 (7 FL apps, 3 gls); Birmingham, (£1,500) Sep 1934-47 (135 FL apps, 63 gls), (war-time guest for Blackpool); Nottingham F, Sep 1947-48 (7 FL apps, 5 gls); Kidderminster Harriers, c/season 1948; Redditch Utd; retired 1950.

Wilson Jones, who went to same school as Tommy Griffiths, turned out for Oswestry in 1931 but left after three matches because the club refused to play him at centre forward. After unsuccessful trials with Blackburn and Bolton, he became a regular in Wrexham's Birmingham and District League side - cycling the 10 miles round trip to the ground - while continuing to work in Brymbo as a cobbler. He appeared mainly in the reserve side at the Racecourse, but his 51 goals during 1933-34 season impressed Birmingham sufficiently for them to pay £1,500 for his services. He made his debut for the Blues a month after joining the club and was an instant success. A matter of months after leaving Wrexham, Jones was back at the Racecourse to play for Wales against Northern Ireland and scored his side's opening goal.

'A leader of real merit', Jones, continued to find the target regularly for Birmingham and had a fine understanding with Fred Harris and Frank White. He briefly resumed his career at St Andrews after the war and it was claimed he scored the first goal of the new Football League season at 3.02pm on 31 August 1946 against Spurs. In fact Foreman of Spurs had bagged that honour seconds before Jones. The Welshman tasted non-league football with Kidderminster Harriers and Redditch United and became a licensee in Birmingham until he retired in 1979. His father, Bill Jones, had played for Shrewsbury in the Birmingham League between 1904 and 1920 - once selected as 12th man for Wales - while Wilson Jones' brother Bert played for Brymbo, Shrewsbury and Oswestry, and another brother, Harold, was captain of Brynmally Rovers.

362 Seymour Morris

B: Ynyshir, Rhondda;
  15 Feb 1913
D: Ynyshir, Rhondda;
  Oct 1991
Winger/inside forward
  (5ft 6½ins, 10st 7lbs)
5 caps (2 gls): (Birmingham) v Eng, Sco 1937; v Eng, Sco 1938; v Fra 1939

Career: Rhondda Schoolboys; Aberaman, 1932-33; Huddersfield T, Mar 1933-35 (6 FL apps, 3 gls); Birmingham, Mar 1935-39 (83 FL apps, 29 gls); retired 1944.

Seymour Morris left school to work as a pit boy but after narrowly surviving an underground roof fall he abandoned the mines and joined the Army. As a drummer boy in the Welch Regiment, Morris was stationed at Cardiff Barracks and began turning out for local soccer teams. Aberaman of the Welsh League saw the gifted inside forward as an investment and he was induced to leave the Army and sign professional forms. The expected approach from a league club materialised and Morris was transferred to Huddersfield for £2,000.

At Leeds Road, the large playing staff meant intense rivalry for senior places and when the opportunity to join Birmingham came along, Morris, guided by England player Billy Smith, took his chance. The first few months at Birmingham were frustrating but Morris got into the first team at the end of the 1935-36 season and kept his place. His style was likened by some to that of Stanley Matthews, but he could also score goals and was Birmingham's leading marksman in 1936-37. One reporter described him thus: 'The young Welshman has the reputation of being a sharpshooter ... he stands well up field and is not afraid to try a shot. When he loses the ball, it is his first endeavour to regain possession'. Morris made a notable debut for Wales, scoring directly from a corner against England in October 1936.

A cartilage operation in December 1937, followed by further knee operations in 1939, put him out of action and his recovery had hardly got underway when war broke out. Morris serviced aircraft at Elmdon Airport during the Second World War, playing the occasional game for Birmingham. He took on the role of coaching youth football in Wales after the war and worked in a tool factory in Crickhowell. In the early 1950s he opened a children's home in Glyncoch with his wife which they continued to run for over 20 years.

363 Herbert Gwyn Turner

B: Brithdir, Rhymney;
   19 Jun 1909
D: Birchington (Eng);
   8 Jun 1981
Right back/half (6ft, 13st)
8 caps: (Charlton Ath) v Eng, Sco, Ire 1937; v Sco, Eng, Ire 1938; v Ire, Fra 1938

Career: Brithdir; Charlton Ath, Aug 1933-39 (176 FL apps, 3 gls), 1946-47 (11 FL apps); Dartford, Aug 1947 (player-coach); Dortrecht FC; Malmo FF, (coach) 1951-55; Malmar FF, (coach) 1955.

Bert Turner was a powerful defensive player who learnt a lot of his football in the Army with the Welch Regiment. Something of an all-round sportsman, he played in the Battalion Rugby Cup final and won medals for athletics and hockey with Army teams. When he returned home to Brithdir, he joined the local club but after only four appearances he was invited to Charlton for trials and a contract followed. Turner made his debut in November 1933 at Norwich, which was the start of a career at Charlton that lasted 13 years and interrupted only by war service with the RAF. In first three seasons at the Valley, Turner filled both full back positions, all three half back berths and the centre forward slot. His versatility was said to be the result of hours of practice to develop two good feet. He had the misfortune to turn the ball into his own net in the 1946 FA Cup final, but within a minute he made amends by netting from a free kick (a feat equalled in 1981 by Tommy Hutchison). A very strongly-built defender, his difficulty keeping his weight under control always demanded drastic measures when pre-season training at the Valley commenced. Turner retired from league football to become player manager at Dartford and later spent some years coaching in The Netherlands and Sweden, where he won two Swedish titles and two Swedish cups, before returning to Britain in 1956 and, for 23 years until 1980, Turner was a licensee in Manston in Kent.

A brother-in-law to Dai Astley, Turner's brother, Ernest, played for Merthyr Town and Southampton.

Honours:
Charlton Ath - FA Cup finalists 1946
            - FL 3rd Div (S) champions 1935

364 John Warner

B: Trealaw, Rhondda;
   21 Sep 1911
D: Tonypandy, Rhondda;
   4 Oct 1980
Wing half (5ft 7ins, 11st)
2 caps: (Swansea T) v Eng 1937; (Manchester Utd) v Fra 1939

Career: Trealaw; Aberaman, 1932-34; Swansea T, Jan 1934-38 (132 FL apps, 10 gls); Manchester Utd, Jun 1938-51 (105 FL apps, 1 gl): Oldham Ath, Jun 1951-52 (35 FL apps, 2 gls); Rochdale, Jul 1952-53 (21 FL apps).

Although Jack Warner would have gained more caps but for the war, he successfully resurrected his career in peacetime and played on until his early 40s, which was hardly surprising for a man who prided himself on his physical fitness. A long spell at Swansea ended in 1938 when he joined Manchester United at the age of 27. His prime footballing years were lost to the war but he made over 150 appearances for United in war-time soccer, assisted with their youth side, and later put his coaching talents to use as reserve team skipper. Warner was unlucky to lose his first team place shortly before the 1948 FA Cup final.

An accurate passer, 'Nippy' Warner prompted his forwards with well made openings and was also a steadying influence in defence where he tackled strongly and exhibited a calm assurance. At Oldham Athletic he became, at that time, the club's oldest debutant, a month before his 40th birthday and played a big part in the improvement in the Latics' fortunes. Warner's ambition was to take up a managerial position when his playing days were over and in 1951 he became player-coach to an Oldham side managed by George Hardwick. The following year he was unwilling to re-sign for the club and Hardwick reluctantly released him to become player-manager of Rochdale, where he made a promising start but the appointment was 'not a conspicuous success' and he resigned in May 1953.

Honours:
Manchester Utd - FA Charity Shield runners-up 1948

365 William Marshall Hughes

B: Carmarthen; 6 Mar 1918
D: Birmingham (Eng);
   16 Jun 1981
Left back: (5ft 10ins, 12st)
10 caps: (Birmingham) v Sco, Eng, Ire 1938; v Eng, Sco, Ire, Fra 1939; v Sco, Eng, Ire 1947

Career: Llanelli Boys Sch; Swansea G Sch; Archer Corinthians; Birmingham C, May 1935-47 (104 FL apps), (war-time guest for Hearts, Arsenal, Queens Park Rgrs, West Ham Utd and Wrexham); Luton T, (£11,000) July 1947-48 (31 FL apps); Chelsea, (£12,000) Mar 1948-50 (93 FL apps); Hereford Utd, 1951-54; Flint T Utd, Jan 1954-55.

After a brief flirtation with rugby, Billy Hughes, an apprentice car mechanic, took up soccer with Archer Corinthians of Llanelli. He was soon spotted by Hayden Price and signed by Birmingham for £5, making his debut aged 17 in January 1936 against Manchester City. The following year he became a regular Birmingham player and, with Cyril Trigg, set up a league record for the youngest pair of full backs when, both aged 17, they faced Aston Villa. Billy took over the Birmingham captaincy from Harry Hibbs in 1938 and during the same season played his first match for his country. In the war years, Hughes switched to centre half and was appointed the Wales captain. Billy's total of 14 war-time appearances was second in number only to Don Dearson.

In peace time, he reverted to his former position and was considered to be the best full back in Britain. He was selected to play for Great Britain against the Rest of Europe, a call-up he first heard about via the wireless. Hughes moved to Luton for a record club outlay of £11,000 and although great things were expected of him, his time at the club was brief. A polished and extremely accomplished defender, he completed his league career at Chelsea but played on into non-league football, joining Hereford then Welsh League (North) club Flint. It was at Flint that Hughes enjoyed an Indian summer. The part-timers, captained by Hughes, defeated Cardiff City in the semi-final of the 1954 Welsh Cup and took the trophy with a 2-0 win over Chester. Immediately after retirement, Billy became landlord of the Blue Bell Inn in Halkyn, in Flintshire, and scouted for Chester before returning to live in central England in June 1969. He worked as supervisor at the Morris Works Recreation Club then became steward at the Wolseley Car Social Club.

Honours:
Flint T Utd - Welsh Cup 1954

366 Edwin Perry

B: Rhymney; 19 Jan 1909
D: Shepway (Eng);
 25 Nov 1996
Centre forward: (6ft, 11st 10lbs)
3 caps (1 gl): (Doncaster Rov) Sco, Eng, Ire 1938

Career: Tredomen Engineering Works XI; Rhymney (Welsh Lge); Swansea T (trial); Mid Rhondda, Jan 1927; Merthyr T, Mar 1928 (am) (1 FL app); Bournemouth & Boscombe Ath, (£200) Apr 1928-30; Thames Association, Jun 1930-31 (25 FL apps, 16 gls); Fulham, May 1931-36 (63 FL apps, 35 gls); Doncaster Rov, Nov 1936-39 (102 FL apps, 46 gls); Chelsea; Brentford (war-time); Fulham, (coach) 1946-56; Southend Utd, (secretary-manager) 1956-60.

Eddie Perry was signed by Bournemouth after impressing against them in an FA Cup tie as centre forward for Merthyr. The amateur gave up his job as a mining engineer but didn't make his mark until after he joined Fulham. Initially, he spent a lot of time in the reserves and gained a Football Combination runners-up medal in 1933. Despite being overshadowed by Bonzo Newton and Ronnie Rooke, Eddie was a regular scorer and became one of the stars of Fulham's progress to the 1935-36 FA Cup semi-finals, including his four goals in the 5-2 fourth round win over Blackpool.

In November 1936, Doncaster laid out a club record fee, said to exceed £2,500, for Perry in an effort to strengthen the side and solve their goal scoring problem. When he moved to Yorkshire, the club were languishing at the foot of the Second Division and experiencing a goals famine. Perry's goals, good ball play and intelligent distribution repaid the club's investment and led to his international selection.

After the war, Perry was one of a panel of coaches despatched by the FA to Norway to help re-establish soccer in the country, after which he spent ten years as Fulham coach, playing a leading role in developing such fine talents as Johnny Haynes and Bedford Jezzard. He was briefly team manager in 1948. Outside soccer, Perry was known as 'a violinist and vocalist'.

Honours:
Brentford - London War Cup 1942

367 George Henry Green

B: Barry; 12 Nov 1912
D: Bromley (Eng); May 1994
Outside left/centre forward:
 (5ft 10½ins, 10st 12lbs)
4 caps: (Charlton Ath) v Ire 1938; v Eng, Ire, Fra 1939

Career: Gladstone Rd Sch; Barry Schools; Mount Stuart Dry Docks FC; Enamel Works FC; Barry T; Charlton Ath, Mar 1934-35; Deportivo Espanol (Barcelona), Aug 1935-36; Charlton Ath, Jun 1936-39 (57 FL apps, 3 gls), (also 94 apps & 13 gls in war-time football); War-time guest player for Fulham (1939-40), Millwall (Feb 1943), Aldershot (1940-

41) & West Ham Utd (May 1940); Millwall, (trainer) May 1946-47; Dartford, (manager) May 1953-Apr 1961); Portsmouth, (chief scout) 1962.

The 12th of 13 children born to English parents, George Green won a Welsh Schools Shield medal during his schooldays and left school to go to sea. He was a mess room boy from the age of 14 to 17 and spent his 15th birthday in Saigon. On returning to Wales he took up soccer again and was, one day, standing by the Barry dressing room when an official came up to him and asked: 'You're Albert Green's boy, aren't you? You play football don't you? Got any boots? Very well put them on and go on that field and play like mad'. Green scored three times for Barry Reserves and signed as a professional for 10s (50p) a match.

In March 1934, Charlton paid £250 for his services and Green made and started impressively, scoring three times against Leicester Reserves and hitting six against Bristol City. However, despite this promising start he failed to make any first team appearances in his first spell there, suffered broken ribs on two occasions and underwent an appendix operation. In 1935, a pal of Jimmy Seed, the Charlton manager, persuaded Green to try Spanish football and he headed for Barcelona, but while on a return visit from Catalonia to marry his fiancée, the Spanish Civil War started and Green decided not to return. Instead, he established himself in the Charlton senior XI and was beginning to make an impression in the Wales side when the Second World War broke out. Green was unfortunate to reach his peak in the war years, during which, as sergeant-major Green, he supervised the physical fitness of the Canadian troops at Godalming.

Green played a handful of matches at the beginning of the 1943-44 season but suffered an injury and, in 1944, underwent an operation which kept him out for 15 months. He returned to action in October 1945, scoring three against Arsenal, but that was his last match in professional football and he retired shortly afterwards. In May 1946 he became trainer at Millwall, and assisted with West Ham 'A' in 1952-3 before embarking on an eight-year spell as manager of Southern League Dartford. Green was a partner in an exhibition metalwork business, then ran a draper's shop which became a bookmaker's. From 1970 he worked in the off-licence trade and then as a clerk for Express Dairies. In retirement, Green continued to take an active interest in the Charlton club and was a keen golfer, at one time playing off a handicap of 15. Green's father played for Barry Unionists and his brother Albert appeared for Barry Town

Honours:
Charlton Ath - League South Cup runners-up 1943

368 Thomas George Ronald Jones

B: Queensferry; 12 Oct 1917
D: Bangor; 3 Jan 2004
Centre half (6ft, 12st 6lbs)
17 caps: (Everton) v Ire 1938; v Eng, Sco, Ire 1939; v Sco, Eng 1947; v Eng, Sco, Ire 1948; v Eng, Ire, Por, Bel, Swi 1949; v Eng, Sco, Bel 1950

Career: Flintshire Schoolboys; Wales Schoolboys, 1932; Primrose Hill Ath, (Flintshire Am Lge); Connah's Quay Amateurs; Llanerch Celts; Wrexham, 1935-36 (6 lge apps); Everton, Mar 1936-1950 (165 FL apps, 4 gls); RAF, 1940-45; Pwllheli, (player-manager) Jun 1950-57; Bangor C, (manager) Jun 1957-67; Rhyl, (manager) Jul 1967-May 1968; Bethesda Ath, (adviser) Jan 1973-74.

Jones' father, who at one time worked for Shotton Water Works, but did not have the finances to keep young Tommy in school and Baden Millington, the youngster's teacher, persuaded the Wrexham manager to take him on as a 15-year-old apprentice. The club duly arranged a position for Jones as an office boy in the manager's office, before turning pro' aged 17. He played most of his football with the reserves in the Birmingham and District League before making his Football League debut in December 1935 against Rotherham United. Discerning judges spotted a future international despite his limited first team appearances and the hard up Wrexham club quickly accepted Everton's offer for his services. 'TG', as he became known, went on to enjoy a long and distinguished career at Goodison Park. He was a thoughtful and neat player who invariably played his way out of trouble. In February 1939 he played for Everton at Birmingham and his performance drew the following comment: 'Not a player on the field could compare with Tommy Jones, the Everton captain, for cool, calculated football. He was the almost perfect half back, stemmed many Birmingham rushes with the minimum of energy and enabled his backs to mark the Birmingham wings so closely that they were blotted out of the game'. 'Fuse', writing in the *Topical Times* was even more effusive; 'Having known Wedlock [26 England caps at centre half between 1907 and 1914] and Roberts' [Charlie Roberts of England and Manchester United] pivotal success and seen all the best men in the position over the years, I beg to claim that T G Jones of Everton as the most astonishing thing seen in any half back line. Height, build, heading skill, long legs to reach out and bring the ball down to earth, a body swerve, cool head and strong shot if called upon to take a spot kick - all these things are packed into Jones' bag.'

Perhaps the greatest complement he was paid came from 'Dixie' Dean when asked to name the greatest footballer he had ever seen: 'For me, he'd have to be an Evertonian - T G Jones' said Dean, 'Tommy was the best all-round player I've ever seen. He had everything. No coach could ever coach him or teach him anything. He was neater than John Charles, for instance, and could get himself out of trouble just by running towards the ball and then letting it run between his legs, knowing his team mate would be in a position to make it'. Tommy Lawton, who had the benefit of TG's presence behind him in the Everton team said: 'He had the great capacity to stroke the ball. He also had the best right foot in the business and so complete was his positioning and balance that he always seemed to receive the ball on the right foot. He was a taskmaster to the team, never satisfied with the finest performance; never happy unless he was driving. His calmness in a crisis was supreme and built as he was, he was very good in the air but also delicate and sophisticated on the ground'.

An ankle injury sustained in 1944 put him out of action and threatened his career. It was several months before he returned to action, but thereafter he was left with a weakened ankle and his relationship with the Everton board had somewhat soured. Back in Connah's Quay, following war service with the RAF, Tommy became one of the founders of the Connah's Quay Juniors club that joined the Northop Junior League for young men aged under 19. In due course, the junior club became Connah's Quay Nomads, in recognition of the amount of travelling they had undertaken in their early years of existence. TG's uneasy relationship with Everton continued and on the return of league football he competed with J V Humphreys for the centre half berth. A potentially lucrative move to Roma in 1948 fell through and eventually he found himself out of favour at the Merseyside club.

It was something of a surprise when, in 1950, Jones turned his back on league football, took a hotel in Pwllheli and joined the local club: by going outside the Football League he avoided a transfer fee. Some observers said that this is where he played his best football with even talk of a recall to international duty but, for many, Tommy Jones will forever be associated with the Welsh League (North) in the early 1950s. His team packed in the crowds at such clubs as Flint Town United, Holyhead Town, Holywell Town and Caernarfon Town. Tommy's Pwllheli team was the one all other Welsh League teams wanted to beat, but few managed it.

In June 1957 he became manager of Bangor City, then playing in the Cheshire League, who had recently had to seek re-election for the second successive season and had been warned that if they applied again they wouldn't get in. After several near misses he steered the club to a Welsh Cup victory, against Wrexham in 1961, while the following season Bangor played AC Napoli in the Cup Winners' Cup and went out of the competition only after a play-off at Highbury. Had the away goals rule, which was not introduced until 1967, been in place, Bangor would have progressed to the next round. In July 1967 Jones was released by Bangor to take over at Rhyl on a three-year contract but the club were already almost £20,000 in debt and it was an ill-starred appointment. At the end of the season he was sacked by the Rhyl board who referred to 'quite a number of factors', none of which were made public. Jones became a soccer journalist for the North Wales edition of the Liverpool-based *Daily Post* and had his own newsagents business in Bangor. T G's final appearance in a competitive match came in May 1963 when he turned out for Bangor against Borough United in the semi-final of the North Wales Coast FA Challenge Cup.

Honours:
Everton - FL 1st Div champions 1939

369 Reginald Horace Cumner

B: Cwmaman, Aberdare;
   31 Mar 1918
D: Poole (Eng); 18 Jan 1999
Outside/Inside left
   (5ft 8ins, 10st 10lbs)
3 caps (1 gl): (Arsenal) v Eng, Sco, Ire 1939

Career: Aberaman Ath, Swansea T (youth team); Margate, Jul 1935-Jan 1938; Arsenal, May 1936-38; (Margate, for development); Hull C, (loan) Jan 1938 (12 FL apps, 4 gls); Arsenal, May 1938-46 (12 FL apps, 2 gls - war intervening); Notts Co, Aug 1946-47 (66 FL apps, 10 gls); Watford, (£2,200) Jul 1948-50 (62 FL apps, 8 gls); Scunthorpe Utd, Sep 1950-52 (104 FL apps, 22 gls); Bradford C, Aug 1953-54; Poole T, c/season 1954; Bridport, May 1955; Swanage, 1957.

Horace Cumner, a Wales schoolboy player, came to the notice of Arsenal in his teens and joined the ground staff in May 1935 as an amateur. He was initially sent to Margate, Arsenal's nursery club, for two years to gain experience and once scored six goals in a match. Cumner was loaned to Hull in 1938 and, after scoring five goals in six Midland League matches, he was promoted to the senior side for his Football League debut. On returning to Highbury, he made his First Division debut against Wolves and scored the only goal of the match. During the early part of the Second World War, Cumner saw service with the Royal Marines and received serious burns at a military base. He recovered quickly and in 1942 scored two goals for Wales in their 2-1 war-time win over England at Wolverhampton.

Cumner resumed his career at Highbury in 1945, but soon moved on and, in 1950, Les Jones, the Scunthorpe manager, signed his former Arsenal colleague from Watford. Cumner was described as 'a direct style of player who does not fiddle with the ball at all, but beats his man and swings across a well-place centre', and 'not afraid to come to the middle when the occasion demands it'. After leaving league football, he moved into the Western League.

370 William John Whatley

B: Ebbw Vale; 12 Oct 1912
D: Greenwich (London, Eng);
   Dec 1974
Left back (5ft 7½ins, 11st 1lb)
2 caps: (Tottenham H) v Eng, Sco 1939

Career: Wales Schoolboys, 1927; Ebbw Vale; Haywards Sports; Northfleet; Tottenham H, (am)

Dec 1929-31, (pro) May 1931-39 (226 FL apps, 2 gls); (also guested for Fulham, West Ham and Stockport in war-time); retired 1948.

A former baker's boy, Bill Whatley joined Spurs in 1929, with Alf Day and Eugene O'Callaghan, and his early time at the club was spent in development with the nursery sides of Haywards Sports and Northfleet, before becoming a first team regular from 1931. When Whatley turned pro' in 1931, the Spurs defence was remodelled specifically to enable him to link up with Felton as his full back partner.

Whatley had a reputation as a very clean defender who seldom gave away a free kick and never conceded a penalty. A model of consistency, he had just established himself in the national side when war broke out, and held the Spurs left back position until almost the end of the conflict, making 112 appearances in war-time football. Whatley's last senior appearance was against Brentford in March 1945, and he retired three years later after sustaining a broken leg in a reserve match, yet continued to serve Spurs as a coach and scout.

Honours:
Tottenham H - FL 2nd Div runners-up 1933
              - FL (S) champions 1944

371 Donald John Dearson

B: Ynysybwl; 13 May 1914
D: Birmingham (Eng); 24 Dec 1990
Inside forward/Wing half
   (5ft 10ins, 13st 3lbs)
3 caps: (Birmingham) v Sco, Ire, Fra 1939

Career: Llantwit Major Jnrs; Barry T, Aug 1932; Birmingham, Apr 1934-39 (105 FL apps, 16 gls); Northampton T, (guest) 1940-42; also Nottingham F 1940-41 & Wrexham 1940-41; Birmingham C, 1946-47 (25 FL apps, 1 gl); Coventry C, (£6,000) Feb 1947-50 (84 FL apps, 10 gls); Walsall, Mar 1950-51 (51 FL apps, 12 gls); Nuneaton Borough, 1951-52; Bilston Utd, 1952-53; retired.

Soccer took second place for Don Dearson until he had completed his apprenticeship as an electrician but, when Barry played Aberaman in a Welsh League match, the Football League scouts turned up to watch Dearson and Bryn Jones for the opposition. Bristol City, Cardiff, Huddersfield and Newport were interested in the youngster but it was Birmingham manager George Liddell who secured his services. Dearson, who had been described as 'one of the finest forwards playing locally today', opted for the Blues because the club arranged for his apprentice indentures to be transferred from Aberthaw Cement Works to BSA.

Once his apprenticeship was completed, Dearson became a full-time professional and was soon a regular in Birmingham's first team. He won the first of his three caps in November 1938 but then war intervened. He joined the Birmingham City Police but gave it up after nine weeks to work in the BSA factory and remained there until 1948. A clever, scheming inside forward he returned to Birmingham City after the war but soon moved on, playing non-league football with Nuneaton and Bilston before retiring to concentrate on his grocery business in Yardley. He sold the business in 1967 and took employment with British Leyland.

Honours:
Birmingham - FL (S) champions 1946

372 Leslie Mervyn Boulter

B: Ebbw Vale; 31 Aug 1913
D: Pwllheli; 14 Nov 1975
Inside left (5ft 9ins, 11st 6lbs)
1 cap (1 gl): (Brentford) v Ire 1939

Career: Willowtown Sch, Ebbw Vale; Wales

Schoolboys, 1927; Ebbw Vale ex-schoolboys; Cwm Ath; Arsenal, (am) Mar 1930; Charlton Ath, (am) Jun 1932, (pro) Sep 1932-39 (167 FL apps, 28 gls); Brentford, (£6,000) Jan 1939-47 (19 FL apps, 1 gl); (war-time apps for Brentford, Blackpool, Cardiff C, Manchester C, Bolton Wdrs & Rochdale); Yeovil T, Jun 1947-48; Pwllheli & Dist, (player-manager) 1948-50; retired.

Les Boulter, a Wales Schoolboy player and ex-pit boy, joined the Charlton ground staff in 1932 and his development in the London Combination team was so swift that he made the senior side in his first season. By early 1934-35 he was out of favour but refused a move to QPR, preferring to win back his place at the Valley, and made a significant contribution to Charlton's rise from the Third Division (South) to the First Division in two seasons. In 1937, he helped the club become First Division runners-up and two years later Brentford paid £6,000 for him. He made his one appearance for Wales when Les Jones cried off because of illness but because of an oversight he never received his cap from the FAW. Following the publication of the original edition of this book in 1991, his family got in touch with the FAW to rectify the oversight and they received his cap in 1992.

Boulter was a stylish player who worked the ball well, had a flair for sending defenders the wrong way and invariably masterminded his side's attacks. After war service in Canada with the RAF, he returned to soccer with a struggling Brentford side but did not get a game during a disappointing season which saw the London club relegated. In June 1947 he joined Alec Stock's Yeovil Town in the Southern League but, 12 months later, he became the first player-manager of Pwllheli in the Welsh League (North). On retirement in 1950, he went into business as a stationer and tobacconist. Boulter returned to London in 1958 to work in insurance and took charge of Charlton's Aetolian League team, but moved back to Pwllheli five years later to open a grocery and provisions shop in the town.

Honours:
Charlton Ath - FL 1st Div runners-up 1937
- FL 2nd Div runners-up 1936
- FL 3rd Div (S) champions 1935

373 George Poland
B: Penarth; 21 Sep 1913
D: Penarth; 6 Oct 1988
Goalkeeper
(5ft 11ins, 12st 4lbs)
2 caps: (Wrexham) v Ire, Fra 1939

Career: Cogan; Penarth Mission; Swindon T, (am) 1934-35; Cardiff C, Nov 1935-38 (24 FL apps); Wrexham, Jul 1938-39 (39 FL apps); Liverpool, Jun 1939; wartime apps for Leeds Utd & Brentford; Cardiff C, Aug 1946-47 (2 FL apps); Lovell's Ath, 1947-48.

George Poland first played soccer as an outfielder and was a goal-scoring centre forward with Penarth Mission before Ted Vizard invited him to Swindon to play as a right winger. At Cardiff, who had earlier rejected him as an outfield player, he was thought of as the club's best keeper since Farquarson in the 1920s and, unusually, was selected for the first team after conceding seven goals in a reserve game.

George Poland was a confident goalkeeper who was agile and safe and commanded his area well. At Wrexham, Poland displaced long-serving keeper Pat McMahon and did so well that at the end of his first season he was capped by Wales. The watching Liverpool scouts saw enough at the Racecourse to recommend the Anfield club to sign him for a hefty £3,000, but his blossoming career was curtailed by the outbreak of war a few months after he had joined Liverpool. During the war he served with the Welsh Guards and while stationed at Esher was a guest player for Brentford. It was during a guest appearance for Leeds in 1943 that Poland broke his arm. The injury troubled him thereafter and he managed just two post-war league appearances with

Cardiff before being displaced by Danny Canning. After retiring from soccer, Poland worked as a postman.

374 John James Williams

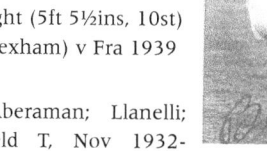

B: Aberdare; 29 Mar 1911
D: Wrexham; 12 Oct 1987
Outside right (5ft 5½ins, 10st)
1 cap: (Wrexham) v Fra 1939

Career: Aberaman; Llanelli; Huddersfield T, Nov 1932-35 (50 FL apps, 14 gls); Aston Villa, Nov 1935-36 (17 FL apps, 5 gls); Ipswich T, Jul 1936-38 (SL), Aug-Nov 1938 (9 FL apps); Wrexham, Nov 1938-39 (27 FL apps, 4 gls); Colwyn Bay Utd, Oct 1945; Runcorn, 1947-48.

A short, dark-haired winger, Jackie Williams, like many other flank men, more than made up for his build with guile and trickery. An amateur with Llanelli, he turned professional two weeks before joining First Division Huddersfield in November 1932 and made his debut in February 1933 in a 1-0 home win over Sheffield United. Playing at outside right, he remained a regular first team squad member for three seasons during which the Terriers finished in sixth place, and then as First Division runners-up to Arsenal in 1933-34.

His consistent play prompted Aston Villa to pay £2,000 for him and he got off to a flying start, scoring two goals on his debut, but Villa were eventually relegated the same season and Williams was not retained. Surprisingly, he moved from the First Division into non-league soccer, and was later a member of the Ipswich team that won the Southern League championship in 1936-37. When Ipswich were elected to the Third Division (South), Williams appeared in their first ever Football League match (v Southend) in 1938-39 before moving to Wrexham after a further eight appearances. Newly arrived at the Racecourse, the winger went straight into the first team and missed only one match in that final season before the war and gained his only cap against France in Paris. He continued to play soccer throughout the war, as and when the opportunity arose, mostly in the regional leagues. When the war ended, Williams joined Colwyn Bay for a short spell in the Welsh League (North) before joining Cheshire League Runcorn where he was also selected to represent the league against the Southern League. Upon retirement from soccer he was employed as a storekeeper for Hunt's Capacitors in Wrexham for many years and played bowls for Gresford Bowling Club.

Billy Meredith (161) proudly showing his honours and caps.

APPENDIX 1

OFFICIAL INTERNATIONAL MATCHES 1876-1939

1876	Mar 25	F	v Scotland	West of Scotland Cricket Ground, Glasgow	4-0	L
1877	Mar 5	F	v Scotland	The Racecourse, Wrexham	0-2	L
1878	Mar 23	F	v Scotland	1st Hampden Park, Glasgow	0-9	L
1879	Jan 18	F	v England	Kennington Oval, London	2-1	L
	Apr 7	F	v Scotland	The Racecourse, Wrexham	0-3	L
1880	Mar 15	F	v England	The Racecourse, Wrexham	2-3	L
	Mar 27	F	v Scotland	1st Hampden Park, Glasgow	5-1	L

v Scotland 1880

Rear: L Kenrick, H Hibbott, E Bowen, H V Edwards, E Manners (FAW secretary).

Middle: John Vaughan, J R Morgan, J Powell, J Roberts (Corwen).

Front: W P Owen, T J Britten, J Price, W Roberts (Llangollen).

| 1881 | Feb 26 | F | v England | Alexandra Meadows, Blackburn | 0-1 | W |
| | Mar 14 | F | v Scotland | The Racecourse, Wrexham | 1-5 | L |

1882	Feb 25	F	v Ireland	The Racecourse, Wrexham	7-1	W
	Mar 13	F	v England	The Racecourse, Wrexham	5-3	W
	Mar 25	F	v Scotland	1st Hampden Park, Glasgow	5-0	L

v Scotland 1882 (Players Only)

Rear: W H Roberts, J Powell, H V Edwards, J Price, W Williams.

Middle: J Roberts (Ruthin), W P Owen, J R Morgan, H Phoenix, J Roberts (Corwen).

Front (seated): John Vaughan.

1883	Feb 3	F	v England	Kennington Oval, London	5-0	L
	Mar 12	F	v Scotland	The Racecourse, Wrexham	0-3	L
	Mar 17	F	v Ireland	Ulster Cricket Ground, Ballynafeigh, Belfast	1-1	D
1884	Feb 9	BC	v Ireland	The Racecourse, Wrexham	6-0	W
	Mar 17	BC	v England	The Racecourse, Wrexham	0-4	L
	Mar 29	BC	v Scotland	Cathkin Park, Glasgow	1-4	L

v Scotland 1884 (Players Only)

Rear: T Burke, F W Hughes, R Roberts (Bolton), C Conde, J Jones (Llangollen).

Middle: W P Owen, W H Roberts, J Eyton-Jones, R A Jones.

Front (seated): E Owen, E G Shaw.

1885	Mar 14	BC v England	Leamington Road, Blackburn	1-1	D
	Mar 23	BC v Scotland	The Racecourse, Wrexham	1-8	L
	Apr 11	BC v Ireland	Ulster Cricket Ground, Ballynafeigh, Belfast	2-8	W
1886	Feb 27	BC v Ireland	The Racecourse, Wrexham	5-0	W

v Ireland 1886 (Players Only)

Rear: R Hersee, R Roberts (Wrexham), W S Bell, S A Powell, H Sisson, J O Vaughan.

Front: J Wilding, W Roberts (Wrexham), H Jones, A Hersee, T Bryan.

	Mar 29	BC v England	The Racecourse, Wrexham	1-3	L
	Apr 10	BC v Scotland	1st Hampden Park, Glasgow	4-1	L
1887	Feb 26	BC v England	Kennington Oval, London	4-0	L
	Mar 12	BC v Ireland	Old Park Avenue, Belfast	4-1	L

v Ireland 1887 (Players Only)

Rear: G Griffiths, E P W Hughes, S Jones, A Townsend, A H Hunter (FAW secretary).

Middle: H W Sabine, R Roberts (Wrexham), H V Edwards, W H Turner.

Front (seated): W Roberts (Wrexham), R Doughty.

| | Mar 21 | BC v Scotland | The Racecourse, Wrexham | 0-2 | L |

| 1888 | Feb 4 | BC | v England | Nantwich Road, Crewe | 5-1 | L |

v England 1888 (Players Only)

Rear: P Griffiths, R Roberts (Bolton), J Davies (Cefn), R Mills Roberts, J Powell.

Middle: J B Challen, A O Davies.

Front: W E Pryce Jones, W Lewis, J Doughty, W Owen.

v Ireland 1888

Rear: R Humphreys, J Davies (Cefn), A O Davies, R Mills Roberts, J Powell, D Jones.

Front: W E Pryce Jones, J Wilding, J Doughty, R Doughty, E G Howell.

	Mar 3	BC	v Ireland	The Racecourse, Wrexham	11-0	W
	Mar 10	BC	v Scotland	Easter Road, Edinburgh	5-1	L
1889	Feb 23	BC	v England	Victoria Ground, Stoke on Trent	4-1	L
	Apr 15	BC	v Scotland	The Racecourse, Wrexham	0-0	D
	Apr 27	BC	v Ireland	Ulster Cricket Ground, Ballynafeigh, Belfast	1-3	W

1890	Feb 8	BC	v Ireland	Old Racecourse, Shrewsbury	5-2	W

v Ireland 1890 (Players Only)

Rear: R H L Roberts, S G Gillam, W P Jones.

Front: W E Pryce Jones, D M Lewis, P Griffiths, H Jones, A Hayes, W Owen, A Wilcock, J C H Bowdler.

	Mar 15	BC	v England	The Racecourse, Wrexham	1-3	L
	Mar 22	BC	v Scotland	Underwood Park, Paisley	5-0	L
1891	Feb 7	BC	v Ireland	Ulsterville Avenue, Belfast	7-2	L
	Mar 7	BC	v England	Newcastle Road, Sunderland	4-1	L
	Mar 21	BC	v Scotland	The Racecourse, Wrexham	3-4	L
1892	Feb 27	BC	v Ireland	Penrhyn Park, Bangor	1-1	D
	Mar 5	BC	v England	The Racecourse, Wrexham	0-2	L
	Mar 26	BC	v Scotland	Tynecastle Park, Edinburgh	6-1	L

v Scotland 1892 (Players Only)

Rear: S Powell, J Wilding, W Owen, R Roberts.

Front: W Hughes, S Arridge, C A L Jenkyns, J Trainer, Ben Lewis, Billy Lewis, T W Egan.

| 1893 | Mar 13 | BC v England | Victoria Ground, Stoke on Trent | 6-0 | L |

v England 1893 (Players Only)

Rear: C Parry, J Trainer, D Jones, E H Williams.

Middle: James Vaughan, E James, J Butler, B Lewis, R Roberts (Crewe).

Front: J Davies (Cefn), E Morris.

v Ireland 1893 (Players Only)

Rear: A Townsend, O D S Taylor, S Jones (Wrexham), A Lea, E Morris, J Evans.

Front: James Vaughan, W Owen, J Butler, G A Owen, E James.

	Mar 18	BC v Scotland	The Racecourse, Wrexham	0-8	L
	Apr 8	BC v Ireland	Ulsterville Avenue, Belfast	4-3	L
1894	Feb 24	BC v Ireland	St Helens, Swansea	4-1	W
	Mar 12	BC v England	The Racecourse, Wrexham	1-5	L
	Mar 24	BC v Scotland	Rugby Park, Kilmarnock	5-2	L

1895	Mar 16	BC	v Ireland	Solitude, Belfast	2-2	D
	Mar 18	BC	v England	Queen's Club, Kensington, London	1-1	D

v England 1895 (Players Only)

Rear: G Williams, C A L Jenkyns, J L Jones, A W Pryce Jones.

Middle: W H Meredith, J Davies (Chirk), J Trainer, H Trainer, W Lewis.

Front (seated): C Parry, D Jones.

	Mar 23	BC	v Scotland	The Racecourse, Wrexham	2-2	D
1896	Feb 29	BC	v Ireland	The Racecourse, Wrexham	6-1	W
	Mar 16	BC	v England	The Arms Park, Cardiff	1-9	L
	Mar 21	BC	v Scotland	Carolina Port, Dundee	4-0	L
1897	Mar 6	BC	v Ireland	Solitude, Belfast	4-3	L
	Mar 20	BC	v Scotland	The Racecourse, Wrexham	2-2	D
	Mar 29	BC	v England	Bramall Lane, Sheffield	4-0	L
1898	Feb 19	BC	v Ireland	Council Field, Llandudno	0-1	L

v Ireland 1898 (Players Only)

Rear: W H Meredith, W Lewis, J H Edwards, G Williams behind Lewis, J Morris, S Arridge, J L Jones.

Front: T Thomas, C Parry, A Lockley, J C Rea.

	Mar 19	BC	v Scotland	Fir Park, Motherwell	5-2	L
	Mar 28	BC	v England	The Racecourse, Wrexham	0-3	L

| 1899 | Mar 4 | BC v Ireland | Grosvenor Park, Belfast | 1-0 | L |

v Ireland 1899 (Players Only)

Rear: George Richards, Horace Blew, Charlie Thomas, E Hughes.

Middle: Kelly, R Atherton, John L Jones, J Trainer, William Jackson, D C 'Chappie' Davies.

Front: Edwin James.

	Mar 18	BC v Scotland	The Racecourse, Wrexham	0-6	L
	Mar 20	BC v England	Ashton Gate, Bristol	4-0	L
1900	Feb 3	BC v Scotland	Pittodrie Park, Aberdeen	5-2	L
	Feb 24	BC v Ireland	Council Field, Llandudno	2-0	W
	Mar 26	BC v England	The Arms Park, Cardiff	1-1	D

v England 1900 (Players Only)

Rear: Joe Davies (Chirk), F Griffiths, A E Watkins.

Middle: M Morgan-Owen, C Morris, E Hughes, D Jones, T D Parry W C Harrison.

Front: W H Meredith, S J Brookes.

1901	Mar 2	BC	v Scotland	The Racecourse, Wrexham	1-1	D	
	Mar 18	BC	v England	St James' Park, Newcastle	6-0	L	

v England 1901 (Players Only)

Rear: S Meredith, L R Roose, C Morris, E Hughes, M Parry.

Front: W J Jones, T D Parry, W H Meredith, M Morgan-Owen, D H Pugh, E Williams.

	Mar 23	BC	v Ireland	Solitude, Belfast	0-1	W
1902	Feb 22	BC	v Ireland	The Arms Park, Cardiff	0-3	L
	Mar 3	BC	v England	The Racecourse, Wrexham	0-0	D
	Mar 15	BC	v Scotland	Cappielow Park, Greenock	5-1	L
1903	Mar 2	BC	v England	Fratton Park, Portsmouth	2-1	L
	Mar 9	BC	v Scotland	The Arms Park, Cardiff	0-1	L
	Mar 28	BC	v Ireland	Solitude, Belfast	2-0	L
1904	Feb 29	BC	v England	The Racecourse, Wrexham	2-2	D
	Mar 12	BC	v Scotland	Dens Park, Dundee	1-1	D
	Mar 21	BC	v Ireland	The Cricket Ground, Bangor	0-1	L
1905	Mar 6	BC	v Scotland	The Racecourse, Wrexham	3-1	W

v Scotland 1905

Rear: G E Davies, J Ll Williams, E Hughes, L R Roose, C Morris, W Nunnerley (FAW secretary), T Kirkham (referee).

Middle: W H Meredith, M Watkins, H Blew, A G Morris, A Oliver.

Seated: A Davies, J Hughes, G Latham.

	Mar 27	BC	v England	Anfield Road, Liverpool	3-1	L
	Apr 8	BC	v Ireland	Solitude, Belfast	2-2	D

1906	Mar 3	BC	v Scotland	Tynecastle Park, Edinburgh	0-2	W
	Mar 19	BC	v England	The Arms Park, Cardiff	0-1	L
	Apr 2	BC	v Ireland	The Racecourse, Wrexham	4-4	D
1907	Feb 23	BC	v Ireland	Solitude, Belfast	2-3	W

v Ireland 1907 (Players Only)

Rear: G Latham, G Williams, J Roberts, L R Roose, Lloyd Davies, Llew Davies.

Front: W L Jones, A Davies, W H Meredith, R Morris, G P Jones.

v Scotland 1907 (Players Only)

Rear: W H Meredith, H Blew, G Latham, H Price, C Morris.

Front: H Morgan-Owen, W L Jones, L R Roose, Lloyd Davies, A G Morris, G P Jones.

Mar 4	BC	v Scotland	The Racecourse, Wrexham	1-0 W
Mar 18	BC	v England	Craven Cottage, Fulham, London	1-1 D

1908	Mar 7	BC v Scotland	Dens Park, Dundee	2-1	L
	Mar 16	BC v England	The Racecourse, Wrexham	1-7	L
	Apr 11	BC v Ireland	The Athletic Ground, Aberdare	0-1	L

v Ireland 1908 (Players Only)

Rear: John Davies (FAW secretary), G Latham, G Williams, M Parry, W H Meredith, H Blew, H Price, Mr Ibbotson, Evan Rees.

Front: E Peake, J Jones, R Morris, M Watkins, R O Evans, T D Jones, A V Hodgkinson.

1909	Mar 1	BC v Scotland	The Racecourse, Wrexham	3-2	W
	Mar 15	BC v England	City Ground, Nottingham	2-0	L
	Mar 20	BC v Ireland	Grosvenor Park, Belfast	2-3	W
1910	Mar 5	BC v Scotland	Rugby Park, Kilmarnock	1-0	L
	Mar 14	BC v England	The Arms Park, Cardiff	0-1	L
	Apr 11	BC v Ireland	The Racecourse, Wrexham	4-1	W

v Ireland 1910 (Players Only)

Rear: E Peake, L R Roose, C Morris, Llew Davies, R E Evans.

Front: J L Jones, Lloyd Davies, W H Meredith, E Jones, A G Morris, E Hughes.

1911	Jan 28	BC	v Ireland	Windsor Park, Belfast	1-2	W
	Mar 6	BC	v Scotland	Ninian Park, Cardiff	2-2	D
	Mar 13	BC	v England	The Den, Millwall, London	3-0	L
1912	Mar 2	BC	v Scotland	Tynecastle Park, Edinburgh	1-0	L
	Mar 11	BC	v England	The Racecourse, Wrexham	0-2	L

v England 1912

Rear: T Robbins (FAW secretary), E Peake, Ll Davies, R O Evans, J T Jones, J Ll Williams, R T Gough (FAW president)

Front: E Hughes, G Wynn, E Jones, W Meredith, L Davies, A G Morris, E Vizard

	Apr 13	BC	v Ireland	The Arms Park, Cardiff	2-3	L
1913	Mar 3	BC	v Scotland	The Racecourse, Wrexham	0-0	D
	Mar 17	BC	v England	Ashton Gate, Bristol	4-3	L

v Scotland 1913 (Players Only)

Rear: T Hewitt, W E Bailiff, W O Davies, Ll Davies

Front: W Meredith, G Wynn, L Davies, E Hughes, J Roberts, E Vizard

	Mar 17	BC	v England	Ashton Gate, Bristol	4-3	L
1914	Jan 19	BC	v Ireland	The Racecourse, Wrexham	1-2	L
	Feb 28	BC	v Scotland	Celtic Park, Glasgow	0-0	D
	Mar 16	BC	v England	Ninian Park, Cardiff	0-2	L
1920	Feb 14	BC	v Ireland	The Oval, Belfast	2-2	D
	Feb 26	BC	v Scotland	Ninian Park, Cardiff	1-1	D
	Mar 15	BC	v England	Highbury Stadium, London	1-2	W

| 1921 | Feb 12 | BC | v Scotland | Pittodrie Park, Aberdeen | 2-1 | L |

v Scotland 1921 (Players Only)

Rear: Fred Keenor, Joseph T Jones, Harry Millership, Ted Peers, Moses Russell, Tommy Matthias.

Front: Rees Williams, Dai Collier, Ted Vizard, T F Hoddinott, Stan Davies.

v England 1921

Rear: T F Hoddinott, H Millership, T Peers, J T Jones, F Keenor, T Matthias.

Front: T Robbins (FAW secretary), D R Williams, I Jones, M Russell, S Davies, E Vizard.

	Mar 14	BC	v England	Ninian Park, Cardiff	0-0	D
	Apr 9	BC	v Ireland	The Vetch, Swansea	2-1	W
1922	Feb 4	BC	v Scotland	The Racecourse, Wrexham	2-1	W
	Mar 13	BC	v England	Anfield Road, Liverpool	1-0	L
	Apr 4	BC	v Ireland	Windsor Park, Belfast	1-1	D

v Ireland 1922 (Players Only)

Rear: Herbie Evans, Moses Russell, Ted Peers, James H Evans, Joseph T Jones.

Front: Stan Davies, Fred Keenor, Len Davies, Jack Evans, Ivor Jones, Tommy Matthias.

| 1923 | Mar 5 | BC v England | Ninian Park, Cardiff | 2-2 | D |

v England 1923

Back: R W Matthews, E J Peers, W Jennings, M R Russell, E Parry.

Front: W J Hole, I Jones, L Davies, F Keenor, E T Vizard, J Evans.

	Mar 17	BC v Scotland	St Mirren Park, Love St, Paisley	2-0	L
	Apr 14	BC v Ireland	The Racecourse, Wrexham	0-3	L
1924	Feb 16	BC v Scotland	Ninian Park, Cardiff	2-0	W

v Scotland 1924 (Players Only)

Rear: H Evans, M Russell, A Gray, J Jenkins, W Jennings, L Davies

Front: W Davies, L Davies, F Keenor, R Richards, E Vizard.

| | Mar 3 | BC v England | Ewood Park, Blackburn | 1-2 | W |

v England 1924

Rear: H Evans, J Nicholls, M Russell, A Gray, J Jenkins, W Jennings

Front: W Davies, L Davies, F Keenor, R Richards, E Vizard

| | Mar 15 | BC v Ireland | Windsor Park, Belfast | 0-1 | W |

| 1925 | Feb 14 | BC | v Scotland | Tynecastle Park, Edinburgh | 3-1 | L |

v Scotland 1925 (Players Only)

Rear: M Russell, S Bennion, A Gray, J Jenkins, J Lewis, R Richards.

Front: R Williams, W Davies, F Keenor, S Davies, E Vizard.

	Feb 28	BC	v England	The Vetch, Swansea	1-2	
	Apr 18	BC	v Ireland	The Racecourse, Wrexham	0-0	
	Oct 31	BC	v Scotland	Ninian Park, Cardiff	0-3	
1926	Feb 13	BC	v Ireland	Windsor Park, Belfast	3-0	L
	Mar 1	BC	v England	Selhurst Park, London	1-3	W
	Oct 30	BC	v Scotland	Ibrox Park, Glasgow	3-0	L
1927	Feb 12	BC	v England	The Racecourse, Wrexham	3-3	D
	Apr 9	BC	v Ireland	Ninian Park, Cardiff	2-2	D
	Oct 29	BC	v Scotland	The Racecourse, Wrexham	2-2	D
	Nov 28	BC	v England	Turf Moor, Burnley	1-2	W
1928	Feb 4	BC	v Ireland	Windsor Park, Belfast	1-2	W

v Ireland 1928

Rear: G O Postle, B Williams, Dan Lewis, T J Evans, S Bennion, H Hopkinson (referee).

Front: W Hole, Willie Davies, Len Davies, F Keenor, Wilf Lewis, Rev H Davies, B John.

| | Oct 27 | BC | v Scotland | Ibrox Park, Glasgow | 4-2 | L |
| | Nov 17 | BC | v England | The Vetch, Swansea | 2-3 | L |

1929	Feb 2	BC	v Ireland	The Racecourse, Wrexham	2-2	D
	Oct 26	BC	v Scotland	Ninian Park, Cardiff	2-4	L
	Nov 20	BC	v England	Stamford Bridge, London	6-0	L
1930	Feb 1	BC	v Ireland	Celtic Park, Belfast	7-0	L
	Oct 25	BC	v Scotland	Ibrox Park, Glasgow	1-1	D

**v Scotland 1930
(The Unknowns)**

Rear: Emrys Ellis, W Crompton, L Evans, W Robbins, W E Collins.

Front: J Neal, T Bamford, W Rogers, F Keenor, F Dewey, W R Thomas.

	Nov 22	BC	v England	The Racecourse, Wrexham	0-4	L
1931	Apr 22	BC	v Ireland	The Racecourse, Wrexham	3-2	W
	Oct 31	BC	v Scotland	The Racecourse, Wrexham	2-3	L
	Nov 18	BC	v England	Anfield Road, England	3-1	L
	Dec 5	BC	v Ireland	Windsor Park, Belfast	4-0	L
1932	Oct 26	BC	v Scotland	Tynecastle Park, Edinburgh	2-5	W

v Scotland 1932

Rear: F Keenor, T P Griffiths, R John, E O'Callaghan, D Richards, B Ellis.

Front: D Astley, W Robbins, B Williams, C Phillips, D J Lewis.

	Nov 16	BC	v England	The Racecourse, Wrexham	0-0	D
	Dec 7	BC	v Ireland	The Racecourse, Wrexham	4-1	W
1933	May 25	F	v France	Stade Olympique	1-1	D
	Oct 4	BC	v Scotland	Ninian Park, Cardiff	3-2	W
	Nov 4	BC	v Ireland	Windsor Park, Belfast	1-1	D
	Nov 15	BC	v England	St James' Park, Newcastle	1-2	W

| 1934 | Sept 29 | BC | v England | Ninian Park, Cardiff | 0-4 | L |

v England 1934 (Players Only)

Rear: D O Jones, S Lawrence, R John, D Richards, R Williams.

Front: C Phillips, E O'Callaghan, T P Griffiths, J Murphy, T Mills, W Evans.

	Nov 21	BC	v Scotland	Pittodrie Park, Aberdeen	3-2	L
1935	Mar 27	BC	v Ireland	The Racecourse, Wrexham	3-1	W

v Ireland 1935 (Players Only)

Rear: C W Jones, B Williams, J Hughes, D Richards, B John.

Front: I Hopkins, J Murphy, L Jones, T P Griffiths, B Jones, C Phillips.

v Scotland 1935 (Players Only)

Rear: R John, S Lawrence, R John, D Richards, C Phillips.

Front: J Murphy, W Robbins, T P Griffiths, L Jones, E Glover, B Jones.

| | Oct 5 | BC | v Scotland | Ninian Park, Cardiff | 1-1 | D |

1936	Feb 5	BC	v England	Molineux, Wolverhampton	1-2	W
	Mar 11	BC	v Ireland	Celtic Park, Belfast	3-2	L
	Oct 17	BC	v England	Ninian Park, Cardiff	2-1	W
	Dec 2	BC	v Scotland	Dens Park, Dundee	1-2	W
1937	Mar 17	BC	v Ireland	The Racecourse, Wrexham	4-1	W

v Ireland 1937

Rear: L Jones, P Glover, H Turner, A Gray, D O Jones, D Richards, F Warren.

Front: I Hopkins, T P Griffiths, J Murphy, B Jones.

	Oct 30	BC	v Scotland	Ninian Park, Cardiff	2-1	W
	Nov 17	BC	v England	Ayresome Park, Middlesbrough	2-1	L
1938	Mar 16	BC	v Ireland	Windsor Park, Belfast	1-0	L

v Ireland 1938

Rear: A Lumberg (linesman), Len Evans (trainer), G Green, E Perry, B Gray, T G Jones, W M Hughes, D Richards, H Webb (linesman).

Front: I Hopkins, B Jones, L Jones, H Turner, F Warren, R E Mortimer (referee).

	Oct 22	BC	v England	Ninian Park, Cardiff	4-2	W
	Nov 9	BC	v Scotland	Tynecastle Park, Edinburgh	3-2	L
1939	Mar 15	BC	v Ireland	The Racecourse, Wrexham	3-1	W
	May 20	F	v France	Stade Olympique, Paris	2-1	L

APPENDIX 2

UNOFFICIAL INTERNATIONAL MATCHES 1876-1946

A. Canada 1891

Wales played the touring Canadians in two unofficial internationals in the autumn of 1891, with both matches taking place at The Racecourse, Wrexham. In the first match, on 21 September 1891, Wales fielded: R E Turner, Di Jones, Seth Powell, Peter Griffiths, Humphrey Jones, Roger Doughty, Joe Davies (Chirk), William Owen, (Chirk) William Lewis (Crewe A), Ben Lewis and John Butler. A crowd of 500 braved the wind and rain to witness a 1-1 draw which ended in controversial circumstances. The referee, former Wales player James Davies, awarded a goal when Garrett, the Canada goalkeeper, had clearly pushed the ball behind for a corner. Canada objected, walked off, then returned, but the dispute could not be resolved and the match ended prematurely. For the second match on 12 October, Wales lined up as: J Trainer, Di Jones, G O Postle (Chirk), William Hughes (Bootle), Jack Mates, Bob Roberts (Bolton W), William Owen (Chirk), W E Pryce Jones, William Lewis (Crewe A), Ben Lewis (Wrexham) and R L Jones (Swindon). Wales won 2-1 in front of what was described as 'a very large crowd'. Only two of the players who appeared against the Canadians were not, or did not, become full Wales internationals: Richard Lewis Jones and George Postle.

Richard Lewis Jones
B: Chirk; 6 Nov 1867
D: Swindon (Eng);
  7 May 1951
Forward

Career: Swindon St Marks; Swindon T; London Welsh; Queens Park Rgrs; London Caledonians; Clapton (as an amateur), Swindon T, Jul 1895-97; Trowbridge T, 1897-98; Swindon Vic; London Welsh; Swindon T

Jones moved to Swindon in 1882 and later took employment as a clerk with the Great Western Railway works in various departments. He was an 'expert at the short passing game' and a fine dribbler. Originally an amateur, he was later declared a professional by the FA and represented Wiltshire on 17 occasions. While playing for Swindon against Ilford, Jones was said to have scored three goals in succession without a member of the opposing team touching the ball. He also captained Swindon Town reserves to a Wiltshire League and Cup double in 1895-96. Two seasons later he led Trowbridge Town to Wiltshire Cup success and, in 1898-99, made it a hat-trick with Swindon Vic. Jones, who was also a prominent athlete and boxer, retired from the GWR in 1927. On his one appearance in a Wales shirt, against Canada, he did manage to get on the score sheet, securing the first goal.

George Owen Postle
B: Acrefair; 10 Aug 1867
D: Acrefair; 10 Feb 1940
Full back

Career: Druids, 1887-91; Chirk, 1891-93; Druids, 1893-96 (also appeared for Rossendale and Gainsborough Trinity); retired

George Postle was connected with Welsh football for over 50 years as a player, referee and finally as an FAW councillor. There was a certain irony in his later respectability in official soccer circles, as he had been a robust player with more than his share of brushes with the FAW. Postle was allegedly the culprit who flattened Arthur Lea in a Charity Cup final, causing a minor riot.

Despite offers to join Rossendale, Heywood and Gainsborough Trinity as a professional, Postle remained faithful to Chirk, eschewing one offer of 'ten golden sovereigns for each of his knees and a week-day job in a slipper factory'. He retired in 1896, to become the trainer at Druids, but soon became involved in refereeing and organising junior soccer in Denbighshire. Postle, who was later employed in a terracotta works, served for many years on the management committees of various leagues, including the North Wales Alliance (secretary) and was a parish councillor. His refereeing career saw him progress to the Combination League, officiating in three Welsh Cup finals, and he ran the line at international matches. In September 1935, his lengthy service to Welsh football was marked with a testimonial fund.

Club Honours:
Chirk - Welsh Cup 1892, finalists 1893

B. Victory Internationals 1919

In 1919 Wales played two unofficial Victory internationals against England. The first match took place at Ninian Park on 11 October 1919, with Wales winning 2-1. A week later, however, England secured a 2-0 victory at the Victoria Ground, Stoke. Only one of the Welsh participants was never recognised at full official international level: William Goodwin.

William Goodwin
B: New Brighton;
 16 Jan 1892
D: Middleton (Eng); 1972
Full back (5ft 8ins, 11st 12lbs)

Career: Mold T; UCNW Bangor; Holywell; Oldham Ath, Jul 1914-21 (40 FL apps); Crewe Alex, Sep 1921-25 (148 FL apps, 2 gls); Oldham Ath, Jun 1925-26 (21 FL apps); Congleton T, 1926-28; Mossley, Jul 1928.

Goodwin was the son of a miner and graduated from Bangor University. In 1913, while playing for Holywell, and the year he was capped at amateur level, Goodwin was described in the following terms: 'His interventions were accurately timed, his returns were beautifully judged, his placing of the ball whether by volley or by place kick was superb. Beyond doubt he is the best full back playing in north Wales today'.

Goodwin combined league soccer with teaching, but his duties as a schoolmaster meant that he missed many of Oldham's mid week matches. Nevertheless, he appeared four times in the team that finished runners-up to Everton in 1914-15.

Although his educational career appeared to be progressing successfully, becoming headmaster at Chadderton Elementary School in 1923, Goodwin and his wife were both jailed for postal order offences in 1942.

C. FAW Tour of Canada 1929

During the 1929 close season, Wales undertook their first overseas tour. A squad of 20 players was selected, almost all of whom were established or were to become international players. The party was accompanied by Ted Robbins and George Latham. [Photo courtesy of Ceri Stennett]

The 1929 FAW touring party to Canada

Rear: S R Bennion, R A Pugh, A Wardell, F Warren, W W Robbins, L Evans, E Lawrence, T H Lewis, A Rogers, A Lumberg

Middle: E Vizard, F Keenor, Ted Robbins (FAW secretary), A Thomas (FAW vice president), M Russell. C Jones, G Latham (trainer)

Front: L Davies, W Jennings, A Gray, J Neal, R Williams

Jun 1	v Montreal and District	Montreal	1-3	W
Jun 3	v Hamilton and District	Hamilton	0-1	W
Jun 5	v Toronto and District	Toronto	1-4	W
Jun 8	v Manitoba	Winnipeg	2-7	W
Jun 10	v Regina and District	Regina	0-7	W
Jun 12	v Calgary and District	Calgary	1-10	W
Jun 15	v Upper (or All) Island	Nanaimo	0-3	W
Jun 17	v Lower Mainland	Vancouver	0-8	W
Jun 19	v Victoria and District	Victoria	0-1	W
Jun 22	v Westminster Royals	New Westminster	1-2	W
Jun 24	v Edmonton and District	Edmonton	1-2	W
Jun 26	v Saskatoon and District	Saskatoon	1-6	W
Jul 1	v Ontario	Toronto	1-3	W
Jul 2	v Hamilton and District	Hamilton	0-2	W
Jul 3	v Montreal and District	Montreal	1-2	W

[Also Jun 28, 'Whites' 2-4 'Reds' in Winnipeg, when each side consisted of eight Welsh players and three Canadian players]

Three of the players who appeared for Wales on the Canadian tour never achieved full international recognition.

Thomas Henry Lewis

B: Walsall (Eng); 21 May 1900
D: Holywell; 1968
Half back (5ft 9½ins, 12st)
1 cap: (junior level) v Ire 1927

Career: St Mary's Greenfield; Holywell, 1924-25; Rhyl, Jul 1925-28; New Brighton, 1928-32 (88 FL apps, 4 gls); Connah's Quay, Sep 1931; Holywell Arcadians, Sep 1932-34; New Brighton, Feb 1932 (11 FL apps); Holywell Arcadians, Sep 1933; Mostyn YMCA, 1936.

In February 1930, Lewis drew the following description: 'A product of the Rhyl Athletic club and now in his third season with New Brighton. He is regarded as one of the most versatile intermediaries the club possesses for he can take any half back berth. He plays a storming type of game and is fast developing as an exponent of the ground pass'. Lewis successfully managed Welsh League side Holywell Arcadians in the early 1930s and was the mainspring of the side, generally turning out at half back or inside forward. He worked as an artificial silk spinner after retiring from soccer and is believed to have died in the Holywell area in 1968.

Club honour:
Rhyl Ath - Welsh Cup finalists 1927

Robert Archibald Lewis Pugh

B: Symonds Yat (Eng);
  16 Sep 1909
D: Newport; Jan 1986
Left half/inside left (6ft, 12st)

Career: Symonds Yat; Whitchurch; Monmouth; Hereford; Newport Co, Sep 1926-29 (66 league apps, 13 goals); Bury, Aug 1929-31 (28 lge apps, 10 gls); Nottingham F, Jan 1931-Aug 1938 (248 lge apps, 19 gls);

Bob Pugh would surely have gained full international honours but, subsequent to the Canadian tour, the FAW discovered that he had been born a few miles the wrong side of the Welsh border and was ineligible. He joined Newport, in the face of stiff competition from Hereford, after being spotted by a County director.

Pugh was once described as: 'tall, sometimes leisurely but always clever and an artist with the ball especially when there is mud around', while another reporter noted him as 'a robust, clever player who goes into every game he plays to enjoy it'. Originally a centre forward, he gave great service to Forest as part of a powerful half back line with Billy McKinlay and Tommy Graham. Pugh was injured playing against West Ham in March 1938 and underwent an operation to repair a cartilage but, on 31 August 1938, he turned out for Forest against Plymouth Argyle and after the game was advised to retire from league football on medical grounds. Pugh, who once saved a boy from drowning in the River Wye, later worked for the Bristol Aero Company then served with the RAF in North Africa. After the Second World War he played for Avro in the Nottingham Spartan League and scouted for Forest.

Albert Wardell

B: Bilston (Eng); 12 Jan 1908
D: Prestatyn; Mar 1987
Forward (5ft 8ins, 11st 7lbs)
1 cap (amateur): v Eng 1927

Career: Hereford Utd; Newport Co, 1926-31 (43 FL apps, 9 gls); Darlington, Aug 1930 (5 FL apps, 2 gls).

'Nip' Wardell, was born in the West Midlands but his parents moved to Newport the following day. A stockily-built but extremely quick player, he represented Wales Schoolboys at both soccer and rugby. Wardell was principally a goal scoring winger but got few first team opportunities at Newport. He was later loaned by Darlington to

Chelsea, and several other clubs, but made no league appearances.

In the 1930s, he was player-manager for Taylor Brothers steel works team in Manchester, where he was also employed. Wardell subsequently worked at a Manchester power station, then became a landlord at a public house in Eccles before following his son to the north Wales coast where his managed Prestatyn FC in the late 1960s and early 1970s when the club operated in the Welsh League (North). His father was Mayor of Newport at one time, and Wardell was a brother-in-law to Alex Higgins, the Newcastle and Scotland player.

D. War-time Internationals 1939-46

Wales played 17 war-time unofficial matches for which players were not awarded caps.

Wales captain T G Jones introduces Deputy Prime Minister Clement Attlee to the Wales players at Wembley (25 Sep 1943)

1939	11 Nov	v England	Ninian Park, Cardiff	1-1	D
	Nov 18	v England	The Racecourse, Wrexham	2-3	L
1940	Apr 13	v England	Empire Stadium, Wembley	1-0	L
1941	Apr 26	v England	Nottingham	4-1	L
	Jun 7	v England	Ninian Park, Cardiff	2-3	L
	Oct 25	v England	St Andrews, Birmingham	2-1	L
1942	May 9	v England	Ninian Park, Cardiff	1-0	W
	Oct 24	v England	Molineux, Wolverhampton	1-2	W
1943	Feb 27	v England	Empire Stadium, Wembley	5-3	L
	May 8	v England	Ninian Park, Cardiff	1-1	D
	Sep 25	v England	Empire Stadium, Wembley	8-3	L
1944	May 6	v England	Ninian Park, Cardiff	0-2	L
	Sep 16	v England	Anfield, Liverpool	2-2	D
1945	May 5	v England	Ninian Park, Cardiff	2-3	L
	Oct 20	v England	The Hawthorns, West Bromwich	0-1	W
	Nov 10	v Scotland	Hampden Park, Glasgow	2-0	L
1946	May 4	v Ireland	Ninian Park, Cardiff	0-1	L

Of all the players who appeared for Wales in the war-time internationals, 13 never achieved full international recognition.

Thomas Arthur Astbury

B: Buckley; 9 Feb 1920
D: Queensferry; 19 Oct 1993
Inside right
(5ft 6ins, 10st 4lbs)
3 apps: (Wales) v Eng, May 1945, Oct 1945; (Wales XI) v Western Command, May 1942

Career: Mold Alex; Chester, May 1938-55 (302 FL apps, 38 gls); Wrexham & Everton (war-time guest); retired

Tom Astbury first played soccer for Bistre N Primary School in Buckley, failed to get selected for his secondary school team, Mold Alyn Grammar School, but was spotted, by Chester, playing for Mold in the West Cheshire League and went on to become one of the club's greatest servants. 'A bit on the small side but a player of exceptional ability', he remained a loyal one-club man throughout his career. On retiring he was given the post of part-time coach with Chester but later worked as a sales representative for a builders' merchant.

Honours:
Chester - Welsh Cup 1947; finalists 1953, 1954
Manchester Utd - FL North Cup finalists 1945

Robert Griffith Davies

B: Blaenau Ffestiniog;
  19 Oct 1913
D: Nottingham (Eng);
  10 May 1978
Half back

6 apps: (Wales) v Eng, Mar 1940, May 1944, May 1945, Oct 1945, v Scotland Nov 1945; (Wales XI) v Western Command, Jun 1942

Career: Blaenau Ffestiniog, 1932-36; Nottingham F, Dec 1936-Apr 1947 (55 FL apps); Blackpool and Leicester C (war-time guest).

A Notts Forest official was sipping a cup of tea while waiting for a train at Blaenau Ffestiniog railway station when he learned there was a game on at Haygarth Park. It was there that he saw the young hairdresser Bob Davies and wasted little time in signing him for Forest. Blaenau were rewarded with a match against the Football League club that raised a pretty meagre amount of £55.

A 'policeman' type of centre half, Davies was selected for a Welsh amateur trial but turned pro' in November 1936 and gave up his chance of an amateur cap. He made his league debut in September 1937 and was soon 'a much-discussed player' and in contention for a full Welsh cap. A big, strong pivot and 'a dominant defender', he was kept out of the national side by Tommy Jones. Davies was called up by the RAF at the outbreak of war and made nearly 300 parachute jumps until an accident threatened his soccer career. He had both legs in plaster but fought back to fitness.

After retiring as a player, Davies became second team coach at Forest and reputedly never lost a game during his seven years in charge of the team. He later became a noted physiotherapist, attending to both Forest players and Nottinghamshire's county cricketers but lost his job, and ended nearly 40 years service at the City ground, when Alan Brown took over at Forest in 1974. Bob then became physio' at Walsall and when he fell seriously ill in May 1978, the club arranged a testimonial match against Aston Villa. Sadly, he died five days later.

William Davies

B: Troedyrhiw, Merthyr Tydfil;
  24 Jun 1910
D: Watford (Eng); Nov 1995
Winger (5ft 7½ins, 10st 7lbs)
1 app: (Wales) v Eng, May 1944

Career: Troedyrhiw; New Tredegar; Watford, Apr 1930-50 (285 FL apps, 69 gls), (122 war-time apps); Grimsby T (war-time guest).

'Taffy' Davies joined Watford in April 1930 from New Tredegar and turned pro' within weeks. Originally an inside forward with Troedyrhiw, he was 'a forceful & skilful winger' who not only centred the ball well but was also an excellent schemer. One report commented he 'puts plenty of life and thought into his game' but also noted his' tendency to hold his ground and pass back instead of taking a direct route to goal'.

A cartilage operation during the 1937-38 season put him out of action until April 1938 and the club did not recover from his loss, missing out on promotion. On his retirement in 1950, after 20 years with the club, Davies was given a benefit cheque of £200. He was subsequently the licensee of the Red Lion, near the Watford ground.

William John James

B: Cardiff; 18 Oct 1921
D: Cardiff; 27 Jul 1980
Inside forward/Centre forward
2 apps (1 gl): (Wales) v Eng, Jun 1941, Oct 1941

Career: Moorland Rd Sch; Cardiff Corinthians; Cardiff C, 1946-47 (6 FL apps, 2 gls).

Billy James was said, in 1940, to have a brilliant future ahead of him in soccer and, in November 1940, he hit 8 goals for Cardiff City against an Army XI, but his experiences in a Japanese prisoner of war camp ended those hopes. He joined the Army at 18 (77th HAA RA) and was later sent out Far East, where he was captured by the Japanese.

James played only a handful of games for Cardiff after the war before being forced to give up the game because of failing eyesight, a legacy of his time in the camps. He was awarded a benefit match in May 1950, when a Billy James XI played Cardiff City. In later years, James, who worked as a salesman for a office supplies company, coached youngsters in the Cardiff area and scouted for City.

Stanley Harding Mortensen

B: South Shields (Eng);
26 May 1921
D: Blackpool (Eng);
22 May 1991
Centre forward/Inside right
1 app: (Wales) v Eng, Sep 1943

Career: South Shields Ex-Schoolboys; Blackpool, Apr 1937-55 (317 FL apps, 197 gls); Aberdeen (war-time guest); Hull C, (£2,000) Nov 1955-57 (42 FL apps, 18 gls); Southport, Feb 1957-58 (37 FL apps, 10 gls); Bath C, Jul 1958-May 1959, retired; Lancaster C, Nov 1960-Mar 1962; Blackpool, (manager) Feb 1967-Apr 1969.

Although more appropriate to an England Who's Who due to his 25 caps for the Three Lions, Mortensen donned the Welsh shirt in September 1943 to take over from the injured Ivor Powell. The Welsh left half had damaged his collar bone and Mortensen, who was on the England bench as 12th man, took his place: he also made an appearance as a substitute for a Welsh club side. Mortensen had narrowly avoided death when the Wellington bomber he was in crashed, while on a training exercise in Scotland, and was sent to Newport to convalesce. 'Mortie' took a day off to watch Lovell's Athletic and Swansea Town contest a League West Cup final and volunteered to help the short-handed Swans.

After the war, he went on to win 25 England caps and formed a memorable partnership with Stanley Matthews at international level and for

Blackpool. He was one of the most dangerous forwards of his period, a fine ball player and exceptionally quick off the mark. After retirement from soccer he went into business in Blackpool and was president of his former club. A career highlight was his hat-trick in the 1953 FA Cup final.

George Murphy

B: Cwmfelinfach; 20 July 1915
D: Leeds (Eng); Dec 1983
Centre forward/Full back
2 apps: (Wales) v Eng, May 1943, Sep 1943

Career: Pontllanffraith; Cwmfelinfach Juniors: Bradford C, Oct 1934-47 (180 FL apps, 43 gls); Hull City, (£1,500) Dec 1947-48 (15 FL apps, 9 gls); Scunthorpe Utd, Aug 1948; Scarborough; Goole T, 1951; retired.

Murphy was discovered in Monmouthshire junior football and made his league debut two months after moving to Yorkshire. He gave excellent service to Bradford, in most positions but principally as a centre forward and full back, was a dangerous player in the penalty area, and although not a prolific goal scorer, he was renowned for his fearless assaults in the goalmouth. He spent the war serving in the RAF and guested for many clubs; Murphy was another player who would have had a strong claim to full honours but for the war. He had a brief spell at Hull after the war before moving into non-league football and, on retirement, Murphy became a licensee and was later a club steward in the Leeds area.

William Joseph Redfern

B: Connah's Quay;
   15 Oct 1910
D: Sep 1988
Inside forward
1 app: (Wales) v Eng, Nov 1939

Career: Holywell Arcadians, 1931; Bangor C, 1933-34; Newry T; Luton T, 1937-39 (41 FL apps, 19 gls); Derby Co, 1939-40 (2 FL apps, 1 gl); Wrexham (61 war-time apps); Chester (war-time guest). Also, Irish League; v Scottish League, 1936.

Billy Redfern played as an amateur between 1930 and 1934, gaining Birmingham & District League experience, principally with Bangor and Rhyl. A latecomer to league soccer, he was a tall forward with an unusual style. At Luton he was looked upon as successor to Joe Payne and was a regular scorer in the London Combination during the 1937-38 season. One reporter commented: 'he is clever at finding openings, good with his head, very persistent and a good leader'. Redfern attracted Arsenal's interest in May 1938 but the move did not materialise. During the war Redfern made a substantial number of appearances for Wrexham. At one time he worked as a barber, then in a butcher's shop, finally running his own grocery business in Connah's Quay.

Ehud Rogers

B: Chirk; 15 Oct 1909
D: Chirk; 25 Jan 1996
Outside right
   (5ft 6ins, 10st 6lbs)
1 cap (amateur): v Scot, 1934
2 apps: (Wales) v Eng, Jun 1941, Sep 1944

Career: Weston Rhyn; Llanerch Celts; Chirk; Oswestry T; Wrexham, May 1934-35 (11 FL apps, 2 gls); Arsenal, Jan 1935-36 (16 FL apps, 5 gls); Newcastle Utd, (£2,500) Jun 1936-39 (56 FL apps, 11 gls); Swansea T, (£700) May-Sep 1939 (3 FL apps); Wrexham, (65 war-time apps, 27 gls); Swansea T, (53 war-time apps, 18 gls); Lovell's Ath & Aberaman (guest); Wrexham, 1946-47 (1 FL app); Oswestry T, 1947.

A light and quick player, 'Tim' was an enthusiastic winger who had a tendency to overdo things. He left school to become a chauffeur for a local businessman, but also began selling newspapers while playing for Chirk and then Oswestry. In June 1934, he signed for Wrexham as a part-time pro' for £4 a week and had some outstanding matches before being transferred to Arsenal for a fee close to £3,000. It was at Arsenal that he was nicknamed 'Tim', because some players had difficulty pronouncing his biblical name: Judges 3 verses 15-27, 'Ehud, the son of Gera'. A fast little forward, he understudied Joe Hulme at Highbury and while on Tyneside, one Newcastle scribe described him as: 'A player with more than a touch of finesse'.

Rogers had played only three matches for Swansea when war broke out and all contracts were cancelled. He joined the RAF and spent three years at St Athan, near Cardiff, before being posted to Egypt in 1944. He was released by Wrexham in 1947, at his own request, to concentrate on his newsagent's business. Ehud's brother Joe played for Manchester City and Shrewsbury Town.

Arthur John Smith

B: Aberaman; 27 Oct 1911
D: Weymouth (Eng);
  7 Jun 1975
Left back/Left half
  (5ft 9½ins, 10st 2lbs)
2 apps: (Wales) v Eng, Nov 1940; (Wales XI) v Birmingham, Oct 1941

Career: Aberaman; Aberdare Ath; Merthyr T, 1927-28 (14 FL apps, 4 gls); Wolverhampton Wdrs, May 1930-34 (30 FL apps); Bristol Rov 1934-35 (4 FL apps); Swindon T, Aug 1935-38 (114 FL apps); Chelsea, Mar 1938-39 (48 FL apps); West Bromwich Alb (war-time guest); Wolverhampton Wdrs, (trainer); West Bromwich Alb, (manager) Jul 1948-52; Reading, (manager) Jun 1952-Oct 1955.

An intelligent footballer who might have become a dentist but for ill-health at the time of his examinations, Smith turned professional with Merthyr two months before joining Wolves. A capable and wholehearted player, he was an excellent passer but spent much of his time at Molineux in the reserves. When given the opportunity of first-team football at Swindon, he proved to be a very consistent performer and made 130 consecutive appearances. Chelsea paid £3,300 for his transfer, plus a further £700 after 12 league appearances, but war very soon curtailed his soccer ambitions.

Smith served as an RAF flight sergeant but any chance of resuming his football career at the end of hostilities was ended by a road accident. In peacetime he became trainer at Wolves and then managed West Brom, guiding them to the First Division in his first season in charge. Smith resigned his post at the end of the 1951-52 season and took over from Ted Drake as Reading manager. The team struggled and Smith was given leave of absence at the outset of the 1955-56 season. Shortly afterwards he resigned and left soccer to run a hotel in Weymouth.

Frank Squires

B: Swansea; 8 Mar 1921
D: Swansea; 1 Mar 1988
Outside right/Inside forward
  (5ft 10ins, 11st 10lbs)
2 apps: (Wales) v Eng, May 1942, v Sco, Nov 1945

Career: Danygraig Sch; Swansea Schoolboys; Swansea T (war-time); Swansea T, 1946-47 (36 FL apps, 5 gls); Plymouth Argyle, (£7,000) Oct 1947-50 (86 FL apps, 13 gls); Grimsby T, Jul 1950-51 (36 FL apps, 2 gls); Merthyr T, 1951.

A precocious talent, Frank Squires captained his school team at both soccer and cricket before joining Swansea Town for £10 a week, in season, and £8 during the summer. He had been capped twice by Wales Schoolboys and was a member of the Swansea Schoolboys side which reached the final of the English Schools Trophy for the first time in 1935. At the Vetch Field, he waited six years for his league debut but gained much experience in war-time soccer, including a trip to Italy with Stan Cullis' team to provide entertainment for the troops. Squires, who had been one of the first conscripts of 1939, served with the 8th Army in the North African campaign and was a member of the same Forces team as Tom Finney and Bryn Jones.

A very good ball-playing inside forward with much creative ability, his skilful work in midfield created a favourable impression at Grimsby. Squires partnered Tommy Briggs, the England B international, at Grimsby and contributed some 'dandy football'. Unfortunately, Grimsby struggled at foot of the Second Division for most of the season and, during the 1951 close season, he left the club for non-league football. Squires later took employment at a sheet metal engineering company and later ran a grocers shop. Frank's nephews Paul, and Wales international, Dudley Lewis also pursued a career in soccer.

George Williams

B: Ynysddu; 19 May 1914
D: Whitburn (Eng); May 1993
Full back (5ft 11½ins, 12st 4lbs)
3 apps: (Wales) v Eng, Apr 1940, Apr 1941; (Wales XI) v Western Command, Jun 1942

Career: Cwmfelinfach Schools XI; Pals XI (Cwmfelinfach); Bolton Wdrs; Charlton Ath, 1934-36; Aldershot, (£350) Jun 1936-38 (55 FL apps); Millwall, (£2,000) 1938-39 (14 FL apps), 1946-47 (14 FL apps); South Shields.

Williams spent three months at Bolton Wanderers prior to being signed by Charlton manager Angus Seed. A solid and steady player, he had earlier been capped by Wales at schoolboy level. Although Williams was a reliable full back, one report commented of his tendency, at times, to give too much room to the winger. He made his league debut for Aldershot in February 1936 against Crystal Palace, but when the club sold him to Millwall two years later a row developed over the fee: the dispute was settled with Charlton receiving 50 per cent. During the war, Williams served in the Police War Reserve, stationed in London, but once peacetime soccer resumed his career at Millwall proved to be short lived and he eventually moved to Whitburn, due to his wife's family connections, and took employment in engineering.

Danny Thomas Winter

B: Tonypandy, Rhondda; 14 Jun 1918
D: Trealaw, Rhondda; 22 Mar 2004
Full back (5ft 8½ins, 11st 7lbs)
2 apps: (Wales) v Eng, May 1945, Oct 1945

Career: Tonypandy Junior Sch; Tonypandy Secondary Sch; Maes y Haf; Bolton Wdrs, 1936-39 (37 FL apps); Chelsea, (57 war-time guest apps); Chelsea, (£5,000) Dec 1945-51 (131 FL apps), also Arsenal, Crystal Palace, Watford & Norwich); Worcester C, 1951.

Danny Winter played outside half for his school's rugby union team on Saturdays and soccer in the Rhondda League in the mid-week. At the age of 16 years and 9 months, having had trials with Arsenal and Bolton, and following family discussions, he decided to join the Trotters, a decision he never regretted. Initially he worked as an office boy until he was old enough to turn professional and graduated from the ranks of the 'A' and reserve teams before, with a number of other Bolton players, joining the British Expeditionary Force that was evacuated from Dunkirk. A very good all-round footballer, he was a tough opponent for any winger and a noted penalty expert. Winter was a stylish player who rarely went in for rough play and seldom got his kit dirty. In 1950, it was rumoured that he might join South American club Bogota but in the event he wisely decided to remain at Chelsea for a further season before going into non-league soccer with Worcester, for whom The Pensioners waived the £8,000 asking fee due to their non-league status. As part of the transfer agreement, Winter was able to return to live in the Rhondda, train locally and join up with his colleagues on match days. An ankle injury at the age of 35 compelled him to call it a day and he joined the administrative side of his brother's building company. When he left league soccer, he thought he might try his luck as a manager but he never had to use the fine reference provided by Matt Busby and Arthur Rowe. Danny's wife was the niece of Harry Nuttall who won FA Cup medals with Bolton in the 1920s.

Honours:
Chelsea - FL (S) Cup 1945

Vivian Woodward
B: Troedyrhiw, Merthyr Tydfil; 20 May 1914
D: Unknown
Wing half/Inside forward
(5ft 6½ins, 11st)
1 app: (Wales) v Eng, Jun 1941

Career: Wales Schoolboys; Aberpergwm, 1927; Glynneath Welfare; Glynneath; Folkestone; Fulham, (£300) Jan 1936-39 (86 FL apps, 25 gls), 1946-47 (10 FL apps); Derby Co, Bradford C, Blackburn Rov & Crystal Palace (war-time guest); Millwall, Feb 1947-48 (42 FL apps, 13 gls); Brentford, Jul 1948-50 (20 FL apps, 4 gls); Aldershot, Feb 1950-51 (54 FL apps, 5 gls); Bedford T, 1951-55; Biggleswade T.

One of six boys, Viv Woodward spent two-and-a-half years at Folkestone before breaking into league football with Fulham after being spotted by one of the club's directors. At Craven Cottage he played in all forward positions but, after 1938, operated mostly at inside forward. In February 1950, Woodward moved to Aldershot where he was the first signing of new manager Gordon Clark who firstly tried him out as a wing half but soon reverted to playing Woodward in his familiar inside forward role. A tough and uncompromising player, Woodward, was soon appointed club captain and was a very good 'general' at the hub of the Aldershot team. His brother Lawrence captained Bournemouth.

E. War-time Wales XI Matches 1941-44

In addition to the war-time unofficial internationals, six matches in aid of war charities were played by teams going under the title of Wales XI or Welsh Servicemen. Two of these matches were against Western Command, two against the RAF and one each against Birmingham and the National Police XI.

1941	Nov 8	Birmingham v Wales XI	St Andrews, Birmingham	2-3	W
1942	May 23	Welsh Servicemen v National Police XI	Ninian Park, Cardiff	3-6	L
	May 30	Wales XI v Western Command	Belle Vue, Rhyl	4-1	W
	Jun 6	Wales XI v Western Command	The Racecourse, Wrexham	2-0	W
	Sep 26	Wales XI v Royal Air Force	The Vetch Field, Swansea	1-3	L
1944	Sep 2	Wales XI v Royal Air Force	The Racecourse, Wrexham	1-1	D

Of all the players who appeared for Wales in these war-time charity matches, 12 never achieved full international recognition.

Robert Norman Victor Daniel

B: Swansea; 1923
D: 24 Dec 1943
Centre forward
3 apps: (Wales XI) v Western Command, May 1942, Jun 1942; v RAF Sep 1942

Career: Swansea Schoolboys; Arsenal, 1938-39.

A brother to Ray Daniel, Bobby joined Arsenal and was reckoned to be a brilliant prospect. He was never able to realise his enormous potential and was reported missing on 23 December 1943 after an RAF bombing mission to Prague. He was one of the nine Arsenal professionals of the 42 players on the club's books in 1939 who failed to survive the war. Daniel, a flight sergeant gunner, had completed 30 operations at the time of his death.

Alun J Evans

B: Cwmbach, Aberdare;
  1 Dec 1922
D: Worcester (Eng);
  Jan 2008
Wing half/Inside forward
  (5ft 7½ins, 11st)
1 app: (Wales XI) v RAF, Sep 1944

Career: Ynysboeth Sch, Hounslow West Sch; Wilden; West Bromwich Alb, Jan 1943-May 1948 (10 war-time apps); 1947-48 (18 FL apps); retired.

A qualified PE instructor and drill training officer, Evans played a lot of soccer for his Army regiment against local sides while serving in India. An assiduous inside forward with neat footwork and precise passes, he was beginning to show great promise when, in 1948, his eyesight failed following a kick to the head. 'Boyo', as he was nicknamed, was forced into retirement, received just £350 from a benefit game but thankfully recovered the sight of his left eye two years later. He subsequently worked in a factory in the West Midlands and retired to live in Kidderminster where he enjoyed watching the career of his son, Alun Evans, who played for Liverpool during the 1970s.

Wyn Rhys Griffiths

B: Blaengwynfi, Maesteg;
  17 Oct 1919
D: Newport; Aug 2006
Goalkeeper (6ft, 12st 6lbs)
1 app: (Welsh Servicemen) v National Police XI, May 1942

Career: Gwynfi Welfare; Cardiff C, (amateur) 1941-44; Arsenal, 1944-46; Derby Co, 1946 (1 FL app); Newport Co, (amateur) 1951-52 (3 FL apps).

Wyn Griffiths was spotted by Cardiff City in January 1940 while playing for Gwynfi against Swansea in a Welsh Cup tie but, unfortunately, his planned debut at Bristol City the following Saturday had to be called off because the ground at Ashton Gate was waterlogged. Griffiths was again contacted by Cardiff in 1941, while studying at veterinary college at Reading, and became their regular keeper for three years.

He appeared for Arsenal in 1945 against the formidable Moscow Dynamos and was kicked in the head by Bobrov after 15 minutes but remained on the field in a concussed state until he was substituted at the interval. Injury also prevented Griffiths from an appearance with Derby in the 1946 FA Cup final. With the regular keeper out through injury, Griffiths secured his release from Cardiff but his hopes of a Wembley appearance were dashed when he cracked his ribs playing for Derby against Aston Villa. A veterinary surgeon in Newport, Griffiths helped out the local club on a few occasions before turning his sporting attention to polo and thereafter he concentrated on his long-standing interest in horse racing, and breeding thoroughbreds. Griffiths was also an experienced radio and television broadcaster in Wales, principally on horse racing and was once the subject of a filmed biography.

Kenneth Charles Hollyman

B: Cardiff; 18 Nov 1922
D: Cardiff; 14 May 2009
Wing half (5ft 5ins, 10st 8lbs)
1 app: (Welsh Servicemen) v National Police XI, May 1942

Career: Cardiff Corinthians; Cardiff C, 1944-53 (188 FL apps, 8 gls); Newport Co, Nov 1953-59 (233 FL apps, 4 gls); Ton Pentre (player-coach). Also, Welsh League; v Irish League, May 1951.

A great servant to Cardiff City, and later Newport, Hollyman - a keen tackler - compensated for his lack of height with skill, industry and determination and was unfortunate not to gain his full cap. Hollyman, who was a member of Cardiff's Third Division title team, joined Newport as a wing half but was successfully converted to full back. A keen baseball player, he represented Wales on several occasions while, outside soccer, Hollyman worked for a firm of metal fabricators in Cardiff.

Honours;
Cardiff C - FL 3rd Div (S) champions 1947
- FL 2nd Div runners-up 1952
- Welsh Cup finalists 1951

Cyril Jones

B: Rhosllanerchrugog; 17 July 1920
D: Wrexham; Nov 1995
Full back
1 app: (Wales XI) v Western Command, May 1942

Career: Johnstown; Wrexham (120+ war-time apps); Blackburn Rov (war-time guest); Chester (war-time guest); Wrexham, 1946-47 (29 FL apps); Blaenau Ffestiniog; Caernarfon T, Mar 1948-49; Porthmadog, 1949-Apr 1951, Dec 1951-52; retired.

A Wrexham stalwart of the war years, Cyril Jones was signed as a part-time professional while continuing to work at Hafod Colliery. Between 1941 and 1946 he hardly missed a match, frequently coming off shift on Friday evenings, and having a few hours sleep before travelling often long distances to an away match with Wrexham. One reporter described him as 'a classical player who tackles strongly, is speedy and distributes the ball to advantage'. Cyril Jones remained a regular feature of Wrexham's team during the 1945-46 post-war transitional season and was something of a utility player. A knee and ankle injury ended his league career so he moved to the Welsh League (North) with Caernarfon Town, from where he was capped at amateur level in 1948. Jones was a miner for 35 years but later assisted in his son's bakery in Johnstown until he retired in 1985.

Dudley Henry John Kernick

B: Camelford, Cornwall; 29 Aug 1921
D: Unknown
Inside forward
1 app: (Wales XI) v Birmingham XI, Nov 1941

Career: Camelford G Sch; Tintagel; Torquay Utd; Birmingham; Charlton Ath, Walsall (war time guest); Torquay Utd, 1946-47 (38 FL apps, 7 gls); Northampton T, Aug-Dec 1948; Birmingham C, Dec 1948; Kettering T; Nuneaton Borough (player-coach, then secretary-manager).

Dudley Kernick was invited by FAW secretary Ted Robbins to play for the Wales XI when winger George Edwards was unavailable. At the time, he was employed in Birmingham in a munitions works, but his mother's birthplace of Hay on Way secured his Welsh qualification for the war-time charity match. The youngster did well in front of a capacity ground of 25,000 and scored one goal in a 3-2 victory.

Earlier, at Camelford Grammar School, Kernick had scored 15 goals in a match, a record that still stands. His career properly got underway after the war and a succession of clubs followed until he took over the reins at Nuneaton Borough. Under his management they enjoyed some great cup runs and defeated Swansea in the FA Cup watched by a 25,000 crowd: huge for a non-league club. A qualified FA coach, he later worked with Jimmy Hill and Alan Dicks at Coventry City and, in 1970, became Stoke City's commercial manager. Kernick coached at many venues in the English midlands, including at the National Recreation Centre at Lilleshall and was a successful after dinner speaker, who divided his time between the UK and Florida and who, in 1976, wrote his autobiography entitled *Who the Hell is Dudley Kernick?*

Idris Lewis
B: Tonypandy/Trealaw, Rhondda; 26 Aug 1915
D: Swansea; Mar 1996
Outside right
(5ft 7ins, 10st 10lbs)
1 app: (Welsh Servicemen) v National Police XI, May 1942

Career: Ton Boys; Gelli Colliery; Swansea T, May 1935-37 (78 FL apps, 4 gls); Sheffield Wed, Aug 1938-46 (21 FL apps, 7 gls); Cardiff C & Swansea T (war-time guest); Bristol Rov, July-Oct 1946 (13 FL apps, 2 gls); Newport Co, Oct 1946-48 (27 FL apps, 4 gls); Haverfordwest Ath.

Idris Lewis, an amateur, joined Swansea, in the face of interest from Chelsea, for £3 a week plus bonuses. He made his league debut at Christmas 1935 and was highly rated by manager Neil Harris. In 1937 he refused to re-sign in a wages dispute and was transferred to Sheffield Wednesday for a substantial sum, where Lewis scored on his debut in a 4-1 win before a crowd of 83,000.

A traditional style winger, Lewis was a wholehearted player who trained hard. He had two good feet and was equally at home on either wing. When war broke out, he became a PT instructor in the Army and served for the duration. Some opportunities for soccer presented themselves and he captained Cardiff City as captain in 1942. He also represented the Army and, while serving in the Shetlands, for Western Command and Shetlands v Scottish Command. In 1945, with the war over, Sheffield Wednesday insisted on giving him a trial before deciding whether to re-sign him. Lewis, who had played infrequently over the previous three years, refused and was transferred to Bristol Rovers. He was unable to get accommodation for his family in war-scarred Bristol, and assumed he'd have to earn a living outside football but Newport arranged a deal with Rovers and Lewis was allowed to live in Swansea with his family. He later enjoyed several happy seasons in the Welsh League before finally retiring in 1954 with suspected cartilage trouble. His brother Cyril was a full back with Grimsby Town.

Honour:
Swansea T - Welsh Cup finalists 1938

John Frederick Beriah Moore
B: Cardiff; 25 Dec 1919
D: Bangor; May 2005
Outside left (5ft 7ins, 10st)
1 app: (Welsh Servicemen) v National Police XI, May 1942

Career: Cardiff Corinthians; Cardiff C (war-time); Cardiff C, 1947-48 (6 FL apps, 4 gls); Bangor C, 1949-50; Newport Co, Jul 1950-53 (121 FL apps, 46 gls); Caernarfon T, 1954-May 1957 (132 apps, 113 gls); Nantlle Vale, 1957-58.

An amateur with Cardiff Corries, Beriah Moore became a part-time professional during the 1940-41 season. He chalked up an impressive number of appearances in war-time soccer but his most notable moment with Cardiff came in November 1945. He was brought in for the match against the renowned Moscow Dynamo because Billy Rees was injured, and had the distinction of scoring City's consolation goal in the 10-1 defeat. Moore joined his former Cardiff captain Fred Stansfield at Newport in 1950, and ran up more than 100 appearances before turning to non-league soccer in the north of Wales. Hugely popular with Caernarfon supporters Moore was a deadly shot and, for a winger, a remarkable goal scorer. He joined Nantlle Vale in May 1957 after helping Caernarfon to one of their most successful seasons. Moore was later a milkman and then a factory worker until his retirement.

Thomas Bernard Olsen

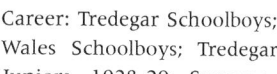

B: Tirphil, New Tredegar;
   13 Jan 1913
D: Swansea; 6 Jan 1973
Outside left
   (5ft 9ins, 10st 4lbs)
1 app: (Wales XI) v Birmingham XI, Nov 1941

Career: Tredegar Schoolboys; Wales Schoolboys; Tredegar Juniors, 1928-29; Swansea T, 1929-39 (195 FL apps, 50 gls); Bury, Jun 1939.

'Tommy' Olsen was of Scandinavian descent and the first Wales schoolboy international produced by Tirphil. A great pal of Jack Warner (qv), he was snapped up by Swansea at the age of 16 and, for a time, he was kept out of the senior side by other players. He did well in the reserves, however, winning South Wales and Monmouthshire FA Cup, and West Wales FA Cup medals. Committed to Swansea, Olsen turned down the chance of a move to a Second Division club in March 1938. During the war, Olsen served with the RAF but once peacetime soccer resumed decided not to continue playing and became a clerk for British Transport Commerce. A keen fisherman, he later ran a grocery shop in Waun Wen, Swansea

Honour:
Swansea T - Welsh Cup finalists 1938

John T Price

B: Shotton; 1918
D: Unknown
Full back
1 app: (Wales XI) v Birmingham XI, Nov 1941

Career: Upton Victory Hall; Manor Athletic; Tranmere Rov, Jan 1941-45; New Brighton (war-time guest).

Price was called up as a last-minute replacement for Bert Turner of Charlton by FAW secretary Ted Robbins. Reports suggested he came from Shotton but it appears he was the product of local league football in Birkenhead. Price turned professional in November 1941 and made one war-time appearance when on loan at New Brighton.

Frederick Roberts

B: Rhyl; 7 May 1916
D: Rhyl; Jun 1985
Outside right
   (5ft 7ins, 10st 2lbs)
2 apps: (Wales XI) v Western Command,
May 1942, Jun 1942

Career: Rhyl Juniors; Rhyl; Bury, Apr 1938-39 (12 FL apps, 5 gls); Arsenal, Everton, Manchester Utd, Chester, Luton T & Glentoran (war-time guest); Bury, 1946-47 (3 FL apps, 1 gl); Leyton Orient, Nov 1946-47 (18 FL apps, 2 gls); Rhyl, 1947-48: Llandudno Junction, (player-coach) 1948-49; Flint T Utd; Colwyn Bay; Caernarfon Town; Rhyl (manager). Also, **N Wales Coast FA** v Scottish Juniors, 1938; **Army** (war-time).

'This Welsh boy, who my old friend Ted Robbins must see as early as possible', noted a press report of his first league match, 'ran like a deer and put the Coventry defence in queer street. He made two goals and scored two in Bury's 5-0 defeat of Coventry'. Sadly the war intervened and instead of looking forward to a possible senior debut for Wales, Roberts became a sergeant PTI with the Royal Welsh Fusiliers. A 'goal getting, flying winger', he appeared for Glentoran and scored a hat-trick when they won the Unity Cup in 1942-43. He was player-coach of Llandudno Junction when they won the Welsh League (North) championship in 1949 and spent some time as manager of his home town club.

Honour:
Rhyl - Welsh Cup finalists 1937

APPENDIX 3

Edward Robbins

Finally, it would be remiss in not acknowledging the role played by FAW secretary Ted Robbins during a large part of the period covered in Volume I. Team selection was the prerogative of the FAW Committee (later Council) until well into the 1950s and matters on the field were left to the team captain. In the 1920s and 1930s FAW secretary Ted Robbins played a large part in selecting the team and during war-time had full control.

B: Wrexham; 4 Aug 1877
D: Wrexham; 17 Jan 1946

Ted Robbins was appointed part-time FAW secretary on 24 November 1909 at a salary of £50 a year and went on to render great service to the association over 35 years.

Although 17 applicants had sought the position, Robbins eventually emerged victorious - having been an unsuccessful candidate when the post had previously been vacant in 1905 - after three ballots and a run-off vote against FAW clerk David W Owens of Rhosymedre.

Robbins, whose father kept the Wrexham Music Hall, began his career as a law clerk but later established himself as an accountant and at one time was auditor to Wrexham Borough Council. A popular amateur comedian, he acquired the lease of the Wrexham public hall, later known as the Hippodrome, and was Instrumental in bringing theatrical touring companies to Wrexham.

His experience of playing soccer was limited to local junior club, Wrexham Ivanhoe, but it was as an administrator that he really made his mark. During the First World War he worked for the Ministry of Food and he kept the association going with R T Gough and T E Thomas. In the early 1920s Robbins attempted to put the domestic leagues in Wales on a sensible and rational basis but the structure did not last, beset by geographical difficulties in mid-Wales and reckless professionalism in the north.

Robbins was described by one FAW council member as an 'entrepreneur, diplomat and showman'. His tact, charm and persuasion helped Wales overcome many a problem in securing the release of players from English Football League clubs and ensured that the Association was able to field a team of committed and enthusiastic players, if not always their first choice.

For the 1929 tour of Canada, Robbins was described as Wales team manager, and this was pretty much his *de facto* role from the 1920s until his death.

APPENDIX 4

Caps Awarded: 1876-1939

48	William Henry Meredith (161)	14	David Jones (109)
			Edward Hughes (186)
32	Frederick Charles Keenor (266)		William Ronald John (336)
			Charles Frederick Parry (134)
28	Charles Richard Morris (199)		
		13	Llewellyn Davies (237)
26	William Lewis (74)		David John Astley (334)
			Cuthbert Phillips (337)
24	Leigh Richmond Roose (203)		
	Albert Gray (282)	12	John Price (16)
			William Pierce Owen (39)
23	Moses Richard Russell (252)		Morgan Maddox Morgan-Owen (172)
	Leonard Stephen Davies (274)		Edward John Peers (260)
	Horace Elford Blew (184)		Thomas James Matthias (262)
			Idris Morgan Hopkins (358)
22	Edward Thomas Vizard (250)		
	John Leonard Jones (160)	11	William Williams (11)
			John Vaughan (35)
21	Arthur Grenville Morris (166)		Joseph Davies (114)
	Tom Percival Griffiths (305)		Richard Morris (214)
	David Thomas Richards (338)		William Davies (219)
	James Trainer (104)		Ernest Peake (246)
			William Jennings (261)
20	William Jones (228)		Eugene O'Callaghan (316)
	Stanley Davies (264)		Walter William Robbins (330)
			Leslie Jenkin Jones (352)
18	William Davies (283)		
		10	John Richard Morgan (15)
17	Brynmor Jones (360)		Benjamin Lewis (128)
	Thomas George Ronald Jones (368)		Robert Owen Evans (210)
	William Owen (66)		Walter Martin Watkins (215)
			George Latham (225)
16	Maurice Pryce Parry (207)		Robert Ernest Evans (231)
	Lloyd Davies (221)		George Arthur Wynn (247)
	Edwin Hughes (232)		Ivor Jones (265)
	John Powell (23)		Samuel Raymond Bennion (296)
			Benjamin David Williams (311)
15	Joseph Thomas Jones (251)		William Marshall Hughes (365)
	Robert Frederick John (280)		
	James Patrick Murphy (349)		
	Humphrey Jones (73)		

9	78, 80, 155, 183, 268, 272	2	1, 2, 5, 6, 10, 13, 17, 21, 33, 40, 43, 44, 45, 53, 61, 71, 76, 85, 98, 100, 106, 117, 121, 122, 129, 131, 132, 137, 146, 156, 171, 178, 185, 190, 192, 193, 195, 196, 197, 201, 205, 222, 226, 227, 229, 233, 234, 236, 239, 253, 254, 259, 270, 279, 286, 320, 327, 329, 331, 332, 335, 346, 348, 357, 361, 364, 370, 373
8	20, 52, 68, 75, 90, 135, 138, 143, 144, 198, 209, 249, 255, 271, 284, 287, 302, 345, 363		
7	29, 79, 105, 153, 167, 200, 248, 340, 354, 355		
6	34, 47, 50, 62, 149, 151, 189, 202, 267, 275, 289, 307, 317, 343, 350	1	4, 7, 9, 12, 18, 19, 22, 24. 25, 26, 27, 28, 30, 32, 36, 37, 42, 48, 51, 54, 55, 60, 65, 67, 69, 70, 77, 81, 86, 89, 91, 93, 95, 97, 99, 103, 108, 111, 115, 118, 119, 123, 124, 126, 127, 136, 139, 140, 141, 147, 148, 154, 158, 162, 164, 169, 170, 173, 174, 175, 176, 177, 179, 181, 182, 187, 191, 211, 212, 213, 216, 217, 220, 230, 235, 238, 240, 243, 245, 256, 263, 269, 278, 288, 290, 292, 293, 294, 295, 297, 298, 301, 303, 308, 312, 313, 315, 318, 319, 321, 322, 323, 325, 333, 339, 341, 342, 344, 347, 351, 353, 359, 372, 374
5	8, 41, 94, 102, 116, 165, 180, 194, 204, 208, 241, 258, 277, 324, 362		
4	3, 46, 58, 63, 83, 88, 92, 96, 110, 112, 113, 120, 145, 150, 206, 218, 242, 257, 276, 285, 291, 299, 300, 304, 309, 314, 356, 367		
3	31, 38, 49, 56, 57, 59, 64, 72, 82, 84, 87, 101, 107, 125, 130, 125, 130, 133, 142, 152, 157, 159, 163, 168, 188, 223, 224, 244, 273, 281, 306, 310, 326, 328, 366, 369, 371		

APPENDIX 5

Goal Scorers: 1876-1939

12	David John Astley (334)	2	William Henry Davies (3)
11	William Henry Meredith (161)		John Richard Morgan (15)
9	Arthur Grenville Morris (166)		William Roberts (29)
			Knyvett Crosse (31)
7	William Pierce Owen (39)		John Roberts (34)
	William Lewis (74)		John Vaughan (35)
	Ernest Matthew Glover (340)		Edward Gough Shaw (49)
			Walter Hugh Roberts (50)
6	John Doughty (90)		Thomas Burke (52)
	William 'Lot' Jones (228)		John Arthur Eyton-Jones (58)
	Leonard Stephen Davies (274)		Robert Albert Jones (63)
	William Davies (283)		Robert Roberts (68)
			Frederick Robert Jones (72)
5	William Davies (219)		John Roach (81)
	Stanley Charles Davies (264)		John Owen Vaughan (83)
	Cuthbert Phillips (337)		Thomas Bryan (84)
	Brynmor Jones (360)		Richard Hersee (86)
			William Roberts (88)
4	John Price (16)		Henry Wilmshurst Sabine (99)
	William Owen (66)		Roger Doughty (106)
	Job Wilding (78)		George Alfred Owen (110)
	Herbert Sisson (82)		David Morral Lewis (122)
	John Charles Henry Bowdler (120)		Albert Thomas Davies (127)
	Walter Martin Watkins (215)		Benjamin Lewis (128)
	Walter William Robbins (330)		Robert Roberts (131)
			Caesar Augustus Llewellyn Jenkyns (138)
3	William Ernest Pryce Jones (102)		Edwin James (143)
	Edmund Gwynne Howell (107)		Thomas Chapman (153)
	Richard Herbert Jarrett (117)		Hugh Morris (157)
	Thomas David Parry (200)		Harry Trainer (163)
	Arthur William Green (209)		David Henry Pugh (167)
	Frederick Charles Keenor (266)		Morgan Maddox Morgan-Owen (172)
	Jack Fowler (289)		Thomas John Thomas (178)
	Tom Percival Griffiths (305)		Robert Atherton (183)
	Wilfred Leslie Lewis (307)		William Thomas Butler (195)
	Ernest Robert Curtis (310)		Richard Jones (197)
	Eugene O'Callaghan (316)		Hugh Morgan-Owen (204)
	Frederick Windsor Warren (317)		John Owen Jones (205)
			Richard Morris (214)
			Lloyd Davies (221)
			Robert Ernest Evans (231)

2	John Love Jones (233)	Ivor Jones (265)
	Ernest Peake (246)	Richard William Richards (268)
	George Arthur Wynn (247)	David John Collier (269)
	Evan Jones (248)	William James Hole (272)
	Edward Thomas Vizard (250)	William Williams (288)
	Moses Richard Russell (252)	Albert William Mays (315)
	David Rees Williams (271)	Thomas Bamford (324)
	Idris Morgan Hopkins (358)	William Evans (350)
	Seymour Morris (362)	Leslie Jenkin Jones (352)
		Thomas James Edward Mills (356)
1	David Walter Davies (254)	Charles Wilson Jones (361)
	John Evans (255)	Edwin Perry (366)
	Walter Otto Davies (258)	Reginald Horace Cumner (369)
	Edward James Roberts (259)	Leslie Mervyn Boulter (372)

APPENDIX 6

Captains: 1876-1939

23	Frederick Charles Keenor (266)	1	Thomas Burke (52)
			John Evans Butler (142)
11	William Henry Meredith (161)		Leonard Stephen Davies (274)
	Tom Percival Griffiths (305)		Llewellyn Davies (237)
			William Davies (219)
10	Humphrey Jones (73)		Henry Valentine Edwards (20)
			John Evans (255)
8	John Leonard Jones (160)		Daniel Gray (6)
	Charles Richard Morris (199)		Harry Hanford (354)
			George Garnet Higham (21)
7	James Trainer (104)		Edward Hughes (186)
			Caesar Augustus Llewellyn Jenkyns (138)
6	John Richard Morgan (15)		William Jennings (261)
	John Powell (23)		David Jones (109)
			Thomas George Ronald Jones (368)
4	Alfred Owen Davies (80)		Thomas James Matthias (262)
	Samuel Llewellyn Kenrick (8)		Hugh Morgan-Owen (204)
	Charles Frederick Parry (134)		Maurice Pryce Parry (207)
	Moses Richard Russell (252)		Leigh Richmond Roose (203)
			Richard Edward Turner (132)
3	David John Astley (334)		Walter Martin Watkins (215)
	Edwin Hughes (232)		
	Herbert Gwyn Turner (363)		
2	Horace Elford Blew (184)		
	Lloyd Davies (221)		
	Stanley Davies (264)		
	Arthur Grenville Morris (166)		
	William Pierce Owen (39)		
	Edward Thomas Vizard (250)		
	Benjamin David Williams (311)		

Note: The Wales captains for 20 internationals during this period have not yet been identified.

APPENDIX 7

Clubs Represented: 1876-1939

61 Wrexham
1, 2, 16, 18, 19, 20 26, 32, 33, 37, 43, 51, 52, 57, 58, 60, 78, 80, 94, 113, 116, 119, 121, 126, 128, 132, 137, 140, 149, 163, 167, 168, 182, 184, 188, 194, 210, 216, 217, 219, 230, 231, 232, 237, 239, 240, 241, 247, 249, 259, 262, 279, 293, 312, 314, 315, 318, 324, 326, 331, 333, 373, 374

30 Druids
6, 7, 8, 9, 10, 11, 23, 31, 35, 40, 46, 48, 53, 63, 68, 70, 90, 108, 112, 145, 149, 188, 189, 190, 191, 195, 208, 214, 218, 222

26 Oswestry T
3, 8, 11, 21, 24, 25, 27, 28, 30, 35, 49, 55, 61, 65, 67, 69, 71, 79, 81, 84, 89, 99, 103, 111, 124, 152, 328

19 Chirk
59, 62, 66, 95, 109, 110, 114, 130, 141, 142, 143, 144, 151, 176, 177, 198, 199, 202, 238

14 Bangor
72, 73, 74, 85, 86, 96, 101, 118, 122, 178, 193, 197, 205, 226

Manchester Utd (Newton Heath)[1]
Man Utd: 161, 271, 296, 300, 308, 364
N Heath: 23, 52, 90, 105, 106, 110, 138, 139

13 Cardiff C
225, 255, 266, 274, 275, 285, 286, 297, 309, 310, 317, 330, 352

Swansea T
265, 272, 281, 283, 289, 291, 307, 311, 336, 345, 348, 354, 364

11 Bolton Wdrs
23, 35, 68, 104, 109, 223, 248, 250, 261, 278, 305

Everton
114, 134, 135, 154, 186, 203, 264, 305, 311, 341, 368

Manchester C (Ardwick)
Man City: 74, 109, 114, 153, 157, 161, 228, 232, 247, 282
Ardwick: 114
Newtown
33, 38, 100, 134, 150, 153, 158, 162, 164, 173, 214

9 Aston Villa
180, 209, 215, 231, 241, 305, 334, 337

Birmingham C (Small Heath Alliance)[3]
Birmingham: 309, 310, 338, 361, 362, 365, 371
Small Heath: 138, 148

Wolverhampton Wdrs
105, 120, 165, 260, 268, 314, 337, 338, 360

Wrexham Olympic
20, 52, 57, 76, 78, 82, 87, 88, 98

8 Shrewsbury T
120, 127, 136, 147, 165, 189, 202, 220

Stoke C (Stoke)[4]
Stoke C: 336
Stoke: 198, 203, 215, 221, 233, 251, 281

7 Aberystwyth T
155, 166, 170, 174, 175, 203, 246

Arsenal (Woolwich Arsenal)[5]
Arsenal: 280, 302, 306, 352, 360, 369
Woolwich Arsenal: 138

Liverpool
207, 214, 224, 225, 246, 273, 277

Middlesborough
128, 183, 233, 295, 305, 317

Ruthin
39, 42, 45, 50, 117, 129

West Bromwich Alb
79, 242, 264, 265, 330, 344, 349

6 Chester
74, 98, 123, 128, 229, 282

Crewe Alex
41, 74, 101, 131, 146, 192, 266

5 **Newport Co**
285, 287, 319, 321, 332

Nottingham F
166, 209, 227, 232, 302

Oxford Univ
5, 14, 171, 172, 204

Rhyl
50, 54, 77, 83, 212

Sheffield Utd
114, 157, 160, 231, 336

Tottenham H
160, 186, 316, 350, 353, 370

4 **Berwyn Rgrs**
29, 34, 46, 56

Blackburn Rov
210, 219, 226, 359

Charlton Ath
322, 334, 363, 367

Clapton Orient
291, 304, 320, 356

Corinthians
92, 172, 204, 294

Grimsby T
157, 214, 269, 340

Leicester C (Leicester Fosse)[6]
Leicester C: 355, 356
Leicester Fosse: 179, 180

Millwall (Millwall Athletic)[7]
Millwall: 180, 234, 258
Millwall Ath: 114

Notts Co
209, 227, 283, 320

Oswestry Utd
152, 159, 189, 200

Preston N E
68, 74, 104, 264

3 **Bootle**
78, 133, 135

Brentford
338, 358, 372

Cambridge Univ
13, 15, 102

Cardiff Corinthians
256, 292, 327

Crystal Palace
242, 251, 253

Huddersfield T
199, 299, 307

Oldham Ath
248, 254, 282

Plymouth Argyle
214, 252, 303

Sheffield Wed
271, 346, 354

West Ham Utd
206, 268, 335

2 **Aberdare**
206, 245

Aberdare Ath
298, 309

Blackpool
196, 334

Bradford P A
273, 347

Bristol C
273, 323

Builth T
107, 125

Chelsea
248, 249

Clapton
116, 211

Corwen
34, 53

Coventry C
210, 352

Derby Co
199, 334

Llanelli
257, 325

London Welsh
169, 203

Merthyr T
252, 271

Newcastle Utd
304, 357

Newtown Excelsior
36, 38

Northampton T
221, 288

Reading
114, 299

Rhosllannerchrugog
131, 156

Rotherham Utd (Rotherham Co)[8]
Rotherham Utd: 264
Rotherham Co: 267
Shrewsbury
116, 120
Shrewsbury Engineers
41, 44
Southend Utd
228, 276
Sunderland
203, 215
Tranmere Rov
263, 282
Walsall
138, 336
Wrexham Civil Service
20, 22

1 **Aberaman**
213
Barmouth
80
Barnsley
342
Bradford C
236
Brecon
185
Brighton & Hove Alb
284
Bristol Rov
235
Burnley
313
Burton Utd
241
Brymbo Inst
165
Burton Swifts
149
Carnarvon Ath
91
Colwyn Bay Utd
329
Crusaders
93
Derby Midland
15

Derby Sch
15
Doncaster Rov
366
East Stirlingshire
73
Fulham
351
Glossop N E
181
Heart of Midlothian
317
Hereford T
185
Hibernian
183
Leeds C
214
Lincoln C
167
Linfield
339
Llanberis
74
Llandrindod
244
Llandudno Swifts
201
Llangollen
29
Lovell's Ath
290
Manchester Central
282
Mold T
268
Motherwell
343
Nelson
301
New Brighton Tower
135
Northwich Vic
47
Nunhead
328
Overton
80

Parkgrove
17
Portsmouth
287
Port Vale
260
Queen's Park
73
Rhostyllen
115
Ruabon
12
Ruthin G Sch
64
Southampton
243
South Liverpool
249
Southport Central
225

St Helen's Recreation
187
St Thomas's Hospital
74
Swifts
80
Swindon T
166
Treharris
254
Wanderers
4
Watford
270
Wrexham Hare & Hounds
58
Wynnstay
112

Notes
1 Newton Heath became Manchester Utd in 1902
2 Ardwick became Manchester City in 1894
3 Small Heath Alliance became Small Heath in 1888, Birmingham in 1905, then Birmingham City in 1943
4 Stoke became Stoke City in 1925
5 Woolwich Arsenal became Arsenal in 1910
6 Leicester Fosse became Leicester City in 1919
7 Millwall Athletic became Millwall in 1903
8 Rotherham County amalgamated with Rotherham Town in 1925 to become Rotherham Utd

APPENDIX 8

Birthplaces of Welsh Internationals: 1876-1939

53 **Wrexham**
1, 2, 16, 18, 20, 23, 32, 37, 43, 51, 52, 57, 58, 60, 76, 78, 79, 82, 87, 88, 94, 104, 113, 115, 119, 121, 131, 132, 140, 149, 154, 163, 165, 167, 168, 171, 184, 203, 210, 219, 222, 232, 237, 251, 284, 295, 296, 300, 305, 318, 326, 331, 333

24 **Ruabon**
7, 8, 11, 33, 35, 40, 48, 63, 67, 68, 105, 108, 145, 176, 190, 191, 195, 216, 218, 221, 257, 273, 320, 328

20 **Chirk**
59, 62, 66, 95, 110, 130, 139, 141, 143, 144, 151, 157, 161, 198, 208, 220, 228, 236, 264, 267

15 **Cardiff**
172, 266, 274, 275, 285, 289, 290, 292, 309, 310, 317, 322, 327, 330, 355

Newtown
36, 38, 41, 102, 124, 150, 153, 158, 162, 164, 173, 214, 225, 242, 286

11 **Aberystwyth**
13, 155, 170, 174, 175, 209, 212, 234, 235, 246, 268

Rhondda
241, 269, 293, 304, 306, 341, 342, 346, 349, 356, 362

10 **Merthyr Tydfil**
265, 271, 299, 302, 323, 338, 348, 351, 358, 360

9 **Bangor**
72, 73, 74, 101, 169, 178, 193, 197, 205

8 **Swansea**
15, 272, 291, 307, 308, 340, 354, 357

7 **Ebbw Vale**
303, 316, 337, 350, 353, 370, 372

Rhyl
54, 77, 83, 204, 229, 233, 276

6 **Llandudno**
85, 86, 148, 201, 329, 344

Aberdare
281, 287, 298, 352, 369, 374

4 **Llanllechid**
39, 64, 118, 183

Rhosllanerchrugog
114, 156, 217, 359

Rhymney
283, 325, 363, 366

Ruthin
42, 45, 50, 92

Pontypridd
248, 288, 364, 371

3 **Barry**
261, 280, 367

Builth
107, 125, 166

Connah's Quay
249, 260, 314

Llangollen
56, 192, 238

Newport
297, 313, 335,

Talgarth
185, 227, 239

2 **Buckley**
253, 258

Caergwrle
137, 279

Colwyn Bay
277, 312

Corwen
112, 117
Flint
181, 187
Llanfyllin
65, 126
Llansilin
134, 189
Llanwnnog
180, 215
Mold
98, 259
Penarth
250, 373
Penrhiwceiber
311, 345
Port Talbot
324, 332
Presteigne
75, 196
Tredegar
252, 282
Aberaman
245
Aberdovey
19
Bala
255
Barmouth
80
Blaina
206
Boughrood
138
Brecon
270
Bridgend
321
Briton Ferry
336
Broughton
262
Caernarfon
91
Caerphilly
343
Carmarthen
365

Cerrigydrudion
74
Chepstow
347
Dolgellau
122
Dowlais
334
Ewloe
278
Gwyddelwern
53
Leeswood
128
Llandrindod
244
Llandysilio
230
Llanelli
223
Llanrhaiadr
61
Llanrwst
294
Machynlleth
213
Pembroke Dock
243
Penmachno
75
Penmaenmawr
96
Pontrobert
142
Prestatyn
29
Queensferry
368
Rhuddlan
160
Rogerstone
319
Saltney
146
Sandycroft
188
Shotton
182

St Asaph
301
Treharris
254
Trelawnyd
179

Non-Welsh Born

57 **England**
9, 10, 12, 17, 22, 25, 26, 30, 46, 47, 84, 90, 97, 100, 106, 116, 123, 133, 135, 136, 176, 194, 224, 226, 231, 240, 268
Oswestry
3, 21, 24, 28, 49, 69, 70, 71, 81, 89, 99, 103, 109, 111, 152, 159, 177, 199, 200, 202, 207, 247
Shrewsbury
4, 27, 31, 55, 120, 127, 147

Usk
5
Ynys Môn
211
Ystalyfera
129

2 **Scotland**
6, 14

1 **Canada**
256
Peru
44

PLAYER INDEX

Adams, Harry (46)
Arridge, Smart (135)
Astley, David John (334)
Atherton, Robert (183)

Baliff, William Ellis (257)
Bamford, Thomas (324)
Bartley, Thomas (181)
Bastock, Archie Middleship (136)
Beadles, George Harold (286)
Bell, William Strafford (41)
Bennion, Samuel Raymond (296)
Blew, Horace Elford (184)
Boden, Thomas Henry (37)
Boulter, Leslie Mervyn (372)
Bowdler, Harry Ernest (147)
Bowdler, John Charles Henry (120)
Bowen, Edward (40)
Bowsher, Stanley James (313)
Britten, Thomas Johnson (17)
Brookes, Samuel James (201)
Brown, Arthur Ivor (298)
Bryan, Thomas (84)
Buckland, Thomas James (193)
Burke, Thomas (52)
Burnett, Thomas Blundell (12)
Butler, John Evans Butler (142)
Butler, William Thomas (195)

Challen, John Bonamy (92)
Chapman, Thomas (153)
Collier, David John (269)
Collins, William Elvet (325)
Conde, Charles (59)
Cook, Frederick (287)
Crompton, Wynne (326)
Cross, Edwin Alfred (1)
Crosse, Knyvett (31)
Cumner, Reginald Horace (369)
Curtis, Ernest Robert (310)

Darvell, Sydney (171)
Davies, Albert Thomas (127)
Davies, Alfred (2)
Davies, Alfred Owen Davies (80)
Davies, Arthur (222)
Davies, David (223)
Davies, David Charles (185)
Davies, David Oswald (126)
Davies, David Walter (254)
Davies, Hywel (312)
Davies, James (18)
Davies, John (32)
Davies, John Edward (69)
Davies, John Phillip (53)
Davies, Joseph (105)
Davies, Joseph (114)
Davies, Leonard Stephen (274)
Davies, Llewellyn (237)
Davies, Lloyd (221)
Davies, Robert (57)
Davies, Robert (70)
Davies, Robert (137)
Davies, Robert Idwal (278)
Davies, Stanley (264)
Davies, Thomas (89)
Davies, Thomas (218)
Davies, Walter Otto (258)
Davies, Walter Thomas (60)
Davies, William (219)
Davies, William (283)
Davies, William Charles (242)
Davies, William Henry (3)
Day, Alfred (353)
Dearson, Donald John (371)
Dewey, Frederick Thomas (327)
Doughty, John (90)
Doughty, Roger (106)

Edwards, Charles (19)
Edwards, Henry Valentine (20)
Edwards, James Alfred (159)
Edwards, John Hawley (4)
Edwards, John Henry (175)

Edwards, Thomas (216)
Egan, Tom William (141)
Ellis, Benjamin (343)
Ellis, Emrys (328)
Evans, David (299)
Evans, Herbert Price (275)
Evans, James Henry (276)
Evans, John (152)
Evans, John (255)
Evans, Robert Ernest (231)
Evans, Robert Owen (210)
Evans, Roger (211)
Evans, Sidney John Vivian Leonard (309)
Evans, Thomas John (304)
Evans, Walter Gwynne (125)
Evans, William (350)
Evans, William Addams Williams (5)
Evelyn, Edward Clement (93)
Eyton-Jones, John Arthur (58)

Farmer, George (71)
Finnegan, Richard Prytherch (318)
Foulkes, Hugh Edward (219)
Foulkes, William Tanat (61)
Fowler, Jack (289)

Garner, John (170)
Gillam, Samuel Gladstone (116)
Glascodine, George William (25)
Glover, Ernest Matthew (340)
Godding, George Alfred (279)
Goodwin, Uriah (40)
Gough, Richard Thomas (55)
Gray, Albert (282)
Green, Arthur William (209)
Green, George Henry (367)
Grey, Daniel (6)
Griffiths, Frederick John (196)
Griffiths, George (95)
Griffiths, Llewellyn (216)

Griffiths, Peter (62)
Griffiths, Philip Henry (341)
Griffiths, Tom Percival (305)

Hallam, John (111)
Hanford, Harry (354)
Harrison, William Clare (194)
Hayes, Abel (121)
Hersee, Albert Malcolm (85)
Hersee, Richard (86)
Hewitt, Thomas John (249)
Heywood, Dennis (26)
Hibbott, Harry (38)
Higham, George Garnet (21)
Hoddinott, Francis (270)
Hodgkinson, Albert Victor (243)
Hole, William James (272)
Hopkins, Idris Morgan (358)
Howell, Edmund Gwynne (107)
Hugh, Arthur Ronald (319)
Hughes, Abel (156)
Hughes, Arthur Howell (238)
Hughes, Edward (186)
Hughes, Edward Percival Whitley (96)
Hughes, Edwin (232)
Hughes, Frederick William (47)
Hughes, John (13)
Hughes, John (224)
Hughes, John Iorwerth (359)
Hughes, William (133)
Hughes, William Marshall (365)
Humphreys, Reuben (108)
Hunter, Alexander (97)

Jackson, William James (187)
James, Edwin (143)
James, Wilfred Bernard (335)
Jarrett, Richard Herbert (117)
Jenkins, Edwin Samuel (290)
Jenkins, John (284)
Jenkins, Thomas (212)
Jenkyns, Caesar Augustus Llewellyn (138)
Jennings, William (261)
John, Robert Frederick (280)
John, William Ronald (336)
Jones, Albert Thomas (227)
Jones, Alexander Fletcher (14)
Jones, Brynmor (360)
Jones, Charles (302)
Jones, Charles Wilson (361)
Jones, David (109)

Jones, David Owen (355)
Jones, Evan (248)
Jones, Frederick Robert (72)
Jones, Frederick William (148)
Jones, Gordon Peace (239)
Jones, Hugh (213)
Jones, Humphrey Jones (73)
Jones, Ivor (265)
Jones, James (293)
Jones, Jeffrey Woodward (244)
Jones, John (7)
Jones, John (56)
Jones, John Leonard (160)
Jones, John Love (233)
Jones, John Owen (205)
Jones, Joseph Thomas (251)
Jones, Leslie Jenkin (352)
Jones, Ralph Stanley (191)
Jones, Richard (101)
Jones, Richard (197)
Jones, Richard (234)
Jones, Richard Samuel (179)
Jones, Robert Albert (63)
Jones, Robert Samuel (154)
Jones, Samuel (98)
Jones, Samuel (149)
Jones, Thomas (300)
Jones, Thomas Daniel (245)
Jones, Thomas George Ronald (368)
Jones, Thomas John (346)
Jones, William (228)
Jones, William James (206)
Jones, William Parry (112)
Jones Evans, Morris/Maurice (65)

Keenor, Frederick Charles (266)
Kelly, Fredrick Charles (188)
Kenrick, Samuel Llewellyn (8)
Ketley, Charles Frederick (48)

Latham, George (225)
Lawrence, Edward (320)
Lawrence, Sidney Wilfred (345)
Lea, Arthur (113)
Leary, Patrick (118)
Lewis, Benjamin (128)
Lewis, Daniel (306)
Lewis, David Jenkin (348)
Lewis, David Morral (122)
Lewis, James John (297)
Lewis, John (235)

Lewis, Thomas (43)
Lewis, Wilfred Leslie (307)
Lewis, William (74)
Lloyd, James William (33)
Lloyd, Robert Arthur (129)
Lockley, Albert (176)
Lumberg, Arthur Albert (314)

Martin, Tudor James (321)
Mates, John (130)
Matthews, Robert William (273)
Matthews, William (229)
Matthias, John Samuel (165)
Matthias, Thomas James (262)
Mays, Albert William (315)
McCarthy, Thomas Patrick (119)
McMillan, Robert John (44)
Meredith, Samuel (198)
Meredith, William Henry (161)
Millership, Harry (267)
Mills, Thomas James Edward (356)
Morgan, John Richard (15)
Morgan, John Tracey (230)
Morgan-Owen, Hugh (204)
Morgan-Owen, Morgan Maddox (172)
Morley, Ernest James (291)
Morris, Arthur Grenville (166)
Morris, Charles Richard (199)
Morris, Edward (144)
Morris, Hugh (157)
Morris, James (103)
Morris, John (177)
Morris, Richard (214)
Morris, Robert (202)
Morris, Seymour (362)
Moulsdale, John Reginald Blackwall (294)
Murphy, James Patrick (349)

Neal, John Edward (329)
Newnes, John (301)
Newton, Leonard Francis (256)
Nicholas, David Sidney (281)
Nicholls, John Barry Lewis (285)
Nock, William (173)

O'Callaghan, Eugene (316)
Oliver, Alfred (226)
Owen, Dennis (26)
Owen, Elias (64)
Owen, George Alfred (110)

Owen, John (139)
Owen Trevor (192)
Owen, Thomas (27)
Owen, William (66)
Owen, William Digby (28)
Owen, William Pierce (39)
Owens, Joseph (217)

Parris, John Edward (347)
Parry, Charles Frederick (134)
Parry, Edward (277)
Parry, Maurice Pryce (207)
Parry, Thomas David (200)
Parry, William (162)
Peake, Ernest (246)
Peers, Edward John (260)
Perry, Edwin (366)
Phennah, Edward (22)
Phillips, Cuthbert (337)
Phoenix, Henry (51)
Poland, George (373)
Powell, John (23)
Powell, Seth (79)
Price, Ioan Hayden (241)
Price, John (16)
Pryce Jones, Albert Westhead (164)
Pryce Jones, William Ernest (102)
Pugh, Allen (115)
Pugh, David Henry (167)
Pugsley, John (322)
Pullen, William John (303)

Rea, John Charles (155)
Richards, Aneurin Glynd r (342)
Richards, David Thomas (338)
Richards, George (189)
Richards, Richard William (268)
Richards, William Edward (351)
Roach, John (81)
Roberts, Edward James (259)

Roberts, James (236)
Roberts, John (34)
Roberts, John (45)
Roberts, Robert (68)
Roberts, Robert (87)
Roberts, Robert (131)
Roberts, Robert Herbert Mills (75)
Roberts, Robert Humphrey Lee (123)
Roberts, Walter Hugh (50)
Roberts, William (29)
Roberts, William (54)
Roberts, William (88)
Roberts-Jones, William (174)
Robbins, Walter William (330)
Rogers, Joseph (168)
Rogers, William (331)
Roose, Leigh Richmond (203)
Rowlands, Alfred Stanley (263)
Russell, Moses Richard (252)

Sabine, Henry Wilmshurst (99)
Savin, George Foulkes (24)
Shaw, Edward Gough (49)
Shone, Watkin William (30)
Sisson, Herbert (82)

Taylor, John (182)
Taylor, Oliver David Shepston (150)
Thomas, Charles Edwin (190)
Thomas, Daniel Edgar (292)
Thomas, George (76)
Thomas, Harry (308)
Thomas, Thomas John (178)
Thomas, William Rees (332)
Thomson, David (9)
Thomson, George Frederick (10)
Townsend, Alfred William (100)
Trainer, Harry (163)
Trainer, James (104)

Turner, Herbert Gwyn (363)
Turner, Joseph Hudson (140)
Turner, Richard Edward (132)
Turner, William Haighton (94)

Vaughan, James, (145)
Vaughan, John (35)
Vaughan, John Owen (83)
Vaughan, Thomas (77)
Vizard, Edward Thomas (250)

Warner, John (364)
Warren, Frederick Windsor (317)
Watkins, Alfred Ernest (180)
Watkins, Walter Martin (215)
Whatley, William John (370)
White, Price Ffoulkes (169)
Wilcock, Albert Richard (124)
Wilding, Job (78)
Williams, Benjamin David (311)
Williams, Bertie (323)
Williams, David Rees (271)
Williams, Edward Houghland (146)
Williams, Ephraim (208)
Williams, George (151)
Williams, George Owen (240)
Williams, Jesse Thomas (295)
Williams, John James (374)
Williams, John William (253)
Williams, Joseph Harry (67)
Williams, Leslie (333)
Williams, Richard Parry (91)
Williams, Ronald (357)
Williams, William (11)
Williams, William (288)
Woosnam, George (36)
Worthington, Thomas (158)
Wynn, George Arthur (247)
Wynn, William (220)

Lightning Source UK Ltd.
Milton Keynes UK
UKHW051117201221
395970UK00006B/253